SENSING SEMIOSIS

Semaphores and Signs

Edited by Roberta Kevelson and Marcel Danesi

Semaphores and Signs ushers in a new age for cross-cultural transdisciplinary semiotics. Each volume of the series will open up traditional areas of inquiry to new dimensions, while presenting both American and Continental views of the field. Cognizant of the advances already made in developing connections between fields of study, the series will seek to unify aspects of the humanistic sciences, the physical sciences, and the arts. *Semaphores and Signs* will use the lens of semiotics as a new vantage point from which to view our world as the approach of the millenium beckons.

SENSING SEMIOSIS

Toward the Possibility of Complementary Cultural "Logics"

Floyd Merrell

MACMILLAN

First published by
MACMILLAN PRESS LTD
Houndmills, Basingstoke, Hampshire RG21 6XS
and London
Companies and representatives
throughout the world

ISBN 0-333-74095-5

A catalogue record for this book is available
from the British Library.

10   9   8   7   6   5   4   3   2   1
07   06   05   04   03   02   01   00   99   98

Internal design and typesetting by Letra Libre

Printed in the United States of America by
R.R. Donnelley & Sons
Harrisonburg, VA

CONTENTS

LIST OF FIGURES AND TABLES

PREFACE

I began this volume in West Lafayette, Indiana, during the fall of 1995. As usual, that faithful brick wall of self-doubt soon loomed large: Who did I think I was to be doing what I thought I was doing? I asked myself that familiar question in earnest and all too quickly gave up on the project entirely. Then there was an opportunity to teach a seminar at the Pontifícia Universidade Católica of São Paulo, Brazil, during the summer of 1996. Brazil. Yes. How could my obsessive cynicism possibly survive a few weeks in Brazil? That hustle and bustle of cultural activity incessantly verging on the chaotic but somehow able to maintain a remarkable dynamism: a flow of bodies, shuffling feet, turning and twisting heads, gyrating hands, darting eyes, an effervescence of polyphonic voices, of laughter and shouts and whistles and whoops and hollers, incessant *abraços*, perpetual rhythmic movement, synchronized swings and sweeps, imbalance in constant self-correction toward melody and harmony, and *syncope*, . . . *syncope*, . . . *syncope*, . . . No culture knows it and does it better than Brazil. It is living *semiosis*, vibrant, throbbing, dancing semiosis. So, ... this volume could not help but move along.

The product, in the most general terms, is a meditation on Charles S. Peirce's basic collection of ten signs. The overriding theme, however, revolves around signs of feeling and of sensing, signs primarily of Peirce's category of *Firstness*, of iconicity, of quality. After all, how could this book be other than what it is? It is semiosis, that is, it is my own very modest dip into the stream of semiosis. But there was a severe problem. In writing a book, one is according to tradition duty bound to describe, explain, interpret—in short, to account for what there is and what made it possible. One must break the whole down into certain constituent parts, elucidate a selection of them thoroughly, and put them together to make up part of the whole or presumably the whole itself in its entirety. According to this formula, I should have ended up with yet another somewhat dreary book on the semiotics of C. S. Peirce. That did not happen. For if, in accord with my professed goals, I was to elucidate the quality, the Firstness, the iconic thrust of signs, how was it possible, really possible, to follow faithfully the standard formula? That is, how could I provide a viable description of particular signs, given the vast, intractable, and ever transient rush of semiosis? There was an even more difficult question, in view of the subtitle of this volume: How could I be so presumptuous as to expect that I could articulate the idea of "complementary cultural 'logics'" if I and you and all of us are inextricably caught within some culture-dependent bit of the entire universe of semiosis without any sextant in order to know with certainty from whence we came, where we now are, and how most propitiously to map out our future journey? What are we that we may know our signs, and what are they that they may allow us the security of our assuming we know them? Indeed, some notion of what signs are all about, however tenuous it might be, was necessary before my story could proceed beyond the first page.

For this reason, I begin chapter 1 by reviewing—as succinctly as I know how—Peirce's basic sign types as the emergence of a combination of three sets of three signs: *qualisigns, sinsigns,* and *legisigns; icons, indices,* and *symbols;* and *terms* (or in the more general sense, individual words), *propositions* (sentences, word strings), and *arguments* (texts, narratives). In an attempt to answer the obvious question, "How comes it that ten classes of signs—a number that is on the surface apparently incompatible with triadicity—can be engendered from three sets of three signs?" I call on the non-Euclidean geometry of Bernhard Riemann, a contemporary of Peirce, whose alternative to classical geometry became the meat and potatoes of Einsteinian relativity. Chapter 2 takes up Nelson Goodman's "New Riddle of Induction" in an attempt to illustrate how "Grue" of the imaginary Grueworlders' language can undergo—apparently for us Realworlders at least—a transformation from "Green" to "Blue." An example is offered of the feeling, sense, and conception of Miguel de Cervantes's *Don Quixote* by virtue of sign *engenderment* and *de-engenderment* (in strict Peircean terms, *generacy* and *de-generacy*) and the possibility of inductive somersaults of the Goodman variety. This leads us by the hand to the edge of the epistemological abyss of Goodman's worldmaking and an image of multiple and the multiplicity of semiosis, where we are given a playful nudge, and consequently we risk all. Such sign engenderment and de-engenderment, I suggest, is feasible solely by way of a genuine conception of triadicity. This suggestion is given support by examples from Paul Klee and other artists and Anton Ehrenzweig and other art theorists, all from a radical view of space and time, especially regarding that semiotic model of models authored by semiotician James Bunn. Chapter 2 ends with a few unexpected words from Oriental philosophy, which, I suggest, substantiates Peirce's variation of classical logic at least as it was outlined in his day.

Chapter 3 outlines the *becoming* of the *being* of consciousness and the self through the *being* of their *becoming*, all within the incessantly flowing, fluctuating effervescence of semiosis. The first five of Peirce's ten signs find surprisingly congenial companions in the five "skandhas" of Buddhist philosophy, and the remaining five signs quite faithfully pattern William James's continuous emergence of consciousness in the mind of the semiotic agent. Thus we have movement from the interrelated, interacting, codependent give-and-take of signs, beginning with the radically free-flowing and *overdetermined* signs of the nature chiefly of Firstness to the ever-incomplete, *underdetermined* signs chiefly of the nature of Thirdness. Indian philosopher Nagarjuna is evoked in an attempt to illustrate that when the whole of semiosis is taken into exceedingly vague and nebulous account, in however inadequate a manner given our feeble intellectual faculties, classical logic is subverted, and any alternative must be free of the restrictive principles of identity, noncontradiction, and the excluded-middle. Finally, regarding Peirce's ten signs, Physicist John Archibald Wheeler offers us the radical sense of an alternative world portrayed by an alternative logic as implied by quantum theory and relativity—both of which have now been almost a century in the making.

Chapter 4 attempts to give further account of the uses of key terms in chapter 3—*space, time, synchronicity*—in light of the syncopation and resonance of signs as a consequence of their interrelatedness, interaction, and codependent arising within the stream of semiosis. This comes about by way of a certain facet of Oriental thought, coupled with the notion of imaginary and complex numbers (which play a role in quantum theory and relativity), as well as zero and Peirce's "nothingness" and Buddhist "emptiness." This special sense of semiosis, I will argue, renders inadequate any and all binary accounts, and most especially information theory formulations, of semiotics. Further allusions to sign engenderment and de-engenderment from the semiosis of everyday living serve to illustrate my contention in this regard. In chapter 5 I display for your contemplation what I call the "Possible Advertising Media Liar Paradox." This move serves to introduce Jean Baudrillard and the unfeasibility of any and all descriptions of the tackiness and the travails of postmodernism that remain trapped in binary principles. While presenting this argument, I allude to Peirce's "Pragmatic Maxim" in order to introduce the notion of what I dub the "Pragmatic Paradox" as an alternative to the "Possible Liar Paradox," with inclusion of sign engenderment and de-engenderment and the Peircean categories of Firstness, Secondness, and Thirdness in terms of the concepts of vagueness and generality and all they imply. The notion emerges that sign and meaning changes occur as a process of translation, of signs incessantly becoming other signs. This move introduces us to chapter 6 with the query, "What, then, is semiosis?" The upshot is that revision of ways of conceiving signs and hence the world must include a sense of both-and and neither-nor, contradiction, inconsistency, and incompleteness. The idea is that no matter to what extent the field of semiosis has been displayed in human thought, there will always be signs of something else—that is, alternative signs—waiting and ready to pop up and present themselves as something other than what might have been taken as valid or even "true" at a given time and place.

Departing from this juncture, we are quickly whisked along. Attention is turned in chapter 7 to the five senses—olfactory, gustatory, tactile, auditory, visual—as a general introduction. In the following chapter *kinesthetics* is given its due share of the spotlight as the mediary agent fusing the suffocating body/mind separation into a more liberating concept of *bodymind* and *brainmind*: an indivisible whole in terms of our participation in the semiosic flow. Syncope, resonance, and complementarity make their way back onto the scene, along with the introduction of *motility* and *haptic* perception—which aid and support kinesthetics—as the most basic characteristics of semiosis. The predominant theme consequently becomes: all is rhythm, the becoming of rhythm and the rhythm of becoming. Then, in chapter 9, Peirce's decalogue of signs is viewed as a direct consequence of the world of the senses, with reintroduction of the notions of *vagueness* and *generality*, *inconsistency* and *incompleteness*. Examples are put forth from the media, especially as they emerge in certain fascinating cases described by neurophysicist Oliver Sacks. The problems of *logocentrism*, *ocularcentrism*, and what I label *linguicentrism* at this point give us a much-deserved slap in the face, especially in regard to their relevance to early studies by Walter Ong and Marshall McLuhan and later by observers of our current "postmodern" turn.

In chapter 10 the undeniable importance of nonlinguistic signs emerges. Signs of tacitness, of embedded, entrenched, sedimented, habituated practices, are signs that the bodymind engenders and processes essentially because it knows how to do so, basically and without the intervention of the imperious, overconfident, and presumably autonomous mind, and in the absence of those so-called higher signs of symbolicity, of language, that stand nary a chance of making their way into the stream of semiosis without their nonlinguistic counterparts. In this light, chapter 11 outlines the severe limitations of the binary view of the postmodern scene—especially as schematically outlined by Baudrillard—and other linguicentric postures. This sets the stage in chapter 12 for a renewed look at the media with a focus on the radical conception of what might be conceived as alternative "cultural logics," which necessarily includes classical logic as a most necessary component. It becomes apparent that semiosis is most genuinely portrayed in terms of interrelatedness, interconnection, and codependence, all in a self-organizing process. As an important footnote, this chapter serves to set the stage for a discussion of specific cases of intra- and intercultural phenomena and crosscultural collisions in the remainder of the book.

In order to develop this discussion, chapter 13 avails itself of Michel de Certeau's notion of the subaltern's "guerrilla warfare" as a response to society's hegemonic power groups and their institutions. De Certeau's thesis is combined with Celeste Olalquiaga's creative account of kitsch within the New York Hispanic-American cultural scene and with the Amerindian response to the conquest and colonization, in light of the implications of an alternative "cultural logic" as suggested in the above chapters. I give all these concepts a specifically Peircean flavor, which serves further to reveal the cultural logics that have been in the process of emerging. Finally, chapter 14 further exemplifies the cultural logics theme with brief allusions to the notorious Murphy Brown versus Dan Quayle confrontation over family values, to the Rodney King beating at the hands of LAPD officers and the subsequent trial, and to pop star, Madonna, as a social phenomenon. The concluding sense of semiosis is it that we are, ourselves, our arrogant, pompous, imperious selves, no more than signs among signs, signs in search of signs capable of knowing signs, signs incompletely knowing themselves. The implication is: our universe is many yet one; it is what it is, yet it is always already something other than what it is/was/will be.

So, enjoy.

ACKNOWLEDGMENTS

My thanks to the Pontifícia Universidade Católica for the wonderfully energetic and inquisitive students it loaned me for a few hours, and thanks to those students who kept me on my toes with their questions and comments and who never registered their exasperation over my struggling Portuguese. I remain grateful to Lúcia Santaella for her very kind invitation, one more time, to visit her country, to all the colleagues of the "Programa de Estudos Pós-Graduados em Comunicação e Semiótica;" and to Michael Flamini and Rick Delaney at St. Martin's Press, for their editorial expertise and assistance in preparing this book. I wish also to acknowledge permission from the editor of *Semiotica* to reprint revised sections of "Do We Really Need Peirce's Whole Decalogue of Signs?" in chapters 1, 2, and 3 of this volume.

Araceli: Yes, this one is truly for you, all for you, always.

1

IS A DECALOGUE OF SIGNS REALLY NECESSARY?

I. TEN SIGNS OUT OF THREES

Even after reconsidering the disclaimers I made in the foregoing Preface, I must declare: "What a strained way to begin telling a tale of ten signs!"

Somewhat in defense of what will most likely appear to be a mania for abstraction in this and the next two chapters, let me say that Charles S. Peirce's concept of the sign has been largely ignored by most philosophers, has been given lip service by a few stalwart social scientists, and has provoked knee-jerks in many humanists due to its antagonizing and apparently forbidden nature. The reasons for this are quite obvious: an exposition of Peirce's ten classes of signs is a daunting task indeed! Consequently, these first steps will in all probability appear more akin to those triple jumps of track and field events than to the baby steps with which we have become accustomed in many books these days that pander to current fads. The leaps are from stone to stone in the ebullient white-water rapids along some stretch, somewhere, in the unruly semiosic cascade. These preliminaries are necessary, however, before we can enter the lulls and the meanderings that hopefully will follow, where smoother narrative will help effectively bear out Peirce's concept of the sign.

Without further ado, then, I list Peirce's three triads of signs qualified by his three categories: (1) qualisigns, sinsigns, and legisigns, (2) icons, indices, and symbols, and (3) terms (words), propositions (sentences), and arguments (texts).[1] These signs combine according to the categories of Firstness, Secondness, and Thirdness[2] to form ten signs as follows (see Peirce CP:2.227–73):

1. QUALISIGN: a feeling, a sensation (for example, the sense of "blueness" upon one's being subjected to a blue object).
    [The qualisign consists of the Firstness of the representamen (somewhat comparable to what is ordinarily conceived of as the sign), Firstness of the "semiotic object" (so labeled in order to distinguish it from the "real object" *an sich*), and Firstness of the interpretant (comparable—or at least comparable enough for our present purposes—to what ordinarily goes by the name of meaning). (Call the qualisign 111, after the numerals depicting the representamen, object, and interpretant, respectively)].

2. ICONIC SINSIGN: something not yet clearly distinguished from something else (a diagram apart from that to which it is possibly related; a shape, however vague it may be at this stage of semiosis).
    [The Secondness of the representamen, Firstness of the object, and Firstness of the interpretant (211)].

3. RHEMATIC INDEXICAL SINSIGN: a recognition or sudden jolt of surprise regarding the existence of the sign (a spontaneous cry, or attention abruptly drawn toward an unexpected object, act, or event).
    [The Secondness of the representamen, Secondness of the object, and Firstness of the interpretant (221)].

4. DICENT SINSIGN: an object of direct experience insofar as it is a sign indicating something other than itself and providing information regarding that something other; in other words, it must be affected in some way by its respective semiotic object (a weathervane, an arrow giving directions, a road sign with a curved arrow giving an indication of what lies ahead).
    [The Secondness of the representamen, Secondness of the object, and Secondness of the interpretant (222)].

5. ICONIC LEGISIGN: a general type of sign insofar as it manifests some likeness with something other than itself and requires each of its replicas to incorporate a definite quality that renders it fit to evoke in the mind the idea of its respective semiotic object (a diagram coupled with and related to that of which it is a likeness, a form and the idea the form is a form of).
    [The Thirdness of the representamen, Firstness of the object, and Firstness of the interpretant (311)].

6. RHEMATIC INDEXICAL LEGISIGN: a general type of sign each instantiation of which is affected by the semiotic object that the sign indicates, but with respect to which that sign remains distinguished

(a demonstrative pronoun, the Mercedes Benz logo in the absence of the car of which it is a sign, an image of a cup standing in for coffee, a photo of Michael Jordan as a replacement for Nike).

[The Thirdness of the representamen, Secondness of the object, and Firstness of the interpretant [321]).

7. DICENT INDEXICAL LEGISIGN: a type of sign, each instantiation of which supplies information in terms of the effect of its object on it and the manner in which that object is apart from it (a street cry such as "Watch out!," commonplace expressions such as "Hi!," "You doin' all right?," "Bless you," or a hand extended to open a door for someone or to shake another hand as a salutation).

[The Thirdness of the representamen, Secondness of the object, and Secondness of the interpretant (322)].

8. RHEMATIC SYMBOL or SYMBOLIC RHEME (TERM): a sign—perhaps in the beginning arbitrary—that is related to its object by an association of a general idea or image in the mind that, due to certain conventional habits or dispositions of that mind, tends to produce a general concept with respect to the object to which it relates (a common noun, an adjective, adverb, or verb).

[The Thirdness of the representamen, Thirdness of the object, and Firstness of the interpretant (331)].

9. DICENT SYMBOL or PROPOSITION (SENTENCE): a sign related to its object by an association of general ideas each of which acts like a rhematic symbol, except that its interpretant represents the dicent symbol as being, with respect to that of which it is a sign, actually affected by its object; that is, the object evokes the calling up of the sign and the sign evokes the idea or image of the object in terms of convention and hence disposition: therefore, the sign's relation to its object is necessarily by convention, if not by other causes (an evocation related to an object, act, or event in the world or the world of signs "out there" and apart from the evocation).

[The Thirdness of the representamen, Thirdness of the object, and Secondness of the interpretant (322)].

10. ARGUMENT (TEXT): a sign whose interpretant is related to its object in terms of that which is conventional and accepted as the general way of the social world (hence also of what is generally perceived and conceived as the physical world). As an argument or text the sign is a genuine symbol and legisign, and a replica of this sign is a dicent sinsign; that is, like a "pointer" or an "arrow," a replica (say, a copy of Truman Capote's *In Cold Blood*) is an indication of

the sign in a general sense at the time of its emergence into the universe of semiosis.

[The Thirdness of the representamen, Thirdness of the object, and Thirdness of the interpretant (333)].

"Too much too quickly," one might wish to retort. However, since reference to these ten sign types by way of the trio of integers depicting them will be made often throughout this disquisition, I am confident that familiarity, and with luck even some level of intimacy, with them will eventually be forthcoming. For the moment, the obvious question to ask is: Why on earth should a combination of three combinations of three classes of signs into nine signs give rise precisely to ten separate classes of signs? Why not eighty-one? Twenty-seven? Or even eighteen? At least those numbers are multiples of nine and three.

In search of an answer, we are drawn toward some of the geometry, mathematics, and logic of the nineteenth century insofar as it has found a place in the twentieth-century view of the world. Above all, it has to do with the shape of space. Of course, in the classical conception space really had no shape to speak of: it was simply an empty container, "out there" and waiting to be occupied by any number of things, the chief stipulation being that two things could not occupy the same part of the whole of space at the same instant. Moreover, space was unlimited: it extended out and out, to infinity, in straight, harmonious Euclidean marching order. In contrast to this classical view of space, the ancients at one time thought of the universe as finite and bounded: it had edges—go too far and you will fall off—or it was a kind of hemisphere, with all the stars and planets sort of hanging down. The twentieth-century view is in a rough manner of speaking a combination of the classical and the ancient views: like an expanding sphere, it is finite, but since there exists the possibility of going around and around that sphere without ever crossing the point of origin, it is unbounded and unlimited.

It might seem that if space is unbounded, then it must be infinite as well. Not necessarily so, however. Take one-dimensional space. If a horizontal line is cut at a point to the right and at another point to the left, then it is of finite length (though it contains an infinity of points if considered as a continuum) and it is bounded. If at the cuts, arrows are drawn that point indefinitely toward the receding horizon, then the line is infinite and unbounded. On the other hand, if at the point of the cuts the line is brought around to meet itself at its two extremities to form a circle, we have finite but unbounded one-dimensional space. This appears simple enough. At the next step of dimensionality, the surface of a sphere, such as the Earth, is an example of two-dimensional space that is finite and unbounded. Walk around it forever, and you will never exactly get to the end, for it doubles back on itself and joins with itself in three-dimensional space.

In his notorious lecture of 1854 entitled "On the Hypotheses that Lie at the Foundations of Geometry," Bernhard Riemann proposed that something similar to the Earth's surface as finite and unbounded two-dimensional space could also be said of the three-dimensional space we inhabit:

> In the extension of space-construction to the infinitely great, we must distinguish between *unboundedness* and *infinite extent*. The unboundedness of space possesses a greater empirical certainty than any external experience. But its infinite extent by no means follows from this. If we ascribe to space constant curvature, then space must necessarily be finite provided this curvature has ever so small a positive value. (Riemann 1854:14–17, quoted in Rucker 1984:93; italics in original)

Space, that is, what we conceive to be our three-dimensional space, is a hypersurface of a four-dimensional hypersphere, much in the manner that the curved two-dimensional surface of our earth makes up a sphere in our three-dimensional space. Of course, consideration of a two-dimensional organism, a Flatlander, and her inhabiting the surface of our earth, is a quite simple feat for us, since we already inhabit the surface of the earth in what we conceive to be three-dimensional space. But imagine how difficult it would be for her to comprehend that she actually inhabits a curved two-dimensional world that exists within three-dimensional space.

"Impossible!" . . . someone pipes up. "How could she mentally jump out of her two-dimensional surface to imagine beings of solid rather than flat constituency? How would it be possible for her to imagine herself in the next dimension looking at her husband and seeing all of him all at once, his front side and his back side and his brain and heart and stomach and intestines, just as we might look at the blueprint of a house and see the arrangement of the rooms from one holistic perspective? How could she get a feel for this higher dimension?"

Difficult questions. If we wish to add fuel to the fire, let us apply them to ourselves. How would it be possible for us to jump to the fourth dimension and create the faithful image of and conceptualize a four-dimensional organism—let us call him Ludwig—who can in an instant see all of us, including our heart and lungs and viscera, in much the same way in which we would gaze upon the blueprint of a house? How can we begin to comprehend how Ludwig would perceive and conceive his four-dimensional world and our impoverished three-dimensional world as well? Getting a feel for ourselves of the viewpoint of a four-dimensional organism is as difficult as a Flatlander's getting a feel for our world. I will not go any further on this topic, since it lies outside the direct interests of this inquiry, and besides, a spate of books exist as self-help programs for understanding the four-dimensional space-time manifold.[3] Suffice it to say for now that an account of our three-dimensional universe from within a four-dimensional space-time manifold is precisely what Einstein was able to offer to the scientific community.

The common assumption has it that Einstein took Riemann's non-Euclidean geometry and put it to use in his General Theory of Relativity. Morris Kline (1980) takes issue with this folk account. He suggests that Riemann's geometry was not necessarily the most adequate mathematical expression for general relativity. It was a matter of Einstein's looking around for a formal expression of the concepts he had in mind; Riemann's work happened to be at hand and it seemed to fit the bill better than anything else, so he used it. Adhocness is more prevalent than most scholars would like to admit. French mathematician Henri Poincaré demonstrated at the end of the last century that ellipses are too simple, and that in a many-body system—such as our sun, its planets, and their moons—the situation is of virtually infinite complexity. Kline's point is that one generation's mathematics does not provide a magical wand for the next generation of physicists, but rather, physicists look around for what shows promise, they try it out, and if it works, they assume the theory ain't broke and discourage anyone from trying to fix it.[4] In a certain sense, the adhocness of theories is both repugnant and useful to physicists. It is tantamount to the biologist's joke about teleology, that, like a second lover, one wants to keep her/him around but doesn't want to be seen with her/him in certain circles.

In sum, there are two enigmas regarding the relation between mathematics and physics. First, the capacity of physicists to invent uses for mathematics, and second, the physicists' uncanny anticipation of "reality" through the aesthetic qualities of mathematics. As a consequence of these two enigmas, there have been frequent and apparently fortuitous unexpected surprises regarding both physics and mathematics, just as there have been in the arts.

Enough preliminaries.

II. THE DECALOGUE AND GEOMETRY

For sure, Peirce's conception of geometry was to an extent influenced by Riemann (Murphey 1961:219). Riemann was arguably the first geometer to consider the two-dimensional surface of the Earth as finite but unbounded, since the space of this surface is bent back in three-dimensional space finally to connect its head with its tail in such a way that it is no longer possible to determine where the head begins and where the tail ends. In other words, from a severely restricted view along the Earth's surface, hardly more can be said except that the center is everywhere and the outer extremities of the surface are nowhere. In the same manner, it is possible to imagine the three-dimensional space of our universe as being bent—as Einstein so conceived it—in four-dimensional space into a hypersphere. This is comparable to the "Fearful Sphere of Pascal," as Jorge Luis Borges (1964:189–92) puts it, or to Nicholas of Cusa's God, whose center is everywhere and whose circumference is nowhere.

In Riemann's conception, consequently, the shortest distance between two points on the Earth's surface is not a Euclidean straight line, but a line that curves along the sphere's geodesics. An equilateral triangle, consequently, has a bulging base and bulging sides such that the sum of its angles are slightly more than 180°. For an easy illustration of the Riemann effect, draw a triangle on a balloon, blow it up, and notice that as the globe becomes larger and larger the sides of the triangle bulge more and more. It is no longer a triangle with three straight lines and three angles the sum of which is precisely 180°. The upshot is that Euclidean straight line geometry is one way of looking at the universe, one with which Newtonian mechanics is quite comfortable. Another, Riemannian-Einsteinian way of looking at the universe is by way of non-Euclidean geometry. And both are equally true and equally false, depending upon the perspective. Regarding this issue, Peirce writes:

> That geometry contains propositions which may be understood to be synthetical judgments *a priori,* I will not dispute. Such are the propositions that the sum of the three angles of a triangle is invariably and unconditionally equal to 180°. . . . But the difficulty is that, considered as applicable to the real world, they are *false. Possibly* the three angles of every triangle make exactly 180°; but nothing more unlikely can be conceived. It is false to say it is necessarily so. Considered, on the other hand, as purely formal, these propositions are merely ideal. Some of them define an ideal hypothesis (in the mathematical sense), and the rest are deductions from those definitions. (Peirce, "Critic of Arguments, synthetic

Propositions *a priori*," p. 1, IB2 Box 12 of unpublished papers; cited in
Murphey 1961:223; italics in original)

Peirce goes on to write that a triangle the sum of whose angles is exactly
180° is an "ideal space" with which "real space approximately agrees." For
Peirce, space is continuous and characterized by "manifoldness," since all
lines are self-returning. What distinguishes space from other continua is
the existence of bodies in space as once-occurring bodies—as *haecceities,* so
they are called in philosophy—made possible by cuts or breaks in the continuum. Peirce's conception of space is in this sense topological through
and through, before the fact of topology as a distinct discipline (Murphey
1961:219–28).

In order finally to get to the meat of the story of a Riemann-Peirce
semiotics, consider a race of Flatlanders on a two-dimensional sheet-uni-
verse that is actually crumpled rather than perfectly flat. Our proud Flatlanders will be found felicitously sliding along on/in their universe,
oblivious to the fact that they are actually wobbling up and down and to
and fro, like some drunk on his way home after the local bar has closed.
Their equivalent of our Isaac Newton might even have invented a set of
laws governing the movement of all the objects in their universe in terms
of the lighter objects' being attracted to the heavier objects—whereas we
can actually see that the heavy objects happen to exist where the two-dimensional sheet dips sharply—due to their additional weight—while the
lighter objects exist at less pronounced dips, so they will naturally tend to
slide downward in the direction of their heftier counterparts. In other
words, from our three-dimensional vantage point we can quite clearly see
that force is a consequence of the topological twists and turns of two-dimensional space, rather than there existing some mysterious force attract-
ing objects to one another (and the same is now said of our
three-dimensional universe: electricity, magnetism, and gravity are the
consequence of the "crumpling" of our three-dimensional universe in the
four-dimensional space-time continuum).

Now, as I naively understand Riemann geometry, the task is that of specifying the "warping" of non-Euclidean space. Take for example a piece of
planar space bending back upon itself and then spreading out to form a
sphere. The surface is two-dimensional, but its curvature takes up residence
in an additional dimension. Riemann introduced a collection of three numbers attached to every point along the surface that describes its bending: two
numbers on the flat Cartesian plane corresponding to the point's location on
the x and y axes, and an additional number pinpointing its deviation from

flat to curved space. If we have a four-dimensional spatial manifold, Riemann found that ten numbers at each point of the three-dimensional space to specify its curvature in four dimensions are required. Why ten numbers? If I may be allowed to simplify the matter—I hope without doing violence to Riemann's very subtle formulation—consider three-dimensional space as the sum of three planes intersecting at the three axes of solid geometry, x, y, and z. A point on each plane needs two numbers, corresponding to the horizontal and vertical axes, and one number specifying the plane's deviation from flatness to curvature. Taking the three planes into account, we have nine numbers. Now, another number is necessary in order to specify the curvature of this three-dimensional space in the fourth dimension. That gives us the tenth number. By Riemann's construction of this geometrical braintwister, no matter how knotted three-dimensional space may be, ten numbers and ten numbers only are sufficient.

Riemann's ten numbers can be arranged symmetrically in what is called a *metric tensor*. Relations in what is known as tensor analysis remain valid, regardless of the system of coordinates used to specify the quantities—or in qualitative semiotics, the values of the signs. Such relations are called *covariant*. Tensors are a matter of vectors, and vectors are regarded as entities that, in n-dimensional space, have n components that are altered according to specific rules. Vectors themselves are independent of coordinates, but they are treated in terms of components with all coordinate systems on an equal footing. For the sake of convenience, coordinates are numbered from 1 to n, and the components of tensors are denoted by letters having subscripts and superscripts, each of which independently takes on the values 1 to n. From metrical tensors it is possible to construct more complicated tensors involving curvature in space. Einstein proposed for his General Theory of Relativity that gravitation should be represented in terms of a metrical tensor of four-dimensional space-time. Once he limited himself to these tensors, he was led to an essentially unique tensor equation for the law of gravitation, in which gravitation emerged not as a mysterious force between physical bodies but as a manifestation of the curvature of space-time. This was indeed amazing. It meant that space is not an "empty container" at all, but rather, it is an "emptiness" that, by its very nature, can give rise to everything that is. There is an important difference here between empty container and emptiness. A bucket, in order to be filled, needs something to be put into it by someone outside the bucket. Emptiness, in contrast, is self-sufficient, self-contained, and immanent. There is nothing and nobody "outside"; in fact, there is nothing at all, there is only emptiness. And emptiness is just that, emptiness.

"Explain yourself," my skeptic protests. "What, in precise terms, are you getting at?" Well, the fact is that in precise terms I'm not sure what I am getting at, for the picture—picture, as an icon, an obsessively ocular image—inexorably remains vague. And, I would expect, relatively few people, physicists included, are *really* sure, that is, *absolutely really* sure, about the implications of relativity theory—to say nothing of quantum theory. Some years ago physicist Arthur Eddington remarked that only three people in the world understood the theory of relativity—Einstein we would suppose, Eddington he obviously supposed, and who knows who the third person might have been. Of course, the theory itself is strange enough. What the theory implies regarding our existence within our universe is virtually beyond imagination.

Actually, the details of Riemann's metric tensor are not necessary. What I find fascinating is a spread of Peirce's basic ten sign types on a Riemann sort of "metric tensor" sheet, as in figure 1.[5] Each sign type is specified by three numbers related to the levels of representamen-object-interpretant and three spatial dimensions with which we are now familiar. Six of these sets of three numbers are mirror images of one another and hence redundant. So although there are sixteen boxes, there are only ten independent semiotic units, as indicated within the heavy borderline. Sign 111 is the initiation of this "semiotic metric tensor" and 333 is the end of the road—though, of course, in the Peirce sense in a finite world there cannot be a final interpretant cut in granite for all time. In this sense these two signs are, from the most ideal view—though not in practice according to good Peircean sign theory—self-contained and self-sufficient. One might say the same of 222. However, since this sign is the first to reach the Secondness of the interpretant (the conception of something other than the sign and its object) it indicates the first important step toward asymmetry, irreversibility. That is to say, 222 is the first clear-cut case of the existence of Secondness, of something other, of otherness, to and for the mind, since we have the Secondness of the interpretant.[6] One might also suggest that signs 311 and 331 suffer for the lack of enantiomorphic—i.e., mirror image—companions within the matrix. However, since these are the first signs to reach the Thirdness of the representamen and the semiotic object respectively, they are, at least in that respect, also self-sufficient—albeit incompletely and ephemerally so, for the semiosic process never stops there, or anywhere else for that matter, but is always already on the go.[7]

Notice that (1) the first two and the fifth sign of the Peircean decalogue, 111, 211, and 311, belong chiefly to the sphere of iconicity, (2) signs three, four, six, and seven—221, 222, 321, and 322—are chiefly indexical

111	112	122	222
211	311	123	223
221	321	331	233
222	322	332	333

Figure 1

in nature, and (3) 331, 332, and 333 are primarily of the nature of symbolicity, though they contain within themselves, as do all signs after 111, the whole of the semiosic process and sign engenderment that preceded them. Notice also that (4) chiefly iconic signs could be characterized as signs of Firstness, of visceral, sensory, corporeal semiosic processing, (5) chiefly indexical signs are characterized by relations of Secondness, of otherness—the self's inner other, its social other represented by the community to which it belongs, and its physical world other, and (6) the last three signs are chiefly of Thirdness, of mediation, of the mind. These interrelations, I would submit, testify to the lack of any mind-body split; rather, there is constant bodymind give-and-take, for body and mind are interdependent, and in fact, part of an inseparable whole.[8]

Riemann's metric tensor made way for the possibility of describing space of any dimension and with arbitrary warps and woofs. It also reveals the possibility of multiply connected spaces by way of what are called in contemporary physical theory "wormholes." Quite significantly, Peirce developed a comparable notion of wormholes in his theory of a "logic of continuity" and in his general cosmology. A tangible illustration of the concept is quite simple—and it rather conveniently falls in line with a Peirce "thought-experiment." Stack a few sheets of paper one on top of the other, and you have various two-dimensional universes as the mere possibility for the construction of art works, geometrical figures, texts, proofs, or just meaningless doodling. In other words, in this state of things the stack of sheets is mere "nothingness," as Peirce puts it (recall the above allusion to space as "emptiness"). Now, from your own three-dimensional universe, with a paper punch make a circular hole in the first sheet—which Peirce calls the "initial sheet of assertion"—and you have entered the second universe. By sliding and warping your first sheet it is possible to enter any spot on the second universe from one solitary point on your first universe. Punch a hole in the second universe, and you can enter the third universe at any point from that hole, which could in turn be entered from the hole in your first universe. Further holes—or "cuts" as Peirce calls them—in this and successive sheets allow you to "pass into worlds which, in the imaginary worlds of the other cuts, are themselves represented to be imaginary and false, but which may, for all that, be true, and therefore continuous with the sheet of assertion itself, although this is uncertain" (CP:4.512).

Peirce invites us to regard the "ordinary blank sheet of assertion" as a film upon which there exists the as yet undeveloped photograph of all the possible "events" of the universe. But this is not a literal picture, for when we consider historically the range of "events" that have been asserted to be "true," we must conclude that this "book" can be none other than a continuum that must "clearly have more dimensions than a surface or even than a solid; and we will suppose it to be plastic, so that it can be deformed in all sorts of ways without the continuity and connection of parts being ever ruptured" (CP:4.512). The initial blank "sheet of assertion" from this book taken in terms of a continuum contains an infinity of possibilities. Cuts as statements relating to events in the world are like a photographic plate that is subject to a scene "out there," which we desire to record. Moreover, since the sheet is plastic, it can be deformed in any way we like so as to yield more or less the world we wanted in the first place. In this manner, an infinity of worlds can come into our semiotic reality according to the manner in which we collaborate with the flow of semiosis, and depending upon our desires, inclinations, preconceptions, and prejudices—our horizon, so to speak.

Hence, Peirce goes on, the original photograph we might happen to take is, more appropriately, a map in which all points of a surface correspond to points on the next surface, and so on successively, and the continuity is preserved unbroken. Each point, each cut, corresponds to the initial "sheet of assertion" where the real state of things (that is, perceived and conceived to be "real" at a given time and place) is represented. All successive sheets, then, represent an infinite set of potential events, many or most of which can, at another time and place, become "real." And, in light of speculations by contemporary physicists themselves, the wormholes alluded to above are capable of connecting one point in the three-dimensional universe within which we live and breathe with another point light years away, and all in virtual instantaneity. This is theoretical speculation, of course, worthy of Alice in Wonderland for whom the wormhole was the looking glass as a passage from one universe to another. Yet it is serious business for physicists, and should not simply be taken with a grain of salt.

Riemann brought about an evaporation of the spell cast by Euclidean geometry over 2,000 years ago. By the same token, Peirce's concept of the sign, if taken straight as pure spirits and without a chaser, is capable of dissolving the smoothly contoured ice of Cartesian vintage floating around in the drink and trying to pass itself off as finely honed, sharply cornered, and beautifully hexagonal crystals of H_2O. The universe of signs is actually as non-Cartesian (and non-Saussurean and non-Boolean to boot) as Riemann geometry is non-Euclidean. Indeed, it can be said that between approximately the years 1890 and 1910 Peirce realized the golden age of his intellectual output, and that literature, the arts, and the sciences realized the golden age of Reimann curved space: four-dimensional geometry. Riemann and other geometers entered avant garde circles in art, literature, and philosophy, and four-dimensional geometry was appropriated by physicists, most notably Einstein with his Special Theory of Relativity of 1905.[9]

But enough of that story also: however intriguing, it remains outside the focus of the present inquiry. Back to Peirce's decalogue.

III. LIKE A FRESHLY CUT GEM?
OR, ARE THE BOUNDARIES INEVITABLY VAGUE?

Notice that, according to the above qualifications of Peirce's semiotics, more complex signs contain less complex signs. In fact, the more developed signs owe their very existence to the signs preceding them and charting the way for their possible navigation on the high semiosic seas. Given this containing-contained relationship, notice also that if we map Peirce's signs in triangular fashion according to figure 2 (*CP*:2.264), we begin with 111 at the upper right-hand corner and move downward diagonally to 222. This would be equivalent to figure 3. The same operation can be carried out for signs 311–333 eventually to yield figure 4.

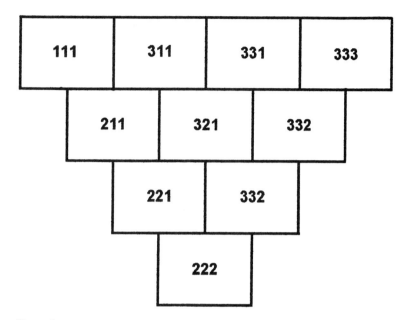

Figure 2

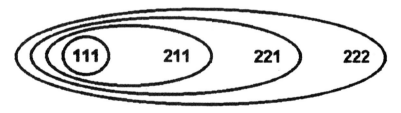

Figure 3

Particularly regarding figure 4, study the relationships between the three families of signs that are chiefly iconic (111, 211, 311), chiefly indexical (221, 222, 321, 322), and chiefly symbolic (331, 332, 333). Observe the containing-contained relations, the subtle overlapping, the embedment of the less complex signs into the more complex signs as if they were a variation of that simile of the onion—albeit an irregular and nonlinear onion in this case—being peeled, shell by shell, until only the core (111) remains. Observe also that the arrows depict sign engenderment from 111 to 333,

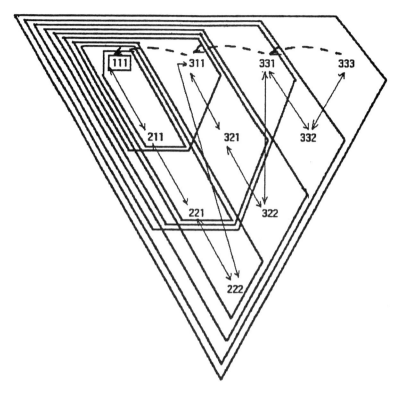

Figure 4

and their mirror-image, sign de-engenderment from 333 to 111 by the long route or by a successive transformation of symbolicity to iconicity according to the broken arrows—to be discussed below.[10] The signs, spaces, and cuts or boundaries in figure 4 bear a relationship to the essentials of what Peirce termed "existential graphs," his own form of logic before the birth of symbolic logic chiefly at the hands of Whitehead and Russell (see Roberts 1973). According to existential graphs, cuts are made in the "sheet of assertion." What appears within the cut is negated, and if two cuts are made, then it is the equivalent of a negation of the negation to produce a positive assertion.

Thus we can construct table 1, which relates classical logic and G. Spencer-Brown's (1979) "calculus of forms" to Peirce's "existential graphs." Notice, in the first place, that in the case of Spencer-Brown and

Peirce's existential graphs, and unlike the notation of classical logic, a single mark or cut is all that is necessary in order to engender the entire edifice of logic.[11] That is to say, the merely possible actualization of an entity, *a*, is negated (by a "cut"), then it is negated ("cut") again, and thus the possibility becomes actualized (*a*). This activity gives rise to the possible actualization of another entity, *b*. Then *b* can be actualized instead of *a* (either *a* or *b*). This gives rise to the possible actualization of both entities (*a* and *b*), and finally to the possible actualization of neither of them, or to the possible implication that if one of them is actualized then the other one will also be actualized (if *a*, then *b*).

This is indeed significant. It ushers in an element of parsimony, of elegance predicated on the negation and on the "not yet decided, needing-to-be-decided" but "not yet merely indeterminate" possibility of Peirce's category of Firstness. Regarding sign relations as they have been described

Table 1

thus far, let us use this primitive form of calculus with only one symbol, a. Assume Firstness to be represented by an uncertainty between actualization into a Second of two different possible instances of a, a_1 and a_2, with the first instantiation preceding the second one by a temporal increment. The expression of the two possible instantiations is $\boxed{a_1\,a_2}$ (= , that is, "nothing," "nothingness"), bearing in mind that neither a_1 nor a_2 has (yet) been actualized as a sign. However, since both a_1 and a_2 are in a state of suspension or readiness to be actualized for some semiotic agent, the equation becomes $\boxed{a_1\,a_2}$ (= both a_1 and a_2, but [still] as possibilities for the agent, since neither has [yet] been fully actualized in consciousness—sign 111). At this stage, conditions of symmetry continue to exist between a_1 and a_2; yet now, there is no priority or privilege of one over the other. Secondness, which demands, in its purest form, distinguishability between each instantiation of a, is expressed by the equation $\boxed{a_1}\boxed{a_2}$ (either a_1 or a_2, depending upon the expectations and inclinations of the semiotic agent—sign 211).

However, since the two items in question are both actualized, albeit during different temporal increments, we have $\boxed{a_1}\!-\!\boxed{a_2}$ (indicating [indexing] that a_1 and then a_2 were actualized [recall that Secondness introduces a primitive form of asymmetry—signs 221, 222]). Although this temporal relationship does not appear in table 1, it is a transitory stage between signs prior to awareness of them as such and awareness of one sign after another, that is, awareness of time. The introduction of Thirdness, largely signified by implication $\boxed{a_1\ a_2}$ (if a_1, then a_2—signs 311 to 333), finally introduces a more genuine form of asymmetry, irreversibility, and "time's arrow"—though the "arrow" in the expression has no bearing on experienced temporality, it is at this point merely a primitive logical construct. In the words of Charles Hartshorne (1970:88–89), Firstness ushers in independence, Secondness direction and dependence, and Thirdness relationality and temporality (the contrast between the "already settled, decided past" and the "not yet decided," "needing-to-be-decided—not yet merely indeterminate—future.") That is, a_2 is not what it *was* but no longer *is*, and what it *is* is subject to anticipation of what it potentially *will be* at some moment in the future.

If we correlate the three Peircean categories as described herein and their respective expressions, we have figure 5. In the most simple manner of putting it—and, I hope, without doing violence to Peirce's subtle concept of the sign—category 1, Peirce's Firstness, is the feeling of what *might be* the case. Category 2, Secondness, is the action, the effect, of that which *is* the case. And category 3, Thirdness, is the relation, the mediation

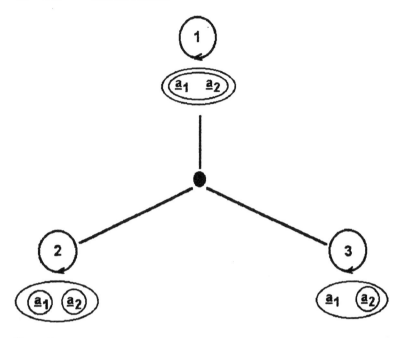

Figure 5

between the other two categories, delineating what *would most likely be* or *will most likely have been* the case in the event that certain conditions are in effect. Category 1 implies "this and that," 2 implies "either this or that but not both," and 3 implies "if this, then that." While 1 is mere atemporal oscillation between symmetrical entities, 2 is linear, hence at least the root beginning of asymmetry, and 3 attains the highest degree of asymmetry and the initiation of temporality. In other words, disjoined terms are symmetrical, the binary operation of combining terms is temporal but purely linear, and, with the triadic relation, legitimate asymmetry and hence irreversibility or temporality begin to exercise their force.

In fact, Peirce's three basic sign types—icons, indices, and symbols—fill the bill quite effectively regarding the categories delineated in figure 5. *Iconicity* is unity, *indexicality* is division, and *symbolicity* is mediation. Relating this triadicity to figure 4, we have signs that are "chiefly iconic" in their nature and their functioning (111, 211, 311), signs that are "chiefly indexical" (221, 222, 321, 322), and signs that are "chiefly symbolic" (331, 332, 333). From 111 to 333 we run the gamut to the most genuine signs of which we feeble and fallible human semiotic agents are capable. Then, in view of figure 4, we can begin peeling off the shells, to signs of de-engenderment, and we finally end up with 111, signs of feeling, sensation, and then with nothing at all, with pure emptiness. At this "pointless" point, this emptiness of all knowing, binary or otherwise, there is no subject-object split, no mind-body rift, no separation of the self from its others, no logocentrism or linguicentrism: all is codependent, interrelated, and in an incessant process of interaction.

IV. THEN HOW IS THE FLOW?

In fact, in figure 6 we have a chiefly iconic circuit (111, 211, 311), a chiefly indexical circuit (221, 222, 321, 322) and a chiefly symbolic circuit (331, 332, 333). Notice that the six signs at the upper right-hand portion of figure 1, as "mirror images" of the signs at the lower left-hand portion, have indexicality in common, but not iconicity or symbolicity. This is an indication that these "enantiomorphic" sign-twins enjoy relations of Secondness to some other to which they must be related in order

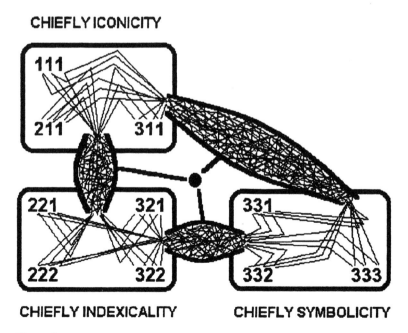

Figure 6

that proper interpretation of the signs may be forthcoming. Notice also that in the sign de-engenderment, 333 → 331 → 311, there is, as depicted in figure 4, one crossing of a boundary in the first instance, two in the second instance, and three in the third instance, thus rendering the crossings equal to the number of Peircean categories.

Figure 6, it becomes quite evident, does not illustrate semiosis as a net or web, but, most properly speaking, as flow, process. In other words, the zone of chiefly iconicity flows, by way of the Secondness of the iconic sinsign (211), into the zone of chiefly indexicality, and by way of the Thirdness of the iconic legisign (311), into the zone of both chiefly indexicality and chiefly symbolicity. Notice also that the Firstness of the rhematic symbol or word (331) is there and with open arms to engulf signs of chiefly iconicity, and the dicent symbol or sentence (332) is ready to do the same with signs of chiefly indexicality. In this manner, the categories and sign types are by no stretch of the imagination static pigeon-holes, rigid boundaries, brilliant gems cut and polished for all time. Rather, they leak, often profusely. Or better, they pour forth one into the others and the others into the one. Semiosis is infinitely more than mere language (hence it is extralinguicentric), and it is infinitely more than the merely visual (hence it is nonocularcentric). More adequately put, as we shall eventually note, it is in large part haptic, kinesthetic, embodied, visceral, of the nature of motility, of somata.

Nietzsche once observed in *Thus Spake Zarathustra* that there is more knowledge in the body than in the loftiest truth. And with reason. In the traditional West within which Nietzsche dwelled the body had been disrespectfully shoved aside to make way for what was conceived to be the more noble mathematical, scientific, logical, and philosophical concerns of the mind and its capacity to mirror the world. Galileo expelled the spheres of auditory, olfactory, gustatory, and tactile sensations from scientific inquiry. Shortly thereafter, primary qualities—objective, measurable, empirical, subject to the gaze of the presumably infallible eye—exercised their hegemony over that relatively messy data gathered by the other senses. Descartes was perhaps the philosopher who most obsessively stressed the importance of everything quantifiable, purportedly of that of which we can be certain. In contrast, figure 6 provides an image of flux and flow, interdependence and interrelatedness, with neither authentic space nor time, at least in the classical sense and taking either of the two in isolation from the other one. Above all, there is in figure 6 predominately neither hegemonically visual nor linguistic signs, but more properly speaking, in addition to the visual and linguistic, there is the haptic, kinesthetic, and embodied sensing in regard to one of a plethora of possible semiotic worlds. There are no autonomous, atomistic signs but rather an effervescent whole: each sign plays the role of a scintillating point making its appearance as an ephemeral, sparkling event. Moreover, meanings of signs within the whole are not in the representamen, the semiotic object, or the interpretant, not in the head of the sign addresser or addressee or in the space between them (pace flowcharts in information theory and semiology diagrams). The meaning of any part of semiosis is inseparable from the whole of semiosis.[12]

As we shall note in more detail, signs 111, 211, and 311, of chiefly iconicity, are those that play the starring role in sensory *qualia* by way of taste, smell, and sound (other than language, music, and other linearly organized sign series). These signs are engendered in the inner self more than in terms of the self's projecting out in order to gather in a harvest of signs in the external world, such as is the case in tactile and especially visual sensory qualia. These inwardly engendered signs are more attuned to nonlinearity, or holism. Signs 221, 222, 321, and 322, chiefly indexical, are more in tune with surface, primarily linear, interrelations. Sights and sounds and touches and tastes and smells enter, one after another, in a linear stream. These signs are the stars in the cosmic game of the semiotically real world, as they race along, their rhythmic movements at their best coming into synchrony with the general flow of things. With respect to these signs, qualities, inner drives and desires, gut feelings and flinchings, visceral huffs and heaves find their place among their counterparts in the physical world "out there," for good or for bad. Finally, signs 331, 332, and 333, chiefly symbolic, are the signs of surface linearity, which, when put into practice, becomes depth nonlinearity. These signs, primarily of sight and sound, of language, reason, logic, and analysis, are signs of mediation at its best. They establish interrelations between all signs and bring the sign components—representamens, objects, and interpretants—into the most effective coordination with one another. These are primarily the signs that have fallen victim to logocentrism, the myth of presence, ocularcentrism, and the fallacies of representation, reference, correspondence, and essentialism, all of which pay due homage to Plato's realm of eternal objects, that ethereal sphere in Western thought so venerated over the centuries.

Moreover, signs of chiefly Firstness at their most basic are what Peirce dubbed "hypoicons," which come in three sorts: images, diagrams, and metaphors. These are signs most closely aligned with the body, signs of body images, of relations with the others of one's inner self, of one's community, and of the hard-core physical world, and signs as figures in terms of "as if" worlds whose nature is such that they are comparable in some re-spect to what is perceived and conceived as the "real." Metaphors in their most primitive functioning, as rudimentary Thirdness, are signs of the mind, thought-signs. When developed into full-blown signs of Thirdness, as linguistic signs, and when on their best behavior, they are capable of giv-ing rise to hypothetical or contrary-to-fact-conditionals, which can then lead to further interaction with the community and physical world others in order to further one's conception of what one's semiotically real world is all about. That is, I refer to the nature and functioning of Peirce's "prag-matic maxim" (briefly to be discussed in chapter 3 [for more see Merrell 1997a]).

V. LIVING SIGNS

But for the moment, please return to the arrows in figure 4, which depict sign engenderment and de-engenderment, or in Peircean terms, "gener-acy" and "de-generacy" (see note 10). Sign engenderment proceeds from 111 to 333; sign de-engenderment goes in the other direction. Engender-ment involves the "growth of signs." This is no guarantee that signs of higher numerical value will be more effective than or superior to their pre-decessors, but rather, they are simply more complex than their younger counterparts—an issue to be discussed later. Signs of de-engenderment are not necessarily signs whose "growth" has been stunted or whose destiny is that of the incredible shrinking man. They are signs that have become em-bedded, sedimented, entrenched, habitualized, to the extent that the mind can engage itself in automatic pilot and leave the body to engender and in-terpret signs in the way it knows best. Consequently, de-engendered signs have submerged within the mind and perhaps even outside consciousness to become tacitly processed: the iconic function takes over where the sym-bolic and indexical functions previously held sway. (I must hasten to em-phasize once again that Peirce by no stretch of the imagination meant to disparage icons in his use of the term "de-generate" signs. "De-generate" signs are actually more fundamental, more essential to communication, than their more "developed" cousins [NE 2:241]).

Briefly put, de-engendered signs are non-genuine. Consummate sym-bols would be in the theoretical long run of things the only authentic signs. Indices and icons are not mere weakened and diluted Secondness and Firstness, however; they contain the potential to bloom into full-blown Thirdness, like the potential within an acorn to become an oak. But . . . no, that's not it, not quite. The Aristotelian simile is actually rather insufficient, for Peirce's concept is mathematical more than ontological, essential, or existential. A simple and more appropriate illustration of Peirce's concept is the map paradox: an absolutely complete map must contain itself ad infinitum. Since each map of the series will be contained within the preceding map;

> [t]here will be a point contained in all of them, and this will be the map of itself. Each map which directly or indirectly represents the country is itself mapped in the next. . . . We may therefore say that each is a representation of the country *to* the next map; and that point that is in all the maps is in itself the representation of nothing but itself. (*CP* 5.71)

This "point" that Peirce refers to is self-sufficient, though not all-sufficient, since it is not a complete representation but only a point on the continuous, infinitely regressive map: it is a map of itself. Like Firstness or what Peirce calls a "monad," the point is related to nothing outside itself. If it were related to another point by a straight line drawn between them, we would have Secondness: the point-map would in turn contain the point to which it was "pointing." And by considering from a higher dimension the entire all-encompassing map as a two-dimensional sheet, we have the triadic relation of Firstness and Secondness mediated by Thirdness. In this manner, "point," "line," and "rectangular sheet" are counterparts to icon, index, and symbol, or Firstness, Secondness, and Thirdness. The map, like the symbol, is a relatively full, or genuine, sign, while the "line" and "point" are either de-engendered signs or signs of engenderment. But rather than being in any way inferior, these de-engendered signs contain, within themselves, the virtuality of becoming complete signs. Just as de-engendered or relatively unengendered signs are destined perpetually to remain incomplete, so also the interpretants of genuine signs must remain incomplete for their finite interpreters, since the absolute fullness of the sign is no more than an ideal; it cannot hope for a place in the starting lineup of the "real" but must continue to play a substitute role on the field of the semiotically real.

Sign de-engenderment occurs in two degrees. A de-engendered sign of the lesser degree has become an index, a sign whose relation to its respective semiotic object is genuine, irrespective of its interpretant—that is, regardless of whatever interpretation may be given to the sign. In other words, the sign de-engendered to this degree is a sign whose possibilities of interpretation have been magnified manyfold, hence there are fewer restrictions for interpretation since the interpretant is at this point exceedingly vague; it has not yet been specified. A sign de-engendered to the greater degree has become an icon, a sign whose effect is due to the sign's quality for affecting the semiotic agent at the corporeal level (*CP*:2.92).[13] In other words, a symbol, the most complex of the basic sign types, can be de-engendered either in the first degree, which involves what I shall term indexicalization, or in the second degree, by way of iconization.

A genuine symbol is in a "conjoint relation to the thing denoted and to the mind" (*CP*:3.360). It is related to its object in terms of a mental association and depends upon habit. Such signs are abstract, general, conventional, and arbitrary. They include the general items of language use and any other mode of conveying judgments. A symbol de-engendered to the first degree has a genuine relation to its object, irrespective of its interpretant (the mind): a sign-object relation. That is, the sign's relation to its object does not lie in a mental association that is governed by habit but rather in a direct two-way physical relation independent of the conscious mind's (Third's) use of the sign. Such an index does not necessarily assert anything, but rather, "it only says 'there!' It takes hold of our eyes, as it were, and forcibly directs them to a particular object, and there is stops" (*CP*:3.361).[14] In other words, it solicits a line of sight between the eye and the object—between one "point" and another—without any interpretation (yet) existing, by the mind, of the object. Isolated demonstrative and relative pronouns are linguistic examples of de-engendered symbols, since they denote things without fully qualifying them. The letters designating the points on a graph before they are connected by a line are also such indices to the extent that there is no dyadic relation in the full sense but merely an object calling attention to itself. Similarly, algebraic symbols distinguish one value from another without specifying those values (*CP*:3.361).

Peirce writes elsewhere that de-engendered Seconds may be conveniently termed "internal, in contrast to external seconds, which are constituted by external fact, and are true actions of one thing upon another" (*CP*:1.365). For instance, a thermometer reacts physically with its environment, and independently of any mind whatsoever, as the mercury column rises and falls with temperature variations. This would occur just the same even if the instrument were entirely forgotten and ceased to convey information to some interpreter (*CP*:5.73). As a de-engendered sign, however, the thermometer's function can also be conjured up in the mind whether or not the instrument is present, even though the interpreter might have learned of its use by verbal instruction or from a written text in the absence of the physical object.

A symbol de-engendered to the second degree is an icon that fulfills its function "by virtue of a character which it possesses in itself, and would possess just the same though its object did not exist" (*CP*:5.73). A statue of a centaur is not an authentic representamen, since there is no such thing as a centaur. Yet it depicts a centaur by virtue of its shape, which it would have according to current conventions whether centaurs existed or not. In this sense, the centaur statue as a sign is self-contained (see Merrell 1983 on Meinong in this regard). Unlike the point-sign (map) "pointing to" another point-sign on the two-dimensional sheet, the centaur-sign is analogous to a point-sign merely *as it is*. Like an unrelated point-map or point on a graph, it involves a sign-mind relation without regard to any semiotically real connection.[15]

The function of icons with respect to the "real" world, as perceived and conceived from a given perspective and within a given context, entails resemblance of the sign to something "out there" to which it might be related (i.e., its possible semiotic object). Since pure icons (or second-degree de-engendered symbols) have not (yet) established a definite link between themselves and that which they resemble, on occasion they can become

> so completely substituted for their objects as hardly to be distinguished from them. Such are the diagrams of geometry. A diagram, indeed, so far as it has a general signification, is not a pure icon; but in the middle part of our reasonings we forget that abstractness in great measure, and the diagram is for us the very thing. So in contemplating a painting, there is a moment when we lose the consciousness that it is not the thing, the distinction of the real and the copy disappears, and it is for the moment a pure dream—not any particular existence, and yet not general. At that moment we are contemplating [a pure] *icon*. (*CP*:3.362; see also 2.92; brackets added; italics in original)

In this process, when construed as self-sufficient, de-engendered signs (iconized symbols or indices) become self-sufficiently semiotically real rather than re-presentations of something in the "really real" world "out there" in the correspondence theory sense. This qualifies them as icons, whether or not they are the equivalent of Hans Vaihinger's (1935) operational "as-if" hypostats, dreams, hallucinations, figments, fantasies, and fictional objects, and whether or not they are found in a book, on a canvas or screen, or in the playhouse. It is as if the infinitesimal point common to each map in Peirce's infinite set of maps were taken to be coterminous with the whole of the territory. The point as such neither points to another point by way of a line between them nor is there any mediation through their contextualization within the entire map. Rather, the two-dimensional map as Third has vanished, as have all relations to any other point. Put otherwise, when indexicalization threatens to produce a symptom—a syndrome in a patient such that what he takes to be real is not so perceived by other members of the patient's community—then iconization becomes imminent.[16] Signs consequently become simply what they *are;* they are self-sufficient and self-contained.

Second-degree de-engenderment is like the sensation of a swatch of cloth, *A,* which is sensed to be the same as (undifferentiated from) another swatch, *B,* though they are actually slightly different; and that second swatch is reported to be "the same as" *C,* which is in its turn "the same as" *D.* However, if *A* were placed alongside *D,* a marked difference—first degree de-engenderment, relation to something else—would now be noticed by a neutral bystander. In the first case, we have a continuum of sorts in which everything simply *is as it is,* in good monadic fashion, without a significant other existing—this and comparable mind-benders have been called the "sorites paradox." In the second case, there is a distinction between *A* and *D;* their dyadic otherness is made manifest as is the potential line connecting two different points in Peirce's map. Regarding the continuum, there is no significant other, only quality; regarding the distinction, Secondness is made evident.

In contrast, if an observer, *X,* notes that *A* is distinct from *C* and *D,* that *D* is distinct from *A* and *B,* and that there is a discontinuous spectrum before her, the relation becomes triadic. It involves an agent (mind) for whom the distinction between *A* and *D* is made manifest. The triad entails a sign's signifying something to some interpreter in some respect or capacity, hence the sign *is* real for someone (*CP*:1.516–20). The dyad and monad, as de-engendered signs, are not any less real than the triads as potentially genuine signs, though the third party of the trio has not (yet) effectively incorporated them into some semiotically real domain.

An everyday example of first- and second-degree de-engenderment is found in a portrait. If you see a portrait and form no more than an exceedingly vague idea of the person it depicts, you are bypassing two stages—the proper interpretant and the index—in the full development of a sign. Your idea of the person in the portrait is merely an icon. However, it is not a pure icon, Peirce would say. You are influenced not only by the icon qua icon but also by knowing that it is an effect, through an artist, caused by the original person's appearance, hence there is an indexical relation of Secondness to the original. A purer form of second-degree de-engenderment is Peirce's case of a person contemplating a painting—or better, viewing a film—and for a fleeting moment losing consciousness that it is not the real thing. One spontaneously reacts to it as if it were actually a real object, as when, for example, a young boy screams when a monster suddenly appears on the screen in the movie house. In such cases, the sign's indexicality (direct relation to its semiotic object) and symbolicity (mediation, through an interpretant, of the sign and its semiotic object) have been suppressed. That is to say, awareness of the sign in terms of its fullness as a Third was either never realized or the sign's Thirdness waned such that it became only tacitly acknowledged. What was or could have been explicit remains implicit; response to the sign has become automatized.

In sum, figure 7 provides a rough diagram of the interdependent interrelatedness of de-engenderment. In first-degree de-engenderment, one of the relations is suppressed, and the other two engage in a two-way connection. If two relations are suppressed (second-degree de-engenderment), the sign functions as if it were a self-contained, self-sufficient icon. Suppressing c highlights a, since the ordinary relation between R (representamen) and O (semiotic object) becomes indexicalized (hypertrophied) by pointing, evoking, or calling attention to something in place of the absent O-I (object-interpretant) relation. In other words, the interpretant-object

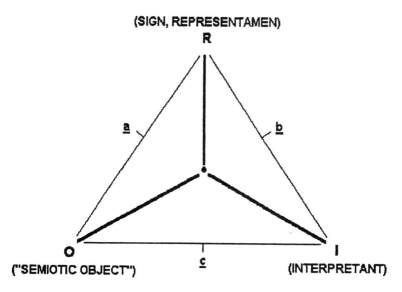

(SIGN, REPRESENTAMEN)
R

a   b

O   c   I
("SEMIOTIC OBJECT")   (INTERPRETANT)

Figure 7

relation wanes, and the object-sign relation is consequently intensified. If, in addition, *a* wanes, the *R-I* relation is iconized (by taking the sign as the real thing) in order to compensate for the backgrounded *R-O* relation. This erasure of the sign-object relation brings about a fusion of the subject and the sign such that, In Peirce's example, the latter may become construed by the former to be real. Hence:

> First-degree de-engenderment: sign → semiotic object (indexicalization).
> Second-degree de-engenderment: semiotic object ⇒ sign (iconization).
> [Where "→" signifies "defers to" and at the same time "differs from," and where "⇒" signifies "becomes tantamount to"] (see *CP*:3.359–62)

Within another context, the first-degree de-engendered sign may be considered a hypoicon of the diagram sort, and the second-degree de-engendered sign a hypoicon of the image sort (see *CP*:2.276–77). One encounters a more complex type of lesser de-engenderment—though as far as I know Peirce does not make this connection—in metaphor. Metaphors involve a combination of indexicalization (evocation of an image as a metaphor) and iconization (virtual identity between an image and a metaphor). But consciously and intentionally constructed metaphorical relations can, with time, submerge into nonconsciousness. When this occurs, the metaphor's indexical function becomes atrophied, and its iconic function becomes hypertrophied. It is now a "dead metaphor"; its quality as metaphor qua metaphor has passed into oblivion.

Notice on the one hand how in figure 4 de-engenderment from 333 to 331, and then from 331 to 311 and 111, undercuts 322 and 222, which 331 doesn't contain, and 321, 311, and 221, which 311 doesn't contain. 322 is exemplified in a commonplace expression, the de-engenderment of an entire phrase that now remains vague and may require for its interpretation a proper context and/or its vagueness made more explicit by the sign engenderer. On the other hand, 222, a weathervane, for example, does not provide the information for a definite indication of the index, but it remains to be determined—made more general—by the sign interpreter. 321, exemplified by "this," "that," and other shifters, likewise requires context and further specification due to its de-engendered qualities. And 221, an abrupt shock, a surprise, or at least a tacit sort of acknowledgment, is a de-engendered sign providing no information with respect to the "what" that is causing the jolt of surprise, or the "why" or the "how" of its so doing. Further determination of the sign calls for engenderment of that which at this particular eddy in the flow of semiosis was found in a de-engendered state. Notice also, once again, that the broken line of sign de-engenderment is one-dimensional, as would be quite proper, and that in the passage from 333 to 331 two crossings are required, in the passage from 331 to 311 there are three crossings, and in the passage from 311 to 111 four boundaries must be crossed. This is not insignificant, I would submit. Firstness is engendered from "emptiness," Secondness is engendered from Firstness, and Thirdness is engendered from Secondness and Firstness. That much is quite unproblematic.

Well, I must say that after this whirlwind of generalities you are undoubtedly ready for the nitty-gritty particulars of our concrete world. These I intend to provide, but not in the conventional fashion, I'm afraid. I will present them through the tainted lens of what will appear to be well-nigh incommensurable—yet they are complementary—cultural and linguistic idiosyncrasies: not the easy-going affairs of everyday life, but that which makes everyday life what it is. Thus I must ask that you bear with me a bit longer.

2

TALKING WITH OR
PAST EACH OTHER?

I. A MATTER OF COMPLEMENTARY SIGN-WORLDS

The contemporary milieu of proliferating signs becomes increasingly problematic when radically distinct culture-dependent signs are taken into account. Consider two signs, "Green" and "Grue." "Green" is for us just ordinary *green*. "Grue," in contrast, is for some strangers from a strange land their equivalent of our "Green," at least up to a certain point in time, then for some bizarre reason it changes into what we would ordinarily consider "Blue."[1] In other words, before time t_0 emeralds are for Grueworlders "Grue," which is equivalent to the color we Realworlders call "Green," but after time t_0 their emeralds, which they still call "Grue," are for us the equivalent of things we would call "Blue."

The Grueworlders have one color term for emeralds, the same as we do, but from our perspective their perception of colors goes awry at a particular point in time. Their inductive capacities become severely warped. However, as far as they are concerned, their world is as stable as can be. For the Grueworlders all emeralds have been, they now are, and there is no reason for them to doubt that they will always be, "Grue," quite clearly and distinctly. For these strange Grueworlders, it is our perceptual faculties that are screwed up; as they see it, it is as if we called emeralds "Green" up to time t_0, and then, for some strange reason, saw them in terms of an entirely distinct sign, our "Blue"—which is for them still "Grue." How can we expect to establish any lines of communication with these kinky Grueworlders? We and they live in completely incommensurable worlds, it would appear. "Green" is for us one thing and one thing only. But for them, what we consider "Green" is entirely unstable. Indeed, it is as if they

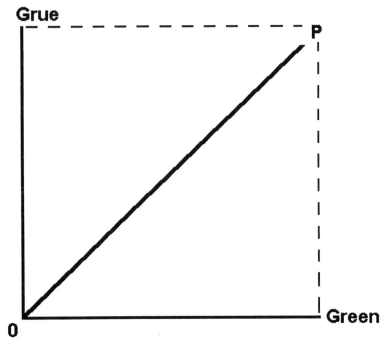

Figure 8

dwelled in another dimension of time and space with which we are entirely unfamiliar.

And so it is. That is to say, in order for us to get into their world it would be as if we were to leap into their world by means of some sort of "wormhole" through another dimension of space. In an attempt to account for just such a leap, I will offer a metaphorical, a rather poetic, account of a transformation through the figure 1 matrix by means of sets of three numbers making up Peirce's sign decalogue. In figure 8, we have the two terms in question, Green and Grue, both as signs 331 within their respective languages. In order to keep things as simple as possible without entering into the details of Riemann curved space geometry, consider the coordinates to lie on a flat plane rather than a curved Riemann sheet, and consider $O-P$ to be equal to the square root of a given value of Grue plus a given value of Green. This is clear-cut enough, I would expect: the Pythagorean theorem. In order to transform Grue into Green we must square Grue (Grue2) and combine it with the square of

Green (Green2), then take the square root of the sum of the two to get O-P. But this is still a study in abstraction, and too much for our taste, no doubt. So consider this:

$$O - P = \text{Grue} + \text{Grue-Green (before } t_0) + \text{Grue-Blue (after } t_0) + \text{Green.}$$

"That is about as clear as mud also," my skeptic observes. However, I would submit that it at least illustrates a very important point. In order to bring about the transformation from Grue to Green, it is necessary to jump completely outside the ordinary taxonomy and perception of both us Realworlders and the Grueworlders (when I say "jump outside" I mean figuratively, of course; in light of above comments, I trust none of us is privy to any otherworldly transcendental grasp of things). In other words, it is the equivalent of a move from the extremity of the Green axis to the extremity of the Grue axis, or vice versa, by a 90° orthogonal flip outside the two-dimensional sheet through our three-dimensional world, where both Grue-Green and Grue-Blue can be quite congenial—albeit otherwise antagonistic—bedpartners. Ah yes, two bedpartners, each with distinct but complementary mental and/or physical make-up and/or sexual prefer- ences. Now *that* we can identify with, can't we? It is a matter not of logic in the sense that A must be A come what may and can never be B, but of a logic in which A is A temporarily playing the role B would ordinarily play, and B is doing the inverse. It is a matter of complementarity, in which something can become something else at a different time or from a differ- ent perspective, and then it can flip back to what it was before.

The method to my madness, and the point to be made, is this. However complicated the above "metric tensor" formulation might be, it describes our world according to the best physics of our times, so we'll probably have to learn to live with it, at least for the time being. It also illustrates two very important points regarding the nature of semiosis: (1) signs as incompati- ble as Grue and Green may be nonetheless intricately and intimately linked in another dimension, and (2) it is possible to exercise a transition from Green to Grue, or vice versa, by means of a "mental flip," at—metaphori- cally speaking—an angle orthogonal to the perspective of the world we are ordinarily caught up in.[2] Transition between the two signs in question, Grue and Green, occurs in steps, through the metric tensors, rather than in one fell swoop. That is to say, first there is Firstness, quality, feeling, pure sensation. The Grue emerald must take on the appearance of something other than what it was at a previous moment. So the representamen un- dergoes a switch (for the Grueworlders), that is, potentially there is a switch, since other onlookers (us Realworlders, for example) might pig-headedly take the emerald *here, now* to be the same as any old emerald, past, present, or future, according to our expectations and our style of reasoning. If the quality of the gem has brought about a sensory switch, however, the next stage is acknowledgment on the part of some semiotic agent that something other "out there" is not what it otherwise would be. And the semiotic object changes from a Green emerald to a potentially—though not actually—Grue emerald. Finally, the interpretant of the item in question forces its idiosyncrasy into the mind of the interpreter, and "Green" becomes translated—in the best of all possible semiotics worlds, at least—into "Grue."

But this is not the complete story, I am afraid. In order that the representamen may undergo a switch in the semiosic space-stream manifold, a series of swimming alterations must come about—I write "swimming" since the entire process is just that, process, with little indication in the mind of the discrete steps involved. These alterations are, as derived from figure 4: $331 \rightarrow 322 \rightarrow 321 \rightarrow 311 \rightarrow 222 \rightarrow 221 \rightarrow 211 \rightarrow 111$ (or, for economy, $331 \rightarrow 311 \rightarrow 111$). Then, the process doubles back on itself and returns to 331, but this time 331 is under a different guise, since the quality of the sign is now something other than what it was. In other words, we might write the transformations necessary for our empathizing with the Grueworlders' off-the-wall term, "Grue," as:

$$\text{Grue}_{331}\text{–Green}_{331} \rightarrow \text{Grue}_{331}\text{–Green}_{322} \rightarrow \text{Grue}_{331}\text{–Green}_{321} \rightarrow$$
$$\text{Grue}_{331}\text{–Green}_{311} \rightarrow \text{Grue}_{331}\text{–Green}_{222} \rightarrow \text{Grue}_{331}\text{–Green}_{221} \rightarrow$$
$$\text{Grue}_{331}\text{–Green}_{211} \rightarrow \text{Grue}_{331}\text{–Green}_{111} \rightarrow \text{Grue}_{331}\text{–Blue}_{111} \rightarrow \ldots$$
$$\rightarrow \ldots \rightarrow \ldots \rightarrow \ldots \rightarrow \ldots \rightarrow$$

The "Grue" signs remain with the same subscripts, though the context is different such that they are always already different signs, and the "Green" signs suffer an alteration of their subscripts, since the sign is undergoing de-engenderment. The series of arrows represents the reverse trend, except that this time "Grue" is in interaction with "Blue" instead of "Green" (I didn't want to spend more of my time and test your patience by completing the entire exercise—and we now know why mathematicians insist on parsimony at all costs). We begin with "Grue (= Green)" and end with "Grue (= Blue)," figuratively through the "wormhole" and into a complementary perception and conception of things.[3]

The de-engenderment of "Green" was from subscripts of symbolicity to subscripts of iconicity and then back again. It was necessary to go back to the beginning, to "emptiness," so to speak, and then start anew, before it became possible to perceive and conceive of things in a different light.[4] As an illustration of this reversion to the "zero-degree" of *semiosis* with each and every sign transformation, observe the zones of "chaos" in figure 6 between iconicity, indexicality, and symbolicity. Observe also that, between everything and everything else, so to speak, we have the "node," the nothingness or emptiness, where there is no foregrounding against a background, no actualization from the range of possibilities, no sign or its semiotic object or its interpretant. It's all just a matter of: emptinessing.

"Yeah, all this is so much ado about nothing, so what's the real point?" comes the yawning reply. Well, I suppose it all appears to be so much mind-spinning. Yet perhaps it is not entirely irrelevant to Peircean semiotics, since (1) Peirce was, after all, a contemporary of Riemann, (2) his most productive years overlapped with the serious inquiries, artistic creativity, mystical insights, wild speculation, and charlatanism over the fourth-dimension at the turn of the century, and (3) his sign typology is curiously related to varying conceptions of space-time (see Murphey 1961). In fact, if the entire figure 1 grid is considered in terms of space, and if another "dimension," a temporal dimension, is added, then we have figure 9, which encompasses the entire set of what we might call "semiosic

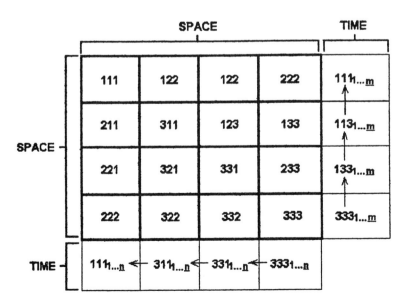

Figure 9

tensors," the mirror-image signs included (compare the arrows here to the broken arrows in figure 4). In figure 9 there is an account of the de-en-genderment and re-engenderment of 333 to 111 and back again, while spatially the signs remain related as they are so related.

Along the bottom row moving from right to left and concomitantly along the right-hand column moving upward, sign de-engenderment can occur either in the normal fashion, or an entirely new sign may emerge. In the first case, the sign appears as a generality without there being any sub-stantial change. Thus, emeralds remain "Green," from the last generation to the present generation, and whether against a black or white back-ground or in the vicinity of lumps of turquoise or finely polished rubies. And with each look at a "Green" emerald our "Green emerald" signs be-come further entrenched and taken for granted. That is, a certain degree of indexicalization and iconization of the signs has occurred such that their interpretants hardly need be explicitly acknowledged. We take them in and make them without hardly giving the activity any thought, since we as-sume emeralds will always be "Green" and need not bother ourselves with any fuss over the issue. In the second case, we have the "Grue-Green-Blue" conundrum. In order to account for the Grueworlders' signs, it was neces-sary for "Green" to become the focus of attention as sign 333. Then it was de-engendered to its bare quality, 111, and re-engenderment was enacted, but this time a different sign and a different interpretant emerged, which in turn altered the conception of the semiotic object, and "Green" became "Blue." Sign de-engenderment occurred in terms of transmutation of one sign into an entirely different sign—i.e., it was realized that after time t_0 emeralds may become for some strange reason "Blue" (that is, "Blue" for us, but they are still "Grue" for the Grueworlder), and from that point on-ward their "blueness" is on the road toward entrenchment, sedimentation, automatization, by way of the de-engenderment of the new sign.

In other words, the predicate "Green!" evoked in the presence of emeralds suffers successive diminution or de-engenderment of its inter-pretant, then of its semiotic object, and finally of its representamen, such that it becomes embodied and embedded within the entire range of one's ordinary perception and conception during the course of one's everyday life. But "Green" could exist as such only insofar as its counterpart, "Blue," now as a nonexistent but possibly actualizable sign, might suffer its own de-engenderment in inverse fashion. Things may appear fine and dandy as long as one does not make too close a comparison between what the sign was, "Green," and what it now is, "Blue." That was the Grueworlders' situation. In contrast, for us Realworlders, the distinction between what is now taken as "Blue" and what would otherwise be taken as a different sign for the same semiotic object becomes quite disrespectfully apparent. As a final observation, notice that our revised grid depicted in figure 9, in contrast to figure 1, illustrates de-engenderment and re-engenderment over time and thus encompasses the essence of figure 4. Notice also that the original portion of the grid—consisting of the spatial dimensions—is just *there*. There are no arrows, there is no change. It all exists as if in a timeless "block." What gives the entire apparatus its flow is the presence of the temporal dimension.

II. AS INDIVIDUAL SIGNS GO,
SO ALSO CONGLOMERATE SIGNS

"Now your discourse has obviously resorted to cute parlor tricks, the equivalent of mere numerology with a tinge of black magic," someone might now wish to rejoin. However, it is not so tricky and not so cute, I would suggest. That is, not when we consider the ramifications of Peirce's sign theory.

Consider, for instance, a solitary word, "Quixote," sign 331. Simple enough. But not really. If the word exists spatially, as a mark in a number of books in a library along with its original incarnation in Spanish and translations in other languages, it appears to be a quite uncomplicated matter, to be sure. It is just a word. However, if it exists in the memory of a Cervantes scholar or the memory bank of a computer, it can be considered for practical purposes just a sign, a word. Yet it is an entire world that contains, within itself, the implications for the engenderment—or re-engenderment, if you will—of an indefinite number of signs, signs of *Don Quijote de la Mancha*. Granted, "Quixote" is only one sign, but it is the sign of possibility implicitly relating to an entire complex novel, to all the articles and books that have been written about it, to all that has been said and thought about it: it is a vastly complex conglomerate sign; it is a tightly packed and condensed "rhizome," to use Deleuze and Guattari's (1987) term. It is simply there, as a Firstness of pure possibility, awaiting its actualization into a sign of Firstness within its respective semiotic sphere of Secondness and then Thirdness.

But this is all mind-numbingly complex, so let us limit ourselves to an imaginary Cervantes scholar. She has obsessively studied the *Quixote* during her long professional career and is quite smug regarding what she knows. The solitary sign, "Quixote," has for her over the years become pregnant with meaning. In fact, it incorporates, in condensed, embedded, entrenched, de-engendered fashion, all the episodes in the entire novel, the narrative strategies, the stylistic devices, the character development, relations to other literary works during the time of the author and back into the remote past and up to the present, relations to Spain of the early seventeenth century, and so on. The sign is replete with meaning in terms of its interdependent interrelatedness with what is for practical purposes, given our tiny minds, an infinity of other signs along the entire semiosic stream. Indeed, our scholar's brain-mind is a vast storehouse of information possibly actualizable for the purpose of pedagogy, or, say, pedantry at cocktail parties, while talking shop with other *Quixote* fanatics, or whatever.

In fact, suppose that at a campus reception and during the course of a conversation outside the context of customary *Quixote* talk someone happens to drop the word "Quixote." Our scholar is nearby, with cocktail glass and hors d'oeuvres in hand, and trying her best to impress the Dean of Liberal Arts who is standing within earshot. She overhears the reference and blurts out: "Ah, yes, the Quixote, Man of La Mancha." An eager graduate student is present and asks her: "You know the work well?" She responds in the affirmative. The Dean turns and makes some trivial mention of Cervantes in order that his ignorance might be camouflaged. Taking what she perceives to be the proper cue, she begins: "As I see it . . ." And she commences to blurt out a stream of verbiage in an effort to impress all those present.

If we put this encounter in a surrealistic framework, time regarding our scholar's and her audience's surroundings could have stopped for all they care, because they are now immersed in another world, as our scholar continues spinning out a linear stream of actualized signs from her storehouse of possible signs. The point is that all these signs were there, embodied and embedded in one condensed sign in the scholar's mind, a sign of sheer virtuality. This sign, "Quixote," a mere sign of 331 that contains within itself the possibility of engendering signs 332 and 333, is also a teeming effervescence of signs, from 322 to 111, which at a moment's notice can quickly emerge from the semiosic flow like nimble dolphins springing from the surface of a body of water. These signs were all there, spatially. They had followed a temporal pathway of de-engenderment such that they had become what they now are. And so they are there, ready for actualization, over time, into one or more of a vast range of possibly actualized signs. This is human semiosis at its best.

Now let's consider another scenario. The fragments of the *Quixote* Pierre Menard wrote—from Borges's (1962:36–44) "Pierre Menard,

Author of the *Quixote*"—were interpreted by a group of presumptuous literary critics as if they composed another work entirely, written during the early twentieth century and with the advantageous hindsight garnered from knowledge of William James, Bertrand Russell, and other philosophers, and the entire history of literary figures and other influences. If we label Cervantes's "Quixote" as an isolated term sign 331_1 and Menard's "Quixote" sign 331_2, the same sign with different interpretants, then we have the possibility for ambiguity. If a literary critic makes a statement about "Quixote," is he addressing himself to the Cervantes sign or the Menard sign? Does the interpretant of a particular sign pertain to Cervantes's work or to Menard's work? Conversely, in the above case of "Green emeralds" in contrast to "Blue emeralds," we have different signs—each following its own pathway in figure 9—as well as different interpretants, which makes for the possibility of incommensurability. Regarding an emerald before them, a Realworld jeweler says "Green," and her counterpart from Grueworld says "Grue," or perhaps an apparently confused Earthling jeweler friend says "Blue." What for one person has become one embodied and embedded sign is something entirely different for another person. The question obviously arises: In spite of the above description of sign de-engenderment and re-engenderment, how can these two people hope to communicate at all? And the hopeful companion query is: Do not the contradictory signs and their interpretants used by the interlocutors affect all other signs within the interdependent, interrelated stream of semiosis as it cascades along, whisking them through a rush of signs all the ramifications of which they cannot possibly be aware?

Yes, each sign does affect the whole of semiosis, at least to a minimal degree, no matter how apparently insignificant the sign. No sign is an island. All signs are all one and the one is in all signs. So there can be communication between interlocutors inhabiting apparently incommensurable worlds after all, though the task is of excruciating difficulty. This virtually unfathomable character of signs bears witness to our fallibility and our limitations.

III. A HOPEFUL RETURN TO TERRA FIRMA?

Well, at least that is one side of the story of Peirce's ten sign types. Another side of the story has to do with a couple of questions. Why is there an added dimension in the scheme representing Peirce's decalogue (figure 9)? Why not simply a sixteen compartment chess game as per figure 1, with ten squares highlighted?—that way life would be considerably less cumbersome.

In response to these queries, reconsider figure 6. The chiefly iconic signs are basically what they are, with little or no relationship to any other signs in the big, wide world "out there." They are, most properly speaking, "nonperspectival" in the sense that there is no conception of them in contrast to some other conception with respect to their relation to some other, some Second, of indexicality, properly developed. They have to do with the world all in one gulp according to the capacity of the semiotic agent's gullet, that is, according to how much semiosis she can take in all at once. Chiefly indexical signs, relating to some other in collusion and collaboration with some semiotic agent, are "perspectival" insofar as the relation's grasp from one vantage point could have been something else from another vantage point. Since indexicality is a matter of here a sign and there something other to which the sign is somehow related, time makes its way onto the scene: now there is the sign here and something other there, now there is something other than that particular other related to what appears to be the same sign, and so on. We simply cannot get rid of time once and for all, no matter how much we try. And we cannot give account of time within time, no matter how much effort we make to jump outside the temporal dimension within which we are trapped.

Along with temporality, since the sign is never identical with that to which it relates, we also have the makings of asymmetry, as suggested above. Moreover, with respect to the sphere of signs of "indexicality," it would be expected that classical logic holds the upper hand: a sign, that to which it relates, and the *relata* can be one thing from one perspective and then another thing from another perspective, but it cannot be both things from both perspectives in the same instant. However, chiefly symbolic signs can at least allow their semiotic agent the smug confidence that she is quite in control of two or more perspectives from within the same perspectival grasp. This situation is comparable to a cubist painting, in which a three-dimensional object is presented from various two-dimensional views as if there were three dimensions spread out and plastered on the canvas. Now, it can rightly be said that it is not a matter of the other to which the sign relates being either one thing or the other, in good Boolean fashion. Pluralism, multiplicity, and the indeterminacy of any and all future signs and their relations is now part of the scene. Consequently, the sign, the thing, and the relation between them is quite possibly neither one thing nor another but something else. Time is now definitely a factor as well, as is asymmetry. Finally, what precedes all these considerations is

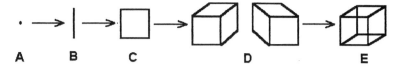

A   B   C   D   E

Figure 10

"emptiness," the equivalent of "0," the undifferentiated flux that precedes all semiotics and contains, within itself, the possibility of all semiosis.

The three areas of figure 6 plus the central "node" can be viewed as three phases of the development of a cube according to figure 10, from A to D. A contains, within itself, the possibility of everything at once: it simply *is as it is*. B is the product of linear engenderment from A. But the view from B is stringently limited: its unidimensionality evinces hardly any indication of what is eventually to become its three-dimensional nature. C presents the countenance, from two particular views, of the surface of the cube as it would appear to the observer limited to a panoramic scanning. E, however, merges the two perspectives of D and incorporates them into a single image. Ordinarily we can see only one of the two possible cubes at a time. Thus, with respect to time, the cube remains polarized: at best we can hardly do more than bring about an oscillation of the cube from moment to moment. The problem is that the very idea of oscillation is a mixed bag. If we mean by oscillation a binary on-off switching from "+" to "−" or whatever, the movement is digital. If we are speaking of something in the order of the up-down periods of a standing wave, then the action is continuous, and, all conditions being equal, each oscillation is a replica of any given oscillation. If we wish to articulate the movement in musical terms from vibrato (a tremulous or pulsating effect produced by minute and rapid variations in pitch) to rubato (rhythmic flexibility within a measure) to glissando (blending of one tone into the next in a scalelike passage) to portamento (smooth uninterrupted glide in passing from one tone to another), we move from fine-grained discontinuity masquerading as near continuity to sheer continuity. None of these movements are sufficiently precise to be caught in the net of musical notation, yet they definitely entail increasingly subtle variations. Since they are virtually of continuous nature, they are left to spontaneous execution on the part of the musician. They contribute to the quality, the mood, the sense of the music, that is, its *tone*—in contrast to the *tokens,* or the discontinuous aspect of the music according to the musical score. They allow the musician to sweep across a range—within certain often ill-defined parameters—of possible pitches and tones. She moves from one otherwise digital stopping point to another, and then to another and another, in an auditory scanning movement, thus taking in what would otherwise be a set of digital, discontinuous micro-elements as if they all composed one continuous whole.

We find the possibility for a visual equivalent of this auditory scanning movement in figure 10. An infinitesimal point engenders a line, an infinity of lines engenders a plane, and an infinity of planes engenders a cube. The cube as presented on a flat plane can have its enantiomorphic twin, and both twins presented as one form the so-called Necker-cube. It is all a matter of sign engenderment. But to the question, "Are we indefinitely limited to a view of one cube or the other?" the answer must be in the affirmative, at least to ordinary Western parlance and regular academic practices.

IV. FUSING COMPLEMENTARITIES

However, let us look further. Paul Klee (1959) conceived of two forms of attention, which can be called figure and ground, inside and outside, positive and negative, here and there, or, in the terms of Michael Polanyi (1958), focal and subsidiary.[5]

A line separates one of the forms from the other one. Ordinarily a line, in the mathematical or geometrical sense, is an invisible nothing. We draw it so we can see it, but that sight is no more than figment, a handy fiction to enable us to get on with the task at hand. For Klee, the artist's line is something else entirely. The line can bring attention to the positive figure it encloses, thus causing that figure to stand out as if it were on a plane above and superior to the negative, or that which lies outside the figure: the line "cuts" the figure out of the ground. Moreover, Klee points out that, with effort, one can highlight the negative in such a manner that it functions much as the positive figure enclosed by the line would ordinarily function. Klee attaches the term *endotopic* to the inside or positive area and exotopic to the outside or negative area. The artist with developed powers of perception and imagination, Klee writes, can willfully bring about an oscillation from endotopic to exotopic and back again. And there is more. A good artist can learn to hold the entire picture, inside-outside, figure-ground, positive-negative, endotopic-exotopic, and focal-subsidiary in a single perceptual-imaginative grasp.

Anton Ehrenzweig (1967, 1975) studies Klee and other artists from a psychological-psychoanalytical perspective. He concludes that what is needed is the concept of "undifferentiated" attention (i.e., of un-engendered signs, possible signs) akin to the "syncretistic vision" of the child before she has become inculcated-indoctrinated by culture so as to be able to cut her reality up in certain predisposed ways. This syncretistic vision is like the process of rapid scanning, rather nonconsciously taking everything in one fell swoop. There is no intentionality here, no willful or conscious thought, no introspection, no analysis or synthesis in the rigorously intellectual sense. All that would be disruptive. Syncretistic vision, rather, is of the content of a scattered sort of attention that appears essentially blank of discrete features and empty of memory. The child's vision is relatively undifferentiated. She learns to differentiate (engender signs from within) her world according to the conventions and practices of her particular culture. After she has become adept at creating a set of "cuts" and "joints" in her reality in conformity with the cultural norms that be, the erstwhile undifferentiated becomes quite inaccessible to her immediate consciousness. The undifferentiated is now entrenched, automatized, embedded and embodied.

While I do not exactly agree with Ehrenzweig with respect to his Freudian interpretation of this process, I would submit that the undifferentiated is comparable to what I have termed the sphere of "nothingness" or "emptiness." The sphere of the differentiated, in all its myriad complexity, is what the "semiotically real" world is all about, having been indicated by some set or other of representamens that are now there and in wait of their respective interpretants. The task of the artist, in Klee's conception, is that of dedifferentiating (i.e., de-engendering) the previously differentiated (engendered) in order once again to approximate the undifferentiated (un-engendered), in other words, to acquire the child's synchretistic vision. This will enable the artist a multidimensional grasp of the line tenderly, tentatively, and delicately set down on the canvas in order to distinguish one thing from another thing but not without leaving open certain possibilities for that other thing to become the predominant thing over the first thing. Multidimensional perception-imagination overcomes the division between figure and ground, as well as all other divisions. This situation is much like polyphonic music, which combines two or more otherwise independent melodic parts, especially when in close harmonic relationship. It is like sweet and sour combined into one taste in the Oriental cuisine; it is like musk mixed with other fragrant aromas and effectively marketed by perfume manufacturers; it is like the smooth touch of silk deceptively produced by a synthetic fabric. And all this wrapped tightly in one package.

Recall figure 10. It might appear that A is a solitary point, an infinitesimal insignificance. This is actually not the case, not by a long shot. A contains, within itself, the possibility for the engenderment, in an infinity of directions and of an infinity of characteristics, of an infinity of figures. But it modestly and rather conservatively engenders no more than a straight line, B. The line, in its own turn, is quite content to engender a flat plane. Yet the plane, in Klee fashion, is an enclosed line "cutting" a space off from everything else in its universe. Consequently, the space within the square, vaguely endotopic, as it were, can give rise to the sensation of a figure in contrast to everything else, the ground. From the square C, a cube, D, is engendered (differentiated). That is to say, two cubes are engendered. That is to say, one cube engenders its enantiomorphic twin, which is the same cube in its mirror-image form. Of course there is actually no cube at all. Culture tells us we should ordinarily differentiate D, otherwise a set of lines on a two-dimensional plane, into a pair of three-dimensional objects, that is, into two objects that we make out to be (construct) as if they were indeed three-dimensional. Consequently there can be a cube and its enantiomorph. Now, in the sense of Klee, the competent artist should be able to dedifferentiate (de-engender) the two cubes such that they become the same cube viewed from different angles. The artist maps herself into a two-dimensional drawing and sees two distinct objects reconstructed as three-dimensional objects in one perceptual gulp and in such a way that they are taken to be the same object but seen from various angles "within" the "depth" of the two-dimensional sheet. Of course the sheet has no depth. But that is precisely the trick: to get inside it and see things within it *as if* it had depth. Once again this is, in essence, the nature of a cubist painting.

Now, notice that B is just a line. It is self-sufficient and self-contained and it does not exercise any form or fashion of hegemony by "cutting" a space out and distinguishing it from everything else and indicating that this space is its own enclosure and belongs to it and to no other line. No. The line is just a line. It is in this sense of pure possibility tantamount to a quite bare yet by no means barren form of Firstness.[6] C, apparently, is of the nature of Secondness. It separates *this* from *that* as a line of distinction in dyadic fashion, albeit in a primitive sense. D, then, should belong to Thirdness, implying yet another dimension. While B can depict some breadth and C can depict an infinite expanse of breadth but very little depth, D's depiction of depth hardly knows any boundaries. For this reason construction of enantiomorphs by means of D sorts of illustrations is an unproblematic task. So in figure 10 we have Firstness, Secondness, and

Thirdness: it is perhaps not mere coincidence that the categories correspond so closely to space as we know it. And it is perhaps significant that
signs of chiefly iconicity are those that correspond most closely to the
essence of the line, signs of chiefly indexicality to the enclosed two-
dimensional figure, and signs of chiefly symbolicity to the conventionally
arbitrated custom of seeing three-dimensionality on a two-dimensional
plane in order that the mind may reconstruct a solid object.

"And what about E?" someone asks. Yes, E, that is where the story becomes most intriguing. The two possible cubes of the ambiguous drawing
are not exactly enantiomorphs—at least they are not from the same angle
of perception. One of the possible cubes, that with the face down, is positioned the same as the left-hand cube of D. The other possible cube has its
face pointing upward, thus it is no mirror-image, but rather, it is incompatible with the left-hand cube of D. However, if we make a copy of E and
rotate it orthogonally—that is, 90°—outside the two-dimensional plane in
another dimension, and then rotate it another 90°, we will have produced
its enantiomorph. Two more flips, and the cube is back in its original position. Interestingly enough, this feat is impossible within the two-
dimensional plane.[7]

"Now why bother with these bewitching tricks?" continues the query.
The bother is worthwhile, I would submit, because the orthogonal
switch is comparable to what in geometry is called the "Argand plane,"
which makes use of an imaginary axis consisting of imaginary numbers
($\pm\sqrt{-1}$, $\pm\sqrt{-2} \ldots n$), quite significantly found in computations in chaos
theory, quantum mechanics, and relativity theory. Moreover, the or-
thogonal switch was the metaphor allowing us a model of sign de-engenderment and re-engenderment in the preceding sections. Of course
allusions to contemporary physics endow the present disquisition with
neither any necessary credibility nor any heightened respectability. The
important point, I would submit, is that the Argand plane introduces
another dimension—a wormhole, so to speak, and as implied above—by
means of which the range of semiosis can be given adequate account.

That is only half of the story. The other half entails time—introduced
in the fifth column and fifth row of figure 9. Notice that when we flip
cube E from one ambiguous possibility actualized to the other, we are seeing an object on a two-dimensional plane as if it were a three-dimensional
object, and we are transforming it into its other as if we were to transform
our perceptual grasp of it into a fourth dimension. This is tantamount to
the impossibility of converting a right-hand glove into its enantiomorphic
twin—a left-hand glove—by reducing it to an infinity of points, passing

the points through a fourth dimension, and then reconstructing the glove into its mirror-image. Of course we could have simply turned the glove inside-out within our three-dimensional world. But that would have been cheating, for we cannot do the same with cube E, since it does not exist in three-dimensional but two-dimensional space. (For a comparable example, draw a right-hand glove and a left-hand glove on a sheet of paper, and notice that the only way you can convert one into the other is by two orthogonal moves in the next dimension.)

Given the fact that the transformation of cube E is logically impossible in three-dimensional space, H. A. C. Dobbs (1972) concludes, after an intricate and convincing argument, that the extra dimension must consist of a mathematically imaginary "time dimension." This extra dimension introducing temporality accounts for the split moment that passes while our mind enacts a flip from one of the ambiguous possibilities of cube E to the other one. A certain duration of time, however brief, transpires, to be sure. After it has transpired, we are seeing something different, something new. Then we can flip back to what was there before, and it's all the same. But no, not really. For memory remains of that which emerged that was in another moment different from what now is—a "difference that makes a difference," to use Gregory Bateson's (1972) key phrase. This new time dimension is tantamount, I would suggest, to the fifth column and the fifth row in figure 9, which is a graphic depiction of temporal process of a sign's de-engenderment from 333 to 111 and its re-engenderment back again. Apparently, time, irreversibility, and novelty are now with us for good.

In another manner of putting all this in light of the above remarks on Ehrenzweig, C in figure 10 is unambiguous. A space is severed from everything else, and that's that. Something has been differentiated from the undifferentiated. D presents two complementary objects, one irreducible to the other from within the same perspectival grasp. Yet we can imagine ourselves in a third dimension walking around the right-hand cube until the equivalent of the left-hand cube comes into view. The same differentiated object has been seen from a different angle. However, in the sense of Klee *via* Ehrenzweig, by scanning and acquiring a "synchretistic vision," the artist can dedifferentiate the differentiated such that the two objects merge into one another to become one ambiguous object, as if it were like cube E, but with both possibilities taken as if existing within her quasi-conscious or nonconscious perception at one and the same time. This is Klee's "multidimensional attention" capable of embracing both inside-outside, figure-ground, and so on. It is like taking in a set of polyphonic sounds both vertically (the paradigmatic dimension, so to speak) and horizontally (the syntagmatic dimension), or like scanning the musical score and grasping it as a dedifferentiated whole. This is also, it bears mentioning, of the essence of Gilles Deleuze and Félix Guattari's (1983) "both-and," their "either-or . . . or . . . or . . . ," and their holistic grasp of the new they outline as three forms of synthesis, all of which serves to subvert classical logical principles. In such dedifferentiating acts, what is ambiguous on a conscious level becomes a rhizomic whole from a quasiconscious or nonconscious view. This dedifferentiating grasp approaches the undifferentiated but can never arrive at that dreamy "oceanic" level. It can never arrive, for the linear, analytic, conscious mind is in collusion and collaboration with the quasi- or nonconscious mind. In other words, the "two minds" are complementaries: one can take control and exercise hegemony over the other and vice versa at the drop of a hat, but both cannot predominate at the same moment, for if they were to do so, the "oceanic," chaotic, nonperspectival state would have arrived, and there would be no consciousness differentiation at all.

Ehrenzweig argues that dedifferentiation (or in the terminology of the previous sections, de-engenderment) is necessary for creative acts, and that creativity entails approximation toward the chaos of the Freudian "primary process." He writes:

> Whether we are to experience chaos or a high creative order depends entirely on the reaction of our rational faculties. If they are capable of yielding to the shift of control from conscious focusing to unconscious scanning the disruption of consciousness is hardly felt. The momentary absence of mind will be forgotten as the creative mind returns to the surface with newly won insight. If however the surface faculties react with defensive rigidity and insist on judging the contents of dedifferentiation from their own restricted focus, then the more scattered, broadly based imagery of low-level [dedifferentiated, scanning] visualization impresses us as vague and chaotic. (Ehrenzweig 1967:35; brackets added)

Mathematician Jacques Hadamard (1945) once conducted a study of creativity among mathematicians and scientists, concluding that it is essential that the creative process cloud the conscious mind, rendering the details somewhat vague (dedifferentiated), in order that novel forms and their combinations might emerge. Poincaré's (1952) particular tactic, it bears mentioning in this vein, is to concentrate intensely on a problem, then engage in some other activity—party, bird-watch, play tennis, make love, or whatever—and let it all gestate. During this lull, the details of the mind's previous activities can become dedifferentiated, and then the spark of creativity can emerge. In other words, a scanning of the whole of things along at least in part nonconscious levels is necessary in order to give things a vague, relatively unfocused tinge. While this scanning sensation is perhaps most effectively articulated in terms of visual imagery, it is by no means strictly visual. To assume so much would be to fall victim to the demands of ocularcentrism. Actually, if we are speaking of visual imagery, scanning clouds the vision and thus places it in close kin to other sensations, especially olfactory and gustatory, but also to an extent auditory and tactile, which are by their very nature to a degree vague.

Wittgenstein gravitated from the "picture theory" of language in the *Tractatus* (1961) to "language games" in his later work—much of which is found in his *Philosophical Investigations* (1953). Language games entail rule following and rule breaking—rules of both the formal and explicit variety and of the tacit variety—and novel strategies and ploys. They are for this reason relatively vague, imprecise, ambiguous, evincing ill-defined pathways of thinking and acting. They include mutually contradictory possibilities that can be held in a comprehensive grasp such that, with relatively undifferentiated focus, the creator can become aware of these possibilities as they emerge into her consciousness and then pick and choose at her leisure. The problem with language games, as I sense it, is that they leave one dangerously open to linguicentric temptations. All is definitely not language. The vagueness and ambiguity of language games and the advantage of a language game theory of creativity, as Ehrenzweig was quite aware, is that articulation of the theory is relatively unproblematic, since the theory, couched in language, is about language phenomena. No intersemiotic transformation and translation is necessary. There is no problem of articulating the unarticulated and perhaps inarticulable. Nevertheless, the extralinguistic—or perhaps we should say translinguistic—must be included within any comprehensive semiotic theory, especially Peirce's theory from sign 111 to sign 311.

In order to begin inclusion of this translinguistic domain within semiotics, let us return to figure 10 for a few minutes.

V. SPACES OF MANY FORMS

In the conventional, polarized mode of perceiving cube E, transition is made from one pole to the other, and the faces are seen as now "inside," now "outside," and back again. But by the act of scanning or dedifferentiation, the two possible cubes are seen as *either* "inside" *or* "outside" at virtually the same moment—or at least what for practical purposes is the same moment. With such fusion, such interrelated, interacting interpenetration, it is in essence as if each face were *both* "inside" *and* "outside," as if all six sides and their complementaries were simultaneously given, as if the move from C to D to E had been from timelessness and symmetry to temporality and asymmetry. Time is in a certain sense spatialized during the process. Yet it is not the same as space, for split moments pass while consciousness is in the act of constructing one cube-world and then its complementary. Time is space, so to speak, but it is also unspatialized time, in another manner of speaking and from the obverse view. In other words, space is also temporalized, for space is a matter of "now this-here," "now that-here," and so on.

Let us make another move by turning the tables in such a way that the entire Necker-cube shebang is given a radically different twist. Take the Möbius strip with a line drawn along it so that its end is its beginning (figure 11). The line is continuous, one-dimensional. The strip is two-dimensional and punctuated by a discontinuous break in three-dimensional space somewhere along the otherwise continuous two-dimensional plane. All this can be seen from three-dimensions as if it were a whole, ideally in somewhat of a dedifferentiated package. Call the whole of the strip taken in one grasp, including the realm of three-dimensional space within which

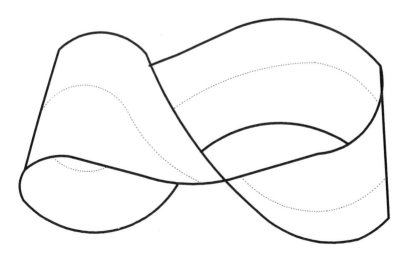

Figure 11

the switch occurs, iconicity. Call the two-dimensional strip itself indexicality, upon which the switch, from the larger three-dimensional view, makes the dyadic distinction between what would ordinarily be "outside" and what would remain "inside," and irreversibility and asymmetry are ushered in. Call the line one-dimensional symbolicity, which is ideally continuous, but in reality it is fractured at some point somewhere due to the Möbius switch (in a manner of speaking, it is marked by Buddhist "flashes," Alfred North Whitehead's "Pulsations," William James's "drops of consciousness"). At the outset this appears to be a bizarre way of looking at the strip. But in a quite fundamental sense that's the way it is, I would submit. There is justification for symbolicity or language as one-dimensional, for indexicality as two-dimensional, and for iconicity as a self-contained whole within three-dimensional space irrespective of time, because symbolicity *does* come in linear spin-outs, indexicality *is* dyadic, and iconicity *does* makes its appearance in whole packages. This essentially entails a pair of steps backward from E to D and then to C in figure 10. In other words, it involves sign de-engenderment, from relative explicitness to implicitness, from consciously and willfully processed signs to entrenched, embedded and embodied sign use.

Dimensionality, in fact, lends itself quite well to the problem at hand. James Bunn (1981) makes ample use of spatial dimensions in constructing his unique "polydimensional semiotics." If I may be allowed to indulge in a brief abstract of Bunn's scheme—and, I hope, without complicating the issue inordinately—we are introduced to a combination of three dimensions and three variables: (1) "highlighted" (foregrounded), (2) "torqued" (brought into action by a sort of orthogonal twist along the Argand plane as described above), and (3) "suppressed" (backgrounded). Bunn constructs

α	3-DIMENSIONS HIGHLIGHTED	2-TORQUED	1-SUPPRESSED
β	2-DIMENSIONS HIGHLIGHTED	3-TORQUED	1-SUPPRESSED
χ	1-DIMENSION HIGHLIGHTED	2-TORQUED	3-SUPPRESSED
δ	3-DIMENSIONS HIGHLIGHTED	1-TORQUED	2-SUPPRESSED
ε	2-DIMENSIONS HIGHLIGHTED	1-TORQUED	3-SUPPRESSED
φ	1-DIMENSION HIGHLIGHTED	3-TORQUED	2-SUPPRESSED

Table 2

a set of six classes of semiotic instruments, tools, and media that function much like a group of permutations (see table 2). Signs come in various flavors, according to whether they are highlighted, torqued, or suppressed. There are "utilitarian signs" consisting of:

α Three-dimensionality highlighted, two-dimensionality torqued, and one-dimensionality suppressed.

[Signs of this sort are Neolithic pots, archaic hand-held implements of war, and modern hand-tools. They require full-blown space for their functioning—they cannot be operated along a line or a plane only—and their proper use. These are chiefly iconic signs of the holistic sort.]

β Two-dimensionality highlighted, three-dimensionality torqued, and one-dimensionality suppressed.

[These signs include the likes of graphs, diagrams, video images, and posters and pictures of all sorts. They can be spread out on a sheet without their losing any crucial aspect of their proper engenderment and interpretation as signs. These are chiefly indexical signs of the dyadic sort.]

χ One-dimensionality highlighted, two-dimensionality torqued, and three-dimensionality suppressed.

[Typical of these signs is writing, speech, arithmetic, and logical and formal sign strings. Their making and their taking is along a linear stream, though their interpreting can be n-dimensional and multilinear, even rhizomic. These are chiefly symbolic signs of the space-time sort.]

A set of signs complementary with the utilitarian class of signs consists of "aesthetic" signs. They can be of:

δ Three-dimensionality highlighted, one-dimensionality torqued, and two-dimensionality suppressed.

[Like hand-held artisan tools, ballet, theater, sculpture, and architecture require, for their proper interpretation, freedom of movement in all directions. The block of marble becomes a statue, the dancer pirouettes around and around while gravitating toward the front of the stage, the action of the drama moves back and forth, forward and backward, and up and down, and the architect works with bulges and cavities and contours and distances in all directions: chiefly iconic signs.]

ε Two-dimensionality highlighted, one-dimensionality torqued, and three-dimensionality suppressed.

[This is the case of paintings, lithographs, silk screens, and so on. The canvas is planar, in spite of its pretending a Renaissance vanishing-point view or a multi-dimensional grasp in the case of the cubist work: chiefly indexical signs.]

φ One-dimensionality highlighted, three-dimensionality torqued, and two-dimensionality suppressed.

[Here we have chiefly musical scores, poetry, and prose, in which signs are displayed one-dimensionally, but many aspects of the medium and its portrayal must be held in check in the mind in order nonlinearly and n-dimensionally to make connections, establish interrelationships: chiefly symbolic signs.]

In sum, a certain number of dimensionalities of the semiotic entity is highlighted, while a variable number of dimensionalities are either torqued or suppressed (Bunn 1981:38–46).

Three dimensionalities highlighted is primarily of the nature of iconicity, such as the entire Möbius strip, including its twist in three-dimensional space. Two dimensionalities highlighted is in the order of indexicality, such as the two-dimensional strip itself. One dimensionality highlighted brings symbolicity to the fore, such as the self-returning line on the strip. This might strike one as a cross-eyed way of putting things, since one might naturally tend to assume that symbolicity should belong to the highest stage of dimensionality. However, symbolicity, of which language is the most supreme manifestation, is a linear engenderment, a slide along the strip, whose very existence depends upon binary relations of signs and their others and unary iconic relations that carry within themselves the possibility of a digital switch from one value to the other. Thus "Green" from one rather artificial perspective on one side of the strip can become "Grue" on the other side of the strip, the incommensurability within the symbolic field having been melted within the iconic field in order that they may be conceived in dedifferentiated fashion as two different expressions of the same universe.

Bunn's trio of variables—highlighted, torqued, and suppressed—also meshes conveniently with Peirce's possibility-actuality-necessity, or Firstness-Secondness-Thirdness triads. When three-dimensionality is highlighted ("α" units or signs), as in the case of a Neolithic pot or a monkey wrench for instance, one-dimensional characteristics are suppressed, while the pot's symmetry depends upon the two-dimensional rotation of the potter's wheel as it is being formed, and the wrench's use entails a twisting motion along a two-dimensional plane. A planar (torqued) surface, then, is paramount in the unit's construction and use. "β" signs illustrated on a flat surface, on the other hand, suppress the first dimensionality, for it is hardly any more functional than in "α" signs, and that which they illustrate—or signify, as it were, in the Peircean sense—occupies three-dimensional space. Thus in Western societies the relatively simple Necker cube—like some of Escher's lithographs ("ε" signs)—is viewed in terms of the ambiguity or visual paradox it evinces solely when the two-dimensional surface is projected onto an imaginary three-dimensional domain. In other words, the cube as a binary either-one-thing-or-the-other affair is a matter of two dimensions highlighted, but such highlighting is not possible without the imagined existence of a third dimension. Display of "χ" signs is necessarily linear. Signs exist in relation of contiguity, but in their composite form, as a text, a mathematical or logical proof, a series of integers, or whatever, they occupy a plane, while their third-dimensional manifestation is shoved under the rug as if it were inconsequential. This linear generativity in the long run, however, requires two, three, and even more dimensions, in this manner incorporating aspects of indexicality and iconicity. Thus we have, in "α," "β," and "χ" signs, a foregrounding of iconicity, indexicality, and symbolicity respectively, with the relatively more complex signs owing a debt to and standing on the shoulders of their more fundamental predecessors.

Signs in category "δ" must be unfolded in three dimensions. Examples are found in the rhythm of a ballerina, the contours of a statue, the Baroque façade of a Spanish cathedral, the movements on stage playing out *Hamlet*. In each case the process of unfoldment is brought about during the time of an artistic work's creation or in the act of an artistic performance along a one-dimensional and temporal "world-line" in three-dimensional space. Two dimensions are highlighted on the painted plane, an instantiation of "ε" signs. In line with "ε" signs, the painting is created along a one-dimensional "world-line," while the three-dimensionality of the item it represents is not of the same consequence as it is for "δ" signs that must model their object of representation in terms of its three-dimensionality. Finally, music or poetry, "φ" signs, highlight the linear continuity of rhythm flowing out in n-directions in three-dimensional space, while the two dimensional page upon which the lines or score are printed are suppressed, since the affect of the aesthetic piece depends upon a synthetic grasp, from beginning to end, of the relations of parts to parts and parts to whole. Once again we have a progressive foregrounding of iconicity, indexicality, and symbolicity, this time from the semiotic entities of "δ," "ε" and "φ" signs.

That is to say, chiefly iconic signs (111, 211, 311), most properly signs of themselves without their (yet) enjoying any definite reference or mediation by Thirdness, highlight three-dimensionality (the pot does not necessarily represent anything, the dance is a dance is a dance—like a rose is a rose is a rose as a representation of itself and nothing but itself). Chiefly indexical signs (221, 222, 321, 322) highlight two-dimensionality (a diagram, graph, or video game picture points to that of which it is a model or simulacrum). And chiefly symbolic signs (331, 332, 333), in their inception partly to wholly arbitrary, and engendered in linear fashion, depend on, and are at the same time superordinate to, signs of relation of Secondness and of monadic Firstness; they are signs that highlight one-dimensionality (logic, mathematics, computer language). In short, iconicity as possibility, indexicality as actuality, and symbolicity as probability or necessity tend respectively to highlight: (1) self-referential, self-sufficient three-dimensionality, (2) two-way, symmetrical planar relationality, and (3) one-dimensional linear development along n-tuple lines (recall the above discussion of the Möbius strip).

Notice that when you scan D of figure 10 there is, in the sense of Ehrenzweig, passage from dedifferentiation (de-engenderment) toward the undifferentiated (un-engendered). Then D can ideally be taken simply as C, as either of the objects or both on a two-dimensional plane (i.e., typical of a cubist picture). This is of the nature of de-engenderment, potentially from sign 333 to sign 111, from Cervantes's entire magnum opus, *Don Quixote,* to the evocation of the image "Quixote," which is at the outset no more than that, an image, a sign of 111, felt rather than cognized, the process of sensation rather than intellectual, an icon rather than a symbol. But it contains, within itself, possible engenderment of the entire novel and all possible interpretations of the novel. The above example of our Cervantes scholar and proud owner of a tightly condensed sign 111 ("Quixote") need hardly do more than put her brain in automatic pilot, and the words come pouring out as an engendering of many actual signs from one de-engendered sign of possibility, the image. It is all there as part of her tacit knowing, what the body knows, *kinesthetics* (body + mind). At this level, bodymind are one; it is a matter of a somatic, motilic "reading" of signs. Within this sphere of Firstness, signs are such as they are because that is the way they are. They are signs of entrenchment, sedimentation, embodiment.

VI. MAKING A DIFFERENCE
THAT MAKES A DIFFERENCE

It all becomes a matter of experience, and our consciousness of it. And of logic, but not the logic with which we are familiar, that is, Aristotelian syllogistic, Boolean, or symbolic logic. Rather, we must become somewhat culture-blind; we must bring about a change of mind-set comparable to considering the Earth as unflat, unstationary, and lost in space rather than the center of the universe. Upon so doing, we must throw language and all its trappings off with a cathartic heave, leaving in its stead the conclusion apparently so unorthodox as to be undeserving of the attention of any self-respecting scholar.

That is to say, what we must be after—this illogical "logic"—is aimed at virtually nothing at all; and it is virtually nameless. This entails anti-intellectualism much in the order of Zen Buddhism, as suggested by Charles A. Moore (1960:289). But, alas, Moore has no alternative but to speak and write, which is the bane and the boon of all of us who find ourselves embroiled in this bogus world of academics. So also, with hardly any recourse myself but to speak and write, allow me briefly to consult Kitaro Nishida, that supreme Japanese philosopher. In *A Study of Good* (1960), Nishida avails himself of William James's term, "pure experience"—the affinities between the two thinkers has been pointed out quite often (for example, Carter 1989). Nishida uses the term "pure" to signify "a condition of true experience itself without the addition of the least thought or reflection" (Nishida 1960:1). It is experience prior to judgment, raw experience with nothing added, and before there has been any distinguishing of subjective and objective elements of experience:

> When one experiences directly one's conscious state there is as yet neither subject nor object, and knowledge and its object are completely united. This is the purest form of experience. . . . True, pure experience can exist only in present consciousness of events as they are without attaching any meaning to them at all. (Nishida 1960:1–2).

Attention to pure experience is in the "now." It does not consist of singularities of experience, but of an interval of the moment insofar as it contains certain memories of the past coupled with anticipations of the future. Nishida writes that pure experience is directly related to the perceiver and is the cause of all "psychical phenomena." So there is no immediacy in terms of the "myth of presence," for one can never be aware of the immediate experience at the moment it enters consciousness, since there is a time differential between the entry of an item of experience into consciousness and one's becoming aware of that item of experience. "First of all," Nishida writes;

> the problem arises of whether pure experience is simple or complex. When we look at it from the standpoint that, even though it be immediate, direct experience, it is a thing which is composed of past experience, or that it can be broken down into its individual elements, it may be correct to say it is complex. No matter how complex pure experience is, however, at the moment of its happening it is always one simple event. Even if it is reconstruction of past experience, at the time when it is unified within present consciousness and becomes one element, acquiring a new meaning, we can no longer say that it is the same as past consciousness. (Nishida 1960:2–3; see also Flay 1985)

We have, then, the problem of the simple and the complex, wholeness and its myriad parts, Firstness and Thirdness, iconicity and symbolicity. Actually, as we are all aware, the topic of simplicity versus complexity is in style these days in the form of fractals, chaos theory, and dissipative structures. It is also paramount in Peirce's thought (see Merrell 1998). Peirce termed *tychism* his view of the universe as a cosmic crap game, mere chance, an aleatory sphere of pure flux. His view of knowledge as evolutionary, toward increasing generality and with all the gaps finally filled and pure continuity of thought realized, he labeled *synechism*. Between unruly tychism and genuine synechism, our familiar world of Boolean binarism, linear classical logic, and "language games" of all sorts beckons. Tychism is of the nature of pure Firstness, synechism ideally of the nature of ideal Thirdness, and, as we would expect, the world we know best is that of Secondness. It is precisely the arising, the emergence, of Secondness from the virtually incomprehensible and ineffable sphere of Firstness—order out of chaos—that must captivate us here in light of a sort of Buddhist Way. This emergence of Secondness is also germane to William James's "radical empiricism," that is, the idea that consciousness of items of experience is based on the raw material of experience as it presents itself (Wild 1969).

It is a matter of the flux, and of the self as here-now, at a certain place and in a certain time. In spite of the perplexing winds of change and of change of change within flowing time—the flux of experience—some form of selfhood prevails, ordinarily. This is what provides for the unity of consciousness, whatever unity there may be. At least this is what we would like to believe. The self, our proud self, that center about which the entire universe revolves for us, that self as recipient of signs that relate to their respective "semiotic objects" so they can be given an interpretant and all will be well in the world, for the self's own interpretants demand it. The haughty individual self standing imperiously above and beyond its world, capable of surveying it, of subjecting it to its will. But actually, for Nishida and Buddhist thought as for Peirce and James, the self is not a "thing" at all. It is inferred, a wishful ideal rather than a fixed reality, ephemeral and transient rather than permanent: it is nothing more than a function (James 1950 I:139). Or better, for Peirce the self is a flow of relations (Colapietro 1990). For Nishida as well, pure experience is a unity of the whole of experience; all is unified through the relations emerging from the stuff of pure experience; neither consciousness nor the furniture of the actual physical world are fundamental, but both interdependently emerge out of the flux of experience. While consciousness is one function of the emergence of somethingness from the flux, physical existence plays out another role, and both collaborate in bringing about the incessant emergence of all that is, for all consciousness and for the world at large.[8] In this light, Charlene Seigfried writes:

> James's thesis of "one primal stuff or material in the world" is meant as a counter-assertion to those who hold to an aboriginal dualism of consciousness. James is not asserting a metaphysical sub-stratum, but he is denying the subject-object distinction as irreducible. Pure experience is neither monistic nor dualistic, it is undifferentiated. (Seigfried 1978:40)

Along comparable lines, Thomas Martland tells us:

> Another revealing but difficult to understand characteristic of pure experience is its "much at onceness" that transcends all separation. As such it is similar to the impression made on the conscious level if a number of impressions, from any number of sensory sources, fall simultaneously on a mind which had not yet experienced them separately. Such a mind would fuse them into a single undivided object. In this case, and in that of pure experience there is no meaning, only a "big blooming buzzing confusion." But in another sense there is meaning because all there is in each case is pure experience . . . on the level of pure experience they mean everything they are. On that level things compenetrate each other, are alive and fuse into each other. (Martland 1963:40)

Regarding James's becoming of consciousness and Nishida's breaking or cutting of undifferentiated pure experience, we have the initiation of

Peirce's semiosis as signs engendering signs of other signs for their semiotic agents in a mind-numbing diversity of respects and capacities. However, once this is actually in the process of occurring, we have semiotics, not semiosis. The former entails the taking and the making of signs; the latter refers to the process itself, which includes a given body of signs' takers and makers, as well as those of all other signs. Semiotics is a broken, cut, fractured, mutilated, impoverished remnant of semiosis. It allows for self/other, subject/object, true/false, mind/body dichotomies, which are all mutually submerged in the soup of semiosis—and hence we have the self as a product of semiotics; by and large it loses its nature as process within the flux and flow of semiosis.

At the outset one might be prone to assume that semiotics is Deleuze and Guattari's arborescence, while semiosis is rhizomic in nature. The metaphor appears at the outset to be on the mark. But it is not, not really. Not really, at least in the manner—quite erroneous I believe—that rhizomicity is frequently taken. It is often and unfortunately assumed that the rhizome is all there all at once, as a vast interconnected tangle. But it is not, for, like an organic entity, it is in a constant process of growth and decay. Like the rhizome-as-organism, semiosis is process, pure process, with nothing necessarily (yet) actualized into the light of day for someone *in* some respect or capacity. Semiosis is the flux of pure experience out of which some semiotic agent carves isolable chunks and signs them. These chunks are most customarily taken as the semiotic agent's proud possession; they are not the property of semiosis. What was the undivided but infinitely divisible sphere of semiosis becomes severed into parts according to the wishes and the needs, the desires and the demands, the intents and the purposes of those living organisms who make and take signs. That severing ultimately makes up what goes by the venerated name of "reality," and the chunks become relatively static fixations selected from the nonselected, which is always already everywhere in flow (see James 1948:50, 65, 73; 1976:4, 13, 263). All this is to say, with both James and Nishida and Buddhism in general, and Peirce as well regarding what he labeled the "logics" of vagueness and generality, that if the very idea of semiosis (process, flow, the continuum of unactualized possibilities) contradicts classical logic, then classical logic is left with no more than a small portion of the entire semiotic-semiosic panorama.

As I have argued elsewhere, this is indeed the role of classical logic within the larger sphere of semiosis.[9] In such case, dualism is dethroned, and classical logic must be content to remain within severely restricted parameters. Consequently, the non-idea, the non-concept, the unthought

thought of semiosis—that is, of pure experience regarding the semiotic agent, the self—is not merely a cute metaphor, a heuristic tool, or the product of so much mind spinning. Semiosis is ultimately the only thing, that is, it is all that is; yet as everything that is it is nothing at all, at least for some sign maker and taker, whether real or ideal. It encompasses the narrow confines of classical logic within its exceedingly more general embrace, like the Möbius strip and its fold that include the linearly engendered line. In short, semiosis is the all of things in terms of sheer possibilities as well as actualities. It is all that is, even including its strange relationship with emptiness.

Carter (1989:10–13) rightly points out that a chief difference between James and Nishida and Buddha philosophy lies in the latter's notion of emptiness or nothingness. Emptiness can perhaps be apprehended during "peak experiences" insofar as the active mind keeps out of the way and lets nature (that is, semiosis) take her course. James, like Peirce, on the other hand, believed that all experience molded into knowledge of the world "out there" is, in a manner of speaking, either flawed and inconsistent or it is incomplete, and hence it is always subject to revision in the light of future experience. Carter alludes to James's allusion to the flow of consciousness and the coming and going of birds in a flock. It (consciousness, an individual bird, or the actualization of minuscule portions of semiosis) engages in a flitty and jerky alternation of flights and perches, all of them tentative, uncertain, vacillating. The resting places are ephemeral flashes of consciousness that make up our awareness, however limited, of whatever we have carved from the possibilities semiosis spreads before us:

> Perchings and flights together add up to our awareness of the whole life-activity of our own life as, metaphorically a bird. Perception and transitive relations together add up to our life of experience. And both are cut out of the infinitely rich flow called pure experience. Substantive "things" and their relations are not ultimately different but arise from the same aboriginal source. (James 1950 1:243)

"Mental content and object" are identical, simply different aspects abstracted out of pure experience for practical purposes (James 1955:246–47). "Subject" and "object" denote different aspects of the same primal flow. The distinction is real enough, for functional purposes at least. But it is certainly not the final word regarding the universe, for, as Peirce and James often stressed, it is no more than a transitory stage in the process of semiosis. Nishida, too, stresses that at the background of any judgment "there is always an event of pure experience." Indeed, pure experience, we are told, rests behind all experience, even the experience of thinking. Relations, thought, willing, feeling are all aspects of direct experience and dimensions of pure experience. In Nishida's words, pure experience and thought "are basically the same event seen from different points of view" (Nishida 1960:17).

Carter writes that if pure experience lies behind all experience of which one is conscious, then it is not available only to states of hallucination, dream, sleep-coma, or to the consciousness of newly born babies, as is usually the common assumption and as James himself occasionally seems to suggest. Rather, it is the recognition of the interpenetrating interconnectedness, or oneness, of things. It is in a sense wider, richer, and more profound, but of basically the same quality, as everyday experience of the minutae of *our* world—that is, the particular world from an uncountable number of worlds that we happen to have made. Indeed, there is only one world, one flowing of experience, semiosis, from which everything is in a process of interdependent emergence. In this sense, generality and particularity, and subject and object, good and evil, truth and falsity, in fact, everything and its presumed opposite, emerge from pure experience, like the temporary perching spot of each pigeon that was previously swirling around with the flock (Carter 1989:11).

A pigeon is "there-now," at rest, temporarily at least. We can see it, darting its head about in constant vigilance and search. It is there for our inspection, our admiration, and then suddenly it is off and swirling around with its neighbors in a flock of flux. In donut fashion each pigeon moves in and out as the entire fluid structureless structure gyrates and migrates, in counterclockwise movement, toward some indeterminable goal: a relatively undifferentiated quasi-periodic attractor or even a "strange attractor," awaiting its re-differentiation into an orderly set of temporarily stable perchings. Classical science and standard logic have focused obsessively on the equivalent of the perchings only—distinctions of perception and thought—while shoving the undesirable unruly behavior and quirks of nature into the dark closet and hoping they will disappear on their own. This practice traditionally demanded a sort of dual consciousness, two distinct views. What the observer saw was what there was, and that's all there was to it: *empiricism.* Or what the solitary cogitator dredged up from the pit of her introspective mind was the only thing that could be accepted without a shadow of a doubt: *rationalism.* In either case, feelings, sentiment, subjectivity, the "reason" of the heart and soul were considered to be another matter entirely and unworthy of serious cogitation.

Then the unseen atom made its way into scientific discourse, in spite of protests from certain phenomenalists and positivists; James, and especially Freud and others revealed that there is much more to consciousness than immediately meets the mind; and with Riemann and other geometers, mathematician Poincaré, and philosopher of science Pierre Duhem, conventions came to be a factor in what was taken as provisional truth rather than what was absolutely true because it seeped into the intuiting mind of the most gifted individual around.[10] Thus:

> Pure experience is carved up, according to our practical needs and purposes, in the myriad ways that constitute ordinary distinction-filled experience, but we should not hold fast to these divisions and distinctions, for they are at best partial glimpses, and at worst distortions of the "aboriginal sensible muchness." Reality presents itself to us as a flow, and as a seamless web, which we then divide up in accordance with whatever principles of focus are important to us. We form concepts of such fixed focuses, and these perchings are not unreal, but proper portions apportioned from the original wholeness. (Carter 1989:14)

While James is unsure whether we can actually ever have "pure" experience, Nishida takes it as given that we can, and that analysis will reveal that all distinctions arise out of an original distinctionlessness. We have, once again, semiotics and semiosis, hopeful bits and pieces carved out of a continuous process.

James and Nishida, pragmatism and Eastern philosophy, is a combination at the outset strange, but it becomes increasingly in tune with our fundamental inclinations as time goes by.

3

HOW GENERAL ARE
THE TEN SIGNS?[1]

I. THE FIRST FIVE SIGNS FROM ANOTHER VIEW

With neither time nor space—nor the necessary apprenticeship in theory and practice—to delve into the intricacies of Buddhism and the vast differences between schools of Oriental thought, from Japan to China to India, suffice it to say, I would hope, that the Japanese variety of Buddhism is more attuned to a positive attitude toward everyday living in the most natural way, while Indian Buddhism tends to be more intellectualist, breaking methods and practices into categories and sets of categories.[2]

In whichever case, at the end of the road there is either a blind alley or a gaping chasm—a blind alley for she who wishes to bask in the diaphanous shine of knowing she knows what there is to be known, a gaping chasm for she who actually expected something, some-*thing*, "out there" passively awaiting its being cognized and now realizes that knowing what *is* is simply not there for the taking. But actually, neither blind wordlessness nor gaping silence are actually what *is*. One must speak, one cannot remain silent, and upon speaking one can do no more than say what *is not* what is, one cannot say directly what *is*. So apparently there is no fruit to be had from obsessively focusing on the "whys." It is a matter of getting on with the "hows" of living. But the "hows" are silent, that is, unless they can be at least partly articulated, and upon their being partly articulated, the "whys" inevitably begin to surface (children learn this at a bright young age with their incessant "whys"). The "hows" are no more than experience (signs 111 to 311), and the "whys" are the saying of that experience (signs 321 to 333). But, pace the Eastern sages with their koans and such, and Western mind-benders from Heraclitus and Zeno to

Nietzsche, Gödel, Bohr, Heisenberg, Wittgenstein, and Derrida, saying the "whys" ultimately lands one in paradox, and remaining in the "hows" turns out to be a pretty solitary game. Actually, from a certain angle the "whys" are much like the "hows." Both are an attempt to probe more deeply into what is not available to surface appearances, what is behind assumptions and presuppositions, behind the feeling and sense of things, to what lies at deeper levels. Ultimately, what is at the surface is *not* what is underneath that surface, so what *is* also *is not,* but what is at the surface, *is,* though it *is not.* So it is neither what it *is* nor what it *is not,* for since what it *is* can always become something else as a result of its interrelatedness with what it *is not,* then it can always be something else, and if it is, then what it *is not* will also have become something other than what it *was.* I did not intend to present a tongue-twister here, not really. The point is that, when taking any cosmology, metaphysical doctrine, method of analysis, or the strategies of practical everyday living to their extreme expression, a theater of the absurd, a hot-bed of paradox, an unruly sea of ambiguity inevitably gives one a slap in the face. That is to say, at the end of the line, the snake stretches around finally to swallow its own tail: the system looks at itself in the mirror, reflects itself. This is the $\sqrt{-1}$ at the "center" of the the/a semiosic field, the undeniable split of pairs without any of them getting the upper hand.

Let me try to put the matter this way. According to certain ancient schools of Indian Buddhism, experience is analyzed into elements labeled *dharmas* (Conze 1962:92–106). A dharma is the term applied to the entire corpus of Buddhist teaching: it is also the "order of the cosmos," the "natural way things are," and it refers to "moral law" governing proper behavior. What *is,* that is, the world in which we live and breathe, consists of dharmas: ephemeral items of experience incessantly flashing in and out with such rapidity that the normal faculties are not aware of them, rather, they appear as a continuous stream. Each dharma is like a Spencer-Brown (1979) "mark of distinction," a Peirce "cut," a James "carving" from the "blooming, buzzing" confusion, in the sense that the semiotic agent isn't immediately aware of the breaks. In a word, an individual dharma is not something that *has* quality, like signs 211 onward; in its purest sense and unrelated to anything else it *is* quality, somewhat comparable to the bare emergence of sign 111. A set of *dharmas* can conglomerate and raise themselves into the consciousness of a semiotic agent to become a sign of Secondness and of Thirdness. But that is another issue. For the bare, fleeting moment, dharmas are simply what they *are,* no more, no less. In Conze's words:

For an understanding of Buddhist philosophy it is vitally important that one should appreciate the difference between 'dharmas' on the one hand, and 'common-sense things' on the other. In agreement with the majority of philosophers, Buddhists regard common-sense things around them as a false appearance. The 'dharmas,' i.e., the facts which are ultimately real, are normally covered from sight by ignorance, and nothing but the special virtue of wisdom will enable us to penetrate to them. No rational approach can be content to accept the crude data of common sense as ultimate facts. The scientific propositions of modern science refer to abstract entities of 'constructs,' such as atoms, molecules, electromagnetic fields, etc., and to their properties, tendencies and habitual behaviour. Common-sense data are thus retraced to, transformed into, or replaced by concepts which are both more intelligible and 'fundamental.' (Conze 1962:97)

Comparable to common-sense data extracted from the flux of experience, Buddhism regards the world as composed of a relentless flow of simples. These simples consist of the dharmas, which are (1) multiple, (2) ephemeral, (3) cold and impersonal (they have not yet been linked to subjectivity), and (4) interdependent, mutually conditioned, and potentially interrelatedly emerging into the consciousness of some semiotic agent or other, whether human or not. In other words, dharmas know of no selfness or thingness: all that comes at a later stage in the semiosic process.

One of the manners in which dharmas have been categorized is into five groups known as *skandhas*, or "heaps," which consist of *form, feeling, perception, formation*, and *consciousness* (Conze 1962:107–20). *Form* subdivides into eleven dharmas (the five senses; that which arises in each of the senses such as colors, shapes, sounds, smells, and tastes; and that which is purely imaginary). It is the only skandha that directly involves the physical world; it offers the world up for the pleasure or the pain, the joy or the anguish of the semiotic agent. However, consciousness is never directly aware of form. It does not "see" a hummingbird in terms of form; it "sees" its experience of the hummingbird. The form makes the experience possible; then, after the fact, the experience is what is "seen." Form, in other words, is roughly tantamount to sign 111. It is there, unrelated to anything else, before it has become a sign of something other for someone in some respect or capacity.

Feeling is what is there and affecting the semiotic agent by way of form. It is a raw, unmediated sensation of discomfort, comfort, pleasure, pain, and so on, or it can even be neutral, and devoid of any conscious, conscientious, intentional, or cognitive interrelations and intermeshing. Feeling is the process of the bodymind as yet undifferentiated, the process of the mind's just-now-beginning to become aware of what the body senses and in a sense already knows, the body's sending what it senses and knows through the nervous channels to dialogue with the mind, that of which the mind is in hopeful expectancy and of which it is dependent upon the body. The mind is just-now-beginning to become aroused. Feeling, then, corresponds directly to none of the ten Peircean signs, but rather it is the commencement of the flow from 111 to 211, without the possibility of its arriving at the next semiotic depot without its passing away into the soup of semiosis, with nary an indication of its having played out its crucial role in the becoming of the being of signs, in the being of its becoming as a sign.

Perception is a matter of discernment, of the bare indication (index) of something other than the sign and/or other than the semiotic self. As the root beginning of an idea or interpretant of the sign, it is the focus of the self's attention as something "out there" and apart from the feeling and sensing body, "out there" and available for interrelation with the mind. It is abstraction, *ab*-straction (ab = from, away, off, away from), to be sure, and it is abs-traction (traction = the act of being drawn, pulled). It is something other, and it is something pulled apart from the perceiving and conceiving bodymind of the semiotic agent. The characteristics of the sign are just-now-beginning to become separated such that the sign, that is, the object to which it relates, that is, both sign and object, can be qualified and identified. Perception is in this sense a flow into sign 211 and along the meandering stream—or onrushing tide depending upon the emergency or lack thereof demanded by the context—and into sign 221. Consciousness of the semiotic agent is on-its-way-toward-becoming aware of the sign as such.

Formation, one might wish to suppose, is the mental register of feeling and perception, signs 111 and 211, and it is consequently the culmination of sign 221. That would be an oversimplification, however. Granted, formation makes up the rudiments of the content of experience. As a "spontaneous cry" in the sense of Peirce, it is "any object of direct experience in so far as it is a sign, and, as such, affords information concerning its Object" (*CP*:2.256). It is an act of recognition, whether positive or negative, simple or complex, and whether accompanying a shock or consisting of relatively passive perceiving. This act of recognition is a *re*-cognition (re = back to a former position or state, a re-tracing, a re-ceding), and it is a re-*cognition* (cognition = knowing, becoming acquainted with). As such it is just that: a going back and a re-calling of what was known, in order to abstract it and relate it to the present sign process so that it may be known anew. It entails a flush from 111, 211, and 221 toward 222, and perhaps even slightly beyond. Sign 222, the object of direct experience and a sign "pointing" to that with which it relates, is the first sign of actual events, of becomings of things, in the world "out there." This it can only do "by being really affected by its Object; so that it is necessarily an index" (CP:2.257). By now there is quite clearly a distinction between sign and its other, semiotic agent and otherness.

Consciousness at least begins the process of ushering in sign 311, the first sign enjoying Thirdness, the Thirdness of the representamen. Consciousness can easily be defined as "pure awareness of an experience," but awareness of the consciousness of that awareness of the experience is exceedingly problematic. This recalls Hume's observation regarding the difficulty of attending to an act of consciousness in the same instant as the occurrence of that act. In Peirce's words, it is there, but stop to think about, to become conscious of it, and it has flown, for it is process (CP:1.357). Consciousness is elusive, chiefly because it is the subject of mental activity, and hence it cannot be made the object of observation, speculation, and knowledge. Once objectified, it ceases to become what it is and is now something else. In other words, when the mind is conscious of itself, it splits into subject and object, and the perceiving and knowing subject can no longer be the object of perception and knowledge. So there is simply a split, without the possibility of the one side of the split knowing the other side in either Baconian or Cartesian fashion. There is nothing but a split. The split *is* as it *is*. It is an icon (the Thirdness of sign 311 is in the sign's First component, the representamen), and as such it is self-contained and not yet related to anything other than itself. Of course, in regards to the split, there is something within the icon that is related to something else, but since at this point the whole of the icon *is* as it *is*, atemporally, the possibility does not exist for the subjective half of the icon to perceive and know the objective half. There is just split, and the split, split *is*.

However, as semiosis flows into sign 311 and then moves on, there is the becoming of some form or other of consciousness, quite definitely, or, that is, quite vaguely, for at this stage there is no more than the split of consciousness without there existing any consciousness of some clearly demarcated other. Consciousness "is that part of ourselves where we are most of all ourselves. It is that in man where he can most easily think that he is himself, alone himself by himself. Pure consciousness, when reached not by way of intellectual abstraction, but by realizing the innermost core of one's self, would therefore be the same as pure and simple 'spirit', by itself in permanent peace" (Conze 1962:113). However, this pure consciousness, once it has come to be its pure self, paradoxically turns out to be nonconsciousness, for there is no consciousness of it as an object by some conscious subject.

So we have now negotiated the rapids from upstream and slightly prior to sign 111 to sign 311 and perhaps even ever-so-slightly beyond. From 111 we have the tacit dimension of the becoming of consciousness, a sense of sight, smell, taste, sound, tactile feeling, and, finally, kinesthesis (or "mind-stuff" in Buddhist philosophy, a sort of sixth sense). There is no propositional knowledge here, nothing explicit, no discursivity, not even any language to speak of, but rather semiosis at its processual best. There is rhythm and rhyme but not (yet) any reason to speak of, learning but hardly any logic or language, knowing *how* to do things without knowing explicitly that those things are done in such-and-such a way (in other words, there is practice without prognosis).

With this processual account of signs 111 to 311 in mind, let us turn to the process of consciousness, that is, to William James.

II. THE OTHER FIVE, THE FIVE OF THE OTHER

James divides consciousness into five characteristics (which I have rephrased somewhat in the spirit and the context of the story I have to tell here):

1. Each thought (sign) tends to exist as a portion of a personal consciousness.
2. Every thought (sign) contained within a personal consciousness is incessantly in the process of change.
3. Within personal consciousness, a thought (sign), all thoughts (signs) are sensibly continuous: they appear as a continuum.
4. Consciousness is consciousness of objects (i.e., signs, and the "semiotic objects," acts and events to which they relate) that are other than that consciousness; in other words, consciousness opens up the possibility of knowing, narrative knowing.
5. Consciousness entails choice and selection, from the potentially infinite number of possibilities of thoughts (signs). (based on James 1950 I:225).

Regarding (1), James writes that every thought is part of a personal consciousness, but that an account of the idea of "personal consciousness" in precise terms is well-nigh impossible. At a political rally, for example, there are myriad thoughts, many of which cohere, since virtually all the individuals present are of more or less like-minded ideological leanings. Yet the thoughts of each personal consciousness are as independent as they are dependent upon the whole. The thoughts are neither separate nor unified, they are neither a random rush of atoms nor a tightly knit molecular conglomerate. Each individual's thoughts, likewise, are neither an aleatory mess nor do they form a coherent package wrapped and tied and ready for delivery. In both cases there is vagueness and ambiguity, usually a bit of inconsistency, and always incompleteness. An individual's thoughts are hers and hers alone, yet they are not exactly hers, for her thoughts happen to enjoy a few affinities with some of the thoughts of those around her. And they are by and large the thoughts of the collection of individuals belonging to the entire party, yet as more and more individuals are concocted into the whole, and as thoughts pile upon thoughts, the whole becomes more and more unruly. At times it may even threaten to disintegrate (i.e., dissipate, as in Ilya Prigogine's "dissipative structures"—see Merrell 1996). In another way of putting it, each personal consciousness lacks definition, distinction, identity, for it is part of a whole, but since that whole is itself vague, each personal consciousness is even more vague and more ill-defined and ill-distinguished from the other personal consciousnesses making up the whole. That is to say, as James would put it, the thought (sign) that tends to be part of a personal consciousness functions much like many pronouns, especially demonstrative pronouns (signs 321). A pronoun specifies, yet it remains indefinitely vague when removed from its context and remains somewhat vague even when properly contextualized. As Peirce points out, it is up to the originator of the thought (sign) to render it less vague. For that reason personal consciousness should stand out, make itself heard, say its piece, argue its point. The favored candidate at the political rally may be able to carry out this task admirably, if she is a great communicator. Less charismatically endowed politicians are destined to relative anonymity, taking the back seat to those who, however wise or egomaniacal, push for their own agenda, or perhaps that of those upon whom their campaign funds or their votes depend.

It might appear that characteristic (2) discards the notion that thought is no more than ephemeral, that it has no duration whatsoever. James denies this. He also eschews the hopeful wish that we enjoy fixed experience of static things in our world. After all, he asks,

> Are not the sensations we get from the same object, for example, always the same? Does not the same piano-key, struck with the same force, make us

hear in the same way? Does not the same grass give us the same feeling of green, the same sky the same feeling of blue, and do we not get the same olfactory sensation no matter how many times we put our nose to the same flask of cologne? It seems a piece of metaphysical sophistry to suggest that we do not; and yet a close attention to the matter shows that *there is no proof that the same bodily sensation is ever got by us twice.* (James 1950 I:231; italics in original)

James concludes that every thought (sign) is, strictly speaking, unique, and that it is no more than the similarity between it and some other thought that allows us to relate the two and put them into the bag of generalities along with a host of other thoughts (signs). This is the commonplace, that which appears to be humdrum; we've seen it before and know it all and hence need pay it little mind. Examples of the commonplace are found in signs 322, which, Peirce writes, furnish at least enough information regarding them and their objects to allow the semiotic agent to relate them to previous signs of the same sort and perhaps to expect signs of a particular sort to ensue in the near future. And so we get along with life (*CP*:2.260). However, James reveals a most Peircean phenomenon: a difference that makes a difference may pop up in the commonplace to shock us out of our lethargy, and in retrospect we "wonder how we ever could have opined as we did last month about a certain matter" (James 1950 I:233). What was commonplace can become unique, what was irreal can become real, what was insipid can become exciting, and vice versa.

Characteristic (3), that each personal consciousness, like the thoughts (signs) within it, appears continuous, forces on us the notion that not only do consciousness and thoughts (signs) change, but that change is an ongoing process. Whitehead's "pulsations" and the Buddhist "flash-dance" are such that there are no gaps but apparent continuity. As a consequence, a thought (sign) and its object are taken as the same from one temporal point to another, and from one spatial coordinate to another. There are changes, of course, but in the ordinary flow of experience, that is, of semiosis, the changes are not so abrupt that they call attention to the incessantly altering nature of whatever is in consciousness. Just as the discontinuity created by our "blind spot" is smoothed over by the exercise of our perceptual faculties, so also perception lards in the gaps marking the occurrence of changes so as to render them inconsequential (*CP*:5.220). Consciousness is in this manner not really a "chain" or a "train," as James puts it, but more adequately put, a "river" or a "stream." The former comes in links and units, the latter does not, it is indivisible, at least by ordinary empirical means.

Thoughts (signs) of characteristic (3) are unary in the sense that, like signs 331—terms, words, or "rhemes" in Peirce's terminology—they are in and of themselves unrelated to other thoughts (signs) of the same class, though they contain thoughts (signs) of the preceding classes. Take a bolt of lightning. It breaks the relative obscurity of the night, giving us a jolt of re-cognition. This unnerving jolt, once we become aware of it and begin remarking on the magnitude of the flash, *is* what it *is* only with respect to what it *is not*, the obscurity, without which there would have been no consciousness of the lightning as such and no language. Moreover, the bolt brings about the expectation that a clap of thunder is sure to follow. And then, suddenly, there it is. But it was not some-thing of which we could have been properly aware and which could have been the focus of our comments without the previous flash. There must have been a transition from one thought (sign) to another one in order to establish the "mark of distinction" between the two. But on so establishing the mark, Secondness has made its presence felt. Insofar as the unrelated lightning goes, there is only a flash, no more, no less, and unrelated to any-thing else. If put into language, this is tantamount to the noun "lightning" before it has been linked with any other word or words to form a sentence and then sentences, many of them. "Lightning," at this point and without any accompanying signs, is no more than a solitary word. Otherwise, it is not "lightning" pure (of course it is never pure in the pure sense, but we are considering the purity of the thought [sign] for the purposes of this inquiry). In other words, it is a replica of the "same" word that has been used with respect to similar events, though it has not (yet) been related to any other parts of the event through thoughts (signs) in this particular context.

Characteristic (4) places us within the sphere of knowing chiefly by way of language after utterances have dealt with objects, acts, and events that are independent of their respective thoughts (signs). Since the utterances have related to other signs, there can now be mediation between the signs as things in themselves and their relation to their objects. This mediation includes consciousness of the otherness of the thoughts (signs) as well as the otherness of the objects, acts, or events with which they interrelate. This nature of double otherness is usually not addressed, as James effectively points out. His words warrant extended citing:

> In popular parlance the word object is commonly taken without reference to the act of knowledge, and treated as synonymous with individual subject of existence. Thus if anyone asks what is the mind's object when you say 'Columbus discovered America in 1492,' most people will reply 'Columbus,'

or 'America,' or, at most, 'the discovery of America.' They will name a substantive kernel or nucleus of the consciousness, and say the thought is 'about'
that,—indeed it is,—and they will call that your thought's 'object.' Really
that is usually only the grammatical object, or more likely the grammatical
subject, of your sentence. It is at most your 'fractional object;' or you may
call it the 'topic' of your thought, or the 'subject of your discourse.' But the
Object of your thought is really its entire content or deliverance, neither more
nor less. It is a vicious use of speech to take out a substantive kernel from its
content and call that its object; and it is an equally vicious use of speech to
add a substantive kernel not articulately included in its content, and to call
that its object. Yet either one of these two sins we commit, whenever we content ourselves with saying that a given thought is simply 'about' a certain
topic, or that that topic is its 'object.' The object of my thought in the previous sentence, for example, is strictly speaking neither Columbus, nor
America, nor its discovery. It is nothing short of the entire sentence, 'Colum-
bus-discovered-America-in-1492.' And if we wish to speak of it substan-
tively, we must make a substantive of it by writing it out thus with hyphens
between all its words. Nothing but this can possibly name its delicate idiosyncrasy. And if we wish to *feel* that idiosyncrasy we must reproduce the
thought as it was uttered, with every word fringed and the whole sentence
bathed in that original halo of obscure relation, which, like an horizon, then
spreads about its meaning. (James 1950 I:275–76)

A sentence is a compound sign, in Peirce's terms a dicent symbol, consisting of various terms, rhematic symbols (331), which, as replicas or instantiations of general signs, are of the essence of rhematic indexical
legisigns (321) and iconic legisigns (311) presented as singular rhematic
indexical sinsigns (221), which themselves are an engenderment of rhematic iconic sinsigns (211) and qualisigns (111). No sign, to repeat, is an
island in and of itself; all signs depend upon all other signs for their emergence into the light of day via the flowing semiosic bootstrapping operation. In this manner, and quite understandably, James hyphenates the
words in his sentence, for they are inextricably conjoined, and their meaning is spread over the entire utterance. However, the properly contextualized sentence, "Columbus-discovered-America-in-1492," is far more
complex than James implies. The sentence must be related to other sentences within the context of its utterance, and those sentences must be related to other sentences of the past, whether in ancient texts in
monasteries, in libraries, in newspapers and magazines, or in memory
banks of computers or the minds of the semiotic agents of a particular
community. Moreover, the sentence must be relevant to whatever propen-

sities there are for sentences to emerge in future moments that may be re-lated to it, either directly or indirectly. All this is of numbing complexity, yet it is of the nature of everyday semiosis.

A pigeon perches. At approximately the same moment somewhere else, a feeling arises in us, evoking an image or idea, which in turn re-lates to other images or ideas. A word surfaces. A sentence is engen-dered, a dialogue is in process, and texts and arguments (signs 333) are forthcoming. By that time the pigeon has departed along with its neigh-bors to pirouette above the buildings and the trees, in a rather unruly swirl, with each pigeon following the silently acknowledged leader, but not quite, for the swirl incessantly threatens to dissipate and disinte-grate. Meanwhile, our images, ideas, sentences, and the entire dialogue are caught up in the flow of semiosis. As the pigeons continue to perch and re-engage their flight, words continue to spew forth. There is con-stant eruption into a turbulence of air currents and a flapping of wings, and an incessant rush of new words and gestures and corporeal feels and visceral impulses and rhythmic swings and kinesthetic sensations. And more words, and then more . . . and more. The darting heads of the pi-geons, constantly vigilant, are on the lookout for new signs. They are incessantly in jerky, uncertain motion. Our words, with some stuttering and restarting, incessantly pour forth. Process, flow, semiosis, signs be-coming signs.

According to James, consciousness is always in some parts of the myr-iad array of possible phenomena to the exclusion of other parts, and it *"welcomes and rejects, or chooses, all the while it thinks,"* by a process of "se-lective attention" (1950 I:284; italics in original). Consciousness would appear, then, to be of the nature of that which gives rise to hypotheses. Hy-potheses are then put to the test, whether implicitly or explicitly, and judged according to how they fare with respect to aesthetic feels, reason-able cogency, and the ethical norms of the day. If these hypotheses pass the test, if the signs of certain tastes, inclinations, ideas, and arguments win out over the antagonistic signs, then they can stand tall, however ephemeral their moment of strident foregrounding may last. If not, they are placed on the chopping block to make way for other candidate signs that are always willing to try out their talents and seek their fortunes. That is to say, from the "infinite chaos of movements, . . . each sense-organ picks out those which fall within certain limits of velocity. To these it re-sponds, but ignores the rest as completely as if they did not exist" (James 1950 I:284). First, a "mark of distinction," a "cut," is made. And as "sign-cuts" pile onto "sign-cuts" a monotonous succession of sonorous strokes is broken up into rhythms, now of one sort, now of another, by the different accent which we place on different strokes. The simplest of these rhythms is the double one, tick-tóck, tick-tock, tick-tóck. Dots dispersed on a surface are perceived in rows and groups. Lines separate into diverse figures. The ubiquity of the distinctions, *this* and *that, here* and *there, now* and *then,* in our minds is the result of our laying the same emphasis on parts of place and time. (James 1950 I:284; italics in original)

In other words, a rudimentary "sign-cut" appears, then it is distinguished in terms of its being what that which is not so distinguished *is not.* A universe of sign-cuts and their absent opposites surfaces. Now the entire spectrum of more developed signs can be advanced, sentences can be engendered, then texts and arguments are forthcoming. However, eventually, as the sign-cuts continue to proliferate, they begin merging into one another, interpenetrating in an inseparable embrace, and distinctions, once clear as day, become foggy, vague, fuzzy. The universe is not only more vast than whatever body of knowledge there may be of it; it is more vast than any knowledge we can possibly have of it. Which is to say that logic, classical binary logic, is grossly inadequate to the task. As James puts it:

For my own part, I have finally found myself compelled to *give up the logic,* fairly, squarely, and irrevocably. It has an imperishable use in human life, but that use is not to make us theoretically acquainted with the essential nature of reality. . . . Reality, life, experience, concreteness, immediacy, use what word you will, exceeds our logic, overflows and surrounds it. If you like to employ words eulogistically, as most men do, and so encourage confusion, you may say that reality obeys a higher logic, or enjoys a higher rationality. But I think that even eulogistic words should be used rather to distinguish than to commingle meanings, so I prefer bluntly to call reality if not irrational, then at least non-rational in its constitution. (James 1967:212–13; italics in original)

In the terms of this essay, when signs of chiefly iconicity emerge and reach the peak of their power to afford a sense, however vague, of the coming and going of signs, then the time is perhaps becoming ripe to "give up the logic" and give in not necessarily to any "higher logic" but to some form of alternate and by its very nature a relatively ill-defined and undefinable "logic," which is also of the nature of process, flow, semiosis, signs becoming signs.

III. MORE THAN JUST EMPTY

In such case, the question inevitably surfaces: What, where, when, how are signs, when considering body as well as mind, self as well as other, sign as well as interpreter, individual as well as his/her community and the world "out there"?

In desperation, we may happen to run onto that Indian counterpart to Heraclitus, Nagarjuna, who counsels that body, mind, self, and world are signs all. The query "To sign or not to sign" is thus no query at all, for all that *is,* is sign. Which is to say that (1) the solitary sign is, but also, (2) it is not, for there is no nonsign against which to gauge it as a sign; in such case (3) it is both sign and nonsign, but if that is the case, then (4) it is neither sign nor nonsign. And yet, if we are to know signs, all four of these possibilities are to be both affirmed and negated! Nagarjuna, by well-nigh inconceivably deft moves, brings about such an affirmation and negation. All is no more than appearance, but it is more than appearance, for it *is,* but if it *is,* then it *is not,* and we find ourselves on the merry-go-round once again. The very possibility of negation is negated, which gives rise to affirmation, but since there is nothing to affirm, then what was affirmed is negated, so it is impossible either to affirm or to negate, which is to say that there is both affirmation and negation and at the same time there is neither affirmation nor negation. In other words, there is only "emptiness." But this is not mere void or "nothingness": the void or "nothingness" does not exist, because it *is not;* neither, for the same reason, does it not exist. In other words void and non-void are reciprocal terms. Each one is as unthinkable as the other. Put the two together and you have "emptiness." It's not a matter of two unthinkables making a thinkable, much as two Hegelian negations make an affirmation. No. For there is nothing, no-*thing,* that is void, and no-*thing* that is nonvoid. To the void, or "nothingness," the same four above-mentioned statements can be applied, hence they must all be *both* discarded *and* affirmed, for they do not apply, for there is only "emptiness."[3]

So signs 111–311, those of the skandhas, are and they are not, for there can be no immediate and all-embracing grasp of them, consciousness of them. And signs 321–333, of James's becoming of consciousness, are and they are not, for consciousness cannot grab itself by its own tail, cannot know itself consistently and completely, in one self-contained, self-sufficient, self-reflexive instant. Either to affirm or to negate a sign would be to affirm or negate a nonsign, and vice versa. It is irrelevant whether one begins with a sign or what is presumably a nonsign, for either way, once there is a register regarding what, where, when, or how it is, there is a sign of it, whether it is a sign, a nonsign, the void or nonvoid, or merely "emptiness." However, the negation of—that is, denial or presumed refutation of, rebuttal to—what has been written thus far in this section cannot by any stretch of the imagination set the foundations for a noble dyadic theory of semiotics from the gush of semiosis. Negation of all signs, both of positive and negative nature, cannot build a hard-rock theory or a solid foundation without contradicting itself. In fact, its very act of negation is in near-simultaneity a self-negation, so it contradicts itself anyway. But at least it does not imperiously presuppose the capacity to negate other assertions while, itself, remaining free of any and all critical gazes, as if it were in possession of some god's-eye grasp of things. By so revealing the implicit contradiction in all adjudications and all pontifications, the only position remaining is a nonposition, a suspension of judgment, and simultaneously a suspension of disbelief and a suspension of belief. Suspension of disbelief, for, even upon suspending disbelief in all things, were that to be possible—which it is not—there must remain a belief in something, that something being the possibility of the act of suspension of disbelief in the first place. And suspension of belief, for the very belief in the possibility of the act of suspending disbelief must be subject to disbelief, for it is by its very nature an impossibility, that is, in the absolute sense.

From within "emptiness"—actually, "within" is a misnomer, for there is no-*thing* "within" which there can be a "within"—there is no saying anything at all about affirmations or negations, or about anything substantial. So "emptiness," well, it's just that: emptiness. It has nothing to do with what we would ordinarily like to think of as "reality," whatever that may be. So it cannot be tantamount to "irreality" either. Hence to speak of "emptiness" as the "reality" of "irreality" can be no more than a play on words. This would be like the child who was terrified while in his dream world, but upon awakening, and with an assuring nod, he gives a giggle and an "Oh, it was only a dream." While in the dream world it was "real," insofar as he could tell while within the dream at least. But it was "irreal" from within his ordinary waking existence. Yet from his somnambulistic wide-eyed logical and rational consciousness in his comfortable physical ambient, he could neither say the dream was "irreal" nor that it was "real" in any clear and distinct fashion. And at the same time in a certain manner he could say that it was both "irreal" and "real." In this vein, perhaps when we awaken from our multiple illusions, we will not regard our previous life with such imperious disrespect, for whatever it was and wherever it led us, it was, after all, *our* life.

Epistémè, according to the long and venerable tradition of Western thought, also involves matters that are either true or false, with nothing in between to muck up the razor sharp categories. However, recent critique of this very idea of epistémè has been notorious from the likes of Derrida, Foucault, Kristeva, Lyotard, and Bernstein and Rorty, and earlier, of even Heidegger, Wittgenstein, Quine, Goodman, Putnam, and others. Many of these critics advocate something on the order of doxa (opinion, and its defense by way of dialogue, whether amiable pace Rorty or a matter of agonistics pace Lyotard). Epistémè hails from theory (*theorein* = sight, a seeing of the ordinarily or previously unseen). It is caught up in the prison-house of the ocular metaphor and the primacy of linguistic signs. Consequently, it has a propensity to give itself up to the eligible semiotic chancellor with the most impressive credentials, capable of the most proper discourse, and willing to muscle his/her way about, perhaps with little regard for those with whom he/she is associated. Doxa, on the other hand, is merely opinion, most often without foundations, and usually emerging from beliefs, inclinations, dispositions, likes and dislikes, hunches and intuitions. As such, it is not likely that we can judge that a given opinion is (1) true, (2) false, (3) both true and false, or even (4) neither true nor false. We cannot even judge at all with the customary confidence that our judgments are perfectly valid because they rest on rock-hard foundations. So all four possibilities of judgment must be denied. But if we cannot judge, then how can we adjudicate, even in a pragmatic sense, between practices that will yield results and practices that will turn out to be futile? And if we cannot do so, then does not the discussion come to a halt, and we are condemned to silence?

Well, not really. Perhaps, that is. For Plato and the young Wittgenstein, as well as for a host of other intellectuals—the list of which is too large for enumeration—in a manner of speaking we are necessarily ignorant of that which is not, of that which we do not know, so we must consign ourselves to silence in the face of such unknowns and unknowables. I would agree, as I suppose would Peirce—he actually did so in so many words—and Nagarjuna. But we must then take the next step. No matter how much we know about that which is, that which remains to be known is a receding horizon, so no matter how much we know, our knowledge will be quite infinitesimal beside the infinite stretch of our ignorance. So we cannot know that which is. In other words, (1) we can know, though (2) our knowledge is ignorance, so (3) it is *both* knowledge *and* ignorance—

unknowing knowing—and hence (4) it is, in the most proper way of putting it, *neither* knowledge *nor* ignorance. And, as a final note, none of the above is valid and it is all valid, that is, we know all the above taken as a whole, but we cannot know any of the above taken as individuals. In other words, we can deny any of the above in favor of some alternative, but if we deny all of the above, then we're left with "emptiness," we're left with nothing at all to see, hear, touch, taste, smell, or kinesthetically to sense. Emptiness is pure form and pure form is emptiness: Nagarjuna said so much. But that is really to say nothing at all, or everything at once, whichever. It is to say that emptiness is as if it were form, and form is as if it were emptiness. But I'm afraid that will not do either. Not quite. So what is it? Quietude? Total inactivity? Pure contemplation? No. There is everyday life, "forms of life," the way we do things while we are embedded in our community practices because that's the way we do them, not very clearly and not very simply. And when we are so acting we do things that, if we think about them, are quite bizarre and we really should be surprised at our acts. But we didn't really expect we would act in this way. So we were surprised that we were not surprised by what we did; and though we did not expect to be surprised, our surprise did not affect our expectations, for we went along generally doing as we would have done anyway.

What, clearly and distinctly, are these daily practices? For sure, by and large they are nothing that can be put into precise terms. On the contrary. They are what we do but cannot really say why or how we know that that is the way we do it because it is just what we do. There, at the edge of thought, that unthinking thinking, and at the edge of knowing, that un-knowing knowing, we find ourselves groping in the dark. No, not really in the dark, but, better said, groping at the boundary. What boundary? Boundary between what and what? And the other side of the boundary? Where is it? How far does it stretch out into the horizon? Where in the world is all this taking us anyway?

Emptiness, cussed emptiness; no, that's too strong a way of putting it, for nothing would be anything without it. Not "really."

IV. NO PLACE FOR BOUNDARIES

Where all this is taking us, perhaps, is toward what physicist John A. Wheeler (1990) dubs the boundary of the boundary. Yes, the secret lies in the "boundary of the boundary." The boundary is where the Zen koan has one hand do the clapping, where the hand catches its own thumb, or in the Western way where there is the silence of John Cage, the blank sheet of Mallarmé, the white patch on a white canvas of Kasimir Malevich, the ultimate limit of the calculus, or, to top it all off, the square root of minus one, $\sqrt{-1}$, the function of which as mentioned above is found in logic, in mathematics and chaos theory, in computer engineering, and in quantum mechanics and relativity theory. $\sqrt{-1}$ is in a sense everywhere and nowhere. It is as if it were emptiness realized, paradoxically.

Consider a media example, which may allow me to introduce Wheeler's idea. At one time in his career blues singer Bo Diddley was somewhat washed up. Then he made a TV commercial with the then baseball and football star Bo Jackson in which Bo D. tells Bo J., "Bo, you don't know Diddley."[4] Subsequently, Bo D. rapidly climbed up the musical records charts, and his career was injected with new life. This massive accomplishment owed a debt to one apparently simple sentence string, an infinitesimally thin line of virtually infinitesimal length when compared to the vast interrelated cultural net engulfing the two actors. The sentence string was a mere sentence-boundary, hardly more than a boundary of a boundary, a sign of itself, from which there emerged an onrushing tide of signs, including filled stadiums and concert halls, music in the air and icons on the sports and entertainment pages, flows of money, cheers and jeers, hot dogs, soft drinks, and a little smoking, deluges of signs in consumers' airy heads, both young and old.

Yes. The boundary of the boundary, the sign of itself, the hinge that allows for all the action: it's from there that the whole show gushes forth. Of course, television is the medium with the unparalleled capacity to highlight and dramatize a plethora of cultural bits and pieces of information, wrap them up in a package, and present them to the public at such breakneck speed that everyone is duped into thinking they constitute a coherent set of signs and that there is an important message there, somewhere. But that's another story for another time. For now, directly to Wheeler.

Wheeler, the quantum physicist—and a rabble-rouser at that in a profession known for hypotheses so wild that they have been adopted by sci fi writers for decades—tells us that a boundary at its simplest best and at its most confoundingly worst begins with a solitary "direct or 'oriented' line"—a one-dimensional "*manifold*" that has for its boundary "the starting point and the terminal point, both zero-dimensional" (Wheeler 1990:10). Such a boundary is a hole cut out of a sheet of paper with a pair of scissors—recall in this light Peirce's "book of assertions." This "book" consists of a two-dimensional manifold, with the cut itself defined as a one-dimensional manifold. So, where is the boundary? At the edge of the paper. What is the boundary, that is, of what does it consist?

Why, nothing at all. It is zero! Zero, "whatever the point at which we consider that line to have started, that is also the point at which the line terminates" (Wheeler 1990:110; italics in original). A debt is incurred at the starting point when the scissors penetrate the two-dimensional manifold, and then that starting point is annihilated, consumed, eaten up. The boundary eats itself up, when the payoff for the debt occurs at the end point. In other words, "the *zero*-dimensional boundary of the *one*-dimensional boundary of a *two*-dimensional region is zero" (Wheeler 1990:110). Which is to say, if I read Wheeler correctly, that if in our three-dimensional world we were to carve out a cube, then, like a square hole marring the Flatlander's two-dimensional existence, there would be a section that would not hold water, or anything else for that matter. Moreover, our cube separating our space from "nothingness," from "elsewhere," would be a boundary consisting of twelve lines (one-dimensional boundaries) and six planes (two-dimensional boundaries) making up a three-dimensional region, and that the sum of these boundaries is zero! Nothing. A nothing that separates what is here-now from mere emptiness.

Wheeler demonstrates his point with a cube (figure 12). Each of the its six faces has an orientation in three-dimensional space. Three spaces give

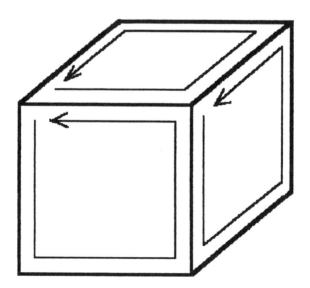

Figure 12

the cube's position, and three more give its movement along its time-line, its world-line. In addition, each face of the cube inherits from the interior an orientation, a swirl, a direction of spin as it moves along its time-line toward the future (in contemporary physics no moving body faces forward and forward only, nor is it Janus-faced, but in constant oscillatory, vibratory, undulatory gyration). The one-dimensional boundary of one of the faces of the figure 12 cube is given a swirl by a line and an arrow. There is a start, wherever that is, and an ending, but the ending ends up at the starting point, and the starting point is the ending, so they cancel each other out: zero dimensions. But isn't the line a boundary? That's one dimension, isn't it? But the line begins eating its own tail, finally leaving nothing. Total washout. Caput.

Actually, we cut the sheet of paper, a two-dimensional universe, with three-dimensional scissors from within our three-dimensional vantage point. The question is, then: What kind of scissors could we possibly use to cut a cube out of our own three-dimensional space from within a fourth dimension? Why, four-dimensional scissors, of course. A big problem. Where do we get them and how can we use them? We don't, and we can't, short of our playing the impossible role of a Maxwell Demon and a Laplace Superobserver all wrapped up into one. So we don't, and we can't. Yet, let's see how far we can go. If two-dimensional space is subject to one-dimensional boundaries and three-dimensional space to two-dimensional boundaries, then it stands to reason that four-dimensional space must be subject to three-dimensional boundaries. Wheeler depicts the whole shebang as in figure 13, a "hypercube." The four-dimensional block of spacetime at the center is bounded by eight three-dimensional cubes according to the orientations of those surrounding the block. Each cube sports six two-dimensional faces, and each face is bounded by four lines. But, as per figure 12, these lines cancel themselves out, leaving zero. By the same token, we would suppose that in four-dimensional space the planes, serving as boundaries in our three-dimensional space, would likewise annihilate each other to yield nothingness.

In a desperate attempt to get a better handle on all this, let us turn our attention once again to Ludwig, our imaginary four-dimensional friend, just for the sake of a "thought experiment." Ludwig would essentially dwell in the central "hypercube" with a vantage point allowing him to peer into our innards and view a stomach ulcer, a kidney stone, some lung crud, and whatever other personal secrets we have stashed away in that blemished temple, our body. How can we possibly identify and empathize with Ludwig? We can't, or at least it is well nigh impossible to do so. So in the

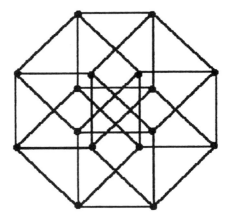

Figure 13

final analysis our handle is like a greased pig: when we think we have it, we don't. Like semiosis, it continues to elude us. So we must concede that while prolonged contemplation of Ludwig would be interesting enough, plenty of meat for a Ray Bradbury story, we really should be addressing ourselves to signs of the sort we can sink our teeth into. A difficult task.

A difficult task, for if we ask ourselves what there is in terms of signs, *our* signs, *ourselves* as signs, the answer must be: Not much, really. We and our signs are virtually infinitesimal in comparison to the entire realm of the possible. In fact, we and our signs are hardly anything at all. On the other hand, we are in a certain sense virtually everything. In this regard, notice what we have in figure 14, if you will. We begin with emptiness, zero, there in the "center," wherever that is. (This, we might speculate, is comparable to Lao Tzu's "Thirty spokes / Share one hub. / Adapt the nothing therein to the purpose in hand, and you will have the use of the cart" [1963:67].) Nothing preceded it and it has no boundaries. Then we move on to the equivalent of the "empty set," a sort of "noticed absence," the absence of something that might have been there but is not, with certain tentatively defined boundaries, or of something that was never there, yet there is at least the suggestion of boundaries, since the set is empty—there is some domain that can possibly be filled by something.

Then we move to sign 111, somewhere along the infinitesimal thin plane within that fathomless cube, our four-dimensional spacetime continuum. But whatever this most elementary sign is, it is not for us, not yet at least. That is, we are not yet conscious of it as sentient and self-conscious

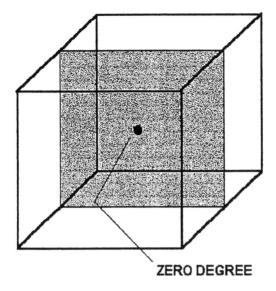

ZERO DEGREE

Figure 14

semiotic agents poised and ready to put whatever there is into the service of the semiosic stream within which we happen to find ourselves at the moment. Such consciousness *of* must await at least sign 211, and if not, one or more of its successive semiotic companions. So we move on, somewhere within the vast expanse, to signs 221 and 222. We have still not definitely set the sign apart from our sentient selves in order to process it as something other, for the representamen remains somewhat less than fully developed, there is no Thirdness. Sign 311 comes into view, and "Lo and behold!" there is a world "out there" awaiting our interaction and participation with it in its self-organizing unfolding; it is there and awaiting our abuse and massive destruction of it, the target of our control and even of our contempt. Then we gravitate toward more developed signs: language eventually comes into view, then dialogue, narrative, discourse.

And at last, we are human! Yes, all too human: perhaps that's the problem. But notice. Signs 211, 221, 222, 321, 322, and 332 are the ones with a mirror-image in the Riemann-inspired matrix-metaphor (figures 1 and 9). In a Wheeler sense we might surmise that they consume themselves, annihilate themselves. So we are left with virtually no more than a straight line in figure 1 from 111 through 311 and 331 and up to 333. And we apparently think we can now bask in the sweet smell of success, the culmination of semiotic progress. But not so fast. Sign 333, to be sure, is the last of Peirce's decalogue. However, the interpretant of 333, or of any other sign for that matter, even though we may have taken it to its third stage, is never final. For, in Peirce's words,

> what anything really is, is what it may finally come to be known to be in the ideal state of complete information, so that reality depends on the ultimate decision of the community; so thought is what it is, only by virtue of its addressing a future thought which is in its value as thought identical with it, though more developed. In this way, the existence of thought now, depends on what is to be hereafter; so that it has only a potential existence, dependent on the future thought of the community.

The individual man, since his separate existence is manifested only by ignorance and error, so far as he is anything apart from his fellows, and from what he and they are to be, is only a negation. (*CP*:5.317)

The process of knowing is ongoing, future oriented; knowledge in the full sense is always in the future and not for us in the here-now. Consequently, the "individual man" (or self), is "only a negation." *Only* a negation? Well, yes. In a manner of putting it. Perhaps there's no other way adequately of putting it. The negation is the negation of a boundary, which boundary is an infinitesimal line, nothing, nothingness, emptiness. Sheer emptiness.

So we are back to that again. But our condition is not as dire as it might appear. We might hope for Peirce's envisioned "ideal state of complete information" as the community consensus that would finally be arrived at in the long run of things. However, our hopes are shattered anew, for, according to Peirce, that community consensus will never come to fruition short of infinite time and an infinitely extended community (i.e., it is a converging series). But, actually, this should give us renewed energy rather than sink us into the doldrums of despondency and despair. The fun should be in the run with everybody else, not in dreaming the impossible dream of sprinting ahead of the pack to break the tape in first place and gloriously lead them all into Paradise, where everybody can sit and gaze for all time at the light of Truth. For us finite, hopelessly and helplessly fallible individuals, Peirce believed, there is no end of the trail. Yet whatever knowledge can be had, however limited, and whether consciously and willfully expounded or tacitly displayed, must be the product of a collective effort.

The final interpretant is not for us.

V. BACKWARD INTO THE FUTURE, THEN?

So which signs of the decalogue, if any, can we know to the letter? Which can be subjected to our control, put into the service of our demands, needs, and desires, our wishes and whims, our vanities and our ambitions?

Sign 333, most developed of Peirce's decalogue, is never interpreted to the extent that it cannot be subjected to further interpretation short of its taking on an infinity of interpretive variations. Let us chalk off 333, then, since in its pure form, containing the final interpretant, it is inaccessible. The tally is now down to nine signs. Signs 211, 221, 222, and 321 enter the scene. These are signs, respectively, of (1) unrelated and unidentified images and diagrams, (2) unintentional and at the moment unconscious and spontaneous recognition of whatever signs may happen to pop up, (3) pointers (indications) directing attention to some other without that other necessarily having been duly registered in, of, and by the consciousness of the semiotic agent, and (4) pronouns (shifters) nothing but momentary heaves of the larynx that in and of themselves provide no concept regarding the semiotic object to which they should relate, are tantamount to the faces of the cube, two-dimensional. They are like Picasso paintings, surfaces on a plane, which, if given a gander from a number of different angles, can make some sort of sense, though each patch of the whole may be virtually unintelligible. These four signs, like 333, obviously spell our limitations and our finitude. Chalk them off too.

Signs 322 and 332 present themselves. Respectively consisting of (1) a polite "Hi! How're ya" and (2) a well formed sentence, at the outset they seem to show a little more promise. However, 322, uncontextualized, doesn't tell us much, and 332, when mirror-imaging its opposite, gives the equivalent of the liar paradox and other quandaries that offer no solution unless they are equally contextualized, thus allowing for the dialogue to carry on with no conceivable end in sight. In fact all the signs—211, 221, 222, 321, 322, 332—and their mirror-images occupying six essential boxes and six superfluous boxes in Riemann's matrix-metaphor (depicted in figure 1) remain basically on the surface. Without context, there's not much there that we can sink our carefully sharpened and polished conceptual teeth into. Sign 333, in contrast, as a well-formed text with body, needs relatively little context—though it remains impoverished without it. The one-dimensional spill of 333 signs, of words following words on two-dimensional sheets to make up a three-dimensional book, or an argument of any other sort, remains, nonetheless, a surface phenomenon. Texts, whether in books or any other chiefly visual form, or whether in tactile form on the order of the hero's reading of Ludmila's body in Italo Calvino's *If On a Winter's Night a Traveler* (1981), are just that: *surface.* Our limitations become even more painfully evident.

We are left with a mere three signs, 111, 311, and 331. Pretty slim pickings, it would appear. Not so, however. Let's go back to the faces of the three-dimensional cubes. If the faces are where the action is, it's a matter of "What you see is what you get, and what you get is all there is." That is a matter of the objective, the quantifiable. In contrast, what is of utmost importance regarding signs 111, 311, and 331 is the qualitative, *quality.* Wheeler tells the tale of a lobster merchant in a little fishing town in Maine. Wheeler bought three large specimens and asked that two be packed in one box and one in a second box, both boxes destined as gifts. When properly packed with Styrofoam insulation, ice, and cold wet seaweed, the merchant forgot which box contained two lobsters and which contained one. He began unpacking a box. Wheeler's wife stopped him, with the advice that he could weigh the contents of both boxes without the need to open them to view. Which he did, and the problem was solved. The moral to the story is that the faces of the cubes, if treated properly, reveal all necessary information, whether it is visible and quantifiable or qualifiable by nonvisual means. The surfaces are where the action is! (Of course, a Ray Bradbury sort of creature, *Ludwig,* inhabiting a four-dimensional realm could have seen inside the boxes without the need to weigh them in order to know their contents, but that, once again, is yet another story.)

What I have dealt with to this point is the making and taking of signs regarding the five basic senses: signs seen, heard, felt, and signs of those other two sensory channels, smell and taste. This is all basically surface, whether of one, two, or three dimensions, and whether the boundaries are of zero, one, or two dimensions. That other mode of sensing, kinesthetic, is another matter. For example, diamonds are diamonds are diamonds, of so many carats, of such-and-such a degree of purity, and cut in so-and-so a manner. And they sparkle. This is actually nothing out of the ordinary. Tinsel on a Christmas tree, sparks from your muffler dragging along the highway because the tailpipe is rusted, and snow on the nearest TV set also give us an effervescence of flashes. But we don't cheat, steal, lie, deceive, and even commit murder to get them. Diamonds have a "deeper" value because they are what they are, culturally and conventionally speaking. We feel this deeper value in the heart and the guts, at times even kinesthetically. Culture and conventions are the issue here: at tacit levels they are a matter of the body's knowing, to a large extent.

As we shall note in the chapters that follow, signs 211, 221, 222, 321, 322, 332, and 333 in their composite form are quite available to sight, sound, smell, touch, and taste. What you sense in these signs is there for the chief purpose of willfully engendering interpretants. A disconnected image or diagram, a cry of surprise, a pointing finger, the grunt of a monosyllabic sound, an isolated utterance, all start with something—a sensation—and end with the conception of something—an interpretant. However, at the boundaries separating each state of this process there is really nothing at all, for, after all, all is process. In contrast, it might seem that signs 111, 311, and 331 have real substance to them. They are often capable of moving you in a much more direct and immediate way than those other signs. You see more than simply a glistening stone when you take a look at the diamond in the jewelry store showcase. In terms of sign 111, you feel, you sense, you become sentimental over the beauty of a diamond, its attraction, its fascination. As the semiotic object evoking the exclamation "Diamond!," you may garner a comparable feeling. "Emeralds," likewise, offer the promise of a comparably pleasant sensation and feeling. Diamond and "diamond," emerald and "emerald," sparkle, and "sparkle," and green and "green" are different ways of saying that there is pleasure in the rocks and their linguistic labels. And this pleasure is viscerally felt before it is consciously sensed by way of any other sensory channels. In sign 311 we have the first Thirdness of the representamen, which, with no more than the Firstness of the object and the interpretant, is *felt* more than anything else; it is chiefly kinesthetic, visceral. Sign 331, proudly donning the Thirdness of both representamen and object, is nonetheless devoid of anything more than the Firstness of the interpretant, thus its affect is in relatively large part kinesthetic also, but now there is full consciousness of the object of the sign as well as of the sign itself. Yet, we must concede that in regards to these signs, vagueness more than ever exercises its omniscient force: there are no clear and distinct, nor are there any complete and consistent, lines of demarcation, for all there is is inexorably indeterminate.

The initiation of kinesthetic feeling from the flow of semiosis, I would submit, is graphically depicted in the central portion of figure 14, where there is nothing more than an infinitesimally thin plane or boundary separating nothing from anything else: it is mere nothingness, emptiness, no more than folds and warps, topological distortions. Yet this nothingness or emptiness contains, "within" itself, the sphere of possibilities that can give rise to the emergence of everything that is in a particular semiotically real world. We could say of semiosis what Wheeler says of geometrodynamics:

This great world around us—how is it put together? Out of gears and pinions? By a corps of Swiss watchmakers? According to some multifaceted master plan embodying an all-embracing corpus of laws and regulations? Or the direct opposite? Are we destined to find that every law of physics, pushed to the extreme of experimental test, is statistical—as heat is—not mathematically perfect and precise? Is physics in the end "law without law," the very epitome of austerity? (Wheeler 1990:120)

Now, what can Wheeler possibly mean by "law without law"? That the boundary is where the action is. And what is the boundary? Once again, zero, zilch, nothing at all. It is a fold, that which is folded within itself, like a cavity that is a cavity of itself, like the origami fold, the paper of which is superfluous, for what is important is the fold itself, a fold of space that is at the same time an enfolding and an unfolding. A hurricane of incessant unfolding of the enfolded and enfolding of the unfolded. At this level, there is no distinction between organic and inorganic matter, between the living and the dead. Thus we are now told by Ilya Prigogine, and even by some fractal geometers and chaos mathematicians, that all is self-organizing (codependent emergence), like the self-organizing universe itself. A geological formation is enfolded into a vein of gold, sheafs and shears of tectonic plates press plants into black carboniferous matter and ultimately enfold that into a diamond, an enfolded chick embryo or an acorn unfolds once, twice, thrice, and virtually countless times.

But please don't get me wrong. The unfolding of the enfolded and vice versa is not simply a matter of tension release and tension build-up, nor is it dilation and contraction, but, rather, it is evolving and involving, developing and enveloping, convolution and involution.[5] A living organism's organs are involved, enveloped, contracted folds that got that way after generation upon generation of evolution, development, and dilation and displaying of what was there all along as a possibility. And now, they are there, within the organism, in the process incessantly of enveloping, involving, enfolding, implicating matter and energy from the outside in order that they may sustain life: that is their charge and their purpose in and for the organism.

This is also, I would submit, quite effectively patterned in the Baroque, in Leibniz, in Bach and Vivaldi, in Cervantes and Shakespeare, in Francisco Goya. It is a matter of seeing through a dark glass clearly, in sensing the disordered order, the harmony of the infinitely chaotic spheres, the inside that is the outside, the surfaceless depth. It is Deleuze's "chaosmos," or the "crapshooting" that "replaces the game of Plenitude," the monad that is now unable to contain the entire world as if in a closed circle that can be modified by projection. It now opens on a trajectory or a spiral in expansion that moves further and further away from a center. A vertical harmonic can no longer be distinguished from a horizontal harmonic, just like the private condition of a dominant monad that produces its own accords in itself, and the public condition of monads in a crowd that follow lines of melody. The two begin to fuse on a sort of diagonal, where the monads penetrate each other, are modified, inseparable from the groups of prehension that carry them along and make up as many transitory captures. (Deleuze 1993:137)

Realization of Baroque forms is a matter of the boundary of the boundary, the fold, the pleated piece of spaceless space in timeless time, the invisible line made visible with a few deposits of graphite on a piece of paper or some phosphor on the monitor. A cell is the product of one-dimensional engenderment according to a few letters and an algorithm in three-dimensional space to create something "here" that is distinguished from everything "there" by a two-dimensional wrap, a relatively smooth fold, a boundary. The entire surface of a solitary living cell takes up a minute piece of three-dimensional space, and at the same time that surface is a boundary in four-dimensional spacetime in the sense of Wheeler. Jumping from our unicellular neighbor to ourselves as a vast collection of living cells doing their own thing generally in harmony with one another, fundamentally the same generalization holds: our body, as a boundary moving along our respective world-lines, makes up an elongated three-dimensional worm stretched out along one dimension of time, from conception to birth to death and decay, and eons before that and eons after that.

"Hold on now!" my skeptic interjects. "Our modest faculties can't hope to be able to conceive of that entire scenario." Fair enough. So let's go back to a particular now, right here at this moment. Your body separates "inside" from "outside." That seems like a pretty clear distinction, no doubt about it. Yet it is only a minuscule portion of the story. In the four-dimensional manifold, your epidermal covering is hardly more than a fold of the Möbius strip giving an indication of the transition from "inside" to "outside," or the fold of an origami bird that doesn't really need that visible slice of paper with which it is dressed. Actually, the origami fold exists without the paper, right there in space, doesn't it? Well, just look at it. There it is, right in front of you. Well, if it isn't yet there, imagine you are Marcel Marceau mimicking the folding of an origami bird for an enthralled audience. It has always already been there for your contemplation and your pleasure, has it not? If you "see" it, that is, "feel" it, you are *in* sign 311, within the fold, within the matrix containing the enfolded knot of everything that can be unfolded, that is becoming unfolded, that is realizing the unfolding of its becoming. As pure space you can't really see, hear, taste, smell, or touch the fold, of course. For it's not really "out there," it's "in here." But, then, it's not entirely "in here" either, for it is at this stage nowhere, that is, it is not anything that can be anywhere, so it is nothing nowhere, it is the emptiness of the empty set. But somehow it's here-now, and you know it, in the guts, kinesthetically you know it, don't you? And if you say it without saying either what it *is* or what it *is not*, or saying anything else for that matter, you are *in* sign 332, but still nonetheless within the fold. You can't really say it, of course, for that would be cheating: once it is said, a host of intuitions, assumptions, preconceptions and prejudices, and inferences, rise to the occasion, and then it is sign 332 no more. It becomes contextualized within an always already incomplete not-so-present presence of sign 333, whether explicitly or implicitly.

So you must somehow "say" it without really "saying" it. Impossible! As impossible as geometrodynamic field equations "saying" how mass—momentum and energy—get a grip on spacetime at the boundary of the boundary. The equations reveal

> how mass, there, bends spacetime geometry, there—deforms it, warps it— as a jumper warps the trampoline beneath his feet. Cupping of the fabric there, however, demands and enforces warping on the canvas in all the domain roundabout. Likewise spacetime geometry there, bent in one way where mass sits or moves, demands and enforces bending of another kind on all the surrounding empty spacetime.
>
> Bending spreads its influence from region to region. The Einstein geometrodynamic influence equation describes and quantifies this spread of influence from region to region. In any region of emptiness, momenergy [momentum + energy] is zero. So is the moment of rotation—because zero momenergy in any locale implies and demands that there the moment of rotation must be zero. (Wheeler 1990:119; brackets added)

In other words, you may be able to describe the function and action of a fold, but you cannot describe the essence of the fold, for in essence there is no essence. The fold itself is the equivalent of Wheeler's zero moment of rotation. How can anything be of zero rotation in a universe in which all movement depends upon frames of reference? Assume we place a cube of ice with a small buck-shot frozen in its center—like a combination of figures 12 and 14—on a skating rink floor. We rotate the cube, which is a quite effortless task since there is little friction between ice cube and icy surface. The cube being well-nigh symmetrical, and all other things being equal, we look at the buck-shot and observe that it appears to be motionless. As a virtually infinitesimal point it has zero moment of rotation. Everywhere else there is force imparted with a certain amount of energy, but this central point has no energy and it exercises no force. It is comparable to the hub of the Buddhist wheel. It is the image of emptiness! "But," someone retorts, "what we have here is a mere point, clearly and distinctly 'nothingness'—if not to say 'emptiness.' You should really get back to the idea of boundary, which cannot be explained away in such sophomoric fashion."

O.K. Assume we have a Linelander gliding happily along her two-dimensional strip-world one extremity of which is given a twist and connected to the other extremity to form a Möbius strip. Easy enough. She is a one-dimensional being residing on a two-dimensional sheet curved and doubled back on itself in three-dimensional space. In essence, she inhabits three dimensional space. Now suppose she stretches herself out along the strip until she encounters her hind quarters and latches onto them (like the line in figure 11). She has become a circle. As such, she is finite but unbounded. Unbounded? Of course. She is apparently a ring, an unbounded boundary that bisects the Möbius strip, separating it into two worlds, this one and that one, the one that is first "above" and then "below," and the other one that is first "below" and then "above." Now *that* is a boundary we can identify with, is it not? We have a one-dimensional line, or Firstness, that, in relationship with its other, the two-dimensional strip, brings about a "cut" in order to construct a binary relationship of Secondness, all by means of the mediating capacity of Thirdness from our three-dimensional view wherein the Möbius strip could become a legitimate Möbius strip.

But wait! Did I not suggest above, following the Möbius strip example in figure 11 and James Bunn's semiotic model, that symbolicity is one-dimensional linearity, indexicality is two-dimensional binarity, and iconicity is three-dimensional unicity? How comes it that the line is not Firstness, most proper to iconicity, and that the entire strip mediating the line and strip is not Thirdness?—actually in passing I implied so much above. The answer to the question is this: if we extend our domains to the maximum and turn the tables entirely, things become their opposites. For instance, let us suppose we bisect our Linelander by taking our scissors and cutting the strip in two pieces precisely where she is lying in apparently so relaxed and carefree a position (like cutting figure 11 along the line). Now we should have two Möbius strips separated by our erstwhile Linelander. To our surprise, however, the strip isn't bisected at all. It remains intact. But it is definitely not the same strip. No, that's not correct, not exactly. In a topological manner of speaking, it is the same, but it is now half as wide and twice as long as it was, and it sports two twists instead of one. Zero sum game again! Then it is the same strip, only evincing a different form. What did our Linelander-boundary separate anyway? Nothing from nothing. The boundary was a zero boundary. While we were cutting the strip, there was a direction, and time passed, irreversible time. But when we finish we realize that there had been no line that separated something from something else, no direction, no irreversibility, and no indication of time. There was no other, nothing distinguishing *this* from *that*.

Now, essentially the whole strip is indivisible if we cut it along its elongated surface. In this sense, it is, most properly speaking, an icon, self-contained, self-referential, unary (it is chiefly of Firstness). The strip itself, then, is indexical insofar as it is capable of incorporating two-dimensionality, directionality, binarity (it is chiefly of Secondness). And the line is symbolicity in the sense that it entails one-dimensional, linear engenderment of signs (it is chiefly of Thirdness). How so? Let us return to our *Don Quixote* example. A few decades in the past, when our Cervantes scholar first read the Spanish masterpiece, she began internalizing a linear sequence of signs, then she read it again and internalized more, and then more signs, . . . and more. After reading a few interpretations of the work, she engendered her own interpretation of it, then a variation of that interpretation, then another one, . . . and anothers. Now, within the image (111) as a de-engendered sign of the *Quixote* in her mind and her body, her bodymind, there is a vague feeling of the Don's fictive presence and his relation to other signs (311), and the mere mention of the sign "Quixote" (331) is at this level of feeling of the nature of iconicity. The image, the sense of relations, and the word are Firsts that contain, within themselves, and timelessly, so to speak, the possibility for linear (re)engenderment of an indeterminately long string of symbols and other signs. But alas. However extensive this linear string of symbols becomes as a boundary encompassing the possibility for knowing and interpreting Cervantes's novel, the entire novel cannot be encompassed. For, the novel as a whole, that entire universe of Cervantes's work, like the Möbius strip, is an infinitely specifiable—though for us always incompletely specified—icon.

An icon in the pure sense is indivisible. Try to sever it with images, relations, and words and it remains as it is, though of a slightly to radically different countenance. Yet virtually nothing has changed. The sum of all changes is no change—the more things change the more they stay the same. In other words, at that infinite and impossible future moment when all possible symbols relating to Cervantes's magnum opus have been engendered, we will have the equivalent of the strip. We will have Firstness, timeless, self-contained, self-referential Firstness. At the infinite stretch of one end of semiosis we reach the other end, which to our disappointment is coterminous with the first end, and there is nowhere else to go. So much for Möbius strip riddles.

But, before gravitating toward other issues, it behooves us to notice what happens to our own world if we apply our Linelander within her Flatland to our own sphere of existence. We take the cube of figure 14, metaphorically tantamount to our three-dimensional universe, and we stretch the right-hand side of it out, give it a twist, and bring it back to its left-hand side and connect it. What we have is a rectangularly shaped sort of skewed torus. Now suppose we split our angular, twisted torus in half along the shaded plane in figure 14. We now know what the yield will be. We are left with a torus half as thick and twice as long as it was. Zero change once again! Total change is no change at all. The iconicity of the whole remains intact. What are we, within this whole concoction, but ourselves minuscule twists, tiny warps, skewed spots, in four-dimensional space?—we are like the buckshot in figure 14, which, if stretched out when the cube is topologically transformed into a Möbius torus, becomes a line, a boundary that separates nothing from nothing.

However, lest nihilism get the better of us, on a positive note we have survived, quite obviously, and it seems that we can learn, especially from our mistakes—i.e., knowing that what we thought we knew we know not, which allows us to re-initiate our game of successive ignorance. In order to illustrate the ways of our knowing, let us once more consult Peirce, this time on what he calls the "pragmatic maxim."

VI. ALL IN A TIGHT EMBRACE

Signs of possibility, signs of convention and hence of necessity, signs of thought and of feeling, of mind and of body (bodymind), of language and of nonlanguage, in fact all signs enter, I would submit, and contrary to the general tenor of many Peirce studies, into the semiosic process Peirce termed the "pragmatic maxim." The maxim is not a matter of language and language alone, or of logic and reason alone.[6] *It is essential to the entire semiosic process.* I must hammer that fundamental idea home with force. There can be no legitimate semiosis, no living semiosis, the semiosis of living processes including all sign forms, without the code-pendence, the interrelatedness, the interpenetrating interaction implicit in the maxim.

According to the standard interpretation of the maxim, in order to determine the truth of a statement we must know its meaning, which is what the maxim is all about—an enabler of meaning, not a royal road to truth. In one of its incarnations, the maxim goes like this:

> Consider what effects, that might conceivably have practical bearings, we conceive the object of our conception to have. Then our conception of these effects is the whole of our conception of the object. (*CP*:5.402)

With neither time nor space to do justice Peirce's subtle concept here, I must remain content with a few comments on what is of importance to the present essay. At the outset, notice that according to the maxim we are to conceive—whether overtly or covertly, explicitly or implicitly and tacitly—of all possible consequences or effects regarding the item in question. And from whence do these conceptions emerge? Ultimately, from what Peirce calls the "nothingness of not yet having been born," from what I have termed, following my slim awareness of Buddhist philosophy, "emptiness" (*CP*:4.512). This is a sort of pre-Firstness from which Firsts arise and then the actuals of Secondness (Baer 1988). Actuals emerge from possibles as part of the process of the codependent arising of all that is from all that might have otherwise been but is not. In other words, everything is inter-related with everything else. The maxim implies so much. Thus the very notion of "the whole of our conception," both actual and possible, whether in the past, at present, or in the future, is mind numbing in its complexity and virtually infinite in all its implications.

Take one of Peirce's favorite examples: "Diamonds are hard" (sign 332). This is one possible evocation from among a number of evocations: "Diamonds are crystallized carbon," " . . . are a girl's best friend," " . . . are the cheapest abrasive for long term use," " . . . are divine," " . . . are a corruption of the Greek word *adamas,* which means 'unconquerable'," " . . . burn just like charcoal briquettes," " . . . are essential to wedding ceremonies," " . . . are nothing but high-falutin' pieces of graphite," and so on. All these statements are entrenched in the "language games" we play when imagining, seeing, thinking, and talking about diamonds. All of them are inter-related, however remote and weak the relationship, and they are all necessary to our general conceptions of diamonds, whether we are in the jewelry story, the machine shop, the minefield, doing philological research, or whatever. Without the most insignificant possible statement regarding diamonds, the entire flow of "diamond-signs" within the general flow of semiosis would suffer a diminution, however slight.

But let's stick to the basics, which, we hope, is what we can at least get some sort of a handle on. Put a finely cut diamond to the test by placing it against a glass plate, applying pressure, and drawing it across the plate. If it cuts the glass, then it is hard. How hard? The answer is simple enough, so it would seem. You just need to extend the experiment. So scratch some soapstone, limestone, marble, quartz, calcite, tourmaline, carborundum, sapphire, etc. with it. If it passes the test, then it is "very hard." Yes, but how hard, precisely? You subject the diamond to more sophisticated tests and come up with the answer: "They rank number ten on the Moh's scale." So they are "extremely hard." Yet no matter how specific you become in your determination of the hardness of diamonds, you will never reach such a refined degree of specificity that you cannot carry your determination a mite further. So you will never know with absolute precision how hard diamonds are (the same can be said of our knowledge of anything else and everything). Thus you cannot be absolutely certain that diamonds are the hardest things around, though your estimation of their hardness has been correct in the past and you are quite certain that it will continue to be just as correct into the remote future. Yet, you cannot be absolutely sure in the most absolutely absolute sense. You might say of the initial statement "Diamonds are the hardest substance in the world" that your knowledge is pretty safe. Still, it is not iron-clad without a shadow of a doubt. There is some chance, however remote, that someday, somewhere, something will pop up with the property of hardness superior to that of diamonds.

In this vein, it might be said that our knowledge regarding diamonds is "neither (determinately) true nor (determinately) false," and at the same time that it is "both (possibly) true and (possibly) false." What we have here are two possibilities for fallibility: *temporal fallibility* and *cognitive fallibility*. In the first case we might say "It may at some moment be the case that the sentence 'Diamonds are the hardest substance in the world' is false." In the second case a complementary statement might go something like this: "The sentence 'Diamonds are the hardest substance in the world' is not known by us to be true in the absolute sense, hence it may possibly be false." The first case violates classical logic's excluded-middle principle, while the second trashes the noncontradiction principle.[7] If both are determinately true, then we know, and we can go from there. But we don't know whether or not they are determinately true, so we don't know, for our knowledge regarding the two cases must surely be as fallible as our knowledge regarding anything and everything else.[8]

At any rate, in order to prevent an extension of this infinite regress argument to everywhere and nowhere, allow me to suggest that both cases are grounded in signs 331 and 311. With respect to 331, "Diamonds," as a condensed, conglomerate sign, much in the manner of "Quixote" as illustrated above, contains, within itself, the possibility of a virtual infinity of evocations, sentences, and propositions, at home and at play, when courting a candidate for conjugal relations, at the office or the minefield, when writing a treatise in semiotic theory, when dreaming, and so on. "Diamonds" evince the possibility of saying it all. With respect to 311, we have ourselves, eager semiotic agents, and our universe of signs, and at a moment's notice our feelings, sensations, emotions, pride, anger, love, and so on can possibly rise up within us. It is this latter emergence of signs, noncognitive and corporeal, even visceral, signs of bodymind, signs that have been the object of contempt and ignored for centuries, that must be given their overdue share of the spotlight.[9]

Signs of the 331 variety and above are chiefly linguistic, and they are engendered in conformity with social conventions mixed with a few personal idiosyncrasies. They are consequently the easiest to define, discuss, break apart and analyze, and theorize. We think we know them quite well. Those other signs, especially those of 311 downward, emerge from somewhere, relatively spontaneously, and often without our desiring their pushing their way into our semiotically real world in the disrespectful manner in which they do so. Yet they keep emerging, whether we at the outset know it or not and whether we like it or not. These signs, of chiefly iconicity, can possibly take on an infinity of countenances. As Nelson Goodman (1972:437–46) puts it, anything and everything is like anything and everything else from some possible perspective. Extrapolating from there, we are forced to the conclusion that the boundaries and categories of all our above figures and tables, well, they're just boundaries and categories: largely arbitrarily selected, abstract, artificial, and divorced from the comings and goings of semiosis, that is, from the comings and goings of our everyday affairs. Social animals that we are, these conventional signs, the majority of them entrenched, automatized, embedded and embodied, are the signs that remain most intimate. They appeal to our dreams and our desires, our wishes and our whims, our feelings, emotions, and sentiments. They are corporeal and visceral, as well as in part susceptible to mindful semiotic processes: they are of the sphere of bodymind, where the one cannot be separated from the other. Hardly next to godliness, I would expect, they are, nonetheless, perhaps the closest we can get to emptiness, that is, to where it all begins, wherever it began, wherever it is and will be in the process of beginning. But that, of course, can be no story at all, because it is an endless story, a boundary that makes no distinction at all, for it is tantamount to the all. So much for stories and boundaries.

What we are left with is a flow of interdependent, interrelated, merging, diverging, and converging signs. Signs all! Semiosis.

4

SIGN, SENSE, CONSORTIUM

I. TIMELESS TIME, CHANGELESS DYNAMISM

I would expect that for a better understanding of the preceding chapters, next on the agenda should be a more detailed account of the concepts, therein alluded to either explicitly or implicitly, of *space, time,* and *synchronicity.* As we shall note in the following chapters, these three terms are closely related, with respect to Peirce's sign decalogue, to *syncopated resonance,* and the interrelated, interpenetrating, codependent arising of signs within the stream of semiosis.

When I write *space* I do so in the sense of form, formation, and in-formation—in-forming of the form formed—and the folded or enfolded set of possibilities coupled with the unfolded, that which has been actualized from the possible. When I write *time* I generally do so in regard to the becoming of the semiotic agent's awareness of that which is formed and in-formed. And when I write *synchronicity* I mean not that of the static Saussurean variety but rather the effervescent, trembling, scintillating, undulating field of the enfolded, the range of possibilities that are there, like a complex standing wave pattern. In other words, space, time, and synchronicity are taken in much the Eastern way and most adequately understood as a psychophysical oscillation-pattern, which makes way for the creation of time itself. That is to say, the *I Ching* trigrams intermingle, in perpetual motion, in clockwise cumulative, spiral, expanding, forming, unfolding movement as time transpires, and in counterclockwise, doubling back, re-enfolding, in-forming, contracting, movement as time goes by. To know the unfolding is to know the present and the past; to know the re-enfolding, the in-forming is to know what possibilities lay in wait for the future. Knowing how the oak tree is contracted into the acorn is knowing the future of the acorn for unfoldment into an oak (Wilhelm 1960:285–86).

Manifestations of the *I Ching*, consequently, evince no linear succession but rather comprise an ordering of possibilities that stands as a whole, in timeless, yet aggressively dynamic, equilibrium. It affords a static image of intense inner dynamism, like a dragonfly hovering in the air, able to do so solely by virtue of a perpetual fluttering of its wings. Its wings represent constant unfolding of the enfolded and re-enfolding of the unfolded, which, as a metaphor of the *I Ching* dynamism, is at the same time a model of the timeless state of orderliness, according to figure 15.[1] Movement occurs from one to four, then crosses the mid-point, passing through five—the axis of the entire diagram, the "navel" of the semiosic universe— then to six and to nine, then it passes through five again in route to one, which can now take on the function of ten as a completion of the first cycle. Then another cycle begins to assert itself.

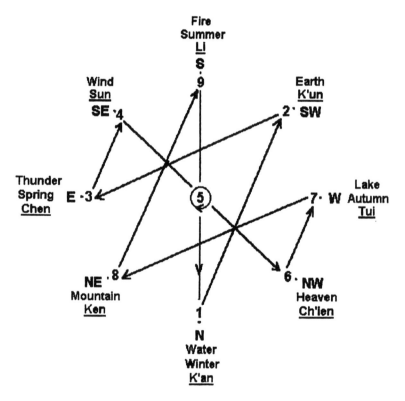

Figure 15

In this regard, time is at its basest a function of static space in perpetual motion, like iron filings scattered on a thin plate placed on a vibrator, or like a computer Boolean algebra glitch when it does nothing but oscillate between a *yes* and a *no,* or between +1 and −1 according to the $\sqrt{-1}$ function.[2] Space is the order of coexistent vibratory, trembling dynamism the sum total of which is null movement; time is the order of succession spiraling ever upward, upward, and back again, but, like an aperiodic crystal, a quasi-crystal, the DNA molecule itself, or the Einstein universe modeled as a giant torus, the return of a cycle never takes things back precisely to the beginning, at least for us, but to somewhere else (Whitrow 1961).[3] Time, according to the long-standing Western tradition, has been metaphorized as a geometrical line representing the series of real numbers. Mathematician Georg Cantor had it that the continuum, the line, is a dynamic staccato-like chain of temporal moments; his contemporary, Richard Dedekind, conceived of a continuum in the order of legato. And the twain could never meet, it was assumed. The staccato series was supposed to consist of discontinuous bits packed together so tightly along the string that at least for practical purposes a continuum was the yield; the legato continuum was an overlapping of erstwhile discontinuous bits to a creamy smooth stream entirely devoid of lumps. Yet, no matter how brief those staccato jolts were made, the yield would never coincide exactly with legato. And legato, no matter how it was sliced, would remain static, and at the same time completely and eternally divorced from time.

II. THE OTHER OF THE ONE: TWO

But all this is inordinately abstract, I fear. We must really consider the time of our "real" world, of the coming and going of the play of the universe.

Let me begin with a Western scientific concept of time in its most elementary form. Time in our days of quantum theory is conceived along the lines of atomic clocks, or wave motion. The watchword, once again I must emphasize, is rhythm. The energy and rhythms of the atoms are of the most constant of constants. In fact, theory has it that the sum of all 1079 or so atoms of which the universe is combined make up one single rhythm, the cosmic wave function. According to this view time is grounded in rhythm rather than the other way round. However, if we relate rhythm to a geometrical line that flows on and on, like the number series—whether staccato or legato—and indeed, we have a picture of rhythm as flow. This is not mere coincidence, for number, arithmetic, from the Greek word *arithmos,* "number," we have *rhythmos,* "rhythm," "flow." The relation of number to time is thus a matter of rhythm, flow, and time. Time consists of the dynamic interplay between numbers in the mandala field, along the line, in the atom, in the organism, in all the patterns that connect (Dantzig 1930). In short, this field, this dynamism within stasis, this rhythm of the universe the sum total of which is null, zero (i.e., physicist John A. Wheeler's [1980] cosmic formula: "0 = 0"), *is as it is*. It is self-contained, self-reflexive, and self-sufficient. It is Peirce's category of Firstness in the most pristine sense of the term. It is coterminous with the number one. But here, there is no real living and breathing time as we concretely know it. This sort of time begins with Secondness.

The number two, the one and the other it reflects, the one and the other with which it ideally enjoys a symmetrical relationship, marks the beginning of asymmetry, difference, disequilibrium—so much has been implied above. The number one entails the symmetry of a sphere: rotate it in any direction and at any angle and it remains the same as it was. Two entails bilateral or mirror symmetry: the right-hand glove becomes the left-hand glove, things become awry. Two marks the initiation of the number series and unidirectional movement, in the order of bilateral symmetry on the geometrical plane (Weyl 1952).

Twoness or duality also stands behind the concepts of imaginary and complex numbers—recall the Argand plane in chapter 2, which integrates both of these types of numbers. The numbers can be depicted as a series of positives to the right side of zero and a mirror image series of negatives to the left side of zero, with zero representing the "empty" field of possibility, the matrix from which both series are engendered. This makes up the x axis on the Cartesian plane. The y axis can be depicted as $+\sqrt{-1}$ ($= + i$) above and $-\sqrt{-1}$ ($= - i$) below and orthogonal (i.e., at a 90° angle) with respect to the horizontal axis. The value of the vertical axis can be nothing definite, but rather, it is an oscillation up and down between the two possible values, with the unity of the two represented as i ($[+\sqrt{-1}] \cdot [-\sqrt{-1}] = i$). This oscillation, if coupled with movement back and forth from positive to negative values on the horizontal axis, will produce a mirror-image series of circles as per figure 16, a "hypercircle," thus engendering a two-dimensional object within three-dimensional space from a set of one-dimensional series (see also Merrell 1991a, following Kauffman and Varela 1980).[4] In an additional step, a third axis projecting inward and outward could produce a series of spheres to yield a hypersphere from two-dimensionality to three-dimensionality in four-dimensional space. And the engenderment can continue, without conceivable end.

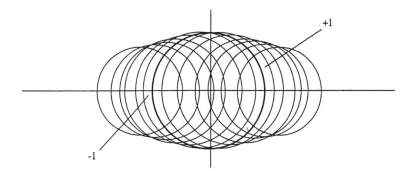

Figure 16

The important point is that this bilateral symmetry in terms of numbers and of space marks the initiation of time. At this stage it is only mathematical time, to be sure. But this "mathematical time," coupled with the image of movement of physical bodies in space, that is, of events, gives rise in turn to physical or chronometric time and psychological time as it *comes into consciousness* (Fraser 1979, 1982; Whitrow 1961). This oscillatory or pulsational basis for the perception of time is in a general sense of the nature of Alfred North Whitehead's (1929) philosophy and is nowhere more evident than in the two-fold symphony of Yin-Yang rhythm. At this level, there is no difference that makes much difference between rhythm and matter (Granet 1968), just as at the quantum and relativity bases of the universe—both of which integrate $\sqrt{-1}$ into their equations—there is no essential difference between number and matter (Dantzig 1930, Eddington 1958). Thus it is that, in Oriental thought as well as process philosophy and quantum theory, the cosmic wave, the rhythm of the universe, becomes/is "reality," that is, our semiotic reality.[5]

I have evoked the phrase "comes into consciousness." How can this be possible merely with the one and its respective other? Does not the very idea of "consciousness" imply an "outside," something other than the one and its other offering a vantage from wherein that one and its other can be recorded? Yes indeed. There must be Threeness, that is, Thirdness must be engendered. Binarity in the full-blown sense can exist as sign only after the act of the semiotic agent's having become conscious of the sign as such (i.e., the makings of the Peircean sign: something related to something for someone in some respect or capacity).

III. FROM ONE AND TWO, THREE

In twoness or Secondness we have oscillatory rhythm engendered from emptiness, or zero, and oneness or Firstness. The rhythmic repetition cuts a path, and thereby the initiation of time by means of a space vector, which at least implies Thirdness. This engenderment is in a round-about way also patterned in Jungian number archetypes, which merit extended citation:

> The number one claims an exceptional position, which we meet again in the natural philosophy of the Middle Ages. According to this, one is not a number at all; the first number is two. Two is the first number because, with it, separation and multiplication begin, which alone make counting possible. With the appearance of the number two, *another* appears alongside the one, a happening which is so striking that in many languages "the other" and "the second" are expressed by the same word. . . . "One" and the "Other" form an opposition, but there is no opposition between one and two, for these are simple numbers which are distinguished only by their arithmetical value and by nothing else. The "One," however, seeks to hold to its one-and-alone existence, while the "Other" ever strives to be another opposed to the One. The One will not let go of the Other because, if it did, it would lose its character; and the Other pushes itself away from the One in order to exist at all. Thus there arises a tension of opposites between the One and the Other. But every tension of opposites culminates in a release, out of which comes the "third." . . . Three is an unfolding of the One to a condition where it can be known—unity becomes recognizable; had it not been resolved into the polarity of the One and the Other, it would have remained fixed in a condition devoid of every quality. (Jung 1958:180)

In other words, from One comes the Other, and, unlike the case of pure numbers, binarism is engendered, which is then endowed with value (right/left, good/evil, etc.), but only by means of a Third.[6] One, wholeness, Two, dynamism and the forging of a path, and Three, value, directionality. The whole package makes up dynamics, periodicity, and movement toward something, somewhere, though that movement is always subject to change, and change of change.

The triad is patterned in another Peircean trio of terms that are germane to our present concerns: position, velocity, acceleration. Position is Firstness. Movement, but without change of movement, is Secondness. And acceleration, constant change of change, is Thirdness. We have constancy, unchanging change, and perpetually transitional change. From Firstness, Secondness, and Thirdness, or the three triads, qualisigns-sinsigns-legisigns, icons-indices-symbols, and terms-propositions-argu-ments, the ten signs are engendered as per figures 1, 2, and 9. But there is never stasis; the signs are incessantly on the go.

However, one might continue expecting, hoping, desiring to see the signs and their respective pigeon-holes strewn out in a static array. After all, sign engenderment, as was pointed out in the preceding chapters, is inher-ent in the Pythagorean tetraktys and in Riemannian tensors, is it not? Ac-cording to the tetraktys, from 1, 2, and 3, 4 arises, and from the combination (sum) of the first tetrad of integers, 10 emerges (see note 8, chapter 1). From the Riemann tensors, sixteen combinations in four-di-mensional space have six mirror image symmetries, which leaves ten com-binations of signs. Triadicity combined with the number four is also found in the move from numbers to planar geometry to solid geometry. Along the number series, every square number can be divided by four to result either in no remainder or a remainder of one. In Euclidean geometry, four points produce the first three-dimensional body. In what are known as "quater-nions," developed in the last century by mathematician William Rowe Hamilton, a rigid body moving in three-dimensional space and one-di-mensional time (i.e., the four-dimensional space-time manifold) can be de-scribed. The same can be said of the sign decalogue: like the universe, it is basically fourfold. This fourfoldness enjoys a long history:

> In all models of the universe and concepts of the divine, from sources as widely separated as the Chinese, the North and South American Indian, the Asiatic Indian, the Incan and Mayan, and such cultures as pre-Christian an-tiquity and the Mediterranean, a fourfold structure dominates. In the Mid-dle Ages of our culture the number four remained—in spite of the Trinity—*the* number of the elements, aggregate states, alchemical steps, temperaments, and so forth. (von Franz 1974:115)

The culmination of four-foldness is also found in quantum mechanics and relativity theory, as well as in the DNA code, in which four "letters" yield, by taking four to the third power (4^3), 64 combinations, the same as the trigrams of the *I Ching* (Schonberger 1979). So the point has been made: whoever we are, wherever we are, and whatever we do, we are beholden to threeness, which, when integrated with temporality, irreversibility, places us squarely within a fourfold semiotic sphere.

This dynamic semiotic sphere, unfortunately, has been grossly mis-represented either in the classical sense of signs of constancy—posi-tion—via structuralism and even in treatises on our postmodern, "hyperreal" milieu, or as signs of unchanging change—velocity—especially via Jean Baudrillard (briefly to be discussed in chapter 6). What all these accounts generally disregard is the semiotic counterpart to acceleration, perpetual change of change. What I mean to say is that much of the recent obsession with monadism and dyadism, and with pluralism by way of dyadism, has ignored genuine triadism. Consequently, there has hardly been any concept of change and change of change, of transcience in the legitimate sense. But before we jump head-first into that issue, a few more preliminaries.

IV. THE SIGN OF INFORMATION-COMMUNICATION THEORY

Roman Jakobson (1960) offers a model of communication based on the "information theory" paradigm pioneered by Norbert Wiener, Claude Shannon, and Warren Weaver during those early, euphoric days of computing when the dream of silicon mechanisms with the capacity of carbon-based human organisms seemed to be just around a few bends in the road ahead.

Actually, there are two models, which, when mapped one onto/into the other, give figure 17. Four sets of terms divided into two sets that are separated by an axis, with an imaginary addresser at one end and an addressee at the other end, make up what at the outset appears to be a handy key for unlocking the doors of feeling and sensing and perceiving with which to conceive culture and texts. The problem is that this key has been abused as well as intensively used over the past thirty-five years or so. While I do not intend to indulge myself in an exposition of the hazards surrounding Jakobson's model, I will at least briefly relate it to Peirce's decalogue in order to illustrate one of its inadequacies. Notice that Contact and Phatic fit quite nicely—though never exactly—with Peirce's "chiefly iconic" signs (111, 211, 311, also primarily olfactory and gustatory), that Context and Referential seem to dovetail with "chiefly indexical" signs (221, 222, 321, 322, also primarily tactile, as well as kinesthetic), and that Message and Poetic are by and large left to the domain of "chiefly symbolic" signs (331, 332, 333, also primarily auditory and visual). This leaves Code and Metalingual, which, it would appear, are by and large limited to signs 10, arguments, texts (textuality, intertextuality). In communication along the lines of Jakobson's scheme and in light of information theory, we have an addresser shooting signs over to the addressee as if through a conduit tube, and the addressee decoding the signs and giving them the canned interpretation that was presumably in the mind of the addresser in the first place. Well and good, it might seem. There can be the image of red (111) which emerges into consciousness (211) and engenders the general percept of redness (311), which in its own turn gives rise to the predicate-evocation, "Red" (331), and then to the utterance, "Her face is red" (332), all of which is shoved through the "conduit tube" to the addressee. Then the process is reversed in order that she get the drift of the utterance: "She is embarrassed." And proper communication has transpired. Or so it would appear.

But there are problems. In the first place, the Jakobson model does not account for the increase of tacitness when we gravitate from code-metalingual to contact-phatic. Neither does it give account of the phenomenon of sign de-engenderment once signs of greater complexity have been engendered. nor of the unthinking thinking, the unknowing knowing, of signs of lesser complexity—that is, signs of chiefly indexical and especially chiefly iconic nature, signs we make and take without our consciousness of the fact of so doing. In the second place, the conduit metaphor simply cannot ride. There is no meaning in the air ripples passing from a mouth to a couple of ears, or from marks on a page meeting up with a couple of eyes.[7] Neither is there meaning in the head that somehow, and rather mysteriously, makes its way from that head into another head, nor is meaning embodied in signs as carriers or messengers.[8] Rather, meaning (interpretants, interpretation) of signs co-arises with the interrelated signs themselves, and indeed, with the semiotic agents—also signs—within the entire context of the signs' making and their taking. This most crucial

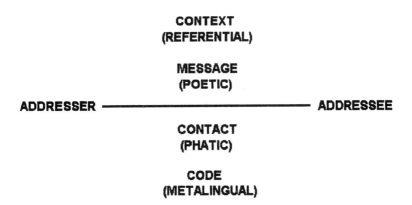

CONTEXT
(REFERENTIAL)

MESSAGE
(POETIC)

ADDRESSER ——————————————— **ADDRESSEE**

CONTACT
(PHATIC)

CODE
(METALINGUAL)

Figure 17

point has three fundamental consequences. First, there can be no genuine metalingual function, for signs, their meanings, and their semiotic agents are embedded within the context that happens to be in the making at a particular spacetime juncture; immanence prevails; there is no transcendence, hence no "going beyond" for an imperious, totalizing god's-eye view of things. Second, given the co-arising of selves (the ephemeral manifestations of the semiotic agents' selves), of signs, and of their interpretations, there can be no set of codes and rules (algorithms) for their combination that is cut in granite and embedded in the minds of sign makers and takers. Presupposition of the metalingual and of codes in a relatively to wholly static sense available to some impassionate observer from an outside vantage point is presupposition by way of transcendence. In contrast, according to the premises underlying this inquiry, semiosis as a co-arising process of selves, signs, and interpretations is a matter of contextualized strategies. Consequently, there can be no outside, no god's-eye view *sub specie aeternitatis,* no neutral observer. But in saying this I am getting ahead of myself. Let us for the moment stick to codes and rules and strategies for their deployment.

Take a billiard match. The conventional and culture-bound billiards code consisting of the signs to be manipulated and the rules for their manipulation—which perhaps have become partly embedded and tacit for the occasional billiard player (by means of his knowing *how* to play the game)—can ordinarily be explicitly described by the specialist (by means of her knowing that the rules are such-and-such, which determine the nature of the game). This is easy enough, the specialist would tell us. And she is right, insofar as describing the code and the rules goes. However, what she cannot do is predetermine the strategies each player will employ against his/her enemy. For example, during a game the configuration of the balls on the table after a shot can ideally be predetermined by mechanical rules of physics, and explicitly formulated culture-bound rules of the game can state a certain range of possibilities open to the players after each shot. However, the actual shot a player subsequently attempts and the general trend of the game cannot be foretold. Culture-bound billiard rules, then, govern a finite set of possibilities, but strategies entail a virtually unlimited number of potential combinations over an indefinite period of time. Such strategies are the product of (partly embedded and nonconscious) knowing *how* to play the game by following culture-bound rules and by adherence to certain physico-mechanical laws. Assume two players, while they are playing the game, carry on a conversation using grammatically correct sentences, although they are not conscious of the grammar rules they are using. These rules are not part of their knowledge, at least when they are engaged in a billiards match. Grammar rules are part of a linguist's knowledge that such-and-such is the case when he reduces them to mechanistic formulation that describes precisely the linguistic possibilities accessible to each player by use of the lexical items, or the code, they have internalized. Yet the internalized code and grammar rules, followed to the letter, are incapable of ordaining *what* each of these players speaks, *when* he/she speaks it, and *where* he/she is standing around the billiard table when he/she speaks it. The utterances he/she can emit are potentially unlimited over time, even though their generation follows a definite set of rules. Consequently, he/she knows *how* to speak without possessing explicit knowledge of the mechanical set of rules he/she follows. And the strategies he/she employs when speaking by use of these rules are the product of (partly embedded and nonconscious) knowledge how to speak in certain situations and in certain contexts. Hence, his/her utterances, like his or her billiard strategies, are unpredictable.[9]

Finally, the third fundamental consequence of the interrelatedness of signs is this. Jakobson's categories simply cannot be clearly and distinctly delineated. They are themselves interrelated, interactive, co-dependent, and they are co-arising. Signs of contact, chiefly iconic in nature, are signs of flux, dance, process. Signs of context are the ephemeral instantiation or actualization (haecceities) here-now and there in the next moment. They are noticed in their fleeting appearance and disappearance act by a semiotic agent, and after the fact, in his/her mind, they can be proper signs of some message to be mediated and given one of a set of possible interpretations—all of which are always dependent upon their co-arising with all the other signs and within some particular context or other. Just as one cannot determine without a shadow of a doubt that here is sign 211, there sign 222, and somewhere else sign 321—for the signs are interpenetrating and can have no clear and distinct boundaries—so also the artificial lines of demarcation between Jakobson's categories are inevitably cloudy. That, precisely, is why there are de-engendered signs, signs of one category taken for signs of another category because consciousness of the signs' function within the first category has waned.

In fact, Jakobson's context(referential)-message(poetic) can be collapsed, since there is no means for determining precisely where the message ends and the context begins, or when language is self-reflexive and when it becomes referential, because however the linguistic signs are made and taken depends in part upon addresser, addressee, and the situation that prevails in the signs' making and their taking. Moreover, contact(phatic)-code(metalingual) are not distinctions at all, but, rather, the demarcation line between them is at best fuzzy and at worst taken as either nonexistent or of virtually no consequence. What is contact and phatic is in large part implicit, tacit sign activity as a result of embedded, entrenched, habitual private and social practices. This being the case, since both addresser and addressee are themselves signs among signs, once again we see that immanence prevails, hence there is nary a chance of a legitimate metaperspective, and the code, whenever it can be at least partly specified, is never divorced from the techniques and strategies of concrete, everyday semiotic activity.

In other words, what is likely the most developed form of a phatic sign, sign 311, an iconic legisign, "is any general . . . type, in so far as it requires each instance of it to embody a definite quality which renders it fit to call up in the mind the idea of a like object. Being an Icon, it must be a Rheme. Being a Legisign, its mode of being is that of governing single Replicas, each of which will be an Iconic Sinsign [211] of a particular kind" (*CP*:2.302) (brackets added). So sign 311 is definitely related to something else, its object, by way of some similarity or other, while sign 211 realizes no such connection but must be content to stand alone, its relation to some other remaining as a potentiality. If code(metalingual) sign there may supposedly be, it must surely be a relatively developed and relatively genuine sign, that of 333, a text or argument. However, there is no argument absolutely devoid of presuppositions, prejudices, and preconceptions—the "new philosophers of science," Norwood Hanson, Michael Polanyi, Paul Feyerabend, and Thomas Kuhn have raised our awareness of this important characteristic even of the most rigorous scientific theories and arguments. Hence within each and every text or argument there lies some remnant of belief, disposition, habit, feeling, sentiment, emotion: quality. That is to say, some signs or some aspect of a conglomerate of signs within a text or argument will be taken implicitly, tacitly, in virtually spontaneous and automatized fashion, as if they were sign 311—of first-degree de-engenderment—and even as if they were sign 211—of second-degree de-engenderment: signs of unsayability, of unthinking thinking and unknowing knowing. As such, one might jump to the conclusion that these signs will be taken as what might appear to be simulacra, as if the signs and their respective objects were one, in much the fashion of Jean Baudrillard (1983a, 1983b, 1988a).

This view, however, is problematic. As we shall note in further detail below, Baudrillard is simply off base in this regard: it is not so much that the signs are "hyperreal" simulacra, and taken to be more real than the "real" itself, but rather, they are signs in co-dependent interaction with other signs and hence they are not merely autonomous and free-wheeling signs of themselves, of iconicity, but they can at a moment's notice be booted up to signs integrating the consciousness of their interpreters. But for the moment it behooves us to look at another aspect of these chiefly iconic signs, 311, 211, and 111, an aspect that marks the beauty of iconicity, but also the possibility of its tyranny.

V. HAVING GRACE

Gregory Bateson calls it "grace," this knowing how to do what is done without the need of any explicit hows and whys with respect to the doing. By grace, he follows Aldous Huxley's special attribute of the term as he interprets it in the New Testament. Communication between animals is of a naiveté, a simplicity, that humans have long since lost (Bateson 1972:128–52).

Our signs, unlike those of the animal kingdom, are blemished with deceit, self-deceit, and self-consciousness. The animals make and take signs as they do because that is the way they do it, with no further ado. We, in contrast, use and abuse our signs for ulterior purposes or for subterfuge. We lie with them, cheat with them, subversively relate them to semiotic objects to which according to convention should not be related in such a manner. We engage in incessant prattle regarding the whys and the hows of our signs. We talk about them as if they had no semiotic objects at all and were completely divorced from their respective contexts and from their addressers and addressees, or as if their interpretants were crystallized for all time, or as if they could give us Truth once and for all. We become ecstatic over them, inject them with our bloated egos so that they may endow us with a false pride, play a chance game of semiotic lottery with them simply for the fun of it, wax romantic and mystical over them, agonize over them when we think they fail to pamper our vanities, create mood swings with them in order to get what we want, engage in warfare with them for the sake of pride, power, territory, prestige, and pecuniary gain.

Umberto Eco writes that what makes human semiotics distinctively human is its capacity for lying (Eco 1976:6–8, 1984:177–82). The fact is that animals can and do prevaricate, though certainly without the ease, the perverse pleasure, and the selfish motives of which we humans are capable (Sebeok 1976:143–47). A lie contains negation at its very heart and soul, such negation serving to create a contradiction out of which tension arises, quite possibly resulting in vicious circularity. Now, negation, contradiction, and vicious circularity are the makings of, indeed the prerequisites for, paradox. We need not go so far as the perennially applauded Cretan Liar Paradox in order to illustrate this characteristic of all lying. When little Johnny tells his mother "I went to school today" when actually he played hooky, he is saying what was not as if it were. At the purely iconic level, we have two possible images relating to the evocations he "went to school" and he "did not go to school," but he "went to school," but he "did not go to school," and so on. Fiction and fact are tied into a knot of meaning such that Johnny's mother either believes him or she does not believe him. If she believes him, she does so in face of the possibility that what she takes as fact could well be fiction. If she does not believe him, her doing so is dependent upon the possibility that she could have believed him. Johnny's utterance might well have been "I did *not* go to school," an utterance that was there with the utterance he chose to spill out as one of many possibilities all democratically fused at the same level. Johnny selected one of the possibilities, but its actualization in his world of signs carries with it the implication that in an alternate world some other utterance could have been actualized. In the sphere of possible utterances (pure quality, Firstness, iconicity) Johnny both went to school and he did not go to school. He could have chosen to go to school, in which case his actualized signs for the day (of quality and indexicality [Secondness] and symbolicity [Thirdness]) would have been what they were in relation to those signs that were not actualized but might have been actualized in an alternate world. But Johnny did not go to school; that is the *isness* or Secondness of his world.

Yet by virtue of his little fib his mother believed he went to school. So the signs she believes were actualized in Johnny's world that day were not actualized, and the signs that were actually actualized were now not up for her consideration, that is, unless she were to reconsider her decision to believe him. In this sense, at the level of the Thirdness of signs, signs that should have been, could have been, and most likely would have been actualized given other circumstances, Johnny neither went to school nor did he not go to school—recall the above on Nagarjuna. Of course he did not go to school: that was his world of isness from all the possible might have beens. But he went to school in his constructed world of deceit, the world within which his mother chose to dwell. And he went to school, yet he did not go to school. That is to say, in the antecedent sphere of possibilities there exists both "go" and "not go"; Johnny's actual world was that of "not go," his world as far as his mother was concerned was "go." Johnny's world was a "go-less" world, that of his mother was a "not-go-less." The interpretant of the sign "I went" is neither exclusively "go" nor "not go," but that of "go-lessness-not go-lessness." In other words, the interpretant is ambiguous; it must embrace two contradictory signs, but not in the same mind or the same world at the same instant: the two signs of the interpretant are complementary.

I've demonstrated my point, I would imagine. And that point is, I'm afraid; What muddles we get ourselves into! With reason the Christian God gave up on humankind on so many occasions: we have lost the "grace" we once had as children, or that we had before we evolved into smug, imperious humans from the lowly animals. As "articulate mammals" with the ability explicitly to describe, interpret, and analyze the hows and the whys of our doing, our thinking and knowing is booted to the highest mountain tops, where we can be satisfied with nothing less than god-like omniscience. What is indeed sublime, however, as Nietzsche's Zarathustra knew so well while in the act of leaping from craggy snow-capped peak to peak, is not the guise of gab but the gift of "grace." In Bateson's attributing "grace" to art, he draws from the "Ames Room" and comparable optical illusions to suggest that what we sense is what we are most predisposed to sense because we simply have the good "grace" (*habit* in Peirce's terms) to sense it that way. He also draws from Freud's theory of conscious and nonconscious processes, and especially the primary process from which dreams, metaphors, and art emerge. At this juncture Samuel Butler makes his entry as well with his suggestion that the better an organism knows something the less conscious it is of that knowledge and of its behavior as a result of that knowledge (the better we know how to drive a car, ride a bicycle, play tennis, and so on, the less we have to be conscious of our actions: tacit, embedded, entrenched, automatized knowing).

The animals have the necessary "grace" to do what they do because it comes naturally. Of course, most of that doing is by way of instinct, but some by Peircean habit taking—such as the notorious case of the macaques in Japan that learned to wash their food and passed this knowledge onto succeeding generations. In contrast, much and most likely most of what we humans do is by the force of habit, of conventional means and modes of doing things. Get behind the wheel of your car and tool down to the nearest convenience store for a loaf of bread: it all comes quite naturally. You just turn on the automatic pilot and let the body do what it does The signs you unthinkingly take and interpret and use are chiefly iconic, they are replicas: 311, 211, 111. You've done what you're doing so many times you simply don't need to think about it. It's all done tacitly, implicitly, nonconsciously, in entrenched, rather autonomous fashion. But years ago, when you were taking a driver instruction class, there were plenty of symbols (333, 332, 331) of explicit instruction from your teacher, and many indexicals (322, 321, 222, 221) as well as icons, when you were behind a mock wheel complete with a monitor in front of you providing a rush of curves and impediments. Then, you had to concentrate, think, sweat, making a carefully controlled series of moves in linear succession. But now, it's all so easy. You know what to do without having to cogitate about it and you do what you do without a moment's notice. In other words, you drive with grace. There is apparently no code or metacode or language or metalanguage here, only grace. Well, I should qualify that statement somewhat: an accomplished driver, when sober, when not compelled to impress friends and associates, when not under the pressure of getting to the airport, or whatever, is at least capable of driving with grace.

Oliver Sacks writes of his encounter with an angry bull in a desolate spot in Norway, which left him with a severely damaged leg. We read the story of his long, anguished, and painful journey back to recovery. Renewed use of his leg came not through explicit instruction (symbols, Thirdness) from his therapist, or by his manipulating his damaged member by use of artificial aids (indices, Secondness). Recovery was forthcoming solely through grace; that is, by rhythm, memories of signs deeply embedded in his feeling for himself and his body in relation to its environment, in the motility, the kinesthetics, with which he had become familiar as a child but had long since forgotten because this form of knowing had seeped into the depths of his bodymind. The stimulus for these long repressed, de-engendered signs was music. Music helped him learn to walk again. He became

> embodied in music, glorious music. . . . It was the triumphal return of the quintessential living "I," lost for two weeks in the abyss, the two minutes in the delirium; not the ghostly cogitating solipsistic "I" of Descartes, which never feels, never acts, *is* not, and *does* nothing; not this, this impotence, this mentalistic fiction. What came, what announced itself, so palpably, so gloriously, was a full-bodied vital feeling and action, originating from an aboriginal, commanding, willing, "I." The phantasmagoria, the delirium, had no organization, no center. What appeared with the music was organization and center, and the organization and center of all action was an agency, an "I." . . . The new, hyper-physical principle was Grace. Grace, unbidden, appeared on the scene, became its center, transformed the scene, Grace entered, at the very center of things, at its hidden innermost inaccessible

center, and instantly coordinated, subordinated, all phenomena to itself. (Sacks 1984:121–22)

You will most likely have observed that replicas of Peirce's more complex signs of his decalogue are signs of lesser complexity. The same, of course, can be said of de-engendered signs. A replica of sign 333 moves to 332, which then gravitates to 222, an indexical, a sign that indicates or points to its semiotic object without the interpretant's needing to be genuinely actualized or made explicit. The sign is seen, its indication is acknowledged, and life goes on, possibly with grace, though there is no guarantee of it. Such is the case of spying a weathervane while driving your car, noting its direction, and carrying on as before with hardly a break in your conversation with a friend at your side. Such is also the case of your friend's phrase embedded within a sentence about talk shows, "Rush Limbaugh is a big fat liar and an idiot." You take the phrase in, perhaps you engender a mental icon, perhaps not, perhaps a typical Limbaugh hyperbolic allusion comes to mind, perhaps not, but at any rate the conversation moves on, without the subject of that phrase having been elevated to the status of a relatively full-blown interpretant.

A lonely word (331) cannot have, as its replica—or de-engenderment—sign 222, for, if you will notice in figure 4, 222 is not included within its sphere of influence. A replica of sign 331 can be no more than 221, typical of a spontaneous register of surprise or at least tacit acknowledgment of the sign's being something other and unexpected. Sign 221 can be replicated in 211, if that other is not even so far as acknowledged by the self-conscious self but passes by merely as part of the scenery. Such would be the case of a McDonald's golden arches on the way home from work. They are there as always, so no big deal. However, if tomorrow when you reach that spot and the establishment has been demolished, a shock of surprise is forthcoming, and an absence of the customarily unnoticed signs become what the signs are *not*, while the signs themselves are booted (de-de-engendered) to a more complex stage. To make a long story short, signs 322 have as their most immediate replicas 222, signs 321 have 221, signs 311 have 211, and 211 have 111. Notice that, per figure 4, this manner of replication—or of de-engenderment—follows a logic of inclusion-exclusion. Notice also that gravitation is toward a "sink" (111), consisting of signification before it has been elevated to the level of consciousness. These signs, signs 111, are signs of greatest grace, signs of pure quality, to which response is most natural when that response is at the level of 211 or 311. A wren inspects the feeder in your backyard, the alley-cat makes her nightly visits, you nonconsciously turn off the light when leaving your study, heavy of eyelids, to make your way toward the bedroom. And so on.

Grace: signs engendering signs, unthinking, unknowing signs of de-engenderment, signs unencumbered by the intentional focus of attention. Thus we have:

$333 \rightarrow 332 \rightarrow 322 \rightarrow 222$
$332 \rightarrow 322 \rightarrow 222$
$331 \rightarrow 321 \rightarrow 221$
$322 \rightarrow 222$
$321 \rightarrow 221$
$311 \rightarrow 211$
$222 \rightarrow 221$
$221 \rightarrow 211$
$211 \rightarrow 111$

(All this, and then there is the possibility of going back again: de-de-engenderment.)

The arrows are pathways of replication, or de-engenderment if you will. It might appear that the parenthetical statement should be deleted, that signs of greater complexity always tend to become signs of lesser complexity toward the "sink" of semiosis, and that's that. So Baudrillard (1983a) has his day, we might suppose. And we have a culmination of the three great "ages of simulation," from (1) the rise of modernity when signs enjoyed representation and were power for those in control of them, to (2) the industrial age and the era of serial production, when signs, like the commodities in capitalist societies, became the product of automation, to (3) today's era of simulacra and nothing but simulacra, signs without representation or reference, signs that are produced and consumed as nothing but signs of hyperreality, which are more real than the real.

Not so, however, in spite of our penchant for believing otherwise. That is, not necessarily so. Let's go back to the beginning of this chapter. Just as signs of Thirdness are engendered from signs of Firstness and signs of Firstness from the nothingness of the signs' having not yet been born into the glitter and glitz of our everyday life, so also signs of Thirdness cannot survive unless they can stand on the robust shoulders of the signs that preceded them. Going in the other direction, de-engendered signs, replicas or simulacra, cannot exist as such unless they carry along a satchel containing vestiges of the more developed signs they once were. Otherwise they would not be de-engendered signs or replicas or simulacra but merely signs that have not (yet) reached the stage of development of which they are capable. Signs 311–111 are chiefly iconic and spatial. That is to say, otherwise incompatible signs can sit side by side without apparent discomfort; hence we have the possible emergence of metaphors and other rhetorical tropes. If there were no fusion of incompatibles, such happy coexistence of signs could hardly occur. Well enough, we might assume. Baudrillard has actually implied so much and Jameson (1992) has said so much. Temporality is introduced with indexicality and it becomes paramount in the playground of symbolicity.

This is no assurance, however, that simulacra simply use a sort of "spatial synchretic logic" of both-and while signs of greater development by and large follow the footsteps of classical logic. Without the both-and there could be no either-or in the first place. This we learned in chapter 2. Moreover, either-or also depends on the neither-nor of that which could have been along a spectrum of possibilities instead of a mere binary pair of choices, also in light of the above discussion of Johnny's little white lie and his mother's somewhat blind faith in his word. In other words, "spatial synchretic logic" there might be if there were nothing more than pure simulacra. The whole display of signs before us would be like a slide show, with no more than traces of connecting links. But actually, there are no pure simulacra, for the so-called signs of simulacra (311–111) more often than not remain laced with traces of their once proud grandeur as indexical and symbolic signs. They are not merely newly born signs of chiefly iconicity. Rather, they are signs of greater complexity that by virtue of their de-engenderment have become signs demanding little attention toward themselves and allowing for greater consciousness on the part of their semiotic agent-collaborator of those other signs that require greater care. For as de-engendered signs they are not as intimately linked with the body as are their counterparts, signs of initial engenderment; they are signs of lesser "grace," so to speak.

If this is the case, then there is no telling when a given semiotic agent will begin reaching out to open that closed satchel and reveal what was hitherto concealed in the sign, to de-de-engender the sign such that it may bloom once again. But it will not merely bloom into the sign it was (a replica), for its context is now something other than what it was: it will be a sign with new possibilities and potentialities. Within the sphere of pure possibilities, and even in those waters navigated by the iconic legisign (311, and the iconic signs it brings along with it, 111 and 211), both-and prevails; something is *both* one thing *and* another thing as possibility of interrelations, or in the realm of symbols, as a possible metaphor or rhetorical device of another nature. Here, consequently, overdetermination reigns. Within the sphere of chiefly indexicality (221, 222, 321, 322) something either is or is not what it is presumed to be or said to be. In other words, there are all the trappings of what conventionally goes by the labels of "representation," "reference," "correspondence," and hence the either-or of standard logic usually manages to exercise its hegemony. In the sphere of chiefly symbolicity (331, 332, 333), what there is is inexorably underdetermined; it is neither exactly what it is said to be nor is it exactly not what it is said to be (i.e., the arbitrariness and indeterminacy of the sign), but something else, that is, possibly or likely something else. So we have the both-and, the either-or, and the neither-nor (please place them in the context of the above on Nagarjuna, and the need of all three sets of relations, I trust, should become apparent). Moreover, with replicas (or de-engenderment), that is, relatively simple signs standing in proxy for more complex signs, we gravitate from signs of intellection, cognition, and reason to signs of perception, empirical and voluntary action, and finally to signs of feeling, sensation, quality. What was explicit becomes relatively implicit; what was willed by and available to consciousness becomes embedded, entrenched, automatized, the product of habit, of tacit inferential practices, of a vague feel for what is to be done, what is correct, what is most natural; in short, it is a matter of grace.

This apparently heretical inclusion of both-ands and neither-nors, I would submit, is very roughly what Fredric Jameson (1992) dubs the "cultural logic of postmodernism" or of "late capitalism." It presumably includes, it seems that we are to assume, somewhat the equivalent of a "logic" of Baudrillard's (1983a) "simulacra," of Bourdieu's "practices" (1990), of de Certeau's "practice of everyday life" (1984), of Deleuze's "sense" (1990), or some rather ill-defined "logic of modernity" (Feher and Heller 1983) or "logic of subalternity" (Spivak 1988, Chow 1993).[10] The bugbear of all these "logics" and the saving grace of the both-and and the neither-nor of the "complementary cultural logic" to be developed herein rests on the relative fixity of the former and the dynamism of the latter. This distinction is due chiefly to the former's remaining caught between the horns of dyadic thinking and the latter's riding the triadic whirlagig of perpetually changing signs, signs in incessant engendering, de-engendering, and de-de-engendering processes, on thinking and unthinking, and knowing and unknowing, levels. These are signs of differentiation in the sense of modernity to be sure, but also signs fusing into one another in de-differentiating processes, interrelated signs of interdependency.

Actually, the signs of tacit de-differentiation are of a transemiotic variety. They include, by and large implicitly, all the sensations of which we are capable. And they contain, within themselves, the wherewithal for re-engenderment into fully blossomed signs of greater complexity that are relatively more accessible to analysis and synthesis. However, unfortunately they are also more susceptible to manipulation and control by semiotic agents guided by ulterior motives. Before moving on to these themes, we must take a closer look at Peirce's concept of the sign and at a particular aspect of the sign, especially insofar as it bears on Eco's notion of semiotics and the lie, but this time with the exercise of what might at the outset appear to be a strange, tangential move.

5

THE POSSIBLE
ADVERTISING MEDIA LIAR

I. ON THE LIAR, THAT IS, THE PRAGMATIC, PARADOX

An advertiser, in an attempt to market his/her client's product, tells us: "X is without a shadow of a doubt the best product on the market."[1] Is he honest or lying through his teeth? That, of course, is for us to decide—assuming we are able to do so, that is, assuming we are not those clapped-out somnambulistic consumers of whom Baudrillard so contemptuously writes.

The common assumption has it that what should be on our minds these days when listening to, or reading, seeing—and even smelling and tasting—this and all advertisement ploys, is:

1. "This message is *possibly* false"

while supposing, we would expect, that the entire message—that is, the utterance plus the numeral designating it—in the final analysis must be determinately "either true or false." This being the case, the possibility that (1) is false entails that it must be true, and if it is true, then it is not false—that is, not determinately false. So if we decide by a leap of nonfaith to take (1) as false, then it must be true, for the possibility of its being false materialized, at least for us. And if we make a leap of faith in favor of its truthfulness, then it is still possibly false, so it is true. In whichever case, we would most likely either see our advertiser as a habitual liar or assume the possibility exists that he is lying. But what are we to do while playing the consumerist game in order to make a decision? Suspend our disbelief? If so, we could eventually spend ourselves into the poorhouse. Categorically disbelieve all sentences of the (1) sort? In such case a decision to buy or not to buy would be indefinitely placed in limbo and we would be left to oscillate between a "Yes" and a "No." Our financial advisor might counsel us to suspend judgment entirely regarding (1) and move on to the next logical stage. In this event, we would have:

2. "This sentence stating that it is possibly false that 'This message is possibly false,' is possibly false."

Now, if it is possible that (2) is false, then it says what is the case, quite clearly and distinctly, so it must be true: it is possible that (1) is false. But if (2) is definitely false, then we couldn't expect that (1) is determinately false. So (2) must be true; in other words, it is merely possible that (1) is false. And the same can be said of (2). If we consider it to be true, it is possibly false, and if we assume it is false, then it is true, for the possibility exists for its being false. We might tentatively conclude that we shouldn't believe (2) nor should we categorically disbelieve it. However, in good faith, we really should give the advertiser some benefit of the doubt. He can't be entirely evil. At least we would suppose that some and possibly even most advertisers are not always evil. For if so, they would invariably lie to us, and the entire economy as we know it would in all likelihood eventually collapse. But doubts remain, for we would like to avoid making purchases we will later regret.

In order to get a better handle on all this, it seems that we have established that it is necessary that utterances (1) and (2) are not false without a shadow of a doubt; they must be only possibly false, so they are most likely true. With this in mind, we may wish to draw up the grand conclusion that:

3. "It is possible that (1) and (2) are false" (i.e., it is for sure that "It is possible that they are false").

Now, statement (3), like (2) and (1), should be true, we must expect. But if it is true, then it becomes painfully evident that we have an infinite regress in the making. For there must be another statement, (4), about (3) and (2) and (1), just as there is a statement, (3), about (2) and (1). And so on. No matter how far we travel along this inferential highway, the Doubting Thomas in us is sure to remain. Or is it merely possibly false that he will leave of his own accord? Or is it merely possibly false that we can voluntarily expel him? How in the world can a decision be made? Well, it can't be made without a shadow of a doubt remaining.

This, then, is the "Advertiser's Paradox." That is to say, it is our conception of the possible meaning of the advertiser's statement about the value of his product. So it seems that we the consumers-addressees have been sucked into the paradox along with the advertiser-addresser. Actually, what we have here is of the essence of Peirce's "Pragmatic Maxim." As we saw in chapter 3, the maxim tells us that we must conceive of all the possible meanings of a term or sign within the context of its use in all possible contexts of human pragmatic give-and-take, and when we have done so—which entails an infinite string of conceptions, practical applications, and their consequences—then we will finally know the "truth" and it will make us free. Pure bliss, semiotic felicity.

But there is a problem here. Assuming our conception of all the possible meanings of a sign by some stretch of the imagination could be realized, there could really be no endgame. In addition to considering all the possible true meanings, we would have to have conceived of all the possible false meanings. That is, we would at least feel compelled to entertain the possibility of their being true before simply discarding them. But that is still not the whole story. Some of the meanings we discarded as false might find their way into our conception of them as possibly true at a different time, a different place, and in a different context. So they were actually only possibly false, were they not? Let us call this conundrum—since we brought the pragmatic maxim into the ballpark of the possible liar paradox—the pragmatic paradox.

The pragmatic paradox avails itself of a weak form of pragmatism. That is to say, it does not entail the equivalent of:

4. "Sentence (1) is either true or it is false, dammit, and if not, then it is merely nonsensical, or meaningless."

That would be the proper response from the hard-nosed classical logician, or perhaps from a logical positivist. In the Peircean sense the logical or positivist statement is most appropriate to the dyadic nature of Peirce's category of Secondness—in other words, it is either true or false, in good binary or dyadic fashion. Furthermore, the pragmatic paradox doesn't even include a statement as strong as:

5. "Statement (1), according to present indications, will most probably prove to be false—or not false—at some future moment."

Probabilities of semiotic happenings more appropriately belong to Peirce's Thirdness. Where Thirdness is concerned, generalities can yield a somewhat comfortable degree of certainty—in other words, the statement would be either true or false, according to the prevailing conditions, those conditions adding a third element rendering the category triadic rather than merely dyadic. The pragmatic paradox must include, in addition to Secondness and Thirdness, a lesser degree of certainty appropriate to the sphere of Firstness, where at the outset everything is vague, sometimes inordinately so, and hence nothing is really certain.

It is no surprise, consequently, that someone's asserting "I know that (1) is false" should be looked upon with skepticism. How can that person possibly know? Is she somehow privy to all the possible conceptions that may arise from (1) in all possible contexts of sign use? Is she in possession of some god's-eye view of things? Of all possibly true statements and all possibly false statements as well? The answer, I expect we would all put forth in unison, is "No!" We are in the signs we are in, and as signs ourselves, we participate with them as we all engage in our boot-strapping, self-organizing semiosic dance. The same applies to our apparently amiable advertiser. He may be sincere in what he says, he may be trying to dupe us all, he may also be duped by the manufacturer of the product in question, or he may just be trying to make an honest buck. We may never know. Nor may he ever know about our doubt. He may never know the manufacturer's true motives, nor may he ever be entirely consciously and conscientiously in tune with his own inner drives and motives, cares and desires, wishes and whims. But, alas, the same can be said of us. It's an uncertain world, to be sure.

II. AND NOW?

In an effort to keep the waning dialogue alive, someone pipes up with the daring idea that "No statement, indeed no sign, can be exempt from criticism and denial, not even this statement." Noble words. But can they really hold water within the pragmatic jousting involved in human dialogic semiotics? That is to say, was this person sincere when she made her statement? Did she actually believe it or believe it was possibly false? The second must be in all likelihood the case. If she believed it was possibly false, then she believed it was true, and if so, then she believed it was possibly false. And we are off to the infinite regress race again. Is there no way out of this dilemma? Are we eternally condemned to our learned ignorance?

Hm. Let's go back to advertising for a moment. Within academia, we properly enlightened consumers and knowledgeable citizens would like to think we know what we are doing. (It is of course the unlettered, barbarous

masses who have all been taken in by the advertising media in good Baudrillard fashion, have they not?) If this is indeed the case, then we should
be able to boot our semiotic enterprise up a few notches to the level of generalities. Given our imperious vantage point from the hallowed halls of the
institution, our minds having been properly cultivated by the Priests and
Priestesses of the Cult of the Scholarly Saviors of the Hitherto Misguided
Masses, we can assume something such as:

6. "Every sentence which belongs to the class Y of sentences referring
    to 'every sentence' is possibly false, including this sentence."

There are, unfortunately, two traps here. First, we commit Bertrand
Russell's (1910) sin of "logical typing," which bars all uses of terms at the
same level as the category of terms to which that term refers. When we
said "Every sentence" in the same breath as "this sentence," we committed such an error. Second, we are caught within the uncertainty of intentions. What, precisely, were our motives at the moment we uttered that
statement—sincerity, arrogance, humility, deceit, honesty? Were your
motives the same as mine and as someone else's? The bottom line is that
we simply can't be absolutely sure when someone says "This sentence is
possibly false" whether she believes it to be true or false, or vague or a generality applicable to all sentences, or all of the above or none of the above.
    "But," comes a voice from the back of the room, "did not Russell vio-
late his own ruling upon stating we cannot use the statement 'Every sentence' as if his own statement were at the same time in the same category
as and applicable to all sentences to which it applies?" Well, yes. He did.
And he did so while remaining quite comfortable with himself, we might
like to assume. The fact is that in the everyday affairs of our common
speech we are so accustomed to violating Russell's interdiction that we
hardly give it any mind. And we usually get along swimmingly, flowing
with the current, leap-frogging the waves here and there, bucking with the
stretches of white-water, and usually managing to survive. "The letter m,"
"the personal pronoun you," "the city Z from among all cities of population greater than 100,000," and such phrases usually present no problems.
Even "all cows," "all pine trees," "all internal combustion engines," and
such are usually relatively safe. Of course when we resort to "all black
folk," "all Jews," and other comparable stereotyping references we are on
dangerous ground. Yet, in our everyday speech patterns it is quite efficient
to use words as if they belonged to a class of words. So why sweat it? Even
William W. Bartley's (1962) "Comprehensively Critical Rationalism,"

"Every rational sentence is criticizable, including this sentence," and Karl R. Popper's (1962) addendum to his "Falsifiability Thesis," "Nothing is exempt from criticism, even the principle of rational criticism itself," are acceptable. And they are quite acceptable according to the venerable tenets of "reason"—but please don't ask me "Who's reason, with what intentions, and how was it conceived?"—that would reopen Pandora's box.

III. SO . . . WHERE?

But unfortunately, we're still in a mist, it appears. Where to go from here, wherever we are? What to do when we get there?—wherever and whenever that may be. Well, as a beginning, perhaps we should get back once again to our advertiser.

"X is without a shadow of a doubt the best product on the market," he tells us. From one point of view—that of the pragmatic maxim as customarily conceived—determination of the truth or falsity of his statement is simple. Put the product in question to the test: if it proves to be the best, then keep it, and if it doesn't, then discard it and warn all your friends about it. But things aren't as simple as that. If we take science itself, that most stalwart fortress of objectivity and clear thinking, Einstein once told us that it is theory that decides what we shall see. Indeed, we have learned from post-analytic, post-positivist philosophers of science over the past four decades of the likes of Hanson, Polanyi, Feyerabend, and Kuhn that what the scientist sees is in large part what she expected to see in the first place, and what she expected to see is in large part dependent upon her theory, language use, and in general the temper of the times in which she lives. In this regard, it could be safe to say that there are more airheads than crystal-clearheads, more glazed eyes and selectively discriminating eyes than innocent eyes. So, criticism and doubt? Where are they in the final analysis coming from? And by what authority or whose authority?

For Baudrillard, the pathetic "silent majority" in the United States can be forgiven, for they know not what they do. They are no more than so many sheep following sheep. But let's not be so quick on the draw. Have not people had the wool pulled over their eyes throughout history? Are the consequences necessarily any more grave now than then? "Yes!," the Luddite, half-crazed over the recent onslaught of cybermedia might be quick to reply. Of course, technology has enhanced the capacity for surveillance, for control, for reaching out virtually to the entire community to an exponential degree in comparison to torpid media channels of the past. That, however, is no guarantee that human control by way of machines is irreversible, or that it is any more overpowering than the human-to-human face-to-face and physical contact of yesteryear.[2] What it does indicate is that in either case humans have been used by humans, whether the use has been humane or inhumane (Wiener 1956). The question to ask is: How, semiotically speaking, can this control come about? The answer, I would submit, is: by and large through sign de-engenderment.

"De-engenderment? That again?" Yes. De-engenderment. Signs, Peircean signs, are engendered from the most fundamental of icons to the most complex of symbols—in arguments, narratives, texts, entire bodies of discourse. Signs of such complexity are de-engendered when they are taken as if they were signs of lesser complexity. Peirce called them "de-generate" signs, using the term in a strictly mathematical sense rather than in the negative and pejorative sense it is given in everyday talk (see note 10, chapter 1). I will not bore you with the details regarding these signs except to say that when a photograph of Bill Clinton, Bob Dole, or Ross Perot makes different people feel good and smile, or perhaps cringe, clench their fists a bit, and tighten their guts a tad, they are reacting to the words viscerally, unthinkingly, nonconsciously and unwillfully knowingly, almost as if the reaction were instinctive. Their reaction brings with it, at tacit and implicit levels, an entire body of narrative and discourse, including nonverbal and verbal signs alike, from within conservative circles, liberal political groups, gay caucuses and feminist demonstrations, aging and paunchy hippies of the 1960s, holdovers from the Marxist-socialist camps, and so on.

When a person looks at the photograph of a loved one, a scene from the Vietnam War, or a portrait of LBJ or Richard Nixon, a comparable body of narrative and discourse applies. The signs are taken as if they were signals, indices of the most rudimentary sort, or as if they were icons the response to which is embedded and entrenched, automatic and unthinking, like the stick figure of a woman or a man as a sign for rest rooms, an "X" in front of some railroad tracks, the golden arches signifying all the signs present at a McDonald's franchise, the letters "NIKE" on the TV screen, and so on. A large number of these entrenched, automatized signs were once learned by relatively explicit means, but now they are unwittingly taken in, and appropriate behavior obediently follows. That is ordinarily the trend. But not always. It is often possible—though sometimes not probable—to break out of the customary pathways of least resistance, when, for example, one realizes the error of one's ways after one has been met with a surprise due to a difference that made a difference in one's awareness in the train of events surrounding one. This can involve so apparently trivial a happening as the awareness that a house on the block has a new paint job, that a pothole has appeared in the street, that the boss has a new haircut, that all politicians are not corrupt. It can also involve the realization of a solution to a problem in mathematics, in family relations, in building a kitchen cabinet, or in putting a new business strategy into effect. In all these cases, expected signs—expected because they had become signs of de-engenderment, signs embedded and entrenched in customary practices—were not forthcoming, with the concomitant awareness that there are signs of alternative possibilities, signs that may now appear more plausible than those signs that were expected but did not materialize.

But these examples are relatively trivial. I am, in contrast, referring to something more fundamental: a world-vision and all it entails. To make a very long story short, if I may, the Newtonian world-model had become convenient. The Cartesian mind/brain and self/world splits, the Galilean-Newtonian mathematization of the universe, Baconian inductivity, and Lockean objectivity thanks to primary qualities as opposed to secondary qualities, aided and abetted the venerated machine model of the universe. Then came Einstein, quantum theory, and all the ramifications thereof, and the machine model suffered terminal burn-out and death. However, although the post-classical scientific view of the universe has been around for almost a century since its disrespectful entry onto the scene, the going has been rough. Einstein, prime mover of the new view during its early years with his Special Theory of Relativity of 1905, later became suspicious of quantum theory, finding it rather disturbing—the universe simply couldn't be a matter of God's tossing the dice. Indeed, the quantum model, if correct, would present problems. Instantaneous travel of information from one place to another remote place in the universe would be possible, which is categorically barred by relativity theory, based as it is on the finite velocity of light, which is the conductive medium for all information travel. Moreover, the quantum world would be an inconsistent world, which provoked knee-jerks in those hopeful scientists seeking a complete and consistent account of everything that is. If knowledge is limited by the Heisenberg uncertainty principle—we cannot know both the position and the momentum of a particle-event at the same instant—and the Bohr complementarity principle—position-momentum and particle-wave are complementary forms of one whole reality, which remains inaccessible to us—then for some disappointed observers we might as well abandon the ship, for it will not lead us to that promised land of milk and honey and absolute knowledge for all. Quite perplexing, all this.

To make matters worse, the mathematics of quantum theory seemed to be a magic trick. To repeat an above scene, the magician takes off his left-hand glove and gives it to a member of the audience and takes off his right-hand glove and keeps it. Then he turns his right-hand glove inside-out to produce a left-hand glove, which should now be the same as the glove the person in the audience has in her hand. But presto! Her glove was turned inside-out in harmony with the magician's glove to yield its opposite, the right-hand glove. In quantum theoretical terms, the other glove automatically turned itself inside-out in order to maintain "parity"; it became its enantiomorphic (mirror-image) twin. This is an impossibility in our macroscopic world. Hold your right hand up to a mirror and it is your left hand in the mirror-image. That's easy enough. However, convert your right hand to your left hand in three-dimensional space and without the use of a mirror. Impossible, unless you turn your hand into an infinity of points and transform each point individually, or unless you are somehow able to make the transformation from within a four-dimensional frame of existence. All this is disconcerting, to say the least. Niels Bohr once remarked that anyone who isn't shocked by quantum theory doesn't understand it. It is so shocking because: (1) it exposes a sharp contrast between our macroscopic world, with which we have become quite comfortable, and the microscopic quantum world, (2) it is ultimately a matter of probabilities and potentialites, with nothing determinate, and (3) in contrast to linear cause-and-effect sequences, quantum theory lives by an entirely interconnected universe where there is no causality in the classical sense (event A affects what can be observed of event B, but this affect is instantaneous and does not depend upon information that travels through a linear channel, and over a certain increment of time, from A to B).

In fact, there is an alternative logic, "quantum logic," a nonclassical, nonlinear, "logic of complementarity." Quantum logic is not voodoo logic, but an answer to a world that is at its roots simply incompatible with the world we have come to know so well. Many observers are now telling us that we will have to learn how to live in an entirely new world that is in line with this quantum world, just as over a few centuries after Copernicus we learned to live in our classical world, as Morris Berman (1981) and Alex Comfort (1984) so adeptly illustrate. The time lag before we get a feel for (a sense of Firstness, an empathy with the quality of) this new world has recently brought on a swarm of buzzing flies as eerie as that notorious play by Jean Paul Sartre, "The Flies" (1989): pop mysticism and pop science, religious fundamentalism, astrology and palm reading, faith healing, radical cults, new age philosophy, tales from the *National Inquirer* and other publications specializing in the bizarre and irrational. This swarm even overlaps with academic pursuits. We have deconstruction, which is hardly more than a search for a model with the playfully joyous yet smug assurance that we will never have a model to end all models. We have Baudrillard, who simply gave up hope, Michel Foucault, the quasi-anarchist; Richard Rorty, the philosopher-cum-performance artist; and the likes of Gilles Deleuze and Félix Guattari's rhizome. Ah yes, the rhizome. Now *that* nonlinear image of radical interconnectedness seems to hold promise. So do chaos theory and Ilya Prigogine's "dissipative structures" as an important component of his "physics of complexity." From the chaos of the swarm there may eventually emerge some sort of order, though at this stage it remains vague and ill-comprehended.

At any rate, let us briefly pursue this idea of order and harmony and swarms and chaos and rhizome in regard to semiosis, that is to say, in regard to a further incursion into the intricacies of the Peircean concept of the sign as briefly outlined in the first three chapters of this inquiry. This, I would submit, is a necessary step before we can successfully embark on the chapters that follow on the beauty and the bounty of nonlinguicentric signs.

IV. ONE, TWO, THREE, . . . INFINITY (OR AT LEAST TOO MANY TO COUNT)

It's a syncopated beat, that sphere of semiosis that gives rise to order from chaos. One-two . . . and then three—pause . . . and a one-two . . . and then three—pause. And the beat goes on, to somewhere, somewhen, there is no knowing exactly where or when. Syncopation is triadicity at its best, and by way of symmetry breaking it ushers in radical asymmetry to the extent that chaos once again threatens.

The Peircean sign is in this respect a far cry from binarism. And it is nonlinear, a syncopated beat. In fact, it is in a manner of speaking rhizomically syncopated in the most radical way imaginable, or perhaps we should say in a radical way that is more than imaginable, or perhaps less than imaginable, depending upon how we care to take the term "imaginable." Does triadicity at its greatest potentially embrace everything? Or at that point can we say that it embraces virtually nothing at all? I have argued elsewhere that ultimately to say that triadicity embraces everything is to say that it embraces nothing.[3] Which is to say that the only thing we can know is the syncopated semiosic beat from a fallible and feeble finite, immanent perspective. No, . . . I'm sorry, . . . that's not exactly right. What

I should say is that the best we can hope for is to get a *feel* for the beat, for it can't be explicitly known. What is it that can't be explicitly known? Well, if we can't explicitly know it, then we can't say it. But perhaps we can feel it. Perhaps. Perhaps not. Now, how can I illustrate this hodge-podge of ineffables and partly articulable but exceedingly vague notions? Perhaps like this, if you will bear with me.

The Peircean sign, we have noted, consists of a representamen, which is something (in the mind, "out there") that is in relation to some other, its semiotic object, on the one hand, and to a mediating interpretant on the other, in such a way as to "bring the interpretant into relation to the object, corresponding to its own relation to that object" (*CP*:8.332). The representamen plays the role of a First, the semiotic object of a Second, and the interpretant of a Third. However, as we noted in chapter 1, there is a Firstness, a Secondness, and a Thirdness of the representamen, of the object, and of the interpretant. In view of this quality of interrelatedness of the Peircean sign, a further word on Peirce's categories is in order. The categories correspond to the triad making up Peirce's set of fundamental relations, which can be given linguistic dressing as follows:

1. *Firstness:* the mode of signification of what there is such as it is, without reference or relation to anything else [a quality, sensation, sentiment, or in other words, the mere possibility of some consciousness of something].
2. *Secondness:* the mode of signification of what there is such as it is, in relation to something else, but without relation to any third entity [which can include the consciousness of the self-conscious self of something other than itself].
3. *Thirdness:* the mode of signification of what there is such as it is, insofar as it is capable of bringing a second entity into relation with a first one [by way of mediation of the categories of Firstness and Secondness].

In schematic form, Firstness is quality, Secondness is effect, and Thirdness is product; and Firstness is possibility (a might be), Secondness is actuality (what is), and Thirdness is potentiality, probability, or necessity (what would be, could be, or should be, given a certain set of conditions). But like all schematic formulations, this one is admittedly somewhat deceptive. In reality, Firstness, in and of itself, is not an identified concrete quality of something (like, for example, the sensation of an apple that we might be looking at at this moment). It is nothing more than a possibility, a pure abstraction—ab-stracted, separated from everything else—as something enjoying its own self-presence and nothing more: it cannot (yet) be present to some conscious semiotic agent as such-and-such. It is an entity without defined or definable parts, without antecedents or subsequents. It simply is what it is, without reservations or regrets.

The "whatness" of that which is perceived belongs to the category of Secondness. It is a matter of something actualized in the manner of *this* entity *here* for some semiotic agent. As such it is a particularity, a singularity. It is what we had before us as Firstness, such as, for example, a vague red patch without there (yet) being any consciousness of it or its being identified as such-and-such. But now, as a manifestation of Secondness, it has at least been set apart from the self-conscious agent, willing and ready to be seen as an apple. But at this point it is not (yet) an "apple," that is, the word-sign identifying the entity in question and bringing with it a ponderous mass of cultural baggage regarding the word "apples" (the particular class of apples of which the one before us is an example, what in general apples are used for, the role of apples in legends, folktales, and myths, and so on). At the first stage of Secondness the apple is hardly more than the possibility of a physical entity, a "brute fact," as Peirce was wont to put it. It is just one more thing amongst the furniture of the self's physical world: it is otherness in the most primitive sense. If Firstness is the pure feeling or sensation of what is as it is, Secondness is pure negation insofar as it is other than what is.

Thirdness, evincing Peirce's influence from Kant and Hegel, is nonetheless not the product of dialectics. It can be tentatively qualified as that which brings about mediation between two other entities in such a manner that they are related to each other in the same way they are related to the third entity as a result of its mediary act. The mediary act is like the spheres of Firstness, Secondness, and Thirdness twisted into an intertwined variation of a Borromean knot that clasps them together by way of a central "node" in such a way that they are "democratically" conjoined (figure 18).[4] Each of them can intermittently play the role of any of the categories, yet at a given space-time juncture, one of the three will be a First, one a Second, and one a Third. In order for this "democratic" process to be played out, (co-)relations between the three peripheral points of figure 18 can exist only by way of the central node or fourth point. As was implied above, you might visualize the node as an axle that holds the spokes of a wheel together. The wheel is in constant motion, but the axle remains fixed: it contains the grease providing for the continuity of movement regarding the whole.

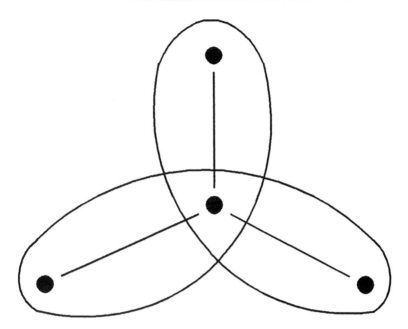

Figure 18

Since the peripheral points of figure 18 can be occupied by any of the three categories, whatever at a given space-time slice happens to be a First is a vague sensation. What is a Second entails bare consciousness of the First on the part of some semiotic agent. And what is Third brings the two together and potentially gives them some meaning as a genuine semiotic entity. That is to say, if Secondness entails the becoming of consciousness to the extent that a red patch of Firstness is seen as an apple, Thirdness entails the becoming of consciousness to the level of awareness that the physical entity apple is the instantiation of a class of things that go by the name of "apples." Consciousness sees that the "apple," like all "apples," provides a certain function in one's life and in the life of one's community, given the attributes that make it an "apple." Thus Thirdness has to do with a sign as generality—the particular instantiations of the sign belonging to Secondness—according to what Peirce called social convention, and as a result of habit-forming tendencies to use the same sign in relation to classes of similar objects in the physical world. In another way of putting it, the word "apple" has become part of our entrenched, embedded, automatized language use when we are relatively nonconsciously making and taking signs. We generally tend to use the sign just as we use it in our everyday activities, with or without much "grace," and without giving our use of it a moment's thought.

We see anew, then, that the interaction of sign, semiotic object, and interpretant is not a "standing for" or "referring to" operation or a "representation" as a binary act. It is an act of *relating to* and at the same time of *interacting with*. There is no essential "represented" or "referred to" or "stood for" quality of signhood; that is, signs are not mere surrogates for something else. For, all sign components are dependent upon, and they collaborate and corroborate with, all other sign components of all other signs. All signs make up the liquid flow of semiosis.

V. THEN WHAT'S ALL THE FUSS ABOUT?

Unfortunately, one of the greatest mistakes of many expositions and applications of Peircean semiotics rests in his triadology being passed off as a combination of binaries. A possible reason for this confusion is that when we think of threes, in spite of our better judgment, Euclidean triangles almost invariably come to mind.

The geometry of our everyday life, speech, and thought processes is Euclidean through and through, and this Euclideanism contrives and conspires with the classical mechanical model of the universe, mentioned above, to endow us, as a result of generation after generation of cultural inculcation, with our Cartesian-Euclidean-Newtonian world image. We are the product of over 2,000 years of indoctrination, with all its presuppositions and biases, of a successive expansion of what was originally Greek metaphysics. However, psychologists have been telling us, especially after the ground-breaking work of Jean Piaget (1973), that children are not simply little Euclidean savages with binary computer minds (see in particular Gardner 1987). Their perception of the world follows models that are most properly classified as *haptic* and nonlinear. They involve a sense of what can be felt, smelled, and tasted in addition to their being heard and seen, and they are in contrast to our adult habits fixated on the spoken word, the straight line on the pages, binocular vision, the sense of depth in painting, TV, and the movies, and linearly developed rhythm in music. We learn from historians and anthropologists that other cultures have not necessarily followed the royal road of converging lines and Pythagorean spheres to "truth," so dear to our own way of living. Traditional societies customarily practice what ethnologist Claude Lévi-Strauss (1966) terms a "science of the concrete"—consisting of the phenomenal world grouped into an intricate set of classes and categories—rather than our more familiar "science of the abstract"—following the ideal of mathematizing the universe. However, the so-called primitives are not simply child-like in their perception, conception, and articulation, while we exist above and beyond them as enlightened savants. As far as they are concerned, and perhaps with more than a modicum of reason, it is the anthropologists studying them who behave like children (Tyler 1987).

Revolutionary thinkers at the turn of the century such as Nietzsche, Frege, Freud, Husserl, and Bertrand Russell remained caught up in classical logical principles, Euclidean lines, Cartesian coordinates, and laws of causality. Nietzsche was obsessed with the eternal return, which was in his conception part and parcel of classical mechanics and simply incompatible with much scientific thought of the present century—and it was rapidly becoming outmoded during his day, evidence of which we find in abundance in Peirce's thought. Freud—especially during the early years of his career—was in certain ways a sort of "romantic mechanist." Husserl maintained faith in our deluded ability somehow to brush inessentials aside and see things as they should be seen. And Frege and the early Russell believed the entire edifice of mathematics could be reduced to a few logical axioms. Even Einstein could not give up his insistence that God did not play dice in his search for an absolutely determinate universe. And to top it all off, we have Saussure's chessboard analogy of language, by and large a digital, dyadic image. But enough digressive wanderings. Back to Peirce.

It is, of course, difficult to express the idea of ongoing process in language, for language by its very nature cuts the world up into discrete objects, acts, and events. Not surprisingly, in this light Peirce's sign triad is generally diagrammed as a triangle (for example, Ogden and Richards 1923). Figure 19 is pleasing to the eye. Its shape is quite familiar to any elementary schooler who has studied a few geometrical figures, and it coincides nicely with our penchant for Euclideanizing the world. But it is not genuinely triadic. It consists of a set of three binary relations, representamen-object (R-O), representamen-interpretant (R-I), and object-interpretant (O-I), no more, no less. There is no genuine triadicity. Figure 20 (engendered from figure 18 [and in memory of figures 5, 6 and 7]), in contrast, ties each sign component to the other two and, in addition, to the relation between them. The relation between R and O, for example, is no relation at all outside consideration of the relations between R and I and between O and I. And none of the relations hold outside the node, the emptiness, or nothingness, as Peirce (*CP*:4.12) put it, connecting them to one another.

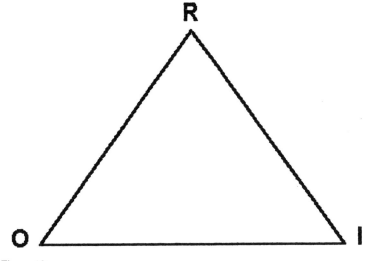

Figure 19

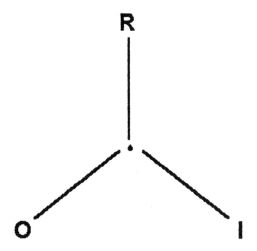

Figure 20

Compare figure 20 to the above definition of the Peircean sign: let your eyes travel from sign component through the node as you recapitulate the verbal definition of the sign, and a sense of its fluid movement will begin to emerge. "But is the node really necessary, or is it no more than a further complication of the sign?" someone interjects. I suppose the best I can do in terms of an illustration is suggest that it is of the genuine nature of emptiness or Peirce's nothingness, as described above.[5] It is nothing, no-thing, yet it is the possibility of everything, every-thing. It is the doorway through which all signs pass during the interaction of their sign components and during their interaction with all the signs. It is a sort of pre-First, the emptiness that holds, within itself, the possibility for everything that can be actualized, past, present, and future, though within it, there is no actualization of anything, for nothing is more than a mere possibility— Peirce, I must add, used the term much in the spirit of Buddhist philoso-phy. It is the set of possibilities that gives rise to the creative stream of semiosis, which is never at a standstill but consists of signs incessantly be-coming other signs (see Baer 1988).

For an image of the ongoingness of this semiosic process, notice figure 21. It offers a more concrete exemplification of the relation between Peirce's sign components. In this instance, the initial sign (R_1) can consist of the word "Joe," which can be manifested either as waves in the air or marks on paper. But to the questions "Which Joe?" "Where?" "When?" "What about him (or her)?" and so on, there is as yet no specification (i.e., hardly any O_1 or I_1). The sign remains inordinately vague, though it can be a sign type or generality of the most general sort, since the word could relate to all the "Joes" of the universe, past, present, and future. Further de-

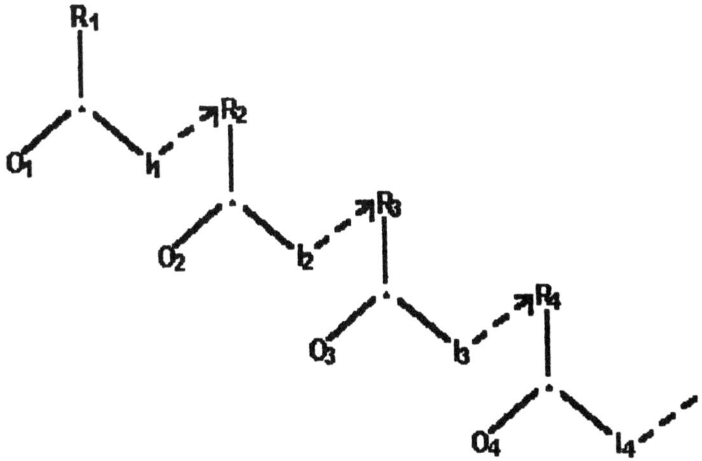

Figure 21

termination of the sign "Joe" as a token in reference to a particular person is left to the addresser. So I will fulfill my obligation by elucidation of "Joe Camel" (R_2) as a giant replica, about 150 feet tall, painted on the side of a building just off Avenida Paulista and Rua Consolação in São Paulo, Brazil. This "Joe" replica is in jeans, a black leather jacket, and dark glasses, and, of course, with the ubiquitous Camel cigarette defiantly protruding from the right side of his mouth. He is on a motorcycle with the handlebars turned slightly to the left in such a manner that the right hand of the fork juts out abruptly to emphasize the cigarette rigidly held in his mouth. Joe's right hand is draped over the right fork just to the left of the handgrip, with his three fingers—quite typically, he has only three fingers and a thumb—sort of dangling in limp fashion, much as does his nose and mouth, which serves further to highlight the stiff tobacco product. The headlight of the motorcycle points downward and directly in the face of the viewer: a protracted and penetrating imaginary column of light that complements the Camel column in Joe's mouth, which is what the image is all about. Underneath the image, and more often than not hidden by the trees at the base of the massive mural, we have the ever-present Brazilian equivalent of the U.S. Surgeon General's warning about the cigarette's death threat, which, the advertisers hope, will be ignored by all potential consumers. Quite significantly—at least for the Camel advertisers, but unfortunately for the public, I would say—the trees shelter a small children's playground, with slide, merry-go-round, and all. From this spot old Joe is a sight to behold, an imposing giant of a figure that cannot help but impress the onlooker.

Enough specificities? I have enshrouded a single sign, "Joe," with a complexity of signs that can be interpreted in many ways (i.e., as I_1 of R_1, or as I_2 after I_1 has become itself another sign, as R_2, and so on). The message to my tale—or moral to the story if you wish—is that figure 20, apparently a simple point with three equidistant lines sticking out, presents what might threaten to be conceived as a static picture: there is no necessary indication of dynamism, movement, process, fluidity. In order to create the proper image of semiosis, the possibility must exist for the I to become another R relating to its O—which is now something other than what it was—and engendering its own I, which is always already in the process of becoming yet another R, and so on. On this account, and in view of figure 20, we can note that in figure 21 a given sign or representamen (R_1, Joe_1) becomes (is translated into) its successor sign (R_2, Joe_2) by virtue of R_1 having transformed itself into another sign, and that sign in turn becomes (is translated into) the next sign (R_3, Joe_3), each with its respective O and I, and while swirling along the semiosic stream. In this manner, each instantiation of the "same" sign (a replica) yields a sign that is now a different sign, even though to a virtually infinitesimal degree: semiosis is never static, but an effervescent, ebullient flow, always bordering on the hyperactive. Solely within the semiosic flow can all the relations in question compose an interrelated, self-organizing whole—a rhizome, interconnected by way of its multiple nodes.

VI. IS A SIGN EVER JUST A SIGN?

Relating this entire process to the concept of sign transformation or translation further, suppose, for example, you don't understand the meaning of the word "world," and, looking it up in a Portuguese-English dictionary, you find "world" corresponding to "mundo." You have now learned that whatever "mundo" means for you, "world" means approximately the same. That is, it may mean something almost negligibly different to other speakers of your language community and something slightly to radically different to speakers of the English-speaking community—not to mention the context of the word's utterance, and the particular mood of the speaker and hearer. Yet you now know more or less how to use "world" in conjunction with other English words you have committed to memory. That is, you know that: (1) "mundo" is a mediating sign related to "world" as a sign of basically the same semiotic object that this mediating sign itself signifies, and (2) "the world" is that object in the firmament upon which we dwell, that to say "world" is more or less to say "mundo," and therefore "mundo" is the interpretant of "world." The two words as general terms denote nothing but a certain form that belongs to itself and itself alone (see Savan 1987–88).

I am not simply ignoring the idea of reference, or better, of relations between signs and things. I am emphasizing the function of translation as more a matter of relations between signs than between signs and things. And since those relations between signs, given translation, include relations between signs and things as a subset, much has been gained and hardly anything lost. In this sense we could say that (a) "'World,' 'monde,' and 'Welt,' have most, but not all, the attributes common to 'mundo' in its relation to that spherical body revolving about the sun on the surface of which we dwell, those attributes being approximately, but not absolutely, identical." Or, from a complementary vantage, we could say that (b) "'Mundo' is spherical, and 'world' is spherical, and 'monde' is spherical, and 'Welt,' is spherical." In other words, (a) evokes the attributes of signs in relation to other signs and to their objects. In so doing, it alludes to what Peirce calls their depth (the complete depth of a sign would contain an enumeration of all its attributes). Thus to say "The 'mundo' is a slightly imperfect sphere and it revolves around the sun in elliptical fashion and it is between Mars and Venus and it is habitable and its ozone layer is becoming depleted" gives the sign in question increased depth. However, regarding translation, which also entails predication (b), a mere list of a sign's attributes would endow it with little substantial breadth. The breadth of a sign entails a set of successive exemplifications (tokens, particular instances) of it such that the sign's generality (as a type, or class to which it belongs) in relation to its object is increasingly substantiated. The complete breadth of a sign, then, would consist of the totality of its possible exemplifications or actualizations, including its relation to all its possible objects in the world "out there" and all its possible interpretants. Statement (b), then, accounts for the applications of a sign, but it hardly affords a glimpse of the depth of the sign, of its rich repertoire of attributes.

But breadth is not to be slighted. Signs can take on additional breadth through increased usage in different settings or by expansion of their meaning when used from within different signifying networks with awareness of their semiotic richness. For example, "'Mundo' for a Brazilian peasant does not entail a global concoction of nations, cultures, and peoples, whereas 'world' for an upper-middle-class penthouser in New York City does not necessarily entail intimate ties between humans and the soil." Awareness of these two possible applications of the two signs in question is an aid to a proper understanding of their depth. It also implies awareness of the breadth of a particular sign (a token) as a generality (a type) that is more or less applicable under a certain set of circumstances. In this sense, proper awareness of breadth demands a complementary awareness of depth: breadth without depth cannot enrich the meaning of a sign; depth without breadth is hardly capable of extending meaning to other signs.

So to extrapolate from our diagram with respect to the concept of sign translation, we have a variation of figure 21, in which R_1 would be "mundo," R_2 would be "world," R_3 would be "monde," R_4 would be "Welt," and so on. The difference is that this time around we are considering translation in the conventional sense, whereas previously, translation involved re-iterations of what could have been taken as the same sign but at different times and at different places. However, just as the same sign undergoes incessant change from one point in time and space (or a "space-time slice") to another, so also a sign in one language and its counterpart in another language, though presumably referring to the same semiotic object, become slightly to radically different signs. From within the two languages in question and their respective cultures, distinct space-time slices are implied, different interpretations are evoked.

"So what happened to Joe?," someone asks. Oh, yes. "Joe." A simple enough sign, it might appear. But upon thinking about it a little, it's really not simply at all. In fact it is potentially of infinite complexity, like all Peircean signs. "Joe" is the same sign (or simulacrum) as a token consisting of a one-syllable ripple in the air between a pair or interlocutors or a few marks on a sheet of paper or on a computer terminal. But in the context of human semiosis, and given infinitely variable times and places and social conventions and cultural values and individual mind-sets, it is a different sign with each and every use. In fact, many of its uses can differ as widely as "mundo" for a Brazilian peasant and "world" for a New York City penthouse dweller. They can essentially be translations of one another. "Joe" can be "Joe Cool" for the ten-year-old in the playground near Avenida Paulista where the huge figure is hovering over him, and he is quite impressed with the animal humanized especially for kids his age. Yes, "cool." In contrast, the street-wise fourteen-year-old neighbor on the block might say of the Camel icon: "Joe? He's nothing special. I can take him or leave him." And he freely offers his opinion with a half-smoked cigarette between his index and middle fingers—it's a camel, of course. The lad's mother has a few harsh words for "Joe," who she believes has influenced impressionable young minds and should be banned. A presumptuous academic, on the other hand, might dash off an article on "Joe" as the product of deceptive advertising and another indication of the postmodern turn according to the "cultural logic" of "late capitalist" societies—and he does so with high hopes that it will help him get tenure at his university. And the possibilities for translation of the solitary sign, "Joe," go on . . . and on. There is no necessary endpoint.

6

WHAT, THEN, *IS* SEMIOSIS?

I. STREAMS AND EDDIES AND
WHIRLPOOLS, HURRICANES AND TYPHOONS

The notion of meaning change or sign translation is commensurate with the trembling, effervescent, "revolving" image implied by figures 18, 19, and 21. An I becomes an R, which interrelates with (revolves around) its own O and I, and either the O or the I in the process becoming another R.

These revolutions might be likened to an image found in many forms in different cultures, often called the "Isle of Man's running legs" (figure 22). It is an ancient sign intended to engender a sense of process, what with the three legs chasing themselves around and around a neutral point, the unmoving node. The problem is that, once again, classical thinking invariably threatens to push its way into the picture. The trio of legs could be packed into the concept of a cyclic group, a form of rotational symmetry. The algebra of such rotations is quite straightforward: move a leg 120° and it is transformed (translated) into its successor leg, then repeat the operation, ad infinitum. In contrast, rotations of the "legs" of the Peircean tripod (figure 20) are almost, but never exactly, coequal. They are the propagators of symmetry-breaking rather than symmetry-making. Each translation of a sign component does not leave an arc on the Cartesian plane but describes the beginning of a spiraloid in three-dimensional space: with each completion of the cycle we are never back where we began but somewhere else along the spiraloid. It is like Maurits Escher's lithograph "Ascending and Descending," consisting of monks going up a staircase that ends where it began. We see that they are not progressing, but from their viewpoint they are moving ever-upward toward the heavens. And it is precisely

Figure 22

their viewpoint that matters, since they, like all of us, are caught within the semiosic flow of the universe.

Now, if asymmetry is the watchword, and if a diagram of rotation is up for consideration, then the question is: In which direction is the rotation and how does it bring about change? "But," my ubiquitous skeptic asks, "why should it matter at all? Right to left, left to right, what's the difference?" The difference is between dextrorotation and levorotation, between lofty symmetry, somewhat blemished symmetry, and rather disrespectful symmetry-breaking. Classical physics actually has little to say about any intrinsic difference between left and right. Position, direction, and left and right are relative concepts. There is little to no preference between the one and the other. Absolute symmetry, likewise, knows no direction and has no preference. A perfect sphere is purely symmetrical. Rotate it however you wish, and it is the same sphere; it occupies the same space and in the same way. Now rotate it in the reverse direction, and things still remain the same.

Mirror-image symmetry, which is somewhat tarnished rather than pure, however, has disconcerted many observers. Kant remained fascinated with it, as did Leibniz and others. Mirror-symmetry is more technically bilateral symmetry, which can be looked upon as the initiation of asymmetry or dyssymmetry. A mirror-image is the same yet different. Hold your gloved right hand to a mirror, and, as mentioned, the glove becomes a left-hand glove. If the glove is a surgical glove, simply turn it wrong-side out and it changes hands. But if the glove is thickly insulated and you cannot do so, the right-hand glove can become a left-hand glove solely by an infinite series of topological transformations. Had Alice in *Through the Looking Glass* looked back through the mirror after she became somewhat resigned to her mirror-image world, she would have discovered that her previous "real" world was now the strange one, and that the world she was now in and had become somewhat accustomed to was more real than the "real." One of the first things Alice looked at upon entering her strange new world was a clock, which is significant. Her mirror-image clock was moving in a counterclockwise direction. Clockwise and counterclockwise are even more clearly differentiated than left and right. Clocks, we tend to assume, must move in the direction in which they move. But actually, the direction is irrelevant, for if it is reversed, the clock could function equally well. Another Lewis Carroll case is that of the pair of identical twins, Tweedledee and Tweedledum. When they shook hands with Alice one extended his left hand and the other his right one. If their bilateral symmetry were true to form, then the left cerebral hemisphere compelling one twin to use his right hand would correspond to the right hemisphere compelling his counterpart to use his left hand. They would be "identical" twins, though the inverse of one another.

Counterclockwise patterns (i.e., right to left instead of left to right) are only very occasionally encountered, either in human cultures or in nature. Most screws are made to turn in a clockwise direction. However, in the United States at least, cars, horses, and people usually run in a counterclockwise direction around a race track. That way our eyes move along the stretch of track closest to us from left to right, in the same way we read a book. Reading Hebrew and certain other languages, however, is from right to left. And in England, where cars are mirror-images of our cars in certain respects, races go in clockwise direction. The words "left" and "right" testify in our language to a right-hand bias, perhaps because of our tendency to use the right hand more than the left. *Sinister* is from the Latin word for left while *dexterous* is from the word for right. *Gauche* in French means awkward or crooked while *droit* means honest and straight. The German *link* is left, and *linkisch* means clumsy, while right, *recht,* means forthright and true. Most of these distinctions, however, seem to be arbitrary, idiosyncratic, and culturally dependent, rather than biologically determined. And what is worse, they are saturated with binary thinking.

More striking and of more interest to our present concerns is the fact that life is asymmetrical. Louis Pasteur was one of the first scientists to notice that the molecules making up life can come in enantiomorphic or mirror-image forms. And interestingly enough, like the DNA asymmetrical helix, they are almost invariably right-handed.[1] The human body, and the vast majority of other organisms for that matter, display bilateral symmetry. Yet there are invariably certain deviations from one mirror-image to the other—one eye is slightly higher, one big toe is a little fatter, one knee-cap has more curvature, and so on. Bilateral symmetry persists in most of the body's interior, but it is broken in the radically asymmetrical placing and shape of various organs—the heart, liver, appendix, pancreas, contortions of the intestines, and so on. Certain organs of humans and animals manifest an asymmetrical twist, called chirality—narwhal and ram horns, snails, seahorses. Chirality usually favors one direction over the other. Snail shells nearly always coil to the right when viewed from above. But few biologists believe chirality in animals is directly related to chirality at the molecular level: left- and right-handed snails have the same kind of DNA, for example. Things could equally have been the other way around; that is, we could have lived in Alice's mirror-world, and our DNA would be the mirror-image of what it is. Otherwise, life would go on in essentially the same way, with the same joys and sorrows, the euphoria and the dysphoria, the loves and the hatreds, the times of war and the times of peace. There are various explanations for the right-handedness of our particular world, some of them ludicrous and others quite plausible. The fact remains, however, that we are in general right-handed.

II. WHAT'S THE POINT?

"So, what's the point?" my skeptic queries. The point is that "true" and "false" in classical logic and logical positivist parlance are binaries. As was mentioned, the positivists took care of anything that did not fall into their neat pigeon-holes by labeling it nonsensical or meaningless and relegating it to the trash bin.

In contrast, the idea in the previous chapter of the paradox of the possible liar opens up an entirely new bag of tricks. If what is true is determinately true, and if what is not true is false, that is, is other, then we have the binary mix of what *is* and what *is not*. This is most proper to Secondness. Then where is Thirdness? One might assume that it is the mediation between what is and what is not to yield the interpretation of the one in light of and in its interrelations and interplay with the other. However, if we follow the new philosophers of science mentioned above, and if we heed the counsel of Ludwig Wittgenstein, Hilary Putnam, and Nelson Goodman, as well as that of Peirce and the pragmatists who succeeded him, especially William James and John Dewey, and even the "perspectivism" of Nietzsche and some of his disciples, Foucault, Deleuze, and to an extent Richard Rorty, we will be forced to the conclusion that what was yesterday's veracity can become today's falsity, and what is today's truth can become tomorrow's folktale. This being the case, there is no knowing for all time what is true and what is false without a shadow of a doubt.

What the *is* and the *is not* need is a healthy dose of Firstness, of possibility, of radical uncertainty. The liar, if a possible liar, gives an inkling of such uncertainty. The watchword is vagueness. A vague sign is a sign whose nature as a generality is virtually infinitely pliable. Peirce suggests so much. Thus "Joe Camel" is now firmly lodged in the annals of commercial hype and propaganda as a general sign or type that enjoys a growing number of tokens. However, in spite of its customarily being taken as a generality, it remains exceedingly vague. As a generality, Joe is either good and cool or bad and a corrupter of tender minds, or both, or neither, depending on whether we are talking to a ten-year-old, a fourteen-year-old, a distressed mother, a tenure-seeking academic, or whomever. Whatever the story, the storyteller will be saying a bit of truth, and at the same time he will be lying a little, whether intentionally or unwittingly. It is up to the sign addressers to render their signs a little less vague. But they can go only so far, as they are whisked along the semiosic stream constantly in the process of change. And it is up to us as sign addressees to give a bit more precise meaning to our signs. But we often find that those signs, like all signs, are as slippery as rainbow trout: they slither along the stream eluding our every attempt to grasp them.

So once again it's a "one-two . . . and then three—pause . . . and a . . ." The syncopated, asymmetrical, spiraloid, liquid gush of the semiosic beat goes on, where to nobody knows. What is certain is that it will continue its creative advance, and we are in it, whether we want to be or not. And Joe? Well, he's just "Joe." Actually he's quite a unique image. He's not to blame for what he does to his interpreters, since he is just a sign. But, after all, his interpreters, all of us, are also just signs, so we are not to blame either, nor are those creators of Joe for that matter. Wait a minute. No. That's not right at all. I really must take back what I just wrote. The fact of the matter is that we must all be held responsible, every one of us, no matter how little our input and our interaction with the general semiosic process, for as signs, we exercise a certain influence on all signs, whether we know it or not and whether we like it or not. If I recall correctly, Jean Paul Sartre said something like that regarding existence. But that, of course, is another story.

The story, for our present purposes, entails an outline of the various sensory modes of perception and conception as a further preliminary step toward an understanding of semiosis when it is putting on its most genuine show. That is the thrust of the next chapter.

7

THE SCANDAL OF THE SENSES

The prose of this chapter might appear inordinately pedestrian in comparison to those that precede it, for my aim is not to offer a technical treatise on signs and sense. Not yet at least. Rather, I wish to give a brief outlay of the senses in terms of their opening our world up to us as we live and breathe it. This step is essential, for just as semiosis is the life of all sign processes as they are engendered and de-engendered along their multiple trajectories, so also living processes trace out minuscule lines in the vast sphere of semiosis.

I. OLFACTORY

Of the senses, smell must be the most memorable of all.[1] Fragrances and pungency are momentary and fleeting. Yet they are capable of conjuring up remote experiences of a Southern California beach, the streets of Harlem, a dung heap at an uncle's farm, the desert after a rare spring shower, a popcorn-stenched movie theater, the sweaty locker room after gym class, or perhaps even a McDonald's establishment. With nary a moment's notice, a complex of olfactory signs leaps out of the undergrowth of our neural network to evoke long past objects, acts, and events. Most notably, we have Marcel Proust's *Swann's Way*. In adulthood, he recalls a moment of his childhood days when he savored the smell of a madeleine chunk floating in a spoonful of hot tea. The aroma of the tea-soaked cake wafts into the warm, cozy room. And he begins writing. More than a million words later, the effects of that scent have finally worn off, and the author has virtually recounted his entire life.

Our five million olfactory cells are quite impressive; they add spice to life. But when we compare our equipment for detecting smells with that of, say, a sheep dog, who sports 220 million cells and can smell forty or so times as well as we can, our sensory poverty becomes painfully evident. What, actually, is the sheep dog capable of smelling? How much of life are we missing out on? How much more enriched would our existence be if we enjoyed heightened olfactory capabilities? Neurologist Oliver Sacks (1987: 156–60) reports the unusual case of a man who, after receiving a blow to the head, experienced an enormous enlargement of his sense of smell. For a period of time, he literally lived in a dog's world, experiencing a dramatic tapestry of olfactory sensations wherever he went.[2] After his scent capacity returned to normal, he was glad to be back. But, he observed, "it's a tremendous loss too. I see now what we give up in being civilized and human. We need the other—the 'primitive'—as well. . . . So vivid, so real! It was like a visit to another world, a world of pure perception, rich, alive, self-sufficient, and full. If only I could go back sometimes and be a dog again!" (Sacks 1987:157–58).

The brain handles information from the nose in a unique way, sending it directly to those parts of it associated with memory and emotion. In contrast, taste, touch, and especially hearing and seeing are routed through the brain's analytical apparatus before reaching deeper emotional areas. Smell, in a manner of speaking, is the most primitive of the senses. Long before animals were spotting lions in the bushes or flying off at the sound of a snapping branch, they were sniffing at the world around them in an effort to figure out what they should move toward and what they should avoid. That was in days long past, before the development of the cerebral cortex, the part of the brain that allows higher animals to perform impressive cognitive feats. Even though we so-called higher animals suffer embarrassment when placed alongside other organisms, smells at least serve to put us closest to our unconscious background. This background undoubtedly includes the range of possibilities from which all the signs of greater development co-dependently emerge. This is why olfactory signs should be of such importance: they give concrete life to the other signs. Without smells, life loses a good deal of its savour. If we could learn more about how the information collected by the sense organs is turned into sensual experience in the mind, we might perhaps all have the opportunity to "live a dog's life" if we so desired. However, in our postmodern milieu we have even lost much of the relatively sophisticated sense of smell even our less remote upright simian ancestors had: they kept noses vigilant, following the seasons by way of fresh to stale smells, labeling food, danger, weather, and rituals according to olfactory sensations.

Literature is notorious for its human olfactory images: in addition to Proust, we have Virginia Woolf's profusion of city smells, Dostoevsky's stench of St. Petersburg, Thoreau's fields of corn and berry patches, Baude-laire's immersion into smells in his *Flowers of Evil,* Zola's catalogue of smells in *Nana,* Shakespeare's multiple flower similes, and so on.[3] In *The Hound of the Baskervilles,* Sherlock Holmes identified a woman by the smell of the perfume on her note paper from among the seventy-five per-fumes he could keep in distinction. Holmes knew his aromas well, and he could integrate them with remarkable aplomb with respect to the affairs of his inferential processes in order to solve a crime, in much the manner in which all organisms solve the problems of their everyday existence accord-ing to Peirce (Eco and Sebeok 1983). However, although the notorious English sleuth could describe the results of these inferential processes to his less semiotically endowed companion, Watson, he would have been hard pressed to give his olfactory images precise linguistic dressing.

In other words, it was not that Holmes's qualisigns and icons were to-tally incommensurable with legisigns and sinsigns and indices and sym-bols, for the relations between all signs are continuous. Rather, it was a matter of a continuous deformation of his qualisigns and icons into signs of lesser richness but greater expressive complexity. If those baser signs often resisted such deformation, it was not necessarily on account of the inadequacies of Holmes's more developed, and especially linguistic, signs, but due to the unspeakable qualities of those more richly endowed signs. In this manner, Holmes's inferential reasoning was not locked into his sense of smell; it pertained to signs of greater complexity. Since smell is the most direct of the senses, there was barely time for his awareness of any representamen in the full-blown sense, or of any semiotic object, at least not yet. There were just scent-signs and identifications, much like signal-stimuli evoking responses in automatic and well-nigh instinctive fashion. The effect of the aromas was almost immediate, and undiluted by lan-guage, conscious thought processes, or sign transformation or translation. Thus odors can often be overwhelmingly nostalgic because they trigger emotionally charged images at the qualisign level before the mind has had time to edit them: they elicit gut reactions, clad with presuppositions, prej-udices, and loves and hatreds and anxieties and pleasures. What we see, hear, and touch may quickly fade into the compost heap of short-term memory, to be mulled over by the mind and restructured to fit into one's ready-made categories of thought. Odors, and even tastes, in contrast, hardly know more than long-term memory (Morris 1986).

Our sense of smell seems to consist of seven basic components, a sen-sitivity to camphoric, floral, ethereal, musky, minty, pungent, and pu-trid odors (Amoore 1971). The values given these smells are not simply a biological and psychological matter, however. They are in large part cultural. Some cultures place greater emphasis on olfactory sensations than others. In fact, some cultures, such as the Ongee of the Andaman Islands of the South Pacific, consider odors to be the vital force of the universe and the basis of personal and social identity—a common greeting among them is not "How are *you?*" but "How is *your nose?*" (Classen 1993:1). In our own culture, smells are the source of dynamic, electrically induced reactions: bad smells indicate filth, evil, what must be avoided or hidden away; good smells are linked with all that is pleasant and desirable. Intimate, emotionally pregnant olfactory experiences ensure that cultural values are interiorized by members of society in deeply personal ways.

By virtue of their proximity to the depths of nonconsciousness and gut responses, scents are becoming increasingly important in commercially pushing commodities in our consumerist societies. Some magazine ads now have pull-off tabs that release scents from the products advertised; clerks in department stores give you a spray of scented matter whether you ask for it or not; scent machines fill stores and offices and homes with artificially contrived fragrances. As early as 1940, lingerie shops sported scented underwear; laundries delivered wash delicately perfumed; paints and lacquers were scented according to the part of the house they would cover; cigarettes were doused with odors of vanillin, geranium, and rum that are released when the products are smoked—recall those sweet-smelling, sweet-tasting Mississippi Crook cigars (Verrill 1940:96). Deodorants and perfumes, as would be expected, lead the parade regarding the West's culture-clad smell. Musk, by English Leather, has been advertised as "the missing link between animal and man," promising to endow its user with primitive, more sexual powers that were lost when "civilization" took over. The perfume 20 Carats appeals to the desire for pecuniary gain with the phrase "Smell rich." Brut has Hank Aaron saying "When I'm off the field, I let my Brut do the talking," thus appealing to the shy person who needs some help in winning the game called sex. Aromatic commodities know no boundaries. In the Amazonian region of Brazil, over 60,000 "Avon ladies" barter their wares from hut to hut in exchange for locally produced goods. In virtually inaccessible mining outposts, men and women alike clamor to buy up colognes with exotic names the likes of Crystal Splash and Charisma, each bottle selling for as much as a gram of gold. In rural villages accessible only by canoe, a roll-on deodorant costs a couple of dozen eggs and a bottle of cologne goes for 20 pounds of flour. For sure, marketing techniques differ in the jungle habitat, but the commodity remains the same (Classen, Howes, Synnott 1994:181–82; Jellinek 1975:10). Ah, postmodern culture at its best.

Scent, in sum, is sensation in its basest form. It is in its bare inception of the nature of qualia, qualisigns, signs of 111 that more or less do as they please without the mind's panoptic surveillance with the intent of controlling any and all signs that happen to pop up. These sensations emerge on their own, compelling the body to react with delightful to deleterious anticipation, whether the mind has been engaged or not. Olfactory signs, it would appear, are closest to the semiosic core of figure 4 before the other rings of the onion have grown around it and enveloped it in their oppressive semiotic prison.

II. GUSTATORY

Adult humans have about 10,000 taste buds that order the world into basically four categories: salty, sour, sweet, bitter.

One of the first Western connoisseurs of the gustatory was Seneca, who, in his *Epistulae morales* (1962 2:281) wrote that food not only nourishes the body, but higher nature as well. Food enters the body, is ingested and digested, and in the process it becomes us and we become it: hence it can help enable us to reason and to judge properly, that is, if we have eaten properly. The mouth and tongue are aids in our taking in the outside world and its engulfing us such that we can know it a tad better. By Kant's day, however, taste had been by and large eradicated from proper mental exercises. "Taste" was now a matter of things of beauty, but it provided no faculty for thinking. With Enlightenment thought, the corpuscular-kinetic Newtonian-Cartesian worldview reigned supreme, which spelled doom to taste as a serious matter of cognition. Olfactory as well as gustatory sensations, and indeed, chiefly tactile and auditory phenomena other than spoken language, were downplayed, and sight and the verbal manifestations of sound were consequently hypertrophied. Montaigne was a misfit within this long venerable tradition. During his final days, he discussed his sleeping habits and kidney stones, his repugnance regarding sweets as a child, and his digestion and indigestion.

In our own day, quite notably, Jacques Derrida maintains that there should be no categorical distinction between the intelligible and the sensible. In *Glas* (1974) his writing is arranged in two juxtaposed columns, to be read in simultaneity for some sort of narrative equivalent of sweet and sour pork—an impossibility, of course, for blocks of narrative do not mix in the same way gustatory and other sensations do, though we have synesthesia, oxymorons, and other such rhetorical devices regarding individual words. On the left side of Derrida's text the reader confronts Hegel (taste in terms of the Enlightenment and as a consequence of theory and quantitative, abstract thinking) while on the right side Derrida depicts Edmond Genet (taste—in the archaic sense—as quality, feeling, sensuality, non-theory). As a result of this strategy, Western traditions are placed in question by means of the author's method of showing (as a matter of taste, in the old meaning) rather than saying (in terms of theoretical discourse: proper taste).

Raymond Williams (1976:264) tells us that the English word "taste" entered the language around the thirteenth century. At that time its meaning was more akin to "touch" (from the French, "tastere") or "feel" than to taste. After that time its meaning slowly suffered an alteration, coming to be associated with rules of proper preferences and proper conduct. Today, "good taste," a matter of social invention and convention rather than a feeling for what is right—or in Peirce's jargon, a matter of Thirdness more than Firstness coupled with Secondness—is quite removed from sensory qualities. In other words, it has become the product of mind-stuff rather than corporeal and even visceral feels and imaginary flights. The word has lost its concreteness to take up residence in the venerable Western tradition of good logic and good reason. Enough on the vicissitudes of taste conceived as an ever-changing metaphor within our Western tradition. Let us take a couple of literal cases of taste, historically contextualized, in order to experience how taste can alter entire cultural conventions.

In Europe the demand for sweets experienced a trigonometric upswing after the introduction of chocolate from the Americas.[4] Hernán Cortés introduced the bitter substance to Europe shortly after the conquest of 1519–21. Liberally mixed with sugar, orange, vanilla, and other spices, its consumers soon became participants in a strange new drug cult. And the craze has yet to wane. One line of thought has it that our craving for chocolate might be related to a chemical produced in the brain, phenylethylamine (PEA), associated with roller coaster fits of passion and love-making, much like an amphetamine high.[5] In whatever case, it is most likely not mere coincidence that chocolate has gained its reputation. Coffee, tea, and tobacco and other stimulants were also introduced into the West during the sixteenth and seventeenth centuries and they quickly percolated throughout Europe. One of the most successful recent tastes has been that of Coca-Cola, a combination of sweetness, caffeine, and a tingling of the palate and nose due to carbonation. Once containing cocaine, it is still flavored with extract from coca leaves, but without the cocaine, and it now comes in dietary form—artificiality built into artificiality (Ackerman 1990:153–57).

Taste and smell, our most fundamentally chemical senses, put us in close contact with the atomic structure of the food we eat, as well as other substances that pass by and into our bodies. Taste, like touch, seems to consist of four separate subsenses. Touch is sensitive to pressure, heat, cold, and pain, while taste entails a sensitivity to the salty, sour, bitter, and sweet aspects of chemical substances that our tongues encounter. However, while touch's sensitivity is a matter of contact with the physical aspects of the things of the world, taste brings the chemical composition of those things into relationship with the sensing body: it involves an internalization of those deeper, nonempirical aspects of those things with which the body comes into contact. Taste is in this sense more akin to smell than to touch. In fact, much of the taste of the food we eat depends on smell. It has even been said that the subtle differences in wines is due not to taste but to fragrance (according to the adage, if you have a head cold, wine will taste like water). It would appear quite reasonable to say that since we taste basically only four flavors, most of what we taste is actually odor. Moreover, many of the foods we think we smell we actually only taste. To cite one instance, sugar isn't volatile, so we can't really smell it, even though it gives us an intense sensation in the tastebuds.[6]

Gustatory sensations' close kinship to aromatic sensations gives them billing as the most likely actors at the core of the decalogue of sign folds in figure 4. There, in the dwelling place of sign 111 and perhaps slightly outward, the almost-but-not-quite-immediate sign sensations and their registry in the storehouse of consciousness are subsequently filtered and pigeon-holed according to a given set of cultural conventions, biological demands, psychological needs, and personal quirks and idiosyncracies, as sign among all the other signs in the flow of semiosis. However these signs may be taken, their rebelliousness regarding signs of more complex nature, especially of the linguistic sort, will maintain their relative unspecifiability, their unutterability, their vagueness and their character of overdetermination. Indeed, given their overdeterminability, they can be mixed quite freely to produce not entirely new signs in most cases, but, rather, signs manifesting contradictory characteristics. As we shall note in greater detail below, contradictory sensations flowing freely one into another end up subverting the noncontradiction principle of standard logical operations.

It might appear that this places the most basic sign manifestations in a dilemma. Not so, however. They thrive on it. That is to say, contradictory sensations within the sphere of olfactory and gustatory signs are not at war with themselves: they coexist, they are codependent, they codependently emerge, thus bearing witness to the interrelatedness of all signs as presented in the previous chapters. The problem in our contemporary societies is the creeping artificiality of the odors and tastes that envelop us. Anthropologist E. T. Hall observes that the "extensive use of deodorants and the suppression of odor in public places results in a land of olfactory blandness and sameness that would be difficult to duplicate anywhere else in the world" (1969:45). That was almost three decades ago. Since then, the problem has been exacerbated rather than ameliorated. Moreover, much the same could be said of the blandness of the tastes imposed on us in our fast lane, fast food lifestyles. To make matters even worse, the hegemony of video, movie, TV, and magazine and poster and store window imagery tends to shove smells and tastes further into the background. Sight becomes, is becoming, more paramount than ever. As Walter Ong has tirelessly argued, the predominance of signs is accompanied by increased emphasis on analysis rather than synthesis, appearance over content or substance, surface over depth. We read that:

> Sight reveals only surfaces. It can never get to an interior as an interior, but must always treat it as somehow an exterior. If understanding is conceived of by analogy with sight alone . . . rather than by analogy also with hearing . . . as well as with smell and taste, understanding is ipso facto condemned to dealing with surfaces which have a 'beyond' it can never attain to. (Ong 1967:74)

Olfactory and gustatory sensations, on the other hand, take things in and enfold them within the folds of the body in a dynamic interrelationship and exchange between exterior and interior. A rose by any other name would smell as sweet and Limburger cheese by any other name would taste as pungent. Or saccharine by any other name would taste as sweet and methane gas by any other name would smell as pungent. Words are often hardly more than mere labels, of course. The point is, however, that smells and tastes are close cousins to signs that don't need to be told they must integrate: they never were, nor could they have been, clearly and distinctly segregated in the first place.

Sights, in contrast, if consisting of an incompatible mix, and even if mixed with signs of smells and tastes, are more properly marked by ambiguity than by vagueness. Ambiguity allows us to have either one thing or the other; vagueness allows for both in one gulp; indeed, it tells us that we must have both, for if not, we are exiled to the sphere of eithers and ors of ambiguity. However, at the long stretch of an ambiguous image, concept, or term, it becomes not a mere matter of either the either or the or, but rather, something else always stands at least an outside chance of popping into the light of day. In other words, no matter how general the two terms of the ambiguity dilemma are conceived to be, a third term can always somehow, and at some spatio-temporal context or other, come between them. In this sense, ambiguity in the pluralistic rather than the limited dualistic sense becomes underdetermined—between two possible terms there can always be a third term, so the excluded-middle principle does not necessarily apply—which complements the overdetermination of vagueness as suggested above.

So much for the tongue and the nose.

III. TOUCH

Touch is actually more than a single sense subdivided into the four sensitivities as outlined above: pressure, heat, cold, and pain. It consists essentially of four distinct roads to sensations, not four dimensions of a single sensation. Unlike colors that combine to yield new colors, the mixture of two touches does not necessarily produce a new, synthetic sensation.

But by this description I by no means intend to insult touch. When at its best, it is a fine-tuned means for detecting subtle differences in our world. Our fingertips are capable of sensing a variance in height as small as 1/10,000 of an inch and can be trained rapidly to read texts encoded as raised Braille dots. Touch is also closely tuned in on a sense of the inner body. Those Chinese chrome balls, which bring to mind the mad Captain Queeg of that classical movie, are designed to induce well-being of the body and serenity of spirit. Athletes, musicians, health nuts, and people tied to the computer terminal many hours during the day consider them great muscle conditioners, and effective for relaxation and meditation, in addition to their chime that soothes the ear and the mind. An exciting but controversial area of tactile research is the development of virtual reality simulations in which a computer generates artificial visual and tactile experiences that are channeled through a video helmet and a dataglove to produce a convincing sense of being able to sense, move, and manipulate objects in a wholly simulated environment.

Touch is sort of at the crossroads regarding the sensory modes. Like taste, it is dependent upon physical contact with the thing in question; like smell and taste, it is there all at once, a whole that is as unanalyzable as it is unsayable. Touch also shares with hearing the successiveness of apprehension, as in music, which comes in a linear stream so that the listener must synthesize the whole as she analyzes the parts as she takes them in (i.e., the analysis-by-synthesis method [Neisser 1967]). Like seeing also, touch comes in what appears as a static presence of things, and it is allowed a synthetic grasp through successive analytic dismemberment (differentiation) of the parts of the whole. Since touch is in this manner at the crossroads of the five basic senses, proper account of it is probably the most difficult of all the senses. In the phenomenology of sense-perception, it is the least specialized: contact most commonly is with the fingertips, but it may be initiated with the toes, the nose, the knees, the elbows, the lips, the head, or the buttocks. In its physiology and achievements, touch is the most compound of the senses. What you see, hear, taste, or smell you take in in its entirety; what you touch you do so in more highly differentiated bits and pieces. Of course, you can squint, cover your ears, sample a morsel of food, or stop up your nose or inhale only slightly. But with touch there is a greater number of variations to choose from: where to touch the thing and with how much pressure, whether or not to explore with the hands or whatever, how the exploration should be conducted, and so on. Quite understandably, Italo Calvino in *If On a Winter's Night a Traveler* has his protagonist "reading" Ludmilla's body during a love scene. Touch, like reading a book, can be linear; one can pause, reflect, skip a few lines or a page, go back to a previous passage, exercise an exploratory incursion into future pages, and so on.

In fact, touch is cumulative insofar as the thing's shape as a whole is not usually accessible at the initiation of contact, but it is a construct that emerges additively from a serial multiplicity of single or continuously blending touch-sensations. A single touch-sensation confined to the point of contact and without correlation to more of its own kind is rather barren of information. Simple tactile qualities such as soft and hard, and even more so rough and smooth, are not really instantaneous experiences but require a series of changing sensations obtained by pressure, friction, and movement. This series of sensations in its very constitution entails a synthesis by way of successive analysis on the part of the percipient. The process extends over the time-span of the series and, by short-term retention, it unifies its elements into one impression. Touch and hearing agree in this respect: their primary objects, the qualities sensed, have process character and are thus essentially time-bound. But in hearing, the process is purely passive, while in touch it involves exploration and to a greater extent (re)construction. Yes, we are aware that we can perk up our ears, raise our nose and take a good whiff, strain our eyes to differentiate the collection of articles in our vision with greater acuity, and savor the delicacy of a fine dish at our favorite restaurant. But in each of these cases there is greater passivity than in the sense of touch. We will recall the Buddhist tale of the blindfolded priests who are led to an elephant: one says the object is a rope after handling the animal's tail, another says it is a tree after wrapping his arms around one of its legs, still another says it is a fan after moving his hands over its ears. Exploration: after perhaps sight, touch is the most adept of the senses at foraying out into the world in an effort to know what it's all about.

It is becoming increasingly evident that contact between humans by way of touch is an essential aspect of cultural life (Macrae 1988, Montagu 1971). Massaged babies gain weight as much as fifty percent faster than unmassaged babies. They're more active, alert, and responsive, more aware of their surroundings, better able to tolerate noise, and they can orient themselves faster and are emotionally more in control. These characteristics are even evident among primates and other of the more intelligent creatures. When infant monkeys have their mother removed from them, they show signs of helplessness, confusion, and depression, and only after the mother is back in their midst do they return to their normal activities. During separation of human infants from other humans, notable changes occur in the heart rate, body temperature, sleep patterns, and immune system functions. Electronic monitoring of these infants shows that touch deprivation causes physical and psychological disturbances. "Did you hug your child today?" is perhaps more to the point than one might think.

Indirectly at least, the self is in part a product of a sense of touch with the entire body. What is a sense of one's self? To a large extent, it has to do with how we feel. Our proprioceptors (from the Latin, for "one's own" receptors) keep us informed about where we are in space, if our stomach is growling in protest, whether or not we are defecating, where our legs, arms, head are and the way they are moving, what we feel like physically from moment to moment. The appropriate term for this awareness of where our body is, what it is doing, and what the conditions are, is motility. Motility is the coordination of mental imagery and body movement, of the mind's workings and the body's functionings, the intimate union of body and mind, in short, of bodymind (see Levin 1985). There are so many signs to know at any given moment in our dialogic interaction with the others of our community that we cannot hope to know them all and much less to be consciously aware of them. Motility affords us a tacit feel or sense of the body's positioning and movement within its environment and the movement of each body part in relation to all other body parts. It gives us access primarily to signs 221 (our gut reactions to the world "out there"), 222 (relations between physical objects, acts, and events), 311 (the relationship between body and inferred self that is now on the periphery of consciousness and the relations between the world's objects, acts, and events), 321 (shifters, indicators, indices bringing the bodyself into linguistic relation with the world), and 322 (the making and the taking of commonplace evocations). In fact, up to and including signs 322, the role of tactile touches and feels, both physical and subjective, are on the increase. A hand shake, a high five, a light embrace with a member of the opposite sex or the same sex, a slap on the back, a "Hi," "What's up?" "You all right?" all are of the nature of feels, without the need of actual physical contact but with a degree of familiarity, camaraderie, fraternity, intimacy.

Without such cultural contacts by way of motility one's sense of self and community is severely impoverished. "How are you?" a passerby asks politely in Kafka's novel *The Trial.* The protagonist panics, paralyzed by the shock of being asked a simple question that he can't answer. The problem is that he takes the question literally, as sign 332, to which he feels compelled to respond with an equally literal, informatively pregnant, explicitly precise utterance. How exactly does he feel? How can he know that how he thinks he feels is really what he feels? How is how he feels distinct from how others perceive and conceive of how he feels? Everyday life includes a host of similar cantankerous questions, ones that ordinarily aren't meant to be taken seriously but are inserted into a conversation like a quarter into the slot of a mechanical horse. "How are you?" a friend will ask, and one might conceivably be tempted to report straight from one's proprioceptors on the state of one's kidneys, nasal mucosa, blood pressure, digestion, cholesterol count, and general adrenal unrest. Of course, ordinarily one doesn't do so. It would be a quick way to lose friends and alienate people.

It has become quite apparent that I consider the tactile as more than the sentient body in contact with things. In fact, tactility is virtually nothing at all without motility: bodymind in its imaginary (Firstness), actual (Secondness), and thoughtful (Thirdness) relations to itself and its world. The bodymind becomes the voluntary agent of that movement that is required for the acquisition of this serial sequence of feelings, impressions, actions, and thoughts. The tactile passes over from suffering to acting: its development is a matter of interrelations of self to inner self, to the physical world, and to other selves of the community, and it may be continued and varied with a view to the signs amongst which it finds itself. Thus imagery, touch-impression, and thought converge, complement one another, and collaborate in the ever-changing process of feeling. There is a basic difference between simply having a tactile encounter and feeling another object, on the one hand, and the motilitic, kinesthetic feels of the individual self on the other. The former is an essential facet, a set of atoms playing out their role in the complex totality of the latter. But this totality is more than the mere additive result of such atomic sensations as a result of physical contact. Through the motilitic and kinesthetic accompaniment of voluntary and involuntary physical contact, the whole of tactility is expanded. Touch-qualities (Firstness) become arranged in a spatial scheme; they fall into the pattern of surface and become elements of form. They then merge into sense-qualities (the Firstness of Secondness) that integrate their own time-series of contact-sensations but now enter as material into the larger unit of spatial order. In this order the manifold concresces into a shape in space-time. This mediated synthesis (Thirdness) involves memory and anticipations, thus including a larger spacetime-span for its performance.

In sum, in the hand there is a tactile organ that can take over some of the perceptual functions of the eye. Also there is a bodymind aspect of the highest performance of the tactile sense, or rather to the use that is made of its information, which transcends all mere sentience, and it is this mental use that brings touch within the dimension of the achievements of sight. Consequently, image—imaginatio, phantasia—and thought collaborate with the data of touch. Thus blind people can "see" by means of their hands and artificial extensions of the hands, not because they are devoid of eyes, but because they are beings endowed with the general faculty of "vision" as a byproduct of the more fundamental faculty of tactility, motility, kinesthetics.

IV. SOUND

The human ear is sensitive to sound frequencies between 20 cycles and 20,000 cycles per second. This is almost ten octaves, compared to the eye's ability to detect a single octave of light frequencies. But the detector for these auditory frequencies is not divided into a small number of primary receptors like the eye. Instead, the cochlea, a small snail-shaped organ inside the ear, consists of tens of thousands of tiny hairs, each sensitive to slightly different ripples in the air.

Designers of music synthesizers try to cover as much auditory space with their sound machines as they can in order to duplicate most of the known sounds and exhaustively identify other sounds that the human ear can experience. The problem is that due to the large number of different auditory receptors, there is no auditory equivalent of the single pair of eyes and no color solid upon which all possible acoustic sensations can be mapped. There is no way of simply displaying all the familiar sounds and of looking for gaps in acoustic space corresponding to sounds heretofore not experienced by humans. Consequently, there may be hundreds of novel sound sensations out there waiting to be heard by human ears and brains. The upshot is that color is a necessary companion of our binocularly focused vision, of the roving, searching, and gazing eye that thinks it penetrates its world, in contrast to the ear, which has no alternative but to sit around in wait of whatever compact and diffuse air patterns the world happens to send it.

There is a close parallel, however, between vision and hearing in terms of synesthesia: both involve sensing the frequencies of certain vibrations. This is especially evident in music and colors (Klein 1926, Wood 1936), in the relation of colors to letters and words—the case of Vladimir Nabokov (1949) being one of the most notable—geometrical shapes and colored hearing (Cytowic and Wood 1982), and sounds and colors in general (Downey 1912, Marks 1974). Just as the sensed visual spectrum loops around, although the physical spectrum is linear, so also a corresponding acoustic loop can be produced in our subjective sense of musical pitch. By playing a three-note chord on a music synthesizer and programming the amplitudes and frequencies of this chord in a particular way, the sensation is created of a sound of constantly increasing pitch that returns again and again to the same aural sensation. This is roughly the acoustic equivalent of the visual color wheel or color solid, of the visual paradox artist Maurits Escher's constructs in many of his lithographs, of the Gestalt psychologists' figure-ground drawings, of the visual effects of Op art, and of optical illusions of various sorts (Escher 1971, Gombrich 1979, Gregory 1966, 1970, 1981). Such oscillatory effects produced by the combination of different frequencies and amplitudes, and by colors or shapes or patterns, helps account for the fact that among synesthetes a fusion of vision and sound is quite prevalent (Cytowic 1989). The relation between reiterative but paradoxical combinations of sight and sound patterns is remarkably illustrated through Escher and Johann Sebastian Bach and given metamathematical framing through Kurt Gödel in Douglas Hofstadter's *Gödel, Escher, Bach* (1979).

In short, A. R. Luria writes, regarding synesthesia:

> Is it reasonable to think that the existence of an extraordinarily developed figurative memory, of synesthesia, has no effect on an individual's personal-

ity structure? Can a person who "sees" everything; who cannot understand
a thing unless an impression "leaks" through all his sense organs; who must
feel a telephone number on the tip of his tongue before he can remember
it—can he possibly develop as others do? (Luria 1968:150)

Quite obviously, given the nature in which these questions are posed,
Luria's response is negative. In such case, the relationship between synesthesia and Peirce's decalogue of signs is intriguing. Smell and taste, it seems
quite safe to say, favor signs of chiefly Firstness, while sound-signs find
their greatest affinity in signs of chiefly Thirdness. As mentioned above,
touch is at the crossroads. In collaboration with kinesthesia, it is the first
of the five basic senses most clearly to establish the inside-outside, here-
there distinctions: the individual comes in direct contact with the physical
world. In synaesthesia any artificially contrived boundaries between sensory modes and sign types "leak," however. In Ehrenzweig's terms, the
synesthete dedifferentiates the differentiated, and is thus capable of "seeing" two or more phenomena ordinarily accessible to distinct sensory
modes as one, by cerebrally scanning and fusing them and bringing about
at least a dissolution of signs into the soup of semiosis.

Sound is usually taken in linearly, over time, and it is given dynamically,
not statically. An abuse of the linear and temporal perception of sound
would be a sustained high C in an absence of background noise. For the
recipient, the noise, discounting memory of past sounds, would be virtually without time and linearity; it would be the purest form of Firstness—
a sign suffering from null relations with other signs—available to
consciousness. At the other end of the spectrum, thunder, canon shots,
firecrackers, car horns, and such are momentary crashes on the ear drums
that are dynamic enough, unlike the monotonous high C, but there is
hardly any temporality as long as no Secondness enters the scene. With
Secondness—prior sensation of lightning, anticipation of the cannon shot
or firecracker effects, the cause of the horn's blare—time suddenly becomes
a factor. Most prototypical examples of linear development are found in
spoken language and music—also, of course, written language and the
musical score, which have to do with sight, but that is another matter.

The wholes achieved by accumulation and by synthesis (i.e., synthesis
by analysis once again) are temporal, and their objective time-measure is
identical with the time of the sense-activation itself: the duration of the
sound heard is tantamount to the duration of hearing it. Thus there is a
coincidence of the extension of object and extension of its perception. The
object is the cumulative string of sounds, and the perception of it is also

cumulative, so there can be a certain mapping going on. In this sense, what a sound immediately discloses is not an object but a dynamical event involving the object, and thereby the object is mediately available to the perceptual faculties of the semiotic agent. The rustling of an animal in the leaves, the footsteps of human beings, the noise of passing cars betray the presence of those things by something they do, by the happening in which they are the primary actors. The immediate object of hearing is the sounds themselves (Firstness), indicating something, some event, "out there" (Secondness), which mediately become something else (Thirdness), a sign in the full sense. Only through Thirdness does the experience of hearing reveal the semiotic object as an entity whose existence is independent of the noise it makes.

I can say that I hear a dog (Thirdness), but what I hear is his bark (Secondness), that is, no more than a sound (Firstness) recognized as the bark of a dog. I hear the dog barking and consequently by inference I sense the dog himself in a certain way. In other words, I sense the effect of the barking dog, the dog doing something; it is not necessary for me directly to perceive the physical presence of the dog. There is an event; that is, there is "eventing" (Thirdness). Consequently, there must have been some action, some other (Secondness), all of which lies outside of icons (Firstness) in their most primitive incarnation. This way of sensing the dog arises and ceases with his act of barking, that is, the act of eventing. By itself the bark does not reveal anything beyond it, an agent of the barking preceding and outlasting the acoustic act I know from information other than the mere sound of barking. The object-reference of sounds is not provided by the sounds as such, and it transcends the performance of mere hearing. All indications of existents, of enduring things beyond the sound-events themselves, are extraneous to their own nature. They are the Thirdness of the barking-event, the eventing that is constructed by myself and combined into a symbolic sign of chiefly Thirdness: "Dog." It becomes quite apparent that sound, and as we shall note sight, are paramount in the engenderment of signs of the more complex sort, which would aid in accounting for the hegemony of sight and sound in Western thought: reading and writing, speaking and hearing, principle sources of logocentrism and linguicentrism, the myth of presence and the subject/object, mind/body, inside/outside, sign/thing dichotomies.

Consequently, sound appears eminently suited to constitute its own, immanent objectivity of acoustic values as such—and, thus, free from other-representative duty, to represent itself. This is problematic. The sound actually represents itself and nothing but itself; that is, it is immediate. In contrast, embodied in the notion of eventing, there is a looseness of external object, of reference, in the traditional use of the term reference, since I don't actually see the dog. Hence there is no immediate object dog; there is only what the dog does, his eventing. In this manner, the physical object is mediate rather than immediate, and rather than reference, there are relations evinced by the eventing. Thus the First of the sign ("bark," a mere icon since it is like other "barks" irrespective of any semiotic objects) presents itself as what it is, and what it is is all it is. If it is related to something else, a Second, then a relation comes into play between the icon and some other, an index. Consequently, some degree of Secondness, if not full-blown indexicality—which is usually the case—also enters the scene. So presumably to perceive and conceive and say the relation between the icon and the other is to bring in mediacy, Thirdness and symbolicity.

Music is something else, since there is not necessarily any semiotic object as in the case of the dog example. In hearing music, our synthesis of a manifold of sounds to a unity of feeling, form, and interpretation relates not to an object other than the sensory contents but to their own order and interconnection. Since this synthesis deals with succeeding data and is spread over the length of their procession, so also in the presence of any one element of the series all the others are either no longer here-now or not yet here-now. And since the present element must disappear for the next one to appear, the synthesis itself is a temporal process achieved with the help of memory. By a collusion and collaboration of memory of comparable past instances of sounds (iconicity, Firstness) and their relation to some other (indexicality, Secondness), and given certain anticipations of probable future sounds (Thirdness, symbolicity), the whole sequence, though at each moment only atomically realized in one of its elements, is bound together into one comprehensive unity of experience. The acoustic semiotic object thus created is a time-object that lasts just as long as the act of its synthesis lasts, that is, as long as the sequence of hearing itself lasts, with whose progress the semiotic object part for part coincides. The semiotic object in this manner has no other dimension than that of time. Time becomes paramount. This is quite unlike the chiefly spatial orientation of smells and tastes, and the spacetime orientation of touch. Now the conflation becomes timespace, a conflation that will become even more apparent in our meditation on sight, which, though apparently spatial before it is temporal, is inextricably caught within temporality in whatever regard it would like to hold for space: différance—temporal deferral and spatial difference rather than mere difference or differentiation.

Hearing, ruled by succession, nonetheless can differentiate juxtapositions of simultaneous acoustic contents, such as polyphony in music or the
separable sound strings of the hubbub at a cocktail party. It is a manifold
of sound patterns, a sort of Fourier addition of sounds that are bisected in
virtually automatic fashion by the brain. They coexist, yet they are a matter of a procession in time. They are there, though they are constantly
moving on, changing; their separation demands qualitative difference (in
pitch, timber, temper: Firstness) the continuation of which in time permits
their strands to be distinguished and indicated (Secondness) and brought
into relation with other sounds (Thirdness). Two musical notes of the
same quality simply reinforce each other, unless there is some kind of
stereo effect; if there are two sounds of different qualities, and if one is
loud and the other quiet, the strongest sound will tend to drown out the
other one, but it will not do so entirely. This is not generally possible with
sight: a spot can't be blue and orange at the same time, a square shape can't
be round; the visual incompatibles can't exist at the same spacetime juncture, that is, in simultaneity. In contrast, the identity of single strings of
sounds in a polyphony, and thus the conservation of discrete simultaneity
through time, is a function of sensed coherence in sound patterns, which
come under the Gestalt principle and thus make the juxtaposition of plurality not a primary datum of the *now* but a feat of ongoing organization.
The product of the sensed sounds is itself a matter of process. Sounds are
dynamic events; they are eventing, not static qualities or essences. Sights
can appear to be relatively static, especially in art—outside Duchamp's
Nude Descending a Staircase and other attempts to dynamize the picture.
For this reason sights tend to be more autonomous, more self-contained,
more independent than sounds. Sounds are more dynamic, more transient, more obviously a matter of becoming.

There is an important feature of sound, briefly mentioned above, that
highlights it and contrasts it with sight: sound, itself a dynamic process of
eventing, intrudes upon a relatively passive semiotic agent. For the sensation of hearing to come about, the percipient is entirely dependent on
something happening—eventing—that is beyond her control, and in
hearing she is exposed to its happening. All she can bring to the event is a
readiness for certain expected sounds to occur (unless she produces them
herself). She cannot let her ears wander, probe, and gaze, as her eyes do,
over a field of possible percepts as possible material for her attention. She
must wait for a sound to come to her. She has relatively little choice in the
matter. In hearing, the semiotic agent is at the mercy of the happenings
"out there" in her environment. The most predominant sounds may not

be stars of an event being played, yet for one reason or another they might seize one's attention from among competing and otherwise more prevailing sounds. Thus sounds are more indexical, more temporal, more linear, a matter of highlighted Secondness, than sights, which are more iconic, more spatial, and less linear.

All this is to say that there is a fundamental difference between the eyes and the ears. Sounds enter the ears; the eyes look. Sounds serve notice that an event occurred, is occurring—there is always action of one sort or another. This is not necessarily the case with sight: it can be of a static landscape, a picture, a photo, a hall full of clapped-out students suffering through an interminable lecture. Ears are always open; eyes can close. Ears can tell the brain during sleep that something is happening, that there is danger, or whatever; eyes open up when the subject awakens, then, what the ears told her before waking can perhaps be apprehended by the eyes. The physical world exercises a relatively large degree of hegemony over the ears; in contrast, it finds more difficulty in doing so over the eyes. Thus hearing demands continual readiness for feeling, sensing, and interpreting, and thus a certain contingency regarding sounds. An important reason for this contingency in the sense of hearing is the fact that it is relatively closely related to eventing and not to existence, to becoming and not to being. In this manner, hearing, bound to succession and well-nigh incapable of presenting a simultaneously coordinated manifold of objects— outside the most notable examples of musical harmony and such—falls short of sight in respect to the freedom that it confers upon its possessor. Hence what is generally taken as an ocularcentric metaphor is of the nature of a noun. It is static: being, identity, generality, permanence. In contrast, the auditory is more akin to a verb. It is more dynamic: becoming, difference, particularity, change. We see the same "Guernica" by Picasso yesterday and today. In a manner of speaking it is always the same, though each time we see it we see it somewhat differently. We also hear the same Bach, yet with each hearing it is somewhat different in its very sameness, and hence we always gain something new from it. Of course the same could and must be said of Picasso, but the difference with each perceptual grasp is of lesser intensity in the case of the visual arts, for all is virtually all there all at once, whereas in music there is the limitation of time, time for the engenderment of subtle variations on the theme being played out, time to develop anticipations and expectations, time for the anticipated to become actualized or thwarted, time for the build up of emotions and tensions, time for the sense of joy, sorrow, pain, contentment, anger, and so on, after tensions have been resolved or become irresolvable. In regards to linear, time-bound unwinding, music evinces affinities with language and the literary arts, and even of logic and mathematics.

The obvious question is, then: Does music have a grammar, like language, or its own set of mathematical laws? If it's principally mathematical, then how come mathematically illiterate people can revel in it? In an essay in *New Literary History* in 1971, composer George Rochberg argued that music is a "secondary language" whose "logic" is closely related to the primary alpha "logic" of the central nervous system itself—that is, of the human body. If Rochberg is on track, then it follows that the perception of music is in large part the process reversed; that is, we listen with our nervous systems and their parallel/serial memory functions. Rochberg alludes to the essential kinesthetic dimension of music, a kinesthetic dimension that remains considerably less intense in language and literature, and especially in logic and mathematics, than in music. In other words, regarding music; *we listen primarily with our bodies.* Indeed, it's hard to keep our bodies still when we hear a familiar bouncy tune—our feet begin tapping, our hands begin swaying, we wave our head back and forth, we pick up an invisible baton, we gyrate in some sketchy dance movements.

Regarding "deeper" classical music, the body is still the principal actor. But now, the ability to articulate the act of musical creation, to intellectualize it, also becomes to a degree essential. This distinction between the creative act per se and articulation of it is illustrated in Peter Schaffer's (1981) play about Mozart, *Amadeus.* Salieri, the established and rival composer, says of a Mozart piece:

> It started simply enough: just a pulse in the lowest registers—bassoons and basset horns—like a rusty squeezebox. . . . And then suddenly, high above it, sounded a single note on the oboe. It hung there unwavering, piercing me through, till breath could hold no longer, and a clarinet withdrew it out of me, and sweetened it to a phrase of such delight it had me trembling. (in Ackerman 1990:212)

Mozart lived his music; he was adept at the task of knowing how to compose it and at the act of actually composing it. But it seems that he was not equally talented at articulating it, of knowing that music is such-and-such and that it must be written in so-and-so a manner—at least he was not prone to articulate the act of creation, whether he knew the thats and the whys of it or not. In contrast, Salieri was relatively literate with regard to music composition, to saying what it is that should be done (though in the act of showing how it was done he paled in comparison to his younger counterpart). In another way of putting it, Mozart was in tune with the Firstness, the iconicity, of his music, and he actualized it into the world of Secondness superbly. Salieri, on the other hand, could intellectualize music quite adequately within the sphere of Thirdness, symbolicity, but this knowledge did not translate effectively into Secondness, for an essential element of feeling, a sense of quality, of emotion, an intimate relation between the self and sounds, was lacking.

Different cultures speak their own unique languages, but whole civilizations enjoy certain forms of music, which we, perhaps too chauvinistically, refer to as Western music, Oriental music, African music, Islamic music, and so on. What we mean is that each culture seems to prefer hearing tones arranged in certain patterns according to slightly different laws. For the past 2,500 years or so, Western music has been obsessed with one polyphonic arrangement of tones, but there are many other arrangements, each as profoundly meaningful as the next and yet virtually incomprehensible to outsiders. "The barriers between music and music are far more impassable than language barriers," Victor Zuckerkandl writes in *The Sense of Music* (1959:84). We can with a greater or lesser degree of effectivity translate from any language into any other language; yet the mere idea of translating, say, Chinese music into the Western tonal idiom is virtually impossible and more often than not produces musical nonsense. Why is that so? According to the composer Felix Mendelssohn, it's not because music is too vague, as one might think, but rather it is too precise to translate into other tonal idioms, let alone into words. Words are chiefly arbitrary. There is not necessarily any direct link between them and the emotions they represent. Instead, words lasso an idea or emotion and drag it into view for a moment in order partially and most often inadequately to satisfy their needs, and then that idea or emotion is on its way again. However, it is worthy of note that during the early years of Greek mathematics, the language of numbers was intended to be spoken like language rather than written; it was a matter of sounds rather than visible symbols (Dantzig 1930). Moreover, in our century mathematics has suffered a "loss of certainty" that at a formal level places it in the same boat as natural languages at informal levels (Kline 1980). Mathematics is not the iron-clad, determinate arbiter of absolute truth that its billing has generally had it, and natural languages are not as inadequate to the task of knowing as logical positivism would like to have had it. So the distinctions between music and language, music and mathematics, and language and mathematics are not those gaping chasms created by the classical picture. There is, rather, constant interplay and interaction between the various semiotic means, modes, methods, and manners of signifying.

Of course, we cannot ignore the fact that we need words to corral how we feel and think; they allow us in an intellectual and conceptual way to reveal our inner lives to one another, as well as to exchange goods and services. But music does language one better in at least one respect: it is a controlled sensation, an expression, and at times even an outcry, from the rambling always-on-the-move herd of emotions all we humans share. Though most foreign words must be translated to be understood, we instinctively understand whimpering, crying, shrieking, joy, cooing, sighing, and the rest of our caravan of cries and calls. It seems quite likely that, in time, they led to two forms of organized sound—words (rational sounds for objects, emotions, and ideas) and music (nonrational sounds for feelings). As Deryck Cooke (1987:86) observes, "both awaken in the hearer an emotional response; the difference is that a word awakens both an emotional response and a comprehension of its meaning, whereas a note, having no meaning, awakens only an emotional response." What sort of response can a few notes of music awaken? Awe, excitement, rage, wonder, restlessness, defeat, love, patriotism, and so on. All these emotions can be given certain linguistic window-dressing, though it is destined to remain incomplete and somewhat inadequate to the task.

Diane Ackerman (1990:202–25) observes that there is an odd sense in which music does not really need to be heard at all. This involves the formalities of composition rather than the sensation of hearing it while creating it or of hearing it once it has been created. Much musical composition involves tonal problem-solving on a very complex scale, an effort undertaken entirely in the mind of the composer. Not only is the orchestra not necessary for that creative feat of legerdemain, but if an orchestra were there to actualize the music during the act of its composition an inferior version of the music would most likely result. People wonder how Beethoven could write his Ninth Symphony so brilliantly when he was stone deaf. In part, the answer is that it was not really necessary for Beethoven to "hear" the music at all. Not as sounds, anyway. He heard it flawlessly and much more intimately in his mind. He heard it perfectly in the resonant chambers of his imagination. His audience then generally heard it emotionally, from inside, more often than not without thoroughly understanding its craft. At the same time the members of the orchestra—arranged according to instruments—heard it also from inside, while they played it, but not as a balanced work in the way Beethoven originally heard it.

As Zuckerkandl (1956, 1959) reminds us in many and diverse ways, polyphony in music coincided with the building of the great Gothic cathedrals, and the birth of harmony with the culmination of the Renaissance and the beginning of modern science and mathematics. In this manner, change of sound perception was accompanied by a change in the understanding of space. This may seem an odd observation, since vision is a chiefly spatial art and music a temporal one. Music unfolds in time. It is dynamic and uses many devices, including syncopation, in which notes appear like hobgoblins when they are not expected and then vanish just as startlingly; or repetition, which snatches the listener back to an earlier pattern or flings her forward into the unknown. Music is not just *in* time, it collaborates *with* time, as if the even flow of time were cut up by the regularly recurrent sounds into short stretches of equal duration. The notes mark time, and they smudge it, then they reassemble it into small groups like a patchwork of cloth remnants making up a quilt. When polyphony was introduced, the only way it could make sense was if each of the voices kept the same time. In this sense the voices, the rhythms, and the beats agreed with one another within the patchwork, though there existed no absolute measuring rod with which each remnant could be measured. In this sense, the music and space were not as far removed as one might think. It became a matter of spacetime or timespace (Ackerman 1990:220).

In short, the nonlinguistic aspects of sound, in music and elsewhere, deserve more visible billing on the marquee announcing the senses of the ear. Otherwise, we are destined to suffer a slide into that bugbear, linguicentrism.

V. SIGHT

It is generally conceded, especially in the West, that our primary sensory connection to the world "out there" is vision. For sure, we are quite sensitive to colors: the experts estimate that we can distinguish more than 100,000 different colors according to hue, saturation, and brightness.

The colors of the visible spectrum have been set out in various schema and diagrams, some of the most common of which consist of various renditions of a "color solid" or a "color wheel."[7] The wheel can be explained by the fact that normal color distinction is based on three different color receptors, whose sensitivities peak in red, green, and blue light, respectively. The relative stimulation of these three receptors defines a unique position within the color wheel. The reason that our psychological color space appears to have more dimensions than the physical spectrum is that our eyes do not detect color like our ears are capable of detecting a single note. What we see is more akin to a three-note chord. We sense a kind of optical harmony: the music of the color wheel. If we happened to possess eyes with four color receptors, the subjective color space would no doubt be four-dimensional, with the pure colors spread out over the surface of a sphere rather than a circle.[8] Although a few poets have speculated about new color sensations outside the human range, it is impossible for us to imagine what a new color would actually look like, visually imprisoned as we are inside the normal human chromasphere.

Since the time of the Greeks, sight has been hailed as the most sublime of the senses. Sight is considered the noble pastime of the mind, *theoria,* theater, sight, that which endows one with the "light of reason." The saying is at its most basic level in the seeing, in what has been called the "eye of the soul," which is presumably the source of the most genuine form of seeing and its translation into well-reasoned saying. Aristotle, in the first lines of the *Metaphysics* (1966), relates the desire for knowledge inherent in the nature of all men to the common delight in perception, most of all in vision. However, neither he nor any other of the Greek thinkers seem to have really explained by what properties sight qualifies for these supreme philosophical honors. Sight appears to be the most complete of all the senses, so the assumption generally has it that it is the most likely sensory channel to support that venerable Western drive toward completeness, axiomatization of all thought, a grand unified theory, total knowledge.[9] Actually, sight is drastically impoverished without the other senses. It requires their complement for fulfillment of its cognitive office. It must lower its goals, its horizon, its vision, in order to collaborate with what have ordinarily been considered those more vulgar modes of sensory commerce. Yet, we would like to consider sight unique, and rather autonomous.

Sight is, or at least it appears to be, well-nigh simultaneous and easily coordinated to the product of the other senses. A look takes in many things; they are juxtaposed, all there for ready analysis. Hardly any cumbersome time is involved; it is virtually instantaneous. In a flash, a glance, an opening of the eyes, there is an entire world of coterminous qualities spread out in space, extending back to give depth. In comparison, the other senses are capable of taking in a unity only by way of a temporal sequence of sensations; they are time-bound and nonspatial. In this regard, the other senses depend more intimately on a cumulative effect, hence any form or fashion of synthesis is always an unfinished symphony, and, a slave to memory, it will always be able to move along only with the movement of an apparently linear stream of sensations. Any available qualities are thus fugitive, fleeting, transient. The content is never all there in the here-now and present as a whole. There is, in other words, no myth of presence. There is no ocularcentrism. There can hardly be any logocentrism. These more temporal senses of sound, touch, taste, and smell therefore never achieve for their object that detachment of its *modus essendi* from their own—of the persistent existence from the transitory event of sense-affection—that sight at any moment offers in the presentation of a complete visual field. We may perhaps best illustrate the difference in the comparison of sight with hearing and touch, the two senses that are apparently closest to sight along the Peircean decalogic spectrum.

I must, of course, properly qualify my above assertions. Sight comes to us only *as if* there were a simultaneity of presentation (the myth of presence) and *as if* the sight were the principal instrument of re-presentation (ocularcentrism). Unlike sight, the other senses are more limited to time-series in the emergence of their qualities (Firstness). Hearing is temporal. It requires analysis-by-synthesis. Music is not only unfolded serially; it *is* serial. So hearing music involves serial accumulation of the series. Touch is capable of taking signs in virtual simultaneity, but it is blind to everything save that which is subjected to actual contact, and successive parts of that everything are available solely through sequences of touches. Smell also comes in virtual simultaneity. Unlike sight, however, there can be two ordinary contradictory sensations at the same moment—the scent of a tulip tree mixed with a whiff from the nearby factory, a combination of popcorn and perfume in a movie theater, gasoline and the interior of your new car at a gasoline station, and so on. Sight cannot cope with such fusions and confusions except by an Ehrenzweig act of dedifferentiation, which requires a temporal process. Taste, like smell, comes in near-simultaneity, and like smell, sensations can be fused into one whole package—sweet/sour, bland/spicy, bitter/sweet, and so on. Moreover, touch, smell, and taste are more dependent on the sensations' relation to other sensations in the memory bank for proper meaning and intelligibility, whereas for hearing this is not so much the case. Sight can appear to be all there all at once, but certain sorts of contradictory information gained by sight cannot easily be reconciled, if at all: something can't be square and round at the same time, nor can it be both green and blue—not even if it is "Grue," according our observations in chapter 2. Contradictories are contradictories, as far as sight is concerned. In contrast, they can live in happy coexistence within the other senses.

Yet, in Western thought, sight retains its unique position (Jonas 1966:142–43). Assumption of the predominance of sight might be quite natural, since it appears to be so straightforward: open your big wide eyes, and it's all "out there," objectively as something other, passively awaiting your cognizing it, manipulating it as you so desire, mutilating it if you wish. But the fallacy of what Karl Popper (1972) calls the "bucket theory" raises its ugly head. Is "reality" simply an "empty bucket"—like our mind was once conceived as a "blank slate"—to be filled as sense data reach us? Or are we inextricably part of that "reality," in interaction with it, in codependence with it such that we and everything that is are in a mutually participatory process of arising. Does the "bucket" and whatever we put in it compose a static set of essences, or is it all, including ourselves, transient, a process of incessant fluxes and flows? An answer to these questions involves further distinction between sight on the one hand, and hearing and touch and smell and taste on the other.

As mentioned above, the ears are always open. In contrast, you have to extend yourself to touch (so it's more active), smells come upon you whether you like it or not, and so do tastes, though in order to experience them you must also extend yourself. Bodily contact is necessary directly with touch and taste, to an extent with smell and sound, though indirectly. But with sight, open your eyes and it's there. It appears there just for you, in all its simultaneity, requiring no time to bring an object into closer approximation for a whiff, a gustatory experience, a feel, or a noise. The apparently simultaneous image allows the beholder to compare and interrelate it to other images; it not only apparently offers many things at once but offers them in their mutual proportion, all objectivity emerging pre-eminently from sight. Proud sight, paramount and imperious signs, the culminating means of access to the most sublime of human thought.

Of course, sight only *appears* available to us in simultaneity. Nevertheless, since it seems quite natural to believe that by way of sight we can collect all the necessary data in the blink of an eye, often we don't think we need any time dimension. The "present" is all that is necessary. This instantaneousness is not possible through the other sensory channels, at least to the same degree, as it is in the case of sight. Since the other senses are more time-bound, they appear more transient, they take in a more transient world. There is not what appears to be the static present available to sight. The other sensations must move on, from the beginnings made in the evanescing antecedent, datum has to follow upon datum to let the larger units of experience in process emerge. Sound exists in sequence, every *now* of it vanishing into the past while it goes on: to arrest this flow and "view" a momentary "slice" of it would mean to have not a snapshot but an atomic fragment of it, and strictly speaking nothing at all. Transience is thus of the very essence of the here-now of hearing, and the "present" is a mere following in the stream of ongoing processes. The situation is similar with touch, only that with touch the sequence is more of active performance than of mere incoming data. In neither case is there a static present as apparently there is with respect to sight. To put this in Platonic terms, the other senses are not of being but of mere becoming, which was traditionally relegated to a subservient position. Only the seemingly "simultaneous" representation of the visual field gives us "co-existence" as such—i.e., an illusory co-presence of things in one monolithic being that embraces them all. The "present," instead of being a pointlike experience, becomes a dimension within which things can be beheld at once and can be related to each other by the wandering glance of attention.

This sort of "scanning" (evoking Ehrenzweig's dedifferentiation), though proceeding in time, articulates only what was present to the first glance and what stays unchanged while being scanned. The time thus taken in taking-in the view is not experienced as the passing away of contents before new ones in the flux of event, but as a lasting of the same, an identity that is the extension of the "instantaneous" here-now and therefore unmoved, continued present—so long as no change occurs in the objects themselves. When change does occur, then time starts rolling visually. Indeed, only the "simultaneity" of sight, with its extended "present" of enduring objects, allows the distinction between change and the unchanging and therefore between becoming and being. All the other senses operate by registering change and cannot make that distinction. Sight, then, provides what appears to be the most adequate sensual basis on which the mind may conceive the idea of the eternal, that which never changes and is always "present." The very contrast between the notions of eternity and temporality rests upon an idealization of "present" experienced visually as the holder of stable contents as against the fleeting succession of nonvisual sensation. In the visual presence of objects the beholder may come to rest and possess an extended here-now. In the "simultaneous" field of vision a coordinated manifold, as yet outside active communication, offers itself to selection by a given semiotic agent for possible action. In this connection, "simultaneity" is tantamount to selectivity, and a major factor in the higher freedom of bodymind interaction with the world and the semiotic agent's awareness of this interaction through motility, as described above.

In touch, taste, smell, and sound, the object seems to enter us more than in the case of sight. In all cases, what enters the senses is ongoing; it is flux, flow, transient process, apparent continuity, in the order of William James's flow of experience. That apparently clear and distinct separation between subject and object is not pressed on us to the extent that it is regarding our entrenched conception of the function of sight. We are not as free, as capable of imposing our will, as we are with our ability to direct our eyes toward the object of our contemplation, curiosity, description, or analysis. Especially on the matter of touch, subject and object are already doing something to each other (you can't touch anything without being in turn touched, as philosopher Maurice Merleau-Ponty argued at length), and in the act the object becomes part of the subject.

Although it appears that there is relatively little intervention on the part of the semiotic agent when hearing, that intervention is actually not necessary, for things are not by their own nature audible the way they are visible; it is not of their nature to emit sound, one might suppose, as it is of the nature of objects to reflect light. To repeat, one can therefore not choose to hear something but must wait until something happens to a part of the environment, until a sound happens to emerge, and then this sound will strike the eardrums whether one chooses it or not. And since it is an event of which sound informs one and not merely the existence of things in their total configuration, one's choice of action is determined by the acoustic information. Something is going on in the surroundings, so hearing "happens," which affects one either as an interested or disinterested party not quite free to exercise any choice on the matter.

It is precisely the apparent absence of such a dynamical situation, of any intrusion onto the sensory organs, that seems to distinguish sight from the other sensory modes. One has merely to look, and the object is apparently not affected by the look. Once there is light, the object has only to be there to be visible, and the semiotic agent is not affected by the reflected light from the object—or so he/she thinks—and yet it is apprehended in its autonomy or self-containment from out of the agent's own autonomy. The object is present to the agent without necessarily drawing him/her into its supposed presence. Whatever dynamic commerce there is in physical fact between source of light, illuminated object, and perceiving eye, this context seems to form no part of the phenomenal result. This presumed complete neutralization of dynamic content in the visual object is one of the major premises of what may be called the image-icon function of sight: the well-springs of knowledge by so-called man, the eminent seeing creature.

The monumental benefit of sight, so the story goes, is the concept of objectivity, of the thing as it is in itself as distinct from the thing as it affects the agent, and from this distinction arises the whole idea of *theoria* (sight, theater) and theoretical truth. Furthermore, the image is handed over to imagination, which can presumably deal with it in complete detachment from the actual presence of the original object: this detachability of the image, of form from its substance, is at the bottom of abstraction and therefore of all thought. This, then, is the presumed gain, thanks to the human use of sight. But for every gain, more often than not there must be a loss. The loss consists in the very feature that makes the gain possible, namely, the elimination of bodymind, of the interrelatedness, the codependent emergence of the entire organism. This elimination is accompanied by the separation of body and mind from everything else, and, given the obsessive priority of mind over body, signs are dichotomized, binarized, hierarchized. Chiefly symbolic signs are granted a privileged spot at the apex of the hierarchically constructed pyramid; chiefly indexical signs are included as a necessary afterthought, then granted only a subservient role; while chiefly iconic signs are left to drag along behind in the best way they can as a rather embarrassing but necessary appendix. And sight reigns supreme. Its presumed neutrality also makes it appear to be the most free and at the same time to afford the most "realistic" grasp of the world. Yes. Proud sight.

VI. RAYS OF LIGHT THROUGH THE DARK CLOUDS

However, according to Peirce, "reality" makes itself manifest primarily as a result of concrete contact, which includes visuality. For obvious reasons, contact is most important regarding touch, the act of one's coming actively into contact with the "brute" Secondness of the physical world.

The Secondness of physical existence is more than mere contiguity: it involves contact, impact, and even clash. Touch—along with taste—is the quality by which force, action and reaction, comes into play in the most direct way. And this force requires that the subject not be merely a passive agent. The subject can dispel suspicions by coming into contact with something that would appear real, but that might be mere apparition; such was the case of Shakespeare's Macbeth in the dagger scene. Macbeth's natural inclination was to reach out and touch the dagger in order to determine its veracity or its quality as appearance. Touch brings the physicality, the Secondness, of the object into contact within the experience of the subject. And external "reality" is disclosed. It is felt at the level of Secondness more forcefully than with contact between the world and the subject through smell, sound, or sight. In this regard, sight is actually the weakest of all the sensory modes, for the gaze is directed toward that which, one hopes, is passive. Sight is relatively effortless, and yet it is apparently the vantage point from which the most control can be exercised.

Seeing demands hardly a smattering of activity, unlike hearing, smelling, and tasting, and especially touching. It would appear that upon the subject's gazing upon the object, neither invades the sphere of the other, and that they simply let each other be what they are, each as if it were a self-contained, autonomous entity. Not so, however. We have it, even from so linguicentric an intellectual—not to say phallogocentric—as Jacques Lacan (1977), that there is an interference set up by the gazer initiating his/her gaze upon the other, and that that other, no matter how neutral and passive we would like it to be, exercises an influence, however minute, on the gazer. The apparent nonactivity of the seen object in relation to the seeing subject is not impaired appreciably by the fact that, physically speaking, action on its part (emission of light) is involved as a condition of its being seen. The singular properties of light are no more than the slightest disturbance, which is hardly of any consequence, one would expect. The causal involvement between percipient and object is not linear causality, nor is it causality in the classical sense of the word: it is nonlinear, nonphysical, non-Boolean, context-dependent, and contradictorily complementary. In a word, it is rhizomic in the dynamic sense the term is given in this inquiry. The percipient remains free from causal involvement in the things to be perceived in terms of physical causality. The causality is a matter of a subject whose emergence is dependent upon the object, and that subject's and that object's dependence on each and every aspect of the entire semiosic stream with respect to the self-organizing of the whole. Everything is interrelated and interacting with, and interdependent upon, everything else. This conception secures that standing back from the aggressiveness of the world that frees one for observation and opens a horizon for selective attention. But it does so at the price of offering a becalmed abstract of reality denuded of its raw power.

The problem is that the object, while remaining within its customarily granted bounds, faces the subject across an apparent gap that the evanescence of the force context has created. Distance of appearance yields a neutral image. This image, unlike an effect, can be looked at and compared with other images, retained in memory and re-called, varied and freely composed and re-composed within the relatively free sphere of Firstness; an effect demands at the very least Secondness and for its result the manifestation of Thirdness. However, the image remains, insofar as its function as image suffers to move toward greater complexity, within chiefly Firstness, and hence it is by and large separated from the

Secondness of existence. The imaginary enjoys a degree of freedom of selectivity that is unavailable from within the sphere of action inhabited by Secondness and Thirdness. In fact, selections made by the imaginary are the appetizers that prepare Secondness and Thirdness for the main course. Without this preliminary sustenance afforded by the imaginary, Secondness and Thirdness would soon wither and fall into a heap, in spite of their occasional registry of contempt for, and even their sporadic rejection of, Firstness, or the imaginary.

Thus in speaking of the presumed and hopeful causal detachment of sight, it must be borne in mind that such detachment can result only by virtue of the causal muteness of its objects. Sight, more than any other sense, withholds the experience of causality: causality is not a visual datum. And as long as percepts ("impressions" and "ideas") are taken as just more or less perfect instances of the model case of visual images, Hume's denial of causal information to them must stand. Vision is not the primary sense, but in the West it is the most prioritized case of sense perception, and it rests on the understructure of more elementary functions in which the commerce with the world is maintained on far more elementary terms. A king with no subjects to rule over ceases to be a king; a sign consisting of an autonomous entity devoid of genuine interrelatedness with some other is no genuine sign at all. The evidence of the eye does not necessarily falsify the world when supplemented by that of the underlying state of experience, notably of motility and touch. However, when arrogantly rejecting touch or any of the other sensory modes, sight becomes barren of semiosis.

For Hans Jonas (1966:150–51), nevertheless, sight is the ideal distance-sense, space-sense, within which the "presentation" of "dynamic neutrality" is possible. Light travels faster than sound, smell wanes at a relatively proximate distance, and touch depends upon the reach of the hand and taste of the tongue. Sight is especially spatial and distance-oriented. Since the best view is not always the closest view, the proper view requires the proper distance, depending upon the context and the objects. Without even thinking about the matter, we have a natural propensity to "stand back" and create distance to get a better angle on things.[10] Sound or smell may report an object as merely distant, without reporting the state of the intervening space. In contrast, with sight, or better, with in-sight, the object faces us across some intervening distance, which in all its potential "steps" is included in our perception of it. In viewing an object there is the situation of a vis-à-vis, which discloses the object as the terminal of dimension leading from us toward it, and this dimension lies open before us.

The facing across a distance thus discloses the distance itself as something we are free to traverse; it is an invitation to forward motion, putting the intervening space at our disposal. The dynamics of perspective depth connects us with the projected terminus.

This terminus itself is arbitrary in each given case, and our glance, even if focused on it, includes as a background the open field of other presences behind it, just as it includes, as a corona fading toward the edges, the manifold co-present in the plane. This indefiniteness with which the visual perception is imbued, an ever-ready potential for realization, is the birthplace, as suggested above, of the idea of infinity, to which no other sense could supply the experiential basis. Touch conjoined with locomotion certainly also includes awareness of the potentially of going on to the next point, and thence to the next, and so on. But touch does not already adumbrate these imminent realizations in its perceptual content, as a marginal part into which the core continuously blends. In the visual field it is this continuous blending of the focused area into more and more distant background-planes, and its shading off toward the fringes, that make the "and so on" more than an empty potentiality: there is the co-represented readiness of the field to be penetrated, a positive pull that draws the glance in as the given content passes into further contents. No such blending of actual and potential content is given in touch; there is merely the abstract possibility of replacing the present by a subsequent content, and the whole results only from the progressive addition of discrete parts. Sight includes at any given instant what appears to be an infinite manifold, and its own qualitative conditions seem to open the way into what lies beyond. The unfolding of space before the eye, under the magic of light, bears in itself the germ of infinity—as a perceptual aspect. Its conceptual framing in the idea of infinity is a step beyond perception, but one that was taken from this base. The fact that we can look into the unbounded depths of the universe has surely been of immense importance in the formation of our ideas.

In sight, then, we believe we sense the notion of unlimited distance, and we gauge this distance, and we inevitably attempt to plumb it. Perceptual distance can become the measuring rod for conceptual distance, mental distance. And here, the possibility of apparent disinterested beholding may emerge, apparent "objectivity" is made possible, and ocular-centric and logocentric biases are sure to follow, leading to that coveted simultaneity of presentation that furnishes the idea of enduring presence, and the contrast between change and the unchanging, between time and eternity. The Western mind has gone where vision pointed it. That has been both its triumph and perhaps its greatest burden.

8

THE BODY: STOREHOUSE OF SIGNS

I. KINESTHETICS

There is also a certain sixth sense, which may well be the most fundamental and hence the most important of them all: kinesthesis. This sense is quite different, I would suspect. It is neither exactly itself nor something else. Like the other senses, it cannot stand alone, for it is integrated, it overlaps and merges with the other sensory modes; unlike those complementary senses, it has no identity of its own but takes a bit here and another bit there from the other senses. Its playground is the area of overlap, the liminality between and the fuzzy lines of mergence, which is present in the interrelationships between the five above-discussed sensory modes. In a word, it consists of the natural complements shared by all the senses, itself included. So it is the complement between the other senses and at the same time it is its own complement between itself and the other complements: it is the complement of complements.

In spite of my somewhat biting comments on language above, I must admit that language, in a manner of speaking, and given all its inherent inadequacies, contains the barest suggestion of the complements and this complement of complements. Language is by its very nature laced with all the senses and all the senses are closely interrelated in language. A term can express one sense, albeit vaguely, incompletely, and quite inadequately, and at the same time it contains, within itself, vestiges of another sense. Originally "to look" and "to see" were based on a root that meant both to see and to say; "touch" is based on the echoic representation of a knock; and, as mentioned, "taste" originally meant to touch. The important point is that we tend to think of language as chiefly visual (discrete marks against a background) and auditory (ripples in the air)—the principle senses in

Western discourse—whereas it actually involves all the senses. Writing is tactile as well as visual, speech is kinesthetic and olfactory and even to a degree gustatory in addition to auditory. So much also for linguicentric biases. Let me begin this chapter in earnest with a tale of two motilities.

It is said that during a conversation between Felix Bloch and Werner Heisenberg while they were walking along the beach, Bloch sounded out his companion about the then new theories involving the abstract mathematical structure of space. Heisenberg listened at length to the pseudo-intellectualizing of his partner, then, finally, losing patience with such imponderables, he remarked: "Space is blue and birds fly in it" (in Cole 1984:209). This story captures the essence of what some scientists consider the most profound facet of twentieth-century physics: Niels Bohr's complementary principle. Complements are a far cry from opposites, dichotomies, or binaries, for they add up to more than the sum of their parts. They are like day and night, which also include dawn and daybreak and sunrise and aurora, on the one hand, and, on the other, sunset and twilight and dusk and afterglow. They are like male and female, each of which contains something of the other and both of which are contained within either one of the two terms and at the same time are themselves and nothing but themselves.

All the colors of the spectrum add up to yield white light, yet all we need is two colors, two complementary colors, say, blue and orange, and we can get the same results. Blue to all appearances contains no orange and orange contains no blue, yet if we subtract orange from white we are left with blue, and taking blue from white, and we have orange. By the same token, remove all male chromosomes from the set of human organisms and we have pure and unadulterated—and in all probability the most incredibly bland—females; remove all female chromosomes from the set of human organisms and we have a mass of equally uninteresting males. Yet females are not simply human organisms minus males. Without female chromosomes there can be no males, and hence no human organisms. The set "human organisms" contains all female chromosomes plus that part of them that is shared with males, and it contains all male chromosomes plus that part of them that is shared with females. What they share is neither exactly male nor female, nor is it either nonmale or nonfemale: it is, in a manner of speaking, female-male-lessness. In regard to female-lessness there is something of maleness, and in regard to male-lessness there is something of femaleness. In other words, the two terms are terms of interrelatedness, mergence of one into the other, codependence. Space, then, is nothing more than a cold mathematical formula, and it is of the loveliest blue, pace Heisenberg, depending how we wish to take it, whether as physicists or poets—Heisenberg obviously was a supreme example of both. Complementarity, in sum, is the Gestalt psychologist's faces and vase image, Escher's ambiguous prints, Yin and Yang, Heisenberg's impossible knowledge of the position and the momentum of a particle at the same instant.

"What has this to do with kinesthetics?" someone pipes up. Actually, it has everything to do with kinesthetics. That is to say, it has to do with rhythm and harmony and symphony and syncope and above all with resonance. The complementary Yin-Yang icon is anything but static: it is a flux of undulating, palpitating, rhythmic movement. There is resonance here. Without the resonance there could be no complementarity, and without the complementarity there could be no movement. The sound of music, any music, as well as the wind whipping through the yellow pines along Southern Colorado mountain slopes, the Pacific waves seen from a distance along California's Highway 1, a dust devil in the Mojave desert, a flash flood along Arizona's Gila River, Pueblo Amerindian chants experienced in New Mexico, all this, and outward, to spiral galaxies millions of light years removed, none of this would exist without resonance.

Resonance is resound, rebound, vibration, reiteration, echo, and all this most likely with a to-and-fro sort of imbalance: syncope. Something begins movement, but it is pulled back by something else, that pulling back compelling the first something to reciprocate with a pull of its own, and the give-and-take goes on, without conceivable end: resonance is also an example of elegant agonistics, the Heraclitean cosmic struggle of the elements. Resonance frequently also becomes synchrony. A tuning fork puts others in the vicinity in motion to the same tune. Each member of a swirl of fireflies at some point gets its turning on and turning off in rhythm with all other members, and the phenomenon of "mutual entrainment" is in effect. A basketball team at the NCAA tournament gets a certain rhythm it has experienced a few times during the long season, and it becomes literally invincible. The list is inexhaustible, of course, but I trust the point has been made. Resonance in the proper tune allows for all parties involved to expend a minimum of energy and realize a maximum of payoff. Out-of-tune resonance can be no more than a wheel-spinning affair, or it can turn into veritable chaos. A gentle nudge with a nightstick by a police officer at a peaceful demonstration might end in a riot and much blood and perhaps a few deaths. In contrast, Martin Luther King's "I have a dream" was capable of bringing many minds into convergence along the same wavelength. Resonance. It is the stuff of life and the staff by which the universe is measured, from subnuclear particles to galaxies.

Kinesthetics is resonance manifested. The manifestation does not, indeed it cannot, make a clear-cut distinction between resonator and resonated, that is, between subject and object. Manifestation of resonance is quite like a paraphrase of Merleau-Ponty on perception, especially his notion of the "reversibility" of perceiver and perceived (or sensor and sensed, as I have been using the terms in this chapter):

> [T]he idea that every perception is doubled with a counterperception . . . is an act with two faces, one no longer knows who speaks and who listens. Speaking-listening, seeing-being seen, perceiving-being perceived circularity (it is because of it that it seems to us that perception forms itself *in the things themselves—Activity = Passivity.* (Merleau-Ponty 1968:264–65; italics in original)

What we have here is tantamount to the interrelatedness, the codependent arising, of dancer-dance during a performance, that is, the act of dancing. The dancer is virtual presence (Firstness), doing the dance, which is actually just-now-pastness (Secondness) in the process of being presented in the here-now (that is, the here-now for the observer), and both come together in the act of dancing, which is future oriented (Thirdness). Dancer and dance are interrelated, they merge into one another, and they are codependent: they are complementary. Thus they reciprocate, interacting so that the action of one on the other is reversed such that the other interacts on the one.

This interaction is what is actually seen as dancing, dancing that is a rhythmic, undulating flow as a result of the reversings of dancer into dance, and dance into dancer. This reciprocation, interaction, reversal of roles, however, is not completable, for Thirdness must remain as an unfinished symphony insofar as finite semiotic agents go. Reversibility is always incomplete, and never realized in its totality. Neither of the two sides of the complementary equation completely becomes the other such that there is identity or absolute parallelism. Rather, there is always some interruption, some hiatus, something lacking in the interaction: that's what the function of the synoptic flip-flop is all about. Perfection is not realizable in our fallible world, it would appear.

However, if the experience of two processes of becoming is never such that the processes can exactly overlap or coincide, this is no indication that

the experience is for that reason blemished, or that the experience is incapable of bringing about a wedding between the two processes. That is by
all means the beauty of experience and its value for us in a world of constant change. It is like an e. e. cummings sort of poetic line, "He danced
his did danced he." It almost contains a mirror-image symmetry, but not
quite, that is, not really. "He danced" is the dancer dancing the dance,
which, once he "did" it while in the act of carrying one with the dance, became a past act overlapping with the act that is not present, but not really,
for before it enters into the awareness of the dancer, it is now almost-but-
not-quite-immediately-past. So the "danced he" preceded the "he danced,"
though not by much, yet it follows "he danced" along the syntactic string,
hence it is neither prior nor posterior but interrelates and interacts in reciprocity, all making up the dance of past performances, the present performance, and all future performances. There is a chiasmus, a "crossing
over," in which process one side does not exactly translate into the other
side, but both retain their uniqueness at the same time that their codependency becomes evident to experience within the consciousness of the
sign interpreter, that is, at the same time that the consciousness of the ex-
periencer arises in codependency with the sign in order that there can be
an interpreter, in order that the sign can construct the interpreter and the
interpreter the sign.

For there can be no subject-object, inner-outer, here-there. These
images intellectually are Cartesian and spatially Euclidean. The proper
model, to use Merleau-Ponty's example, is topological: a glove that, if
fit for the right hand, can be turned inside-out to fit the left hand. Like
the Möbius strip or the Klein bottle, there is no inside-outside or two-,
three-, or four-dimensional space, but always something in between
(Cohen 1984). In all these cases space is like a fabric with continuous
folds in extraspatial dimensions, which allow for interpenetration of
folds. Such is the nature of the dancer, a surface consisting of contours
and folds and cavities and twists and turns in space of the Möbius strip
sort, and at the same time it is interrelated with the dance in terms of
codependence and mutual interpenetration. The dancer (present, Firstness) is there for the seeing, hearing, and smelling and feeling if the observer is close enough—in the case of her partner(s). But the dance
(past, Secondness) is never exactly either here or there but is a past unfolding that was then enfolded and is now in the process of once again
becoming unfolded as a nonempirical presentness-becoming in interrelation with the dancer who is in the now—that is, never exactly now
but always the product of anticipation and necessity that is in the

process of receding into the past—dancing (Future orientation, Third-ness) the dance, which is neither here nor there but always already somewhere else.

How in the world can we more adequately account for this process? Perhaps we can't, that is, I can't, at least in ordinary language and standard logic. Just as we cannot see our seeing, think our thinking, know our knowing, when engaged in the very acts of seeing, thinking, and knowing, so also the dancer cannot dance his/her dancing. It is a three-way process. Rather than saying "The dancer is dancing the dance," better say, "*It* dances." This is like saying "It rains," or "Live it up" or "Just do it," for there is no identifiable subject, no gender . . . but . . . No. . . . That's not it either. There is a subject, however unidentifiable, which we want to do away with entirely. So what about "There is rain going on"? But . . . that's still not it. Where, or what, is the "there"? There can be none. And to whence is it "going on"? How can there be any direction? There can't be. Not really. So how do we say it? We can't. That is, unless we have some sort of temporal and nonmodal logic and some sort of logic devoid of identity and capable of embracing terms that happen to appear in the middle ground between contradictories.[1]

Let us try to begin anew, then. The dancer is to some extent and to a greater or lesser degree subject to sensory data of the standard five classes: visual, auditory, olfactory, tactile, gustatory. While being seen, he/she plays the role of the Secondness of signs, the becoming of "sign-events out there." The dance, in contrast, is nonempirical. Yet it is subject to past experience of the same sort of dance performance or at least anticipations governed by expectations regarding what might or should transpire. This involves quality: emotions, feelings, sensations, evoked by inclinations, wishes, desires, beliefs, customary ways and means of doing things. Now we are in the domain of the Firstness of signs, what "has not yet become but might be in the act of becoming." The becoming of the dance, which involves the act of dancing toward the realization of some wished for, desired, expected performance as the result of "mind-signs in here," is of the province of the Thirdness of signs. Now, finally to get to the meat of the matter insofar as that may be possible, it is this Firstness of things that is most appropriately kinesthetic, if indeed it is possible to place kinesthesia in any category at all. Kinesthesia is in the body but it projects outside. Within the body, of course, there are natural rhythms and flows: the brain-mind engenders wave patterns, muscles expand and contract, cells subdivide, the heart beats, the lungs heave, the guts undergo peristalsis, the bladder inflates and deflates, the liver takes in and puts out.

In terms of brainmind processes there are uncountable instances of kinesthetic rhythms and flows: from Hadamard's (1945) study of creativity in mathematics to Italo Calvino's "Blood, Sea," "Mitosis," "Meiosis," and "Death" in *T Zero* (1969), and from the painful rhythms of Beckett's characters in *Molloy, Malone Dies, The Unnamable* (1955) to the free flow dynamics of Cuban writer Guillermo Cabrera Infante's *Three Trapped Tigers* (1970). In terms of brainmind processes engendering bodymind processes, some of the most effective instances are found in fictional or imaginary situations in TV and film. I allude to the *camera lenta*. In *Butch Cassidy and the Sundance Kid,* when the two main characters—played by Paul Newman and Robert Redford—kill some Bolivian soldiers, it seems to take forever for them to fall. With eyes fixed on the screen, you can feel the violence, the pain, the anguish, you feel it in the guts, your body reacts to it, you are moved. During Tom Cruise's effort to walk in a scene in the Veterans' Hospital in *Born on the Fourth of July,* you sense your own legs contracting, your torso twists slightly, your jaws tighten somewhat, your head moves a little to one side, your shoulders become a tad tense. You watch, the character makes futile efforts to overcome his paralysis, dragging his inert legs along the floor. Where are you, actually, while you are engrossed in the scene? When are you? Who are you? Rent the moving film *My Left Foot,* shove it into that familiar cavity in your VCR, and sit back and watch: your entire bodymind can't help but become involved. Of course, the TV is no faithful substitute for the big screen, but you'll get some of the basic effects. The main character suffering cerebral palsy sucks you into his excruciating agony when trying to accomplish what would otherwise be the most simple of tasks.

Of the five customary sensory channels, for obvious reasons touch is most closely related to kinesthetics. That, at least, is Merleau-Ponty's conclusion, and I would tend to concur. With respect to touch, Merleau-Ponty scholar Sue Cataldi writes that touch is

> the mother of the senses; and our skin is the oldest, largest, and most sensitive of our sensory organs. Our sense of touch was the first to develop and through it we acquired knowledge of a vast array of textures—from the scratch of wool to the sleekness of satin, from the slipperiness of soap to the goo of glue, from the scrub of a beard to the down of a feather. Through touch we are also sensitive to pressure; differentiations in shape; variations in weight and thickness; fluctuations in fluidity, aridity, and temperature; and distinguishable styles of movements. (Cataldi 1984:125)

Tactile sensations—and in an exceedingly more specialized way, gustatory sensations—are unique insofar as there must be an object body in actual contact with the subject body. But it is ambiguous also, since, as Merleau-Ponty argues in great detail, there is no absolute distinction between the touching body and the body touched. The right hand touches the left hand. Or is it the other way round? What is touching and what is being touched? A hand caresses a cat; the cat arcs its back so as to push against a hand that happened to appear, and the cat begins purring. A hand holds a flower; the flower comes in contact with a hand in terms of something that can aid it in its reproductive process, that will consume it, that will brush against it and pass on, . . . or whatever, depending on the touch of the stroker. A hand picks up a stone on the beach; the stone comes in contact with a hand in such a way that its concrete existence at this space-time juncture becomes manifest before its general essence as merely a stone among other stones makes its way into a universe that was, is, and will be just what it is. In every case the touched interacts with the toucher just as the toucher presumably exercises its hegemony over the universe of the touched.

There is a reciprocity, a reflexivity, a reversibility that is not in effect to the same degree in seeing, hearing, and smelling, since concrete physical contact is not as pronounced—of course gustatory sensations usually involve physical contact, but it is limited to a specialized, and relatively small, portion of the body's surface (Merleau-Ponty 1962, 1968).

II. MORE THAN MERELY TACTILE

However, there is more to the issue than merely touch, the tactile, with regard to the kinesthetic. There is haptic perception, which is chiefly tactile, but it also includes certain aspects of all the sensory modes. Haptic perception is to a degree the touched environment, to be sure. But the touching also includes a spatio-temporal sense of the environment in terms of its possibilities for being seen, heard, smelled, and tasted.

Wolfgang Yourgrau (1966) presents an extraordinarily perceptive paper, arguing that a non-Euclidean sense of space and spatial relationships is more fundamental than and precedes Euclidean geometry in the development of the human mind. In his words:

> [T]opological relations are grasped much earlier and more easily than Euclidean shapes. Our education and our environment make us believe that there is a smooth, natural continuity between perceptual and representational relationships. . . . [T]he predominance of Euclidean geometry in our training has created deeply entrenched misorientations. There is a

tremendous gap between haptic perception and mental representation, since the latter invokes the existence of objects in their physical absence. Semantic relations, image, thought, differentiation of diverse signs or symbols not only occur after haptic experience, but they differ fundamentally from it. (Yourgrau 1966:498)

He then goes on to summarize:

> [T]he observation of . . . children's behavior patterns suggests that the "India-rubber" world of the topologist and of Einstein, though highly abstract to the uninitiated, and the haptic perception of the child are much closer to one another than haptic perception is to Euclidean shapes and spaces with their rigid properties. . . . [T]he child recognizes objects haptically at an early age. But once the level of representation is reached, the aid of speech is invoked and thereby all doors opened to Euclidean commitment. (Yourgrau 1966:500)

It hardly needs saying that this haptic perception—perception of an object through a sense of touch, in the absence of visual stimulation—most properly pertains to Firstness and its extension into Secondness, while Euclidean geometry and Galilean science fall within the private domain of that imperialistic form of linguicentric Secondness extended into Thirdness, which lies behind—or is it beyond?—the world of haptic perception and visual appearances. Yourgrau's words also remind us that Einsteinian finite but unbounded space is more closely aligned to the pre-Euclidean finite but boundless sphere of certain Greek thinkers than it is to classical conceptions of space. In a certain manner, it can be said that Euclidean space is to an Erector set as non-Euclidean or Einsteinian space is to a lump of clay that can be kneaded, twisted, stretched, and distorted. Nevertheless, rigid Euclidean space, with its infinite extension as a void, a receptacle to be filled with those autonomous, indivisible, impenetrable spheres, the atoms of the universe racing to and fro, was destined to become over the centuries firmly entrenched in the West's history.[2]

Yourgrau alludes to studies by Geza Révész (1957) and Jean Piaget (1973) demonstrating that haptic perception is more fundamental and prior to visual perception and hence prior also to Euclidean space as a homogenous medium than has been conceded by Western thought. Things in the haptic space of the child are synchretic, unanalyzed wholes, whose parts are as yet unrelated. Interrelations between the parts come later, when the child has been properly indoctrinated into Euclidean space of boundedness and connectedness. Only then do notions of rigid shapes and sizes, distances, angles, and projective relations become part of the child's perception, which is now chiefly visual, haptic perception having waned in the process. Studies by the likes of Jerome Bruner (1956, 1986, 1987), Howard Gardner (1983), and Richard L. Gregory (1966, 1970, 1981) further elaborate and support this view.[3]

The direction we now seem to be taking might suggest that haptic perception is intimately related to the body while visual perception is closer to the affairs of the mind—though actually, there is no mind-body distinction here. If the West has come increasingly to prioritize mind over body, and as a logical consequence the visual over the haptic, language over other communicative media, propositional knowledge over schematic and imagistic knowledge, and symbolicity over indexicality and iconicity, perhaps the time is ripe, I must repeat, for a more balanced conception. This balance is most effectively forthcoming through a bodymind interrelatedness, interactivity, and interdependency rather than the traditional contradiction between body and mind. The bodymind complementarity pervades all levels, from inner to outer and from biological to psychological to phenomenological. In this sense I concur with Mark Johnson when he writes:

> [M]eaning includes patterns of embodied experience and preconceptual structures of our sensibility (i.e., our mode of perception, of orienting ourselves, and of interacting with other objects, events, or persons). These embodied patterns do not remain private or peculiar to the person who experiences them. Our community helps us interpret and codify many of our felt patterns. They become shared cultural modes of experience and help to determine the nature of our meaningful, coherent understanding of our "world." (1987:14)

The "embodied" and "felt [i.e., haptic] patterns," having become "shared cultural modes of experience," are precisely what the meaning of one's environment is all about. Though all the sensory channels are brought into play with respect to haptic perception, the tactile is paramount, given its demand for concrete contact.

Touch involves haptic sensations, and haptic sensations are intimately involved in kinesthetics, especially since the time and space of affectivity regarding the entire bodymind is most apparent in the time and space of tactility. There is more overlap between the touched and the touching than between the seeing and the seen, the hearing and the heard, and so on. The felt object is never entirely divorced from the act of feeling, which projects out into the environment and at the same time draws inward: there is proximity and at the same time distance; there is a there and at the same time what is there is here; there is an unfolded outside that at the same time enfolds with the enfolded bodymind inside that is unfolding in order to sense the unfolded outside (Merleau-Ponty 1962:316). This oscillating there-here, outside-inside, touched-touching is a continual shifting, a vague, rhythmic dynamic of ambiguous reversibility of experience. In Sue Cataldi's Merleau-Ponty vocabulary, this spiraling, shifting, undulatory to and fro of experience occurs

> because the two sides of tactility are immediately and directly *experienced* as occupying or as sharing *between* them, the *same* common space—the same flesh. Tactile experience is corporeal experience, and in tactile experience, we cannot deceive ourselves about the extent to which our bodily flesh is embedded and engrossed in the flesh of the world or about the extent to which the flesh of the world is engrossed and embedded in us. (Cataldi 1984:119; italics in original)[4]

Touching is neither entirely active nor entirely passive. It is movement that touches and movement that is touched. What is apparently now the outside of the Möbius strip is the inside from another view (Merleau-Ponty 1968:256). So depending on the view any spot on the strip is in a manner of speaking either one or the other, both one and the other, and neither the one nor the other. However, cutting a hole in the strip provides access from outside to inside and vice versa, and the one is enfolded into the other while it unfolds out to the other in order to sense it. Topologically, there is no absolute priority of either "outside" or "inside," "enfolded" or "unfolded," "here" or "there," "now" or "then." Topologically, everything is connected with everything else in a codependent, interrelated, mutually interpenetrating way.

While this characteristic is most evident regarding tactile sensations, it is by no means absent in other sensory modes. You are, for example, struck by the brilliant array of an Arizona sunset, a rendition of a Bach fugue, the smooth tang of a fine wine, the aroma of a freshly cut rose. You are apprehending the phenomena and they are taking hold of you; you feel them and they are the felt that is entering you; you are enfolded in them and they enfold themselves in you; they are the "outside" that is becoming "inside" and you are the "inside" that projects "outside." You are affected, "touched," but not tactually or tactically. You are "touched," but "touched" haptically, you are "touched" kinesthetically, both inside and outside. Your entire past condenses into this affectivity here-now, the entirety of your surroundings converges into your being "touched" now. You, like "I," make a mark, a distinction, between some aspect of your surroundings and everything else, and you indicate (index) it as such-and-such; that which was distinguished and indicated is in turn that which makes of you a distinction and an indication setting you apart from your surroundings. The "I"-other distinction, however, is artificial. The "I" before the distinction is what it is (icon), just as the other is what it is (icon). As repositories of Firstness, they converge and merge with one another, they mutually penetrate each other, they are interrelatedly codependent, such that any distinction remains exceedingly vague unless a somewhat arbitrary line of demarcation is made.

Now, what I have written appears to be a matter more of body than of mind. But I repeat, body and mind are inseparable—they are bodymind—in this process of enfolding and unfolding, of the outside becoming the inside and vice versa. It is a matter of body awareness, of the mind's mindfulness of what it is doing in conjunction with the body's doings. Like eyesight and hearing, the degree of body awareness varies widely from person to person. Some people are highly body-conscious; others relatively body-blind. Psychological factors often distort our internal body maps, causing certain parts to appear larger or smaller than they really are. Drugs, fever, and delirium may radically alter our sense of the shape and size of the body. By far the greatest mismatch between body image and body fact is the phantom limb phenomenon, in which an amputated arm or leg still appears to be present. An amputee patient may claim he feels a wristwatch on his missing arm. Admiral Nelson, who lost his left arm in the Battle of Trafalgar, continued to feel its presence for the rest of his life—he actually regarded the existence of his phantom limb as proof of the existence of the soul.

Attempts to create maps of human bodily possibilities have been few. Outside the field of human factors engineering, the work of Rudolf Laban and later that of Ray Birdwhistell is particularly noteworthy (as is that of E. T. Hall and Gregory Bateson during the 1950s and 1960s). In 1928 Laban published *Schrifttanz* (Written Dance) in Vienna, introducing a new graphic system for mapping the possibilities of human movement (Laban 1975).[5] Laban visualized the dancer enclosed in a "kinesphere"—the space of all dance possibilities, the martial artist's "danger zone"—inside of which the joints of the body traced complicated paths. To Laban these paths resembled ribbons winding through a crystalline lattice. Because of the body's symmetry, a common "dance crystal" for these somatic meanderings was the idosohedron, the regular twenty-sided platonic solid.

As developed by Laban and extended by his followers, "Labanotation" continues to be one of the most used body alphabets for the choreography of modern dance.

Ray Birdwhistell is an American anthropologist specializing in nonverbal communication. The goal of his "kinesics" project, initiated in the early 1950s, was to develop a methodology that would exhaustively analyze the communicative behavior of the body (Birdwhistell 1970) He found that Labanotation, originally developed for the annotation of dance movements, was not entirely suitable for the analysis of casual face-to-face communication. He began his own system of kinesics by dividing the body into eight zones and inventing symbols to describe the motional possibilities of each zone. One of the advantages of a comprehensive movement map such as kinesics is that it increases one's skill as an observer by drawing attention to normally ignored gestures such as subtle neck and shoulder movements. Birdwhistell, who claimed to be able to distinguish fifteen different degrees of eyelid closure, used his system to describe various styles of symptom presentation in Kentucky clinics, the American adolescent "courtship dance," body change when speaking a foreign language, and interruption strategies during therapy.[6]

Undoubtedly some of the most awkward experiences that the new mind-link technology might be expected to engender will be the presentation to human consciousness of nonhuman body images. It may not be so difficult to take on the body schemas of dogs and cats, since their body plans are not dissimilar to our own, but to put on the body of a centipede or octopus may be a real challenge to our kinesthetic imaginations. More difficult still will be the experience of mindlinking with microorganisms. Amoebas, for instance, have no fixed limbs at all, moving about, exuding pseudopods, and engulfing food particles by controlling the local viscosity of their cellular contents. What would it feel like to move around as a conscious bog of goo? The possibility of assuming the body image of so formless a creature would demand development of an entire new kinesthesis, a new sense of haptic perception, a completely new bodymind.

III. BODY, MIND, WORD, WORLD

Maurice Merleau-Ponty was a great admirer of Paul Cézanne. Common ground between them consists of their rebellion vis-à-vis the long-standing Western-Aristotelian dictate that the world is "out there," available to the properly cogitating mind "in here." Merleau-Ponty and Cézanne believed that to know the world is, in the terminology of this inquiry, to know the codependence, the mutual interpenetration, the convergence and interrelationships and interactions, with respect to "inner space" and "outer space," "inner time" and "outer chronometric time," or in a semiotic way of putting it, between "thought-signs" and "sign-events" (Merrell 1991c, 1995a, 1996).

Cézanne and Merleau-Ponty, like few painters and philosophers, challenged the West's inner/outer and subject/object and mind/body dichotomies. Merleau-Ponty writes that "quality, light, color, and depth which are there before us are there only because they awaken an echo in our body and because the body welcomes them" (1964:22). And he tells us of Cézanne that "we cannot imagine how a mind could paint. It is by lending his body to the world that the artist changes the world into paintings" (1964:16). Sensing, genuinely sensing—I must continue to write "sensing" rather than "perceiving," "seeing," or some other term in order to avoid the customary stereotypes and premises—is a matter of "sensing" from the "inside," which is really no "inside," for the "inside" is everywhere. And that which is "sensed" is "outside," but there is really no "outside" in the traditional manner of speaking: it is nowhere, for it knows no limits—limits of which we can be aware, that is—and it is everywhere, for it is "inside" and at the same time it is elsewhere. Merleau-Ponty cites Paul Klee, for whom the painter does not simply sense the world, but, in reciprocity, the world senses the painter, and the painter's act of painting is a breaking out from the "inside," which is to say that the "outside" breaks into the "inside" (1964:31). There is no Lacanian or Foucauldian "gaze" here, nor is there merely "sensor" and "sensed." Rather, it is a process of "sensing happening," a "happening of sensing," a simultaneous enfolding and unfolding of some "here happening" and some other "there happening," but there is really neither "here" nor "there," there is just "sensing happening"—relate this to the act of dancing as discussed above. To give my language a Deleuze-Guattari (1983, 1987) slant, the bird-watcher's binoculars give her visual sensing capability approaching that of the keen-eyed exotic bird, and they meet, they interrelate, interact, interpenetrate, they are codependent, they are "happening," they are "becoming-events." The bird-watcher happens to become who she is becoming because of the bird's becoming; the bird is becoming because of the bird-watcher's becoming. Their becoming is codependent with the becoming of their immediate surroundings, their remote surroundings, the continent, the oceans and other continents, the earth, the planets and the sun, the universe. An apparently insignificant becoming is all-becoming.

More adequately stated, perhaps, it is all a matter of rhythm-becoming. A sense of rhythm-becoming is as instrumental in breaking down customary habits of thought as is the inside/outside, subject/object dissolution. There has been surprisingly little investigation of musical rhythm on any scientific basis, but it seems clear from what is known that rhythm is an alternative means for transmitting an experience in such a way that the experience is re-created in the person receiving it. This re-creation is not merely an abstraction, but a physical effect on the organism—on the heart beat, on the breathing, on the entire body, on the physical patterns of the brain. From the sheer intellectual force of Bach's re-creating the Pythagorean harmony of the spheres to so-called primitive music and the likes of jazz, which according to Theodore Adorno (1973) is evoked by a desire to transcend reason and surrender to the body; from Plato's exclusion of music of the body—of women, slaves, teenagers—and St. Augustine's suspicion of music of all forms; to the guttural outpourings at a rock concert; the same tension exists. A tension between what should be—ideal perfection, the mind's imposition on nature—and what might be—natural rhythms, the body in tune with itself.

This tension is hardly anywhere more evident than in the scandal caused by New World music and dance, in part of Amerindian and African origin, upon its introduction to repressive Old World practices during the seventeenth century. The *ciaccona,* for example, of Peruvian Amerindian and perhaps also of Afro-American origin, was introduced into Spain at the turn of the century, and shortly thereafter it sparked a dance craze throughout Europe. Susan McClary writes of the *ciaccona* that:

> On the one hand, it was celebrated as liberating bodies that had been stifled by the constraints of Western civilization; on the other, it was condemned as obscene, as a threat to Christian mores. But most sources concurred that its rhythms—once experienced—were irresistible; it was banned temporarily in 1615 on grounds of its "irredeemably infectious lasciviousness." . . . Nor was social pedigree a sure defense against contamination; even noble ladies ere said to succumb to its call. Like soul music at a later historical moment, the *ciaccona* crossed over cautiously guarded class and racial boundaries. Whatever the *ciaccona* signified in its original contexts, it quickly came to be associated in Europe (by friends and foes alike) with forbidden bodily pleasures and potential social havoc. (McClary 1995:87).

What seems to be most disconcerting in the *ciaccona,* the *sarabande,* and other music and dance imported to the Old World from the Americas is, to re-evoke the term, syncope. These rhythms are a dance between hesitation and assertion, affirmation and denial, stability and instability, continuity and discontinuity, regularity and unsuspected breaks, motion and suspended animation. The body experienced tentative hoverings, the disequilibrium, the reestablishing of stability, the unanticipated detour through one beat and into another one, the bold entry of a new cadence and delicate nuances. This sort of music, as would be expected, met resistance at the pens of the Pythagorean purists of Enlightenment ideals. But the bulges and cavities, the somewhat symmetrical but flawed contours and the flows of the body resisted the crystalline purity of ideal musical forms. McClary concludes her essay with the observation that relocating music in the body is the most adequate way of understanding music history. Music, she says,

> can only maintain its Pythagorean purity if we erase the bodies it shapes and that shape it. To be sure, studies based on contingencies such as the highly mutable body are bound to seem messy in comparison with the mathematical charts we like to flaunt. But they also promise to make visible and audible the power music has exercised in the social world. And because of the extraordinary specificity of musical artifacts, such work also can contribute heavily to projects seeking to reconstruct the history of the body. (McClary 1995:101)

The body. Flows and folds. Function and form. Series and breaks. Continuities and fissures. The seat of rhythm, vibrations "in here" in sympathy with vibrations "out there." Once again, ultimately it's a matter of resonances, and unbalanced syncopated ones at that. During the humdrum of everyday life we are hardly aware of the resonances surrounding us. The earth and moon are resonant with the sun and the entire solar system, which is resonant with other systems within our galaxy, which is resonant with other galaxies. Chlorophyll molecules in plants vibrate to the tune of red and blue light and absorb them, reflecting the remainder, consisting of the green frequencies. These same plants absorb green and reflect other colors during the autumn season. The colors of white light pass through countless droplets of water to spread out into a prism that is magnified into a rainbow. Ultraviolet light vibrates in harmony with the molecules of glass that allows only visible rays to get through; suntan lotion absorbs that same ultraviolet light before it gets to the skin, thus preventing painful sunburn. Electrons in one state resonate with electrons in another state of the same atom provisionally to keep it in harmony with its surroundings. From the microscopic to the cosmic, resonance rules.

But we are oblivious to many of these empathic vibrations. The earth spins around its center at 1,600 kilometers per second and around the sun at 110,000 kilometers per second, but we don't feel it. A 747 zooms through the air at four or five hundred miles per hour, but when inside it you are hardly aware of the movement. You don't ordinarily notice your blood flow, heart beat, lung heaves, small muscular twitches. But when the aircraft hits an air pocket, when the asthmatic's air passage becomes congested, when the heart goes into irregular syncopations, awareness of disrupted resonances abruptly makes its entry. We mindlessly and blissfully go through life assuming things are as they should be, unaware of most of the violent Heraclitean struggles of the universe. Mindfulness is the exception, rather than the norm, it would appear. The trick, however, is to enhance mindfulness and minimize mindlessness. How so?

In search of an answer, let us further integrate Peirce's sign decalogue with the senses as discussed in this and the last chapter.

THE DECALOGUE VIEWED FROM
THE WORLD OF THE SENSES

I. SCENTS AGAIN, AND SIGN 111

The revelation of paradox (of the both-ands and the neither-nors from preceding chapters) does not mark disaster but, rather, opportunity. When such opportunity knocks, it customarily knocks only once. It has no patience with indecision. It wants to be where the action is. And the action is where paradox is embraced. If not, the party is soon dead, and rigor mortis begins to set in.

Peirce's decalogue is nothing if at its heart it is not vague, ambiguous, even contradictory and inconsistent, but always incomplete. So there is no hope that we will have the truth and the whole truth, wrapped, sealed, and ready for delivery. But the good news is that there is really no need for hope ever to wane. The vaguest of the vague in regard to the decalogue is found, as would be expected, in the beginning, with sign 111, and the vaguest of the vague in regard to the senses are undoubtedly olfactory signs. Smells, I suggested in chapter 7, are the closest of all to "speechless sense" (Howes 1989, 1990). They are by nature relatively formless, hence they naturally resist all attempts at classification or articulation. They are liminal, not easily classified; therefore they are easily the focus of taboos (Douglas 1966:95, Leach 1972, Turner 1967:97). In fact, it has been suggested that odors bypass all forms of coded communication; in addition to their lending themselves so readily to social taboos, they are also highly individual, idiosyncratic, and have much to do with personal history (Sperber 1975:118). And yet, Lewis Thomas (1980:42) could write that "the act of smelling something, anything, is remarkably like the act of thinking itself." This "inarticulate thinking," thinking of the implicit, tacit sort, we must suppose, is what one knows how to do without being able to say that it is done in such-and-such a way.

Smells are at their level best of the nature of quality or qualisigns, feeling, sentiment, emotion, icons. In other words, they are relatively continuous, in contrast to discontinuous signs, the paradigm case of which are found in linearly developed language strings. They therefore specialize in signs 111, 211, and 311. From that point we move on to signs of taste, sound, touch, and sight—the most abstract and dichotomizing of them all—not to mention kinesthetics. By no means, however, do I wish to give the impression that signs of the senses fall into a neat set of pigeon-holes. Nothing could be further from my intentions. The signs in question converge and merge, they fuse into one another, they intermingle, they are codependent for their very emergence into the light of day. Hence if olfactory signs are the most basic (continuous), this is no indication of their inferiority or superiority. It is a matter of the prevailing socio-economic conditions, and of the nature of customs, conventions, peer pressures, power groups that be, oppressive church and/or state, a domineering father, or whatever. At any rate, it is most likely a safe bet that smells are closer to 111 than any other type of sign arising out of the senses.[1]

Scents: so near and yet so far, so familiar and at the same time so remote, given their zone of unsayability. They get you in the guts. They appeal to the most "primitive" of emotions, desires, needs, demands. Thus they necessarily border on the ineffable; they exercise a collective as well as deeply personal appeal; they are quite comfortable with their dwelling place in signs 111 and slightly outward. Of course, the other senses begin at that point as well: the almost immediate sensation of bitterness, the soft texture of silk, the piercing qualities of a prolonged high C note, a vague image of blueness. All mark the beginning of something that might prove to be interesting, hence at 211 they become dimly sensed as something other, at 221 they grab us, and so on.

At the deepermost zone of 111 where scents are at their best, I would submit, each of us is in a certain manner of speaking both everybody and nobody. This is reminiscent of Jorge Luis Borges's Shakespeare, who, after having become everybody, realized he was nobody, of Nietzsche's and Walt Whitman's "I" that is everyone and everything. Oliver Sacks writes of patients suffering from Tourette syndrome, people who become everybody and in the process lose their own self, becoming nobody. Lacking normal protective barriers of inhibition and a line of demarcation between self and other, the Touretter's ego is destined to a life of bombardment by selves from all angles simultaneously. If any form or fashion of identity can be had by them, it is hardly more than a David Humean fiction and can last no more than a fleeting fraction of a second. Like Zelig from Woody

Allen's movie of the same name, they ephemerally take on the personalities of all those around them. They become a whirlwind of identities, their own identity having been lost in a labyrinth of gestures, glances, and voice inflections. Sacks concludes:

> The super-Touretter . . . is compelled to fight, as no one else is, simply to survive—to become an individual, and survive as one, in face of constant impulse. He may be faced, from earliest childhood, with extraordinary barriers to individuation, to becoming a real person. The miracle is that, in most cases, he succeeds—for the powers of survival, of the will to survive, and to survive as a unique inalienable individual, are absolutely, the strongest in our being: stronger than any impulses, stronger than disease. (Sacks 1987:124–25)

At this level of gushing, fluctuating sensations, there is no lasting differentiation, no (iconic) distinctions in terms of self-other have been made, no (indexical) indications in terms of what that other may be. There is no more than flux, sheer possibility. Here, we would suppose, the silent primal scream of scents, within the domain of spontaneous gut actions and reactions, is on its home court and giving its most accomplished performance.

II. OTHER ICONS

If odors are at their best beginning with sign 111, within the sphere of sign 211 kinesthetics begins putting on its most proficient act, though in academic circles these signs of the body have often been ignored—Howard Gardner (1983), for one, puts bodily-kinesthetic knowing in his seven classes of "multiple intelligences"—though he virtually ignores smells and tastes.[2]

A mime performance by the great Marcel Marceau draws on a form of intelligence that we all know but ordinarily do not notice, that we can recognize but ordinarily cannot adequately describe, for it is virtually indescribable. Kinesthetic knowing is by and large tacit knowing, knowing that in many instances can be taught by example, but hardly by explicit instruction. It is learned not exclusively by explicit means but by following examples, mimicking the master, imagining and feeling the body going through certain motions and then actually bringing about those motions—like the athlete imagining his/her performance before actually stepping onto the track to do it. Motility all. (Think of comedians—Chapman,

Keaton, Cantinflas, Tomlin, Carson, Burnett, Cosby, Williams—and their extralinguistic, kinesthetic capacity for sending signs to their audience.)

Regarding this kinesthetic knowing, there is not (yet) any clear-cut distinction between the physical and the mental, the active and the reflective, feeling and intellection, or between tone (Firstness) and token (Secondness) and type (Thirdness). These distinctions are not as sharp as they are in our Western cultures. Indeed, perhaps no culture in the history of humankind has suffered from our preconception, so deeply embedded as it is in our very psyche as a result of the Cartesian legacy, that thought is the universal imperative, and everything else trails along behind as best it can. But we do not and cannot live by the force of mind alone. The body has its own form of knowing and thinking much of which is to the mind unknown and unthought. This form of knowing and thinking is paramount in skilled activities. Take the basketball player in action on the court, the machinist at her workbench, the surgeon conducting an operation. They are tunnel-mindedly focused on the task at hand and the signs it involves—a drive toward the basket, the diameter of the piece on the lathe, the brain tumor now revealed to the eye.

At the same time, they are subsidiarily attuned to a myriad array of signs in the near vicinity—for example, the opposing small forward moving over to take a charge, the piece's diameter here in relation to its size and shape elsewhere, the signs on the instruments nearby (focal and subsidiary awareness, from Polanyi 1958). The skilled performance submits to the performer's central control tower, and in near simultaneity signs are picked up from the environment, with awareness that the unexpected always stands a chance of occurring. Although after the fact the performer may be able, with a greater or lesser degree of verbal aplomb, to describe and explain his/her actions, during the performance the body did what it does best, in many instances with hardly a nod to the mind, which was simply not nimble enough to keep up with the action. Along these lines, Ruth Benedict reports on teaching children calligraphy in Japan. The instructor takes the child's hand and guides her through an ideograph, thus giving her a "feel" for the activity. This exercise is carried out before words of encouragement and explicit instruction enter the picture. In this manner body learning to a degree precedes mind learning, implicitness precedes explicitness, signs downward from 311 precede signs of greater complexity (Benedict 1946:269).

Playing a musical instrument, dancing, acting out a part in a play or a movie, going through a gymnastics sequence, all are more kinesthetic than cognitive, more a matter of feeling than form, more the product of action

than reason or reflection. And they are, during the course of their enact-
ment, chiefly wordless, symbolless. Iconicity is paramount, with an occasional tinge of indexicality. In this vein, Norman Mailer writes of the
boxer:

> There are languages other than words, language of symbol and languages of
> nature. There are languages of the body. And prize-fighting is one of them.
> A prizefighter . . . speaks with a command of the body which is as detached,
> subtle, and comprehensive in its intelligence as any exercise of the mind.
> [He expresses] himself with wit, style, and an aesthetic flair for surprise
> when he boxes with his body. Boxing is a dialogue between bodies, [it] is a
> rapid debate between two sets of intelligences. (in Lowe 1977:255)

The body, intelligent? Yes. An intelligence of which, when the body is
doing what it does, the mind is in large part unaware. Dialogue? Yes also.
Silent dialogue. Semiotic give-and-take without the need of words, like
two squirrels playing hide-and-seek around a maple tree, like two pigeons
doing their courtship thing, like two dogs nipping in a mock fight. There
is a show of signs and a response, which elicits a counterresponse, and the
action goes on. Detached, subtle, and comprehensive? Of course. The
mind is too slow to become actively involved. The movements are of an at-
tenuation, a refinement, that defies language; they are more subtle than
the most carefully honed rhetorical figure, which, however finespun, still
depends upon language. And comprehensive, for the body can take in, and
react to, a barrage of signs with hardly a moment's notice, quicker than the
most powerful computer. Motility: an inner sense of movement, the visu-
alizer who imagines pole-vaulting at 20 feet and then does it, a kinesthetic
feel for things, the body in harmony with the mind: bodymind.

The act of doing science is much different than boxing, of course. But
the process goes through the same semiotic channels. French philosopher
of science Pierre Duhem puts it thusly: Suppose we ask a layperson who
has never studied physics to

> Enter a laboratory; approach the table crowded with an assortment of ap-
> paratus, an electric cell, silk-covered copper wire, small cups of mercury,
> spools of wire, a mirror mounted on an iron bar; . . . the iron oscillates, and
> the mirror attached to it throws a luminous band upon a celluloid scale; the
> forward-backward motion of this luminous spot enables the physicist to ob-
> serve the minute oscillations of the iron bar. But ask him what he is doing.
> Will he answer "I am studying the oscillations of an iron bar which carries
> a mirror"? No, he will answer that he is measuring the electric resistance of

the spools. If you are astonished, if you ask him what his words mean, *what relation they have with the phenomena he has been observing and which you have noted at the same time as he,* he will answer that your question requires a long explanation and that you should take a course in electricity. (Duhem 1954:248; italics in original)

Before all the items of the physicist's laboratory could pull together, cohere, and organize themselves for—allow themselves to be organized by— the physicist, he was required to undertake countless hours of apprenticeship. It is not that the physicist and layperson saw the same things but did not make the same thing of them. The layperson ignorant of physics could make hardly anything of them at all. If the physicist wished to teach his visitor everything he knows about his experiment, he would have to begin at the beginning with crash courses in mathematics and physics, and end with the theory of electricity. He must verbalize his knowledge, including his actual physical activities at his place of work. Only then will the layperson be equipped with the necessary intellectual tools to put the cluster of objects before her eyes in their proper place. And, I cannot overemphasize, this instruction is necessarily linguistic, consisting chiefly of symbolic signs (which, we must not forget, contain within themselves icons and indices).

Studies of perception, cognition—especially of the "propositional" variety—and language have dominated psychology and neurophysiology over the past decades, while body intelligence, tacit knowing, and implicit meanings have been relegated to the back seat. Physical doings pertain to the "primitive" function of the brain, whereas "high" cortical functions are the domain of the mind. At least that has been the customary story. However, Roger Sperry (1969, 1970) and a host of psychologists argued a few decades ago that mind works should be considered means to ends, those ends being executed actions by the brain or the body—the problem is that this formulation maintains a mind/brain and mind/body split, which I do not. Instead of physical activity as a subsidiary form playing out the role designed by "higher" focal, cognitive imperatives, cerebration should be considered a means of giving possible future direction in order to enhance performance and for survival value (see Clynes 1978, Evarts 1973).

It is worth noting that at the so-called lower levels the senses are fused and confused. This is suggested by the roots of the words we use in artificially classifying the senses: as we have observed, to hear is based on a root meaning of to look, to see originally meant both to see and to say, to touch comes from the notion of an echo such as results from a knock, taste was in the beginning a touch. The interrelations are hardly exhaustible. Newly born infants do not make the distinctions with which we have become so familiar. Babies will try to look at and grab a sound, and there is relatively less distinction between taste (contact with the tongue) and touch and sight (Rivlin and Gravelle 1984:85–86). At this level, it seems safe to say that kinesthetics is intermingled with all the senses, especially those of chiefly iconic nature.

In part for this reason bodily-kinesthetic activity is of numbing complexity. Howard Gardner (1983:210) writes that it calls upon "the coordination of a dizzying variety of neural and muscular components in a highly differentiated and integrated fashion." For example, quickly toss a ball against a wall and retrieve it. There is intricate interaction between the eye and the hand. They work in coordination with one another, from feedback to response and anticipation of more feedback. Voluntary movements demand almost instantaneous comparisons and contrasts and action regarding similarities and differences. The eye and hand codependently rise, arise, to the occasion in order to do their thing in rapid-fire fashion, while the mind can do no more than trail along behind them. If you're a little rusty at this sort of thing, practice it a little, and your game will improve. It will improve because your relatively sluggish mind has had time to appraise the situation—at conscious as well as nonconscious levels, and perhaps linguistically and perhaps not—and formulate instructions to the brain-body so next time they will perform with greater aplomb:

> Much voluntary motor activity thus features the subtle interaction between perceptual and motor systems. At least some activity, however, proceeds at so rapid a clip that feedback from perceptual or kinesthetic systems cannot be used. Particularly in the case of overlearned, automatic, highly skilled, or involuntary activities, the whole sequence may be "preprogrammed" so that it can unfold as a seamless unit with only the slightest modifications possible in light of information from the sensory systems. Only such highly programmed sequences will allow activities of the pianist, the typist, or the athlete, each of whom depends upon lengthy sequences of movement that unfold at great speed. (Gardner 1983:211)

Some exceptional youngsters, "idiot savants" or autistic children, may be totally cut off from their community in terms of symbols. But with respect to indices and especially icons, they may have remarkable powers, especially in the area of kinesthetic activity and spatial knowledge. Their paintings may be worthy of the greatest surrealists, their feats as *bricoleurs* are astounding, such as creative electrical wiring, making a windmill out of a clock, creating musical compositions, reading a map to perfection with one perceptual grasp, giving the tally of a few dozen marbles strewn on the floor after a second or so. There is need of little to no language here. No talking is necessary. There is just sensing, knowing with the bodybrain, feeling what there is to feel in the bones, knowing with the certainty of the so-called lower organisms who have not learned disbelief, skepticism, cynicism, nihilism. In other words, there is no negation, contradiction, vicious circularity, paradox. There is just grace, the good grace of simply and very subtly doing what there is to do.

As I suggested in the foregoing chapter, no performance activity calls on bodily-kinesthetic signs of 211 and downward more than dance. No art form makes such use of the body; few recreational activities place more emphasis on form; few athletic events stress aesthetics so much; no ritual is more into rhythm more than dance. Dance is a patterned sequence of nonverbal body language that has a purpose, but it is hardly utilitarian. The language is intentional, though the intention hardly involves more than rhythm, it is aesthetic though there is rarely any material product "out there"; the product is manifested by the body itself. No two art forms can be more effectively combined than dance and music, though each form can do quite well without the other one: whether listening to music or dancing, dance and music can be respectively in the bodymind, nonetheless.

Hardly any art form, moreover, is more attuned to everyday life than dancing. Professional dancer Deborah Day is one of the foremost proponents of the "dance-live" union. She is of the opinion that every minute of every day, from the moment one gets up, is potentially a dance. Dance is everywhere, in the tree branches waving to and fro, the cars whisking by, people darting, shifting, and pausing on the sidewalks, a newspaper blowing across the street, a couple of birds landing on the telephone wire. The fluctuations, the pulsations, the ebbs and flows of everyday life partake of some vast universal order to create an empyreal rapport that can be almost mystical. Dancing, for Day, is a matter of being conscious of one's movement as part of the cosmic flux of things. To live her life as dance, she cultivates her appreciation of the forms and rhythms of mundane activities like sipping coffee, eating, washing the dishes, combing her hair. All is dance, rhythm, performance. Day has picked much of her philosophy of dance and of life, it bears mentioning, in light of chapters 2 and 4, from her study of Oriental religions and Chinese martial art forms, particularly *t'ai chi ch'uan* (Foster 1986:6–8).

It is worthy of note that within the sphere of signs 211, devoid as it is of language, acts of deceit and subterfuge become well-nigh impossible for all save perhaps an expert mime. As Nietzsche once remarked, we can lie out of one side of our mouths, but, if accompanied by a grimace we nevertheless tell the truth. Oliver Sacks tells the story of a group of aphasiacs who, while hearing a speech by then president Ronald Reagan, saw through the act. This Great Communicator, this actor with his practiced rhetoric, had many of them howling with laughter, while others were bewildered and some outraged. Sacks reports that while they understood the President's words only to a nominal degree, they understood his nonverbal cues and clues to the letter. And they knew he was lying through his teeth. In other words, they were considerably less than adept at signs of the 331–333 variety, but give them signs from 111 to 311 and they can see right through you. In this, then, Sacks concludes, lies the aphasiacs' "power of understanding—understanding, without words, what is authentic or inauthentic. Thus it was the grimaces, the histrionisms, the false gestures and, above all, the false tones and cadences of [Reagan's] voice, which rang false for these wordless but immensely sensitive patients" (Sacks 1987:82).

The aphasiacs of which Sacks wrote suffered from a disorder of the left temporal lobe, which impaired their linguistic ability in terms of types (Thirdness) and tokens (Secondness), of which language offers the most effective examples. However, they were supremely gifted in their capacity for deciphering tones (Firstness), with which they were especially sensitive. What would be the comprehension of patients of an entirely opposite kind? Sacks asks. There were a number of such patients, also in the aphasia ward, that did not have aphasia but agnosia, a disorder of the right temporal lobe. These individuals understood language more effectively than the average speaker. Their problem was that tone, timbre, and a proper feel for the words they heard were virtually nonexistent. Upon listening to the President's speech, this type of patient could not tell if the voice was angry, cheerful, sad, or whatever, since voices lacked expression. They could understand the words and nothing but the words. That is to say, while they were masters of signs 331–333, they were babes in the woods regarding signs 111–311. (Unfortunately, this magnificently complex range of signs is almost entirely ignored by many semioticians, and also by the great majority of our current prattling, dialogic propagators of textualism. Given this posture, they remain linguicentric through and through; they choose to overlook that vast field of signs without which language would be entirely devoid of meaningful meaning.)

Sacks tells another story of a patient with an IQ of 60 who could not function with language as an abstract system (use of the left cerebral hemisphere) but who was a "natural poet" (use of the right cerebral hemisphere). Striking metaphors and other figures of speech would come to her naturally. Moreover, her sense of rhythm, her haptic perception, her capacity for motility, all of her kinesthetic qualities were remarkable. Sacks speculates on the IQ test that this patient, Rebecca, failed miserably.

> I had the strongest feeling of two wholly different modes of thought, or of organization, or of being. The first schematic—pattern-seeking, problem-solving—this is what had been tested, and where she had been found so defective, so disastrously wanting. But the tests had given no inkling of anything *but* the deficits, of anything, so to speak, *beyond* her deficits.
>
> They had given me no hint of her positive powers, her ability to perceive the real world—the world of nature, and perhaps of the imagination—as a coherent, intelligible, poetic whole: her ability to see this, think this, and (when she could) live this; they had given me no intimation of her inner world, which clearly *was* composed and coherent and approached as something other than a set of problems or tasks. (Sacks 1987:181)

Rebecca was aware of the rich tapestry of the world but was unable to articulate the design. She apparently dwelled chiefly in signs 111, 211, 221, 222, and 311, but did not have the language, the indices and symbols (321, 322, 331, 332, 333) with which adequately to dress the design in the necessary abstractions for communicating them to "normal" people. Was she privy to a special form of knowledge? Yes. Is this sort of knowledge given its due share in our obsessively linguicentric, textualistic cultures? Obviously not. There is something seriously lacking; we are missing out on something terribly important. Rebecca's world was a world exclusively of "concrete reasonableness," to use a Peircean term. It was a form of thought wholly different, wholly separate, from our abstract, schematic, linguicentric modes of reasoning. While she was "out in right field" and could not take in the whole picture, we have pushed ourselves "out in left field," given our linear thinking, our reason, our "logic," consequently we cannot take in that part of the whole picture that is common nature to Rebecca. Her concrete, extralinguistic powers gave a sense to her world of which we are largely ignorant; our hyperlinguistic fixation gives a sense to our world that is of value, to be sure, but it is sorely lacking, incomplete.

III. FINALLY, THE GRANDDADDY OF ICONS

Then there is taste. From scent to kinesthetics to taste. The second has been the object of frequent study but the first and third have not. As we observed above, even Howard Gardner excludes olfactory and gustatory knowledge from his seven multiple intelligences. Gardner reveals his Western, linguicentric bias when he writes that acute use of sensory systems "is another obvious candidate for a human intelligence. . . . [But] when it comes to keen gustatory or olfactory senses, these abilities have little special value across cultures" (1983:61). Such omissions are also found in the likes of Rudolph Arnheim (1969:19), who highlights "visual thinking" over "verbal thinking," but who writes that "one can indulge in smells and tastes, but one can hardly think in them." So what does Arnheim do? He virtually ignores them. They are for him unworthy of any and all sober-minded considerations of thought.

Scents originate "out there," somewhere, and they are taken "in here," where they are processed with hardly any further manifestations. Kinesthetic feelings emanate from "in here," and from here they make a show of themselves for all to see, if they happen to be so disposed and if they are sufficiently perceptive. Tastes, in contrast, require contact, like touch. It is significant that the word taste came into the English language around the thirteenth century with an original meaning closer to touch or feel than the modern "taste." However, once taste messages had become a matter of contact and were considered "in here" and processed accordingly, there could be hardly more than "Oohs" and "Ahs," and perhaps "It's almost like . . ." There could be little more insofar as language goes, for, like smells, tastes by and large dwell in that cloudy area of the ineffable. For obvious reasons they have generally been pushed into the musty closet of intangibles by Western logic, reason, and language.

The bottom line is that tastes and smells are difficult to corral, hog-tie, and conceptualize. As noted, tastes are generally classified in the English language into salty, sour, sweet, and bitter. Quite elementary, it would appear. But actually, not simple at all. There is after a fashion some element of synesthesia between smell and taste. The former contributes grandly to the latter. Without smell, wine would still dizzy and lull us, but much of its exotic appeal would be gone. Teen-agers would drink more of it just to get drunk, I would suspect, like other more mundane beverages and spirits. At any rate, swirl the wine around gently. If your surroundings are devoid of distracting noises, perhaps there is the gentle sound of a little fizz, perhaps not, depending upon the type of wine. The scent of wine reaches the taster before it is actually tasted, which is enough to put the taste buds in a thrilling state of expectation. As a sip of the nectar is rolled around in the mouth, the scent lingers, which adds to the savor: that is what wine is all about. One must allow it to caress one's tongue, enjoying it to the fullest.

Potato chips are another matter of synesthesia, certainly without the aesthetic attraction. The plastic wrap can hardly be opened without destroying it, ripping, slashing, and tearing it. The more racket the better, for just as with a noisy container, so also the act of munching on the crispiest and crunchiest product. Potato chips are to be eaten voraciously—they are so thin many of them must be placed whole in the mouth in order to get a substantial portion—ideally with the mouth at least partly open, and in as noisy a manner as possible. So the bag has been opened. Now the greasy aroma of junk-food attacks the nostrils, and the tastebuds are properly prepared for a healthy dose of cholesterol. Hogheaven. Notice that in our two examples of synesthesia, wine and potato chips—and especially with the latter—we have smell, sound, taste, and sight, running the gamut from 211 to at least 311 via the first fully developed Secondness of the sign components, 222. Multiple channels are open and receptive, you are receiving messages of many sorts, you are primed for the occasion. And nary a word (symbol, 331) has appeared on the scene—that is, if you disregard my incessant chatter of marks on these pages.

Are these nonlinguistic aspects of semiosis a form of intelligence in spite of Howard Gardner's prejudices? Certainly. Disability if a human being is deprived of taste or scent? Of course. "Wild" or "feral" children raised outside human cultures enjoy hypertrophied senses of smell, taste, and sound, which is understandable since they have been "talking with the animals." They are consequently able to distinguish between a remarkable variety of subtle difference in olfactory, gustatory, and auditory signs, selecting what is important to them and paying little heed to the rest (Classen 1993:38–40). In comparison, regarding the basic sensory channels of these children, we are relatively impoverished. Indeed, our sensorium can be considered as a whole as an "operational complex" (Ong 1991), or to use McLuhan's (1962:55) metaphor, a "kaleidoscope." We know our world through a combination of the five senses, of the decalogue of signs. Avoidance of any part of this "kaleidoscope" cannot help but impoverish our world considerably.

One particular index of impoverishment, regarding taste, is found in the omnipresent advertising campaign organized by Coca-Cola, in which, like in other soft drinks, artificial imitations have completely replaced natural flavors. In order to create a larger than life savory delicacy, Coca-Cola resorted to a practice that is not at all uncommon today: the number of components of natural flavor was actually reduced. The artificial flavor was now less than the "real" or natural, yet it was passed off as more real than the "real." In Baudrillard's words (1983a:3), the world of Coca-Cola has come to be "artificially revived as though real," and it is then mass produced "an indefinite number of times." To top it all off, the synthetic product is paraded as "The real thing," for "Coke is it!" Yes, right on! We love our Coke, don't we? But what a minute. Coke is *it?* Coke is *what?* Actually, it is neither "real" nor is it natural. It is sham, like many other products on the scene. But in a manner of speaking, it *is* "real," that is, "hyperreal." Is it not? Well, yes. It is as "real" as most of our other commodities, which are sham but "real." In fact, the "real" of many of the commodities on the market is in tatters and shreds, and the papier-mâché fake standing in its stead is the only "real" we often have, imagineered and engineered to dupe us into taking it for "real."

Perhaps, as McLuhan (1964) once warned us, we are drifting so far away from the taste of genuine life that we are beginning to prefer artificiality to the real item: we are becoming content to eat the menu descriptions rather than the food. However, the not-so-sweet smell of success is relatively tasteless. The body, if we could only for a moment suffer the humiliation of listening to it, actually tells us so much. The problem is that the mind generally won't listen, for it is more attuned to the symbols (Baudrillardian signifiers, binary linguistic signs) of our world. Actually, Baudrillard is right, but for all the wrong reasons: as we shall note in chapter 11, the world was never binary and it never will be. It is we who bifurcate it, I would suspect much in the order of Alfred North Whitehead's (1948) grand Western "bifurcation of nature." The world of signs of a customarily presumed lesser semiotics are still there, with open arms waiting our return home after a few centuries of epistemological wandering. Perhaps the way home can be initiated through our getting in better touch with touch.

Touch, for sure, brings us closer to the body, to the two-dimensional surface of the body. That remarkable philosopher of the senses, Helen Keller, tells us that touch "brings the blind many sweet certainties which our more fortunate fellows miss, because their sense of touch is uncultivated. When they look at things, they put their hands in their pockets. No doubt that is one reason why their knowledge is often so vague, inaccurate and useless" (Keller 1909:42). In other words, Keller seems to be saying that our knowledge invariably remains "vague, inaccurate and useless" because it is overly mediated. It is of the vagueness of Firstness mediated by signs of Thirdness, chiefly language, which only serve to intellectualize and render underdetermined that which was overdetermined but at instinctive and habituated levels known and acted upon without a shadow of a doubt.

I alluded above to the importance of contact, of touch, in living organisms, especially humans and primates (Montagu 1971). In fact, as we have observed, a healthy adult life is not possible without much tactile stimulation. Touch places us squarely within sign 311, the sign as token (Second) of a type (Third), the first indication in the decalogue of a genuine sign component, the representamen having raised itself to the status of a Third. The self, within 311, is apart from the other. But not really. The sign itself is other, and it is a Third, conceived as a sign. There is, however, only a Firstness of the semiotic object and the interpretant, no Secondness. They and the semiotic self are still at one with each other. Replicas of 311 are limited to 211, where kinesthetics, smell, and taste are paramount, but touch has suffered a certain de-engenderment since the self-other indication (index) is even less pronounced. Within 211, there can also exist de-engenderment of sight and sound, which brings all the sensory channels into communion and collaboration.

Signs of 311, then, are pivotal. We saw this in the *Ho'tu* model of the *I Ching* (figure 15). And 311 signs, in regard to touch, and especially kinesthetics, are fundamental. It is perhaps in large part for this reason that professional touchers (faith healers, doctors, hairdressers, massagers, dance instructors, cosmeticians, barbers, chiropractors, manicurists, prostitutes) often run the risk of becoming intimate with their clients. Touch *is* intimate, of course, whether with the hands or the tongue or any part of the sexual anatomy. It is considerably more intimate than smell and sight and the sound of words, which serve as sexual come-ons for touching. Yes, touch. A sensitive issue. More sensitive in most animals than in us, as evidenced especially in the cat's whiskers, the cockroach's antennae, and so on. Folk science has it that certain animals can foretell an earthquake, a tornado, and other disasters. There might be some truth to this. Their skin is drier than ours, and they have considerably more hair. With a change in the electrostatic energy of the air surrounding them, they can feel very slight tingling at the extremities of their body hair. As we put it in English, their hair "stands on end." We are not as cleverly endowed as are our animal friends in this respect. Yet we humans are still quite sensitive to touch. The presence of a loved one, for example, can often be "felt," though unseen and though separated by a few feet. This is a sign of 311, the sign is there and "felt," in spite of the fact that the object of the sign remains explicitly unacknowledged and there is hardly more than a tinge of an interpretant. The sign is there, and one knows it, though it is not directly and unmediatedly before one. This is an instance of what Classen calls the "myth of perceptual transparency" (the idea that the senses give us direct, unmediated access to "reality") (Classen 1991).[3]

IV. THE SOUND OF MUSIC, AND OTHER NOISES

The close relationship between music and bodily and gestural languages—other than dance—hardly needs mention. Music is often thought of as an extended gesture, the sound pattern depicting body rhythms—or vice versa, according to the way of the looking and the thinking. Quite understandably, in this regard, Stravinsky believed music should be seen in addition to its being taken as sound. Thus he was partial to the ballet and to the creation of bodily motion to the accompaniment of music, no matter what the situation or the context (Stravinsky 1956).

Ties between music and space are hardly less genuine that those between music and motion. The apparent fact that music perception and space perception are predominantly "right brain" functions gives us a clue in this regard. This might account for another difference—be it genetic or culturally inculcated—in female and male perception: the importance to women of touch over "gaze," of space and polydimensional time over linearity of space and unidimensional time (Harris 1978). Howard Gardner reports that a musician with extensive right hemisphere damage remained capable of teaching music, and he even wrote books about it. But he lost the ability and the desire to compose music. He could no longer retain a feel for the whole piece, nor a sense of what would be aesthetically satisfying and what not. The mechanics of music was still there in the "left brain," so to speak, but a proper "feel" had been lost. The symbolic equivalent of music composition (signs 331, 332, 333) were retained, but the iconic dimension (signs 111, 211, 311) had been impaired.

This suggests the often-discussed relationship between music and mathematics, patterned in the ancient quadrivium—music, arithmetic, geometry, astronomy—in contrast to language, which is found in the medieval trivium—grammar, logic, rhetoric. In Gardner's view, there are affinities between music and mathematics that should not be minimized. In order to appreciate the operation of musical rhythms, one must be in control of basic numerical concepts. Performances also demand sensitivity to recursive series, regularities, and ratios that can become quite complex. This is especially evident in Douglas Hofstadter's (1979) monumental study bringing Bach to bear on the work of Maurits Escher and Kurt Gödel. Stravinsky, in this vein, comments that musical form is "far closer to mathematics than to literature . . . certainly to something like mathematical thinking and mathematical relationships. . . . Musical form is mathematical because it is ideal, and form is always ideal . . . though it may be mathematical, the composer must not seek mathematical formula" (Stravinsky 1971:34, cited in Gardner 1983:126). Indeed, mathematical patterns and regularities are evinced in music ranging from Bach to Schumann in a playful exploration of possibilities of combination. It is said that Mozart even composed some pieces on the basis of a roll of dice. Gardner concludes that in an important respect the musician's task and that of the pure mathematician differ greatly:

> The mathematician is interested in forms for their own sake, in their own implications, apart from any realization in a particular medium or from any particular communicative purpose. He may choose to analyze music and even have gifts for doing so; but from the mathematical point of view, music is just another pattern. For the musician, however, the patterned elements must appear in sounds; and they are finally and firmly put together in certain ways not by virtue of formal consideration, but because they have expressive power and effects. (Gardner 1983:126–27)

Even Stravinsky finally comes to the conclusion that at the most fundamental level mathematics and music are not alike.

Signs 331–333 for music and for mathematics differ primarily because, I would suspect, they are at odds with the sphere of signs 111–311. What for one process is ultimately an aesthetic affect giving rise to and satisfaction to vague feelings, sentiments, and emotions, for another process is an aesthetic affect, equally embedded in vague feelings, sentiments, and emotions, but specifically geared toward satisfying precise formal expression. The aesthetics of mathematics is formal, looking for precision, though any and all relatively rich mathematical edifices of generality of the most general sort cannot but be either incomplete or inconsistent, pace Gödel. Musical aesthetics, however, is properly informal—which does not take anything away from the mechanics of composing a well-wrought fugue or whatever—and its appearance stems from vagueness as an outgrowth of essential tension. At the one end of the spectrum we have a primacy of sight—mathematical symbols—although in its inception, as noted above, mathematics was to be recited rather than written. This sight must evince precision, an ordered sequence culminating in a conclusive wrap-up (sign 333). At the other end of the spectrum we have emphasis on sound—though if there is a score it is necessarily in abstract symbols. This sound embodies quality, of the type that entrances its audience, and it bids its farewell not with a capstone of proof, but with an overriding sense of uncertainty, since the vague tension existing as a product of inner contradictions remains (→ sign 111). At the midpoint between the two extremes, there is something in the order of $\sqrt{-1}$, or its equivalent thereof (such as the Liar Paradox, say), where things must be either one or the other. Attempts to resolve the irresolvable equation into an undeniable generality moves one up the scale toward the final interpretant of 333 and formal precision, but, alas, incompleteness will always prevail, and if not, out and out inconsistency. Embracing $\sqrt{-1}$ as i (= $\pm\sqrt{-1}$) all at once and in iconic fashion entails acceptance of the inner ambiguity and an aesthetics of vagueness, of uncertainty, consequently inconsistency and contradiction will remain.

So between the crystals of mathematical precision and the sense of music there is the noise of either one thing or another with no decision procedure or an impossible both one thing and the other. In another way of putting it, there is noise, noise or chaos from which order is duty bound to arise sooner or later.

V. SIGHTS TO BEHOLD,
BUT IS THAT ALL THERE IS?

As I have intimated, the West has been excessively ocularcentric for some time. In this Grand Age of Information, the Civilization of the Image, the syndrome has become endemic: a disease of the eyes and of the mind. It has been said that if we do not come to our senses, we may soon forfeit the chance of replacing our fixation on the image with any alternatives (Howes 1991:4). Richard Kearney sums up the problem thusly:

> [T]he image *precedes* the reality it is supposed to represent . . . This reversal is evident at a number of levels. In politics, we find presidents and prime ministers being elected because of the media image they represent. . . . [At] the economic level, it is now a well-documented fact that our consumerist society . . . can sustain material production only by means of the 'hidden persuaders' of new brand-images and ever more elaborate advertising campaigns. Even at the everyday social level, we notice the image taking pride

of place over the real, as in Boorstin's humorous anecdote about the contemporary suburban housewife who responds to a neighbour's compliment to her child with the boast: "Yes, he is lovely, but you should see the photograph." (1988:2)

Yet sight, the image, continues to expand its turf by leaps and bounds, and real children, indeed, all people for that matter, and food and clothing and furniture and all aspects of the media, are becoming no more than a pale reflection of their technologically constructed images.

From Alberti's Renaissance "vanishing point" perspective to Dürer's notorious etching of a "Man Drawing a Reclining Woman" scene to our Baudrillardian postmodern culture of "hyperreality" (an apocalyptic interpretation of which is remarkably offered by Robert Romanyshyn [1989:31]), the individual spectator gradually becomes ensconced behind his/her window to the world, like a monad, and the body, in isolation from the self, becomes no more than another image among images. There are hardly any smells or sounds or tastes or textures here. From the Alberti view there is only a window with a grid, an opening, a hole like the camera eye through which the entire world is presumably seen exactly as it is, objectively, detachedly, dispassionately, and coldly. That linear, binary model of subject and object, mind and mirror of the world, saw its quite natural culmination in a formless mass of simulacra vomiting forth more simulacra. In addition to this pictorial (ocularcentric) image, we have recently been engulfed by the onrushing tide of textuality. First there was the "linguistic turn," then the "interpretive turn" (Hiley et al. 1991). Even ethnographers, who I would expect should know better, have occasionally been caught up in that presumed and presumptuous "text of the world," of "culture," of the "mind." The ethnographer wishing to interpret the other culture takes that culture as a "text." It is not that culture is merely *like* a "text," it literally *is* a "text," much in the manner in which for the Renaissance painter the grid through which the world is seen is tantamount to the world: it *is* the world. For Clifford Geertz's "interpretive anthropology," culture and the people it holds are "texts" to be "read" (1975:452). For James Clifford (1986:12) ethnography is "dialogical" and culture is a "theatre" of voices. This is a "discursive rather than a visual paradigm" in which "the dominant metaphors for ethnography shift away from the observing eye and toward expressive speech (and gesture)."

David Howes, after quoting Geertz and Clifford, among others, maintains that "the shift from the ocular to the oral must be accompanied by a further shift, which takes in the gustatory, olfactory, and tactile modalities as well. With these other senses in mind, it becomes possible to think of cultures as contrasting in terms of the distinctive patterns to the *interplay of the senses* they present" (1991:8; italics in original). This new turn was initiated earlier by the likes of Edmund Carpenter and Marshall McLuhan (1960) and Walter Ong (1977, 1982) and is fortunately being revived by Howes, Michael Jackson (1989), Paul Stoller (1989), Stephen Tyler (1987), and others. In order to enact a shift from the oral to the sensorial there must be a retreat from what Ong dubs "Great Divide" theories—i.e., those that are firmly grounded in one pole or the other of the ear/eye, oral/literate, text/world dichotomies. This move has also been at least implied in the work of Finnegan (1988), and Goody (1977).

An important aspect of the McLuhan-Ong thesis is that emphasis on particular sensory channels by the different communications media force us into a twisted experience of the world. In some cultures, scents take on heightened importance; for others, nonlinguistic sounds are more important—African drum messages, whistle messages among the Huichol Amerindians of Mexico and the native peoples of the Canary Islands. Aztec pictographic writing requires a different mind-set than do Mayan or Egyptian hieroglyphics, and those require different mind-sets than Oriental writing or Western linear phonological writing. For the Mayans, time is of utmost importance in their creation myths: it preceded everything that is; the Tzotzil of Mexico believe that temperature is the basic force of the cosmos (Classen 1993). Within our own culture, individuals vary in terms of the sensations they tend to foreground. Musicians cultivate their ear; chefs and wine-tasters their nose and palate; card sharks, typists, and pianists their fingers; painters and sculptors their eyes; dancers their body kinesics; actors their gestures and voice inflections—and professors, of course, their forever flapping mouths. In every case, signs that most effectively distinguish one culture from another are signs of habit, tacitness, de-engenderment, replica-replication, entrenchment, embedment, automatization. It is no wonder that translation presents so many problems, that ethnologists are confronted with apparently insurmountable barriers, that incommensurability between scientific paradigms, social conventions and values, and cultural forms of life is so enticing.

Yet we tend to remain through and through ocularcentric. Most of us in Western societies at least. According to McLuhan's thesis, the road has been long, arduous, and not without pitfalls. First was the oral stage, when speech was the mass medium and thought was forced into an audio bias. Hearing was hypertrophied to take on undue importance at the expense of other possible media. Moreover, people must be present in order to communicate orally, hence tactile, proxemic, gestural, kinesic, and even olfactory modes tended to take on increased importance. The age of chirography disrupted oral-aural cultures. Most notably, phonetic writing brought about an atrophying of the ear and heightened emphasis on the eye. With the invention of the printing press this transition from the ear to the eye became fully consummated. Gradually, books began to be read in silence. Since eventually everyone could in principle have his/her own copy, there was no longer any need for the master of the book—who might be the only literate person present—to read to a group. While hearing is polydirectional, synthetic, and relatively unfocused, sight is unidirectional, analytic, focused, and relatively more distancing. Sound penetrates the listener from all angles, whereas the gazer is the penetrator, the spectator of the spectacle, choosing what he/she wants to see.

The culminating stage of the trend toward lingui-ocularcentrism and the de-engenderment of those more fundamental signs has been ushered in with the grand age of electronics. The new media re-introduce those senses that had previously been suppressed. Telegraph and the written word made for the possibility of sign transmission at a velocity unimaginable to previous generations; telephone and the oral-aural modes brought signs together from a distance and in virtual simultaneity; radio and sound introduced signs into a media that could be adjusted and tinkered with, experimented with, listened to or turned off, but there can be no immediate response to the signs received, for the listener was a relatively passive recipient. Above all, TV brought the sign-image into the living area. Foods, clothing styles, furniture, homes, music, art, architecture, and language and customs from diverse cultural and ethnic groups have become quite familiar to, and even intimate with, the viewers: the entire world can now become a "tribal village."

McLuhan suggests that if we are to attain any valid degree of cross-cultural understanding, we must attend to the manner in which other cultures emphasize and de-emphasize, and use and abuse, the various sensory modes, fully comprehending the other, whether the gap between knower and the desired known is incommensurable or not. However, this task is more problematic than McLuhan and other social critics would like to believe. In the first place, McLuhan deals almost exclusively with the ear and the eye, thus ignoring the other "intelligences." In the second place, he does not pay due heed, in my estimation, to the complexity of the analyst-analysand relation. But, then, this failure is not unique to McLuhan; it is quite common amongst scholars studying other social classes and other cultures. For example, Baudrillard (1988b) takes a quick trip through the United States and then writes a penetrating book about the American Way of Life. Umberto Eco (1986) does the same. Roland Barthes (1972) journeys through some magazines from the newsstands and in "Paris Match" he spies a photograph of a black Algerian soldier that he analyzes to reveal what the numbed, clapped-out bourgeois masses are incapable of seeing. Claude Lévi-Strauss (1976) journeys through the wilds of Brazil and returns to civilization with a tale about the Amerindians and us and why we are the way we are and they are the way they are. Geertz (1973) offers various possible "readings" of a Balinese cockfight but says little about the "dialogic" encounter between ethnographer and the other, or about that which is sensed in modes other than "reading" and that which resists the very idea of "textuality."

Tales all! Written by captivating narrators and nimble rhetoricians, to be sure. But these views, whether supercilious or sincere, whether vain or humble, are stories. And stories are stories. Who is to say that any of the above-mentioned stories reveal the hitherto concealed bare-bones reality of the other that can serve to enlighten us common folk? Rather presumptuous, as are by and large our own efforts to capture the essence of the other. I would dare say that it behooves every ambitious elucidator of "deep" cultural meanings to read the post-analytic debates on problems of incommensurability, reference, meaning, translation, and interpretation.[4] This should bring their attention to the barriers between languages and cultures and even individuals (of the latter Oliver Sacks has made us painfully aware). Moreover, there is a pluralism of possible "styles of reasoning" (Hacking 1985), it appears, that are language and culture dependent, and recent cognitive research suggests that "perceptual styles" and "intelligences" depend upon specific languages and cultures (Gardner 1983, 1987).[5] Back to visuality for a moment.

Sacks, in *Migraine* (1985), reports that patients with severe cases of migraine headaches suffer from visual hallucinations. Images come to them in staccato flickering fashion, as if they were subjected to a rapidly moving slide show rather than the continuous cinematic vision with which we are ordinarily familiar. These series of stills are reminiscent of Jameson's (1992) "hyperspace" endemic in our postmodern cultures, and of the rapid-paced images flashing at us on MTV, TV commercials, and quickly becoming the norm in TV programs, movies, and even juxtapositions of images presented in static form in magazine ads. In their most simple forms, these hallucinatory images take the form of a dance of brilliant stars, sparks, flashes, simple geometric forms, or simply radar-like blips across the screen. In their more complex and subtle manifestations, they are comparable to a scintillating kaleidoscopic succession of cubist paintings, pre-cubist works such as those of Cézanne and van Gogh, Oriental tapestry, Arabic tessellated mosaics, and Huichol Amerindian designs made after mescaline-induced experiences.

These phenomena, it would appear, are pure images devoid of any linear temporal sequence: chiefly iconic signs (111–311) with little indication or indexing (222) and with few pointers (321–322), and they are for sure nonlinguistic (331–333). More importantly, these hallucinations are invariably accompanied by scotoma (blind spots or areas in the visual field), whether scintillating or somewhat stationary. At the risk of climbing out on a limb, I might venture to say that resonating scotoma, which Sacks occasionally terms "nothingness," are comparable to the "node" in the semiotic tripod (figure 20), that "nothingness" of which Peirce often wrote, the "emptiness" of Oriental philosophy (a far cry, I must emphasize, from the "nothingness" of Sartre and other Western philosophers [Nishitani 1982, 1990]). More a propos still, migraine-induced hallucinations are not exclusively visual, but also tactile, auditory, and even gustatory and olfactory. But it is the visual scotoma that at times threaten to bring the patient to a state of horror (Sacks 1985:55–66).

Scotoma are not limited to one sensory mode, nor are they limited to all the sensory modes if they are considered in isolation of the mind, the entire body, and, indeed, the personal history of a particular subject. Sacks brings this point home "loud and clear" (a commonplace expression highlighting the ear and the eye!—I should also say, in addition to "loud and clear," "palpably precise and tastefully tart and of undeniable scent"). A few lines in his autobiographical *A Leg to Stand On,* to which I referred in chapter 7, merit citation. Sacks writes that after his accident with the bull in the mountains:

> The scotoma, and its resonances, I had already experienced—frightful, empty images of nothingness, which surged, and overwhelmed me, especially at night. As a bulwark against this—I had hoped, and supposed—would come the genial understanding and support of my doctor. He would reassure me, help, give me a foothold in the darkness.
>
> But, instead, he did the reverse. By saying nothing, saying "Nothing," he took away a foothold, the human foothold, I so desperately needed. Now, doubly, I had no leg to stand on; unsupported, doubly, I entered nothingness and limbo.
>
> The word "hell" supposedly is cognate with "hole"—and the hole of a scotoma is indeed a sort of hell; an existential, or metaphysical, state, indeed, but one with the clearest organic basis and determinant. The organic

foundation of "reality" is removed, and to this extent one falls into a hole—
or a hell-hole, if one permits oneself consciousness of this (which many patients, understandably, and defensively, do not do). A scotoma is a hole in
reality itself, a hole in time no less than in space, and therefore cannot be
conceived of as having a term or ending. As it carries a quality of "memory-
hole," of amnesia, so it carries a sense of timelessness, endlessness. The quality of timelessness, limbo, is inherent in scotoma. (Sacks 1984:84–85)

During his period of hopeful but excruciating convalescence, Sacks
sensed "nothingness" in his bones (that which is prior to all signification),
and his doctor says "nothing." There were no soothing words of comfort
(an absence of signs). Sacks, consequently, felt himself "sinking" into the
abyss that engulfed him. He was "sensorially and spiritually" affected by
the "silence," on the one hand, and, on the other, by the "infernal din"
(noise) of "hell." Outwardly there was "soundlessness and noise," and inwardly "a deadly inner silence—the silence of timelessness, motionless-
ness, scotoma, combined with the silence of non-communication" (Sacks
1984:85–86). As was revealed above, music brought him out of the
"hole." "Sweet music," no spoken or written words, no indexicals or any
other direct linkings to the physical world, just music. Music, chiefly
from sign 111 to sign 311.

Science and logic and reason could not talk to Sacks of "nothingness,"
of "not" in the absolute sense. There is no place for it in their descriptions
of what presumably *is*. Neither could music "talk" of "nothingness." But it
could give Sacks a "feel" for life, a "feel" that could lend him a hand and
lift him from the dark depths of "nothing" (that is, "nothingness" in the
Western nihilistic sense, in contrast to the "nothingness" or "emptiness" of
which I have written above). "Suddenly, wonderfully," Sacks writes, "I was
moved by the music. The music seemed passionately, wonderfully, quiver-
ingly alive—and conveyed to me a sweet feeling of life" (Sacks 1984:93).
He now knew he would soon have a leg to stand on.

10

MORE THAN WORDS CAN TELL

I. EVERYTHING IS NOT IN THE EYE

Yes, there is life before sight and before sound and language. It is the initiation of time and the life of time of which I wrote in chapter 4; it is the time of our lives, of the life of the entire body, of bodymind, of all signs rather than merely language, textuality, intertextuality, hypertextuality, hyperlinguistic dialogic; it is the life of all sensations rather than almost exclusively those of the eye and the ear.

Some of the most fascinating cases of nonlinear, extralinguistic or prelinguistic, and nonvisual sensory worlds are also reported by Oliver Sacks: patients without speech, without time, without the ability visually to remain focused or whose visuality is in one sense a set of camera-ready copies and in another sense terribly fragmented, patients without traditional linguicentric concepts of reference, representation, correspondence, signs as a mirror of the world.[1] There is the case of the autistic artist, José, who, with a photographic memory, can draw things he has seen to the most minute detail. That is to say, he can draw anything he has seen, but distorts the details, for each instantiation of an object is for him another object altogether. He draws a watch, and each number is different, some large and others small, some of Roman, Gothic, Modern, or Block sort, and others only vaguely represented. As with many autistic individuals, this patient is lacking, or indisposed to, the general: he composes his pictures as, and indeed his entire world is no more than a set of, particulars (i.e., types rather than tokens). He lives not in a universe but in a radical sort of William James pluriverse. He is like Borges's "Funes the Memorious," a Luria mnemonist who was

almost incapable of ideas of a general, Platonic sort. . . . In the teeming
world of Funes, there were only details, almost immediate in their presence. . . . No one . . . has felt the heat and pressure of a reality as indefati-
gable as that which day and night converged upon the hapless Ireneo
[Funes]. (Borges 1962: cited in Sacks 1987:229).

José lives in a world of fleeting images of particulars, each one with its
unique "qualities." He "feels" they afford him a certain "grasp of things."
Their "feel," is strikingly brought out in his drawings. There is "an odd mixture of close, even obsessive, accuracy, with curious (and, I felt, droll) elab-
orations and variations" (Sacks 1987:215). These "qualities," these "feels,"
are a sequence of Firsts, of iconic images, without internal interconnectiv-
ity (of Firstness), external interrelations (Secondness), or conceptual or interpretive input in the customary human sense (Thirdness). José dwells in
his own world. He is an island, enclosed within itself. He is a self-contained,
self-reflexive sign of himself, the consummate icon. However, in certain
ways he is more human than are most of us; in fact he may be all-too-
human for our tastes. For this reason he does not live in our world. He can't,
for his world excludes those complex signs of the so-called more developed
sort. We can perhaps begin to approximate his world by peeling away the
signs, from 333 "downward," in order to get at those of 311 and "downward." But, alas, unlike José's signs, these signs for us are not pure signs but
de-engendered signs, signs of a lesser semiotics—"lesser" insofar as our culturally inculcated tastes go, at least. Our de-engendered signs cannot help
but remain burdened with memories of those semiotic peaks they once
scaled, a burden that severely limits their ability to evince those "lesser"
signs in their pure form. We are, in our own way, as crippled as José.

Then there is the case of Ms. B, a former research chemist who suddenly
suffered a radical personality change after which her thoughts were a free association of ideas. At least that is how her mind appeared to her friends and
the nurses. Sacks, after much effort, finally came to see the working of her
mind in another way. One day he suddenly realized that Ms. B saw him as
a priest (because he had a beard), as a nun (because of his white uniform),
and as a doctor (since he carried a stethoscope), and it was all the same to
her. As far as she was concerned, a sign in its multiple variations, like the
right glove or the left glove, or any enantiomorphic form for that matter,
consisted of the same sign. She did not distinguish between them. There
were no dichotomies or incommensurables; everything took on the same
value. A metaphor or metonym was just as "real" and just as "irreal" as anything else for here. She "had been voided of feeling and meaning. Nothing

any longer felt 'real' (or 'unreal'). Everything was now 'equivalent' or 'equal'—the whole world reduced to a facetious insignificance" (Sacks 1987:117). More surprising still, she was entirely unconcerned over her bizarre nonconception of things; it didn't bother her a whit.

Is this flattening of everything to the same level comparable to our contemporary postmodernist "flattening" gone completely mad? Is Ms. B's "indifference" and "equalization" tantamount to the most extreme form of simulation, of tolerance for the most radical form of pluralism within a multicultural milieu? Whether it is or not, Ms. B's world of meaninglessness not only is found almost entirely lacking in Thirdness, in interpretants for the symbols she uses, it is also impoverished regarding Secondness in terms of distinctions established between things and between the semiotic agent and her world. In other words, Ms. B also lives in a world for practical purposes devoid of Firstness properly actualized into an array of Seconds. There are only Firsts and nothing but Firsts, without value, without their being distinguished from one another. The autistic child, José, lived in a world of nothing but particulars, but each particular was its own island and clearly distinguishable from all other particulars, even though they remained unclothed in a genuine garb of Thirdness for him. Ms. B's rather pseudo-particulars, in contrast, can at a moment's notice take on any one of a range of possible qualities as a First, and in the next moment it could be something else, though there was really no difference that made any difference between the two as far as she was concerned. José's world consists of clearly distinguishable Seconds without the possibility of their belonging to any class of things; Ms. B's world consists of Firsts without the possibility of their becoming Seconds in terms of their relations to other Seconds. Ms. B's Firsts are as deprived of Seconds and Thirds as José's Seconds are of Thirds and Firsts, it would appear. Accordingly, for José there is sheer linearity, sequentiality of signs without generalities. In contrast, for Ms. B there is a Brownian movement of virtually pure Firsts without their standing a chance of becoming Seconds as particulars or Thirds as generals, hence her world remains of the utmost vagueness.

With this view of iconicity and indexicality enjoying no more than impoverished interrelationship with other signs, let us move on to the idea of completely isolated indexical signs.

II. SECONDS WITHOUT A PAST

At least José remembered the items that popped into his experience, and he could at a later date draw them in remarkable detail. The "charming, intelligent, memoryless Jimmie G," as reported by Sacks, could not. The Seconds of his experience were here now and gone forever in the next moment. He simply could not remember his feelings, thoughts, memories, reflections.

Sacks suggested that Jimmie G keep notes every day of his experiences. At first he kept losing his diary. Then it was attached to him, and he kept it as best he could. But after a day's notetaking, if he went back to the previous day's he could not recognize anything, nor could he even recognize his own handwriting. There simply was no "previous day" for him. His mind appeared to have been "reduced to a sort of Humean drivel, a mere succession of unrelated impressions and events" (Sacks 1987:35). He was like Borges's Funes, but without time. Funes was apparently aware of his past sensations and of his self experiencing the objects, acts, and events that produced those sensations. Jimmie G could not. He could not, for he had in a manner of speaking lost his self. If one loses an arm or a leg there will be memories of that loss, to be sure. Jimmie G, in contrast, had no memories of his having lost all memories, because, quite simply, he had lost all memories. The Seconds of his experiences, shorn of all feeling, all qualities, all Firstness, and never having been charged with meaning, with Thirdness, entered his mind and flew out again, gone forever. They were nothing but completely disconnected Seconds, as signs of 222 without iconic input—from signs 221, 211, 111—and never having enjoyed the fullness of a healthy ingestion of symbolicity—from signs 321, 322, 331, 332, 333. His signs were like a Cheshire cat that was nothing but a grin in the first place and then the grin disappears without a trace of its former existence as an index of what it never was. Nothing but virtual "nothingness" remains of the past.

Jimmie G was lost in "spatial time," the "timeless time" J. M. E. McTaggart (1927) labeled B-Series time consisting of "before" and "after," but no mobile "now." However, he seemed to be at home in A-Series time, the flowing time of Henri Bergson (1911) consisting of a knife-edge "now" incessantly moving from "past" to "future," except that for Jimmie G there was no "past" and hence hardly any anticipation of the "future." He could briefly find pleasure in the mental challenge involved with puzzles or games of calculation, but he would fall into the abyss of nothingness and amnesia once he lost interest. Sacks reports that he would usually be found fluttering around, bored and lost. But at times he could be deeply attentive to the beauty of the world around him. This leads the ever-sensitive neurologist to ponder:

> I had wondered, when I first met him, if he was not condemned to a sort
> of 'Humean' froth, a meaningless fluttering on the surface of life, and

whether there was any way of transcending the incoherence of his Humean disease. Empirical science told me there was not—but empirical science, empiricism, takes no account of the soul, no account of what constitutes and determines personal being. Perhaps there is a philosophical as well as a clinical lesson here: that in . . . dementia, or other such catastrophes, however great the organic damage and Humean dissolution, there remains the undiminished possibility of reintegration by art, by communion, by touching the human spirit: and this can be preserved in what seems at first a hopeless state of neurological devastation. (Sacks 1987:39)

Signs 111, 211, 311, and to an extent 221 are closest to the senses, to sensation, experience, feeling, sentiment, emotions, desires, wishes, inclinations. They are closest to the body, to what the body knows without our needing to be conscious of its so knowing. So we walk and talk without giving the acts much mind. And so our mouth goes out of control because we fail properly to engage it. And we walk to where we want to go without the act of going in mind but what we are going to do when we get there. Our nonconscious, tacit walking and driving usually serve us quite well, thank you, but we really should be more mindful of the ways of our talking. Mindfulness, however, is another issue.

The point is that many of the things that are most important for us are hidden from us because of their familiarity, like Edgar Allen Poe's "Purloined Letter." It remained concealed because it was so open to view. We will recall that K, in Franz Kafka's *The Trial,* was once asked "How are you?" He was paralyzed, frozen in his tracks. The question is of the ordinary sort that should elicit a canned answer. It is a question one asks without giving it any thought because the asking is done nonconsciously, tacitly, and a simple response of a few syllables is given in the same way. How was he? Obviously miserable. But how could he articulate his state of mind and of being clearly and distinctly? He couldn't, given the very nature of his state of mind and of being. He was like the parable about the centipede that was asked how he coordinated all his legs at once when he walked, and when he stopped to think about it, he was frozen in his tracks.

We listen to our favorite piece by Mozart, Bach, Beethoven, Vivaldi, the Beatles, Duke Ellington, Bon Jovi, Michael or Janet Jackson, Whitney Houston, or whomever, and we listen to it again and again and never seem to tire of it. That is music appreciation at its best. We feel it in the guts, these signs of 111–311. Now, if we break the music up into its smallest parts, part *a* might have little to no meaning for us, nor does *b,* nor *c,* and so on. So while listening to the music for the *n*th time, how is it that we are able to reintegrate the parts into the whole such that it is made meaningful for us? We do it at the level of feeling, at a visceral level where those baser signs dwell. Hermeneutic circles aside, this level of feeling-thinking, of unthinking-thinking, is the perennial dilemma of reductionism and analysis. If a and all the rest of the atoms are just that, disconnected atoms as Seconds with no Firstness, then there can be no feeling for them as there is our vague feeling for the whole of these integrated atoms. In a nutshell, there is no Firstness regarding the whole if each atom has no genuine Thirdness—which is presumably the case in hard-nosed analytical thought. And it hardly needs saying that there can be no genuine Thirdness—mediation between Firsts and Seconds—if there is no Firstness. Kafka's K could not say how he was, though he felt it in the guts, he was an existential mess. Articulating his lousiness was another matter. Where to begin? How to begin? Where to go from there, wherever that might be? How to know where to go in the first place, if there is no known goal? Without Firstness or Thirdness there is only what *is,* that is, what *is* is what happens to be the focus of attention at the moment, with no awareness of what lies at the periphery. This was Jimmie G's dilemma.

"Tacit knowledge," Michael Polanyi (1958) calls this nonconscious form of knowing that is revealed in what we just do without having to think about it or will our body to do it. It is Charles Sherrington's (1940) "sixth sense," Mary Douglas's (1975) "implicit meanings," Wittgenstein's (1953) "forms of life," Hans-Georg Gadamer's (1975) "horizons," Bateson's (1972) "grace," and it variously goes by many other names and takes other forms. It is that which is known without one's necessarily being conscious of so knowing it. And what one does by way of this knowledge one does as if it were second nature, and in a sense it is. When limiting ourselves to a consideration of what the body knows, we might stick to Sherrington, as does Sacks. Sherrington labels this hidden sense by a term introduced above, proprioception. Proprioception is indispensable for our sense of ourselves, and of our body, its position, its moves, some of which are involuntary or implicit. It has to do with kinesthetics, with motility. What our body does is of utmost importance, though we hardly give it a thought. What it does it does, almost of its own accord and usually without our conscious intervention. Perhaps in part for that reason we would like to consider our body in terms of some other. It is "my body," "my leg," "my arm," and so on, as we say in English. The body and body parts tend to be taken as Seconds, in other words, as if they were something other, other than the self, part of the self's possessions, with the self, in the most ideal sense, as a disembodied, disinterested bystander. This is the Cartesian split in its most vicious form.

This is also why the person Sacks calls the "disembodied lady" is so disconcerting. Christina had a dream that she had lost control of her body, and after awakening, sure enough, she began progressively to lose control of her body, to become "disembodied." She lost all proprioception. From top to toe, she had hardly any sensations at all, though she maintained some awareness of temperature, light, and pain. She could focus her eyes and keep tabs on a conversation, but while doing so she had no idea what was happening to her body. In fact, if while ambulating across the room she closed her eyes, she could lose all control and fall into a heap. Her movements had to be consciously and very carefully monitored, perhaps because the body had forgotten what to do; that is, perhaps the mind had forgotten implicitly how to send directions to the body to tell it what to do; that is, perhaps the body has ceased taking orders from the mind in a silent act of rebellion. Or whatever. Given Christine's problem, it becomes well-nigh impossible to separate body from mind.

Perhaps a couple of Polanyi's terms regarding tacit knowledge can help: focal attention and subsidiary attention. The mind ordinarily focuses on the task at hand, while it remains subsidiarily aware of other activities— the proprioceptive body-model—which are left to take care of themselves. Thus when hammering a nail into a board, the carpenter is focused on the head of the nail, while the left hand holding the shaft of the nail, the right hand grasping the hammer, the biceps and triceps, the angle and bend of the elbow, the angle of the hammer and its weight, the nail now leaning slightly to the left with the third blow, the board sliding approximately one inch forward due to the hammer blows, and more remotely, some hammering next to him, the circular saw that just kicked in some ten yards to the right, perhaps a jet plane flying overhead, all this belongs to subsidiary attention. These subsidiary activities are more immediate and less mediated. That is to say, they are closer to the sphere of Firstness and further removed from Thirdness. These are tantamount to signs 222. A weathervane, for example, indicates the direction of the air current whether anyone is around or not to acknowledge the sign as a sign and properly interpret it. In a sense, the weathervane "knows" what to do and does it, because that is its nature. That is its "habit," as it is the "habit" of the hand that wields the hammer that hits the nail that is driven into the wood. Suppose the hammer has been around for some years and the head is loose. While the tool is being used the head gives a little. Its owner stops hammering and shifts his focal attention to take a look. The hammer's head is now the sign of his focal awareness, and his left hand itself has become the subsidiary sign 222 that moves the hammer shaft that causes the hammer's head to wobble slightly for his focal attention. The hand knows how to do this, just as it knows how to hold the hammer when engaged in the act of hammering, because that it its "habit." The tool is inspected and tossed in the junk heap: time to buy another one anyway. Focal attention was redirected and part of what previously constituted subsidiary attention fell out of the picture.

Christina, to repeat, lost her proprioceptive capacity, her subsidiary attention had become virtually null, and she was capable of hardly more than focal attention. Consequently, she had no body image, no sense of the body's interrelation to and interaction with the signs in its immediate environment. At the same time, however, as compensation, she acquired especially acute hearing. Normally, while speaking, our voice inflection and tone remain subsidiary. In contrast, since Christina had lost her capacity for subsidiary attention, she found it necessary to concentrate on this aspect of her speech. At first there was difficulty in doing so, but gradually she made progress, and her conversation took on a more "normal" countenance. Christina applied this same type of retraining to her body. Since she had very little proprioceptive awareness, she found it necessary to compensate for this loss by paying close focal attention to her body's posture. She was eventually able to improve on the positioning of her body. The problem was that her pose appeared forced, willful, and histrionic, "like a dancer in mid-pose." Nature having failed her, she resorted to artifice, "but the artifice was suggested by nature, and soon became 'second nature'" (Sacks 1970:49–50).

In other words, signs 222 had been part of Christina's subsidiary awareness and its scant interrelations to and interactions with the signs around it, allowing focal awareness to rest on signs of more immediate importance (221, 321–322, and 331–333 during a conversation). Now, given her lack of proprioception, she found it necessary to bring signs 222 into her focal awareness as well, and as a consequence they appeared unnatural, as if coming about in automaton fashion. Her compensatory act, having become available to her without her having consciously to think about it, became part of her nature, yet she was still lacking in natural proprioceptive awareness, so it appeared to onlookers to be unnatural. What for us are signs 222 of our proprioceptive awareness she found she must boot up to signs 321 and 322—to indexical and linguistic "pointers" or "indicators" (321, or pronouns) and customary and entrenched or embedded language use (322, "How are you?"). However, while we habitually take signs 321 and 322 in and process them as part of our sub-sidiary attention and in automaton fashion, she was required to concentrate on them, hence her moves actually appeared to be those of an automaton. Now, since replicas of 322 and 321 are 222 and 211 respectively, that is how we take them, for they have become second nature, they have become part of our "habits of thought and of action." Christina, in contrast, could not afford the luxury of their becoming replicas: each actualization of signs 322 and 321 must be taken as if they were there for the first time, and she reacted accordingly. Her self necessarily remained apart from them. In contrast, ordinarily there is hardly any distinction between our self and our sign replications; we take them all in our stride and act appropriately and proprioceptively. Christina, as a consequence, felt that her body was "blind and deaf to itself," that it had "no sense of itself."

Sacks observes that neither she nor society has words to describe her strange condition:

> The blind, at least, are treated with solicitude—we can imagine their state, and we treat them accordingly. But when Christina, painfully, clumsily, mounts a bus, she receives nothing but uncomprehending and angry snarls: "What's wrong with you, lady? Are you blind—or blind-drunk?" What can she answer—"I have no proprioception"? The lack of social support and sympathy is an additional trial: disabled, but with the nature of her disability not clear—she is not, after all, manifestly blind or paralysed, manifestly anything—she tends to be treated as a phony or a fool. This is what happens to those with disorders of the hidden senses (it happens also to patients who have vestibular impairment, or who have been labyrinthectomised). (Sacks 1970:51)

Christina, in short, is condemned to dwell in an indescribable, unimaginable world. It is a "non-world," which Sacks refers to once again as "nothingness." She has lost all sense of her identity with respect to her body, ultimately she has no body-ego. Whenever she wishes to use her hand, she must reinvent it as her "hand" (signs 331, then 322 and 321) and then concentrate on using that otherwise alien appendage for a specific purpose (as sign 222). She has succeeded in being able to "operate" within her surroundings, but she cannot simply "be," she cannot be "herself," her-self. Her signs of chiefly Secondness have no past; they must be re-actualized in the present as if they were there for the first time. Yet she has learned to survive, an indomitable, irrepressible, and impressive human being.[2]

III. "HIGHER" SIGNS?

It is now notorious that in the West there is a long-standing bias in favor of the so-called left-brain functions (logic, linear language use, reason, mathematics, the linear mechanics of music composition). While left-hemisphere syndromes have been thoroughly documented, right-hemisphere syndromes, even though they are as common as their counterparts, have received relatively little attention. And for a good reason. They remain pretty much a mystery, since they cannot be accounted for in logical, rational terms. Likewise, our biases have favored what are generally conceived to be the equivalent of "higher" semiotic processes (signs 321–333). Now these signs are important. They are the best ones to think with, to reason with, to talk with, and to present fool-proof arguments in order to win other people over to our way of thinking—often with hardly a thought to other people's way of thinking in defense of which they also present fool-proof arguments.

The strange case of Dr. P, an accomplished musician and "the man who mistook his wife for a hat," falls into the category of right-hemisphere syndromes (Sacks 1970:8–22). Dr. P had a quite normal grasp of the mechanical aspects of language use, but he had lost virtually all capacity for visualization, for imagination. He could speak of things but could not construct a mental image of them while he spoke. Novelists visualize and animate their characters, who actually exist only in words. Dr. P could remember narrated details about a novel without difficulty, and he retained an undiminished grasp of the plot. But he could not visualize the characters and the scenes. They were for him no more than so many words. When clothed in their gala best, these words were signs 331–333, to be sure, but Dr P. often managed to take them for something other than what we would ordinarily take them for, since we avail ourselves of visual imagery and he could not do so. He could not relate words with their conventional sensory items. Consequently, he had even more trouble with signs 321–322, since they are vague to begin with. Dr P. could quote the original descriptions of the visual aspects of characters and scenes, but they lacked sensorial, imaginal, and emotional reality in relation to his own sensed, imaged, and emotional self. (Sacks contrasts Dr. P's case to that of Helen Keller, who, from the verbal and metaphorical, had developed a keen feel for the sensorial and the visual even though her visual cortex had never been stimulated.)

While Dr. P, due to his visual agnosia, was lacking in body-image and all other forms of imagery, he had body-music. In fact, he conducted the entirety of his comings and goings through a stream of inner music he incessantly played for himself. He did everything while literally singing to himself. If for some reason that inner music were halted, he became confused and completely out of step with his outer world. His world was not a world with which his signs interrelated, it was a world of music, which had no interrelationship with the furniture of the world, but which, nonetheless, allowed Dr. P to develop his own personal modus operandi. Without these interrelationships, he was lacking in the concrete and the "real" in terms of quality, Firstness (signs 111–311). Consequently, he had trouble recognizing faces, even those of his wife and children. He had difficulty even recognizing himself in a mirror. In fact, while shaving, he often questioned whether it was really his face that was gazing at itself. If we wish to call signs 321–333 signs of a "higher" type, well enough. But can we forget that the signs of a "lower" type are the body and shoulders upon which these signs stand? And that without those other, largely tacitly acknowledged signs, our world would be seriously impoverished?

For sure, signs 331–333 require a dialectical-dialogical leap from images and image-concepts (that is, particulars) to the generalizing power of words. Words as generals do not relate to individual semiotic objects but to classes of objects. Each word is always already a generality before it is used in relation to a particular thing. As a generality, it relates the many aspects of the world as they should be perceived, conceived, and described according to the set of generalities shared by the members of the linguistic community. As a particular, it is limited to a sensation within a specific context and given a specific situation. The inability to use words as generalities (loss of speech, or aphasia) inhibits and can even prohibit the use of symbols of the 331–333 variety. Such is the case of people suffering from prelingual deafness, and their thinking can appear incoherent and stunted (Sacks 1989:1–35). It would seem that language for such unfortunate individuals is limited to 222 and 221, and at the very most, to 322 and 321, which would be replicas of 333, 332, and 331 for ordinary speakers. The chief, and very important, difference is that these replicas are for the linguistically impaired not replicas at all. They are the extent of language; they are for the linguistically impaired taken as the real thing. How could it be otherwise? Like Borges's Funes, they see and name only particulars. Their signs relate to specific things in specific contexts and for specific purposes as individuals, particulars, and no more.

Of particular note is the pair of autistic twins, John and Michael. They are like enantiomorphs, mirror images, Tweedledum and Tweedledee. These twins specialized in "calendar arithmetic." They could be given a date, any date, say, July 6th of the year 1099, and they could in short order produce the day of the week to which it corresponds. Yet, with an IQ in the 60s, they could barely manage with the most simple of mathematical computations. If a bunch of toothpicks were tossed on the floor they could look at them and quickly respond in unison, "Seventy-nine," or whatever the sum of the toothpicks might be. They saw entire arrays of things, including numbers, holistically, and at a glance. Their perception was something like that of Funes, who in one perceptual grasp could catch all the leaves, twigs, branches, and contours on the trunk of a tree. Yet they were very much unlike Funes, for they inhabited a world of numbers, not things. They would nod and smile upon recognizing certain numbers, as if savoring a fine wine. They felt a special affinity, even an intimacy, for particular numbers and combinations of numbers, like a child with a teddy bear, a teenager with a car, an adult with a recently purchased boat.

> The twins live exclusively in a thought-world of numbers. They have no interest in the stars shining, or the hearts of men. And yet numbers for them . . . are not "just" numbers, but significances, signifiers whose "significance" is the world.
>
> They do not approach numbers lightly, as most calculators do. They are not interested in, have no capacity for, cannot comprehend, calculations. They are, rather, serene contemplators of number—and approach numbers with a sense of reverence and awe. Numbers for them are holy, fraught with significance. (Sacks 1970:207–08)

Their universe of numbers consisted of signs 111, 211, and 311, to be sure, since they had an intimate feel, an emotional attachment for, the abstract, arbitrary signs surrounding them. And they had a holistic grasp of numbers within the equivalent, their own equivalent, of signs 221, 222, and 331. But they could not use algorithmic properties to combine their signs into strings comparable to 322 and 333, they could not calculate. They were also deficient in their comprehension of signs 321 and 322, I would suspect, since they were incapable of taking replicas (tokens) and using them as genuine signs (types). Their world was enriched beyond our wildest imagination, on the one hand, and on the other, it was impoverished in a way we can hardly begin to imagine.

Borges's Funes once devised his own system of enumeration. Since he could not conceive of numbers as an ordered series, he substituted ordinary nouns for them. For example, 5 might be "oak," 13 "pampa," 27 "quebracho," 286 "plata," and so on. Since he could hold them all in his mental checking account holistically, they were easily retrievable and quite efficient for his purposes. Kurt Gödel, author of the now notorious "incompleteness theorems," once speculated that numbers could serve as "markers" for people, ideas, things, events, or whatever, which could pave the way for an "arithmetization" of the world (Nagel and Newman 1958). With this in mind, Sacks concludes:

> if this does occur, it is possible that the twins, and others like them, do not merely live in a world *of* numbers, but in a world, in *the* world, *as* numbers, their number-meditation or play being a sort of existential meditation— and, if one can understand it, or find the key . . . a strange and precise communication too. (1970:213)

And with this thought I take my leave as far as this chapter goes. I see no need in further meditation on signs of symbolicity, of natural languages or formal languages. After all, our Western civilization has been obsessed with them for centuries. What could I possibly add to these particulars?

Well, perhaps this . . . just perhaps. Peirce tells us that interpretants of signs 332 look much like signs 322 (their de-engendered replicas), and replicas of signs 322 are signs 222 of a particular kind. Replicas of 333 are also ultimately 222 of a particular kind, while replicas of 331 are 321, pronouns; but then pronouns are more often than not taken as mere simulacra, de-engendered signs, so they are hardly more than signs 222. Particulars from signs 222 can de-engender further to drop out of consciousness altogether. Yet they are always there, now, as possibilities that at a moment's notice can pop up to interact with other actualized signs, or to caress, frustrate, or taunt their interpreter.[3] Then, they may be able to engender signs 222, 321, 322, 331, 332, and 333. It's up and down the semiotic staircase, sign engenderment and sign de-engenderment: an ongoing process. The conclusion that in the final analysis forces itself upon us, it would appear, is that most of our signs are used tacitly. They are part of our tacit knowledge, of our knowing how to do what we do without the need explicitly to explain the whys of our doing. In other words, most of the signs we use and abuse willingly and voluntarily are a mere tip of the iceberg.

I now take a turn to this characteristic of signs, that, ultimately, paces us squarely within linguicentrism.

11

SIGNS, SIGNIFIERS, SIMULACRA: LINGUICENTRISM

I. LIFE IN THE FAST LANE

According to many observers, during the last half of the present century an entirely new "language" began to emerge in response to the rapidly changing socio-politico-economic postmodern environment. Mark Poster (1989, 1990) calls it the "mode of information," which has served, for better or for worse, to "detotalize the social world," thus providing impetus for dispersing and decentering the self. This loss of the self and the accompanying decentering process are chiefly a consequence of recent electronically mediated lines of communication "which are increasingly being substituted for both face-to-face and written communication" (Poster 1989:79).

The postmodern "gaze" tends to reduce the length and breadth of cultural experience to a carnival of two-dimensional (e.g., dyadic) spectacles, an effervescent race of captivating images and seductive surfaces. This phenomenon is an unbridled fetishism, and of the illusion of a forever inaccessible virtuality-immediacy, of the depiction of naked power, ribald sex, and unremitting violence, of relentless speed and break-neck acceleration of the imaginary (and, by extension, the semiotically real), of a blaze of spatial segments and temporal increments the total concoction of which becomes fused and confused into nothing more than a random mish-mash of suggestive signifying glimpses. Television, and especially its ads, we are told, are by consensus the prime offenders. The boob-tube is the most natural medium of information transfer in this near-chaotic setting. In fact, TV is not merely the chief medium, but the most active propagator of the new mode of information. While one stares glassy-eyed at the tube, images fly past images with staccato, rapid-fire cadence. It is up to the mind to somehow find a way to construct some sort of legato flow from the staccato series, an ominous task when considering that the barrage of messages is projected forth at multiple levels, some of which remain virtually inaccessible to the conscious mind: they are in part subliminal (Jameson 1984).

Examples are of course multiple, and I trust I need not pursue the issue further. The point to be made is that Marshall McLuhan's "the media is the message," announcing the impending electronic age, renders centralization, linear specialization, analysis of components to the detriment of wholes, isolation and the cultivation of detachment, all of the machine age, quite obsolete. Meanings merge with messages, and messages become inseparable from channels of information; in fact, information is highlighted more and more, while meaning tends to fall by the wayside. The electronic media creates conditions of decentering within local confines, interdependence on a global scale, and a visual and auditory world of simultaneous events. What is more, the mise en scène rapidly overtaking us apparently defies linearity, hence in its radical nonlinear logic of differentiation it appears synonymous with irrationality (Smart 1992:115–20).

At this juncture it might seem that the media, by and large one-dimensional, even regarding visual imagery—parcel and product of Boolean linearity—with its machine-gun rapidity, gives rise to virtually limitless possibilities in our three-dimensional sphere of things (life games, virtual reality, semantic nets, and other wonders of cybermania). Nothing seems to be absolutely barred, everything is apparently possible by way of some sort of joyous Nietzschean free-play of signs, to rephrase Derrida. We are, it would seem, at last liberated from those awful tyrants—logos, representation, presence, immediacy—and can now bask in the life-giving warmth of semiosis, unfettered by our previous hang-ups.

But this is not exactly what we are being told by those self-proclaimed hypersensitive contemplators of our present scene. Critics charge that TV rhetoric, above all, undermines the viewer's residue of reason, transmuting well-tempered thought processes into the baser metal of desire for frivolous consumption and attraction into the mixed messages underlying dizzy rhetorical cajolery. Advertisers, politicians, and reporters, so the story goes, stop at nothing in their efforts to grab a larger share of the market, rate higher in the polls, and pursue that elusive Pulitzer Prize. Advertising has most especially shifted from being informative, with the presumption of an intelligent, thoughtful consumer, to being the irrational manipulation of the consumer. This transformation is the result of what has been termed a collapse (1) of (dyadic) referentiality—it enjoyed unwarranted privilege anyway—, (2) of (triadic) meaning, the dream of a Grand Transcendental Signified loaded with semantic ammunition—actually, it never really existed in the first place—, and (3) of language in general, the language of "presence," of "(phal)logocentrism," of unadulterated "Truth." Consequently, a decentering of that artificially propagated idea of the paramount individual Cartesian subject standing apart from its world as supreme objective arbiter is brought about, which further serves to undermine the traditional distinctions between subjectivity and objectivity, true and false consciousness, science and nonscience, and appearance and reality.

So far, so good, it would seem: the Derridean critique of our coveted Western standards stands out bold and robust. But let us look further.

II. IS THERE REALLY NO REAL MESSAGE?

The transformations wrought in our contemporary milieu are hardly anywhere more evident than in the writings of Jean Baudrillard. The early Baudrillard saw society as organized around unnecessary conspicuous consumption and the lavish display of commodities by means of which one could acquire identity, prestige, and status in the community. The more flashy one's cars, house, clothes, and assorted toys, the higher one's standing. During this stage of his thought, Baudrillard made efforts to combine Saussurean semiological theory in terms of a "critique of the political economy of the sign" with a Marxist critique of capitalism (Baudrillard 1975, 1981). For the later Baudrillard, labor is no longer a force of production but has itself become just another sign among signs. Production is nothing more than the consumerist system of signs referring to themselves (Baudrillard 1983a, 1983b, 1988a).

Baudrillard's mass media have generated an inundation of images and signs the consequence of which is a "simulation world" (of signs 111 and 211), which erases the age-old distinction between the real and the imaginary (between signs 221, 222, and 321 and other signs). Fredric Jameson (1979, 1983) calls this world the product of a depthless, schizophrenic posture capitalizing on a plurality of styles, idiosyncrasies, fads, and fashions, the end-product of which is "pastiche"—hollow imitation, "blank parody," empty masks (especially signs 111 and 211). I expect Baudrillard would not exactly disagree with this estimation, though the French intellectual remains more aloof regarding Marxism than his North American counterpart. Both he and Jameson allude to a progressive abstraction—in fact, a fetishism of the abstract—of cultural signs (signs of Firstness and Thirdness devoid of relations to signs of Secondness). However, in a certain sense he does Jameson one better. He factors his equation to the next stage: the "logic" of contemporary commodity capitalism is not merely depthless, it breeds a malignant Nietzschean sort of nihilism (i.e., the negative side of "nothingness" as illustrated above). The privileged domains of modernity—science, philosophy, labor, private enterprise, social programs, and, above all, theory (Lyotard's [1984] "metanarratives")—are sucked up by a whirlwind of vacuous signifiers and into a black hole. The age-old cherished illusions of the referential sign vanish, as signs and their objects implode into mere disembodied signs (Baudrillard 1983a:1–4).

Consequently, the commodities of postmodern culture organized around conspicuous consumption have lost their value as material goods; they exist only in the realm of semiotic value. Like signs in Saussure's differential system of language, we are told by many observers of postmodernism, they take on value according to their relations with all other sign-commodities in the entire system. Everything is flattened to the same level, that of signifiers existing in contiguous relationship with other signifiers (i.e., dyadic semiology). Ultracommercialized goods having become signs are centrifuged, homogenized, desiccated, and shoved onto a gullible public in the form of a pabulum diet the totality of which composes a vast tautological system whereby individual needs are created by the very system responsible for satisfying those needs. In fact, individuals are nothing more than socially invented agents of needs. Each individual becomes tantamount to any and all individuals. The individual, like any given sign-commodity, is equal to no more than any and all other sign-commodities of the same name and value. That is, individuals are hardly more than gas molecules rushing about at random in an enclosed container, yet, as an aggregate, the collection of individuals is statistically determinable.

Three "orders of simulation," Baudrillard writes—and as briefly mentioned in chapter 4—have gradually come to dominate our mind-numbing postmodern social life. They were introduced with (1) the order of the counterfeit (the natural law of value), which coincides with the rise of modernity, when simulacra implied power and social relations, (2) the industrial revolution, when serial production and finally automation (based on the commercial law of value) opened the door to infinite reproducibility, and machines began to take their place alongside humans, and (3) our present cybernetic society (based on the structural law of value), when models began to take precedence over things, and since models are signs, signs now began to exercise the full force of their hegemony (Baudrillard 1983a).

This third order simulation is obsessively binary or dyadic in nature—which is to be expected, for, after all, Baudrillard's own model is linguicentric, Saussurean. The story has it that language, genetics, and social organization are analogous (in the order of structuralism, the DNA code, and semiology). All are governed by a binary (cybernetic, Boolean) logic underlying social models and codes controlling institutional and everyday life. Consequently, an individual's range of choices and responses is severely regulated by programmed and precoded messages. In contrast to classical theories of social control, Baudrillard's theory prima facie appears radically indeterminate: there is no grand omniscient administrator with a master plan in hand, but, rather, everything resembles "a Brownian movement of particles or the calculation of probabilities." Such is, for example, voting in democratic cybersocieties, "as if everyone voted by chance, or monkeys voted." Party distinctions have been flattened. It really "makes no difference at all what the parties in power are expressing historically and socially. It is *necessary* even that they represent nothing: the fascination of the game, the polls, the formal and statistical compulsion of the game is all the greater" (Baudrillard 1983a:132; italics in original).

Power can be absolute in this system only if it is capable of diffracting into a spectrum of variants, each defined in terms of binaries: remove something here, put something else there; change this, and reciprocally alter that, and so on. This applies to brands of soap as well as to the peaceful coexistence between superpowers. Two superpowers are necessary to maintain control; one superpower standing alone would soon crumble.[1] The macrolevel binary opposition between them is regulated by manipulating myriad series of binaries within the system to retain the image of equilibrium. Though at local levels a flurry of diversified activity appears to reign, the matrix, by its very nature, remains intractably binary and does not change on the whole. It is "always the 0/1, the binary scansion that is affirmed as the metastable or homeostatic form of the current system" (Baudrillard 1983a:135). Everything apparently comes in twos, whether giving the appearance of opposition or identity (simulacra). In either case, the sign purifies itself by duplicating itself, and on so doing it destroys its meaning and its referent. Andy Warhol demonstrates this with his multiple replicas showing "at the same time the death of the original and the end of representation" (Baudrillard 1983a:136). In short, cybernetics triumphs by reducing everything to binaries that are not really binaries at all but oppositions fused into differences ultimately destined to be canceled entirely. And sameness will surely rule the land. That is, Baudrillard seems to be telling us—though he is far from explicit on the matter—that signs will suffer de-engenderment to the extent that they will function as if they were signs of Firstness: icons.

On Baudrillard's radical semiological view, signs and modes of representation rather than representation itself come to constitute "reality." Consequently, signs begin to take on autonomy. They become mere atoms, having lost their nature as signs interrelated and interacting with all other signs in the codependent process of emerging into other signs. These lonely, hermetic signs make up a new type of social order; they mandate the future of commodities, consumers, and society, all of which are in the final analysis nothing more than signs flattened to the same base level. Signs become charged with meaning only in relation to, and take their rightful place in the language of, the media, with respect merely to other signs in the entire interwoven, variegated, labyrinthine tapestry. Signs are destined to float in an undefinable space of their own making—all of which is Saussurean poststructuralist idealism with a vengeance.

Thus the era of rational thought and discourse meets its demise. As a result, the individual is left with an idealist, relativist universe composed of the imaginary (thought-signs) more than the "real," that is, the semiotically real (sign-events). It follows, Baudrillard writes, that: "All the great humanist criteria of value, all the values of a civilization of moral, aesthetic, and practical judgment, vanish in our system of images and signs. Everything becomes undecidable" (Poster 1988:126–28).

III. YET, STRANGE CONSONANCES

What we have in Baudrillard, it would appear, is a sort of "ultra-" or "hypernominalism," disconnected signs, signs of radical de-engenderment. Signs as discrete, referenceless atoms rush about in a constant collision course with one another, their apparent relation to each other and to the whole of things having been lost in the maelstrom: pure particulars, nomadic signs with neither subject nor object, only naked signs. In fact, Baudrillard's signs have been de-engendered to the extent that they are signs of Firstness and nothing more than Firstness, which is actually quite alien to Peirce. These signs are incapable of producing authentic Peircean symbols of mediated Thirdness, for they have submerged into the domain of Iconicity (simulacra, basically signs of 111, hardly capable of entering into signs of the 211 and 221 sort), with little degree of freedom at their disposal.

In neo-Saussurean parlance common to poststructuralism, a sign is a concept and an image, both of them mental—idealistic nominalism—with hardly any association between sign, meaning, and referent. In other words, the putative postmodern subjectless subject consumes signs, not things. As we have noted, Peircean triadic semiotics, in stark contrast, entails a sign (representamen), its meaning (roughly, the interpretant) and its respective object (which is semiotically real, not "really" real). Peircean meaning is not immediate, but always mediated. It is never what is directly perceived and in the same breath interpreted *as* such-and-such, but, rather, perception and interpretation come into consciousness during an increment of time, they are never direct—which by a hair's breadth salvages the Peircean concept of the sign from out-and-out logocentrism. In Baudrillard's view, when in the postmodern world signs are exchanged between minds they become "symbolic" (i.e., "autonomous"). Their meanings float—ambiguously and vaguely, as it were—between minds, and thus they remain divorced from the furniture of the world. Signs do not carry along a satchel replete with meanings to put in some sort of order such that one can say "Here the sign, there the meaning," nor is there any necessarily motivated link, natural or conventional, between signs and things. Rather, "meanings," if we dare even use the word in this context, indiscriminately and randomly wander in and out of minds: a hustle-bustle of activity, aleatory signification, anarchic information generation. Manipulation of these cultural signs equals manipulation of the public. It is no longer a matter of exchanging commodities in the orthodox Marxist sense, for the commodities have become themselves mere signs. We are, it appears, submerged in the "mode of information."

In this fashion, television is capable of displacing confessionals, therapy, family encounters, fireside chats, private periods of silent contemplation, public events such as checkers, scrabble, and poker marathons, adventurous outings, and even puttering around the yard or cleaning the garage. During sitcoms, commercials, CNN broadcasts, dreary soaps, I-told-you-so miniseries, and even so-called educational TV, the onlooker is presumably formed, fashioned, and artificially refabricated into a passive consumer, numbed into an apparently semicatatonic state by incessant unidimensional bombardment of visual and aural rhetoric. In the process, floating signifiers are slapped onto unnecessary commodities not because of some intrinsic relation between them but for the purpose of fulfilling desires created by that very rhetoric. In comparable fashion, through e-mailing or internetting or teleconferencing or mere surfing, electronic mediation heightens the artificiality of the communicative track, giving the subject the sense of a false presence, an illusory immediacy, a hereness and nowness of the communicative act (and all this without the mediated inferential process of Thirdness, since the semiotic agent, on reflection, knows better—or should know better—than to think all this is anything more than ersatz, mock, sham representation of frivolous commodities).

Thus with the term "mode of information," Poster, in part following Baudrillard, is able to reinvest Marx's "mode of production" and place it in the contemporary context, while eschewing such terms as "age of information," which usually pretend to hail the ushering in of something new and refreshing. "Mode of information" designates the field of pure linguistic experience, "whose basic structural relations change from period to period just as do those of the mode of production" (Poster 1989:82). It takes into account recent critiques of representation, intention, and the univocity of language, while remaining in tune with Marxist assumptions and the unique tenor of the media since the cybernetic revolution beginning in the 1940s and 1950s with Alan Turing, John von Neumann, Norbert Wiener, and Claude Shannon and Warren Weaver.

The important facet of Poster's work—via Baudrillard—to the present inquiry stems from his idea that the electronic mode creates a surface of signs referring only to themselves in delirious bliss, finally embracing the self, which in the process becomes itself a full-blown sign. Language is no longer a mere tool but includes the interpreting self and thus becomes its own mechanic tooling the semiotic machine, from "software" (mind) levels to "hardware" (brain) levels. In this vein, Baudrillard's study of the nature of signification in advertising emphasizing the separation of signifiers and signifieds from the commodities that were the focus of their erstwhile relation is multiplied manyfold by the electronic media. The result is that everything can be somehow construed to relate to everything else, in a bewildering and at the same time, in some masochistic fashion, delectable confusion.

The upshot is that the Boolean computer language underlying the electronic media—the most obstinately linear, digitalized language imaginable—ultimately gives rise to unlimited associativity along n-ary lines in n-dimensional spatiality. The problem stems chiefly from Baudrillard's idea that in our postmodern milieu, signs, Saussurean signs, have been injected with a massive dose of autonomy—an autonomy of actualized atoms, bordering on Secondness as it were. As largely arbitrary, autonomous signs, they enjoy virtually unlimited freedom, no doubt—in terms of their emergence along multiple one-dimensional lines within a three-dimensional sphere—and they can consequently take on a "life" of their own, it might appear. This "life," however—and herein lies the problem—has been supposedly granted them by those of the multimedia in charge of manipulating the public. Signs take on "life" because they have become autonomous; the mediamongers use, and are thereby used by, these signs for the purpose of duping the common folk into lavishing themselves with more and more unnecessary commodities. But the commodities have themselves been replaced by the signs, which are now more "real" than the real, they are "hyperreal," as Baudrillard reiterates time and again. The common folk gobble up the signs dished out to them as if they were real; and they are "real," the only "reality" available to a superhyped malaise.

Now, if Baudrillard's signs with a "life" of their own were indeed to have become autonomous, the yield would be devastating; the so-called common folk's semiotic freedom would be severely shunted. These very autonomous signs enjoying authenticity worthy of the most dignified symbols would actually have become mere signs of de-engenderment. As such they would be "dead" signs, much like "dead" metaphors and all other signs mindlessly consumed as a result of entrenchment, embedment, automatization, habit. They would not be signs engaged in interaction with active consciousness but signs out of mind and rooted in matter, neither genuine thought-signs nor sign-events but simply signs blindly pushed and shoved here and there, randomly moving in and out, while engaged in an aleatory dance to the screech of some sort of heavy-metal-like tribal cadence.

In contrast, relatively authentic, "growing" Peircean symbols spiral "ever-upward"—though in fits and jerks, and with occasional setbacks. These are indeed "living signs." For the "common folks" of Baudrillard's discourse, in contrast, parameters of choice are fundamentally limited to de-engendered symbolicity (that is, to iconicity), autonomous signs having become merely self-contained, hollow, and isolated signs. Active, mediating Thirdness is "life." In contrast, self-sufficient iconicity of de-engenderment without the collaboration of interactive interpretative communities of semiotic agents suffer slow "death." The rampaging semiosic river is dammed, a reservoir builds up, and winter arrives, freezing it into a solid block from which signs sublimate into a random gaseous hustle and bustle with neither rhyme nor reason. If Baudrillard's signs were indeed autonomous in the full-blown sense, then the manipulated ordinary citizens could not but consume them at most in linear Boolean fashion—Baudrillard himself admits that they do so as robots—as if there were no choices, as if there existed *this* sign in the immediate here and now and nothing more.

Fortunately, "living" Peircean signs ipso facto exercise, and will continue to exercise, some degree of autonomy; if not, they would not be "alive." But rather than being mere islands unto themselves, they are also perpetually open to their environment. There is constant give-and-take, disequilibrium, imbalance, tension. The process is ongoing. This tension of tensions there will always be: a tendency toward symmetry, equilibrium, balance ("death"), versus an opposing tendency toward asymmetry, disequilibrium, imbalance ("life"). If "death" were to reign supreme, then there would be only crystallized stasis. On the other hand, if there were only "life" and nothing but "life," then pure chaos would erupt—Nietzsche's eternal return, nothing new under the sun—within which "life" as we know it, and perhaps as it can only be known, could not continue to sustain itself. There must reign, in the final analysis, disordered order, ordered disorder: being always becoming and becoming never quite becoming authentic being.[2]

In short, there is an ongoing process of de-engenderment as well as engenderment of signs. If signs can become indexicalized and then iconized to their basest form such that they are made and taken in mindless fashion, they can also be de-iconized and de-indexicalized in such a manner that their use and abuse on the part of both sign makers and sign takers can emerge into consciousness. Then there can be feeling and sensing and experiencing and thought and talk about the signs, and dialogue and speculation and even theories about why they are the way they are and why we are the way we are. The very important point is that for such signs to be possible, there must be semiosis; that is, there must be Thirdness, sign mediation.

IV. WHERE IS IT ALL TAKING US?

Nevertheless, in Baudrillard's conception of things, whether at work or play or rest, whether in the family, the church, the schools, leisure activities or travel, complex and perplexing new levels of interconnectedness afforded by the electronic media promise virtually unlimited possibilities to the media manipulators, thus enhancing their control over the manipulated. Exchanges of messages between humans and between humans and machines are subject to radically fewer space and time constraints— consequently, McLuhan's "global village" now appears technically feasible. Silicon-based communicative facilities become increasingly efficient, giving credence to compelling arguments demonstrating that human relations are undergoing radical alterations. Negotiations regarding the conduct of social life—who belongs up and down in the hierarchy, who can speak with authority, who must listen, who makes decisions, who is free to choose, who commands credibility and who not—are subject to new rules and strategies.

This is not simply a current phenomenon, of course. It began with the light bulb, the telephone, and other early technological developments, and it is only now beginning to exercise its full force (Marvin 1988). According to this conception, the bonds limiting traditional discourse were severed. Since the Renaissance, art, science, intuition, thought, and even everyday affairs had been ordered along specific lines and patterns, like the iron filings on a vibrating flat surface when a magnet is placed under it. Everything, it now appears, is somehow, and mysteriously by invisible lines of force, connected to everything else. All experience is part of a whole; each individual consciousness is all consciousness. What appeared to be the undesirable chaotic element of the universe, feared by scientists obsessed in their pursuit of truth at all cost, is not merely that random, unplanned, catastrophic anti-Christ, the adversary of all that is good and Godly. It is a new form of order under the statistical headings "indeterminacy," "uncertainty," "fractals," "fluctuations," "dissipative structures," "asymmetry," and so on. From modernity's insistence on law and order, balance and harmony, on collecting all the information and putting each bit in its proper place, we now have postmodernism's ruthless rush of time, reckless abandon in space, and experience through n-directions in virtual simultaneity (Hassan 1980, 1987; Schechner 1982:109–28).

In Baudrillard's interpretation of the postmodern milieu, what we have is actually not symbolicity at all in the Peircean sense. Rather, the unfettered freedom promised by the equivalent of James Bunn's one dimension committed and three dimensions free (Firstness) has been de-engendered to the point that few degrees of freedom remain. That is to say, communication is by way of symbols, clearly enough, but symbols tied down to tunnel-like linear production rather than free-rein n-dimensional engenderment. To repeat, they are de-engendered symbols, their symbolicity is processed in robotic fashion as if they were icons. Of course, Heraclitus of old was privy to such paradoxes. He knew that the sphere of semiosis is not resolvable into a harmonious noncontradictory whole. Postmodernism also admits, embraces, and needs an uncertain system of a contradictory complementarity sort. It has learned—must learn—to accept, even embrace, inconsistencies and incompleteness. For the unattainable and inconceivable whole within which we dwell is multicentric, whether we like it or not. Everything and nothing is at the center, which is everywhere and nowhere, depending upon the perspective—that is, radical perspectivism. Experience is in this view quite free-wheeling. It flows, alternating between reflexivity of the flow without stopping it and subjectivity to the flow without the capacity to analyze it. This alternating of the current serves further to foment an embrace of the inconsistency-paradox horns. Upon their being so embraced, the process of knowing and being known are inseparable: all observations are participatory acts, and all participatory acts are to a degree creative—or constructive, as it were. In this light, it must be conceded that the alternative currents of experience—reflexivity, subject-object, knower-known—cancel the possibility of exclusively autonomous signs. Rather, an oscillatory autonomy-dependency process is incessantly acted out, annihilated, and re-enacted.

Thus it becomes exceedingly problematic to speak of absolutes. The direct, unmediated seeing of things "Exactly as they are on no uncertain terms, Dammit" of modernity becomes a postmodern flux of experience, given the moment and nothing but the moment. The only specifiables, if specifiables there be at all in a rather loose sense, are found solely in relations—in triadicity, and Peirce wins yet another round over binarism. The alternation of flow and reflexivity, of openness and autonomy, of self within other and self set apart from other cannot but result in fragmentation *and* holism. There is not the one without the other. And they are themselves mediated by a third term, like the complementary wave-particle and "wavicle," or sign-object and interpretant, First-Second, and then Third. The dancer cannot be separated from the dance; they are both included in the happening being unfolded, unfolding itself. This is to say that symbols de-engendered by indexicalization and iconization into signs of lesser complexity do not speak well of themselves when parading around in the guise of Baudrillardian simulacra. In fact, that is the problem: they do not speak at all; they are signs of chiefly indexicality and chiefly iconicity as discussed above, and appropriate to bodymind practices. When linguicentrized, typical of Baudrillardian and other binary practices, these signs are disguised as something they once were and can once again become, but for the time being no longer are.

Although this palaver about postmodernism may still strike some observers as light-years removed from Peirce, as I argue elsewhere (Merrell 1995a, 1996), Peirce is in some respects quite in tune with our times. However, in other respects he diverges radically from much current thought, especially in regard to the essence of Baudrillard's three orders of simulation and the (dis)location of the self in contemporary language, discourse, and everyday language games. In order more adequately to illustrate the relevance of Peirce to our contemporary milieu, let us turn to a further consideration of media signs.

12

MEDIA, MESSAGE, SIGN:
AN INSEPARABLE TRIO

I. THE MEDIA AND THE SELF

Instead of offering an Ong-McLuhan historical survey of the transformation from sound to sight to extended sight and finally to hypersight, from orality to chirography to typography and to electronic media, and from temporality to hyperspatiality, I would rather attempt to place the progressive de-engenderment of the stream of semiosis over the various Foucauldian ages in a critical light.

The story might go something like this. In *Peirce's Semiotics NOW* (Merrell 1995b) I proposed a patterning of Western painting, literature, and science from medieval times to the present as a transition from qualisignification to sinsignification to legisignification and then a move back again to spatialization or qualisignification in our century, but this time from a plurality of perspectives. Now I will attempt to offer a tale regarding how it is that we make and take our signs and how they allow us to do the things we do with them, eventually reaching the conclusion that it is fundamentally because they do things *with*—not *to*, notice—us at the same time that we do things with them, whether we know it or not and whether we like it or not. We are all in an interrelated, codependent, complementarily contradictory process of self-organization.

What must become the focus of attention is the semiotic body, its kinesthetics, and more concretely our sense of feeling by way of touch (contact). Touch, to reiterate, is a shorthand of the eyes. It senses what the eyes can only infer if the phenomena are new, and if they are old, they are like the familiar pathway through your home: you know all the three-dimensional angles, impediments, contours, squeaky spots in the woodwork, worn spots in the carpet, and so on; the inferences regarding their existence and their nature took place many moons ago, and since then your perception of them has become tacitly acknowledged and your moves second nature. Regarding the act of seeing an object for the first time, you look at it and you infer that it is three-dimensional and that the back side will be so-and-so because the right and left sides are such-and-such. Touch, in contrast, leaves you with no such need for so many mediated inferences, and it brings with it less doubt and under ordinary circumstances less chance of error. Touch allows you the essence of a cubist view of things. It is two-dimensional and cannot be more; it brings you into acquaintance with the surface of things. By virtue of touch and by moving your hands, you can know the front side, the left side, the right side and the back side of an object, all in terms of their two-dimensional surfaces. Sight, in contrast, requires your focusing your eyes on the object from a series of different angles from different positions of the body. Picasso presents fundamentally this picture of a three-dimensional object on a two-dimensional plane. His paintings are of sight more than touch, which is quite proper, for they are paintings.

Feeling that is more than surface is available to our kinesthetic sense, a sort of sixth sense, a tacit sense of ourselves and our interrelations and our involvement and at times even our entanglement with our world. In fact, it is largely what gives us a sense of self. In a certain manner of speaking the self is the product of how we "feel" about ourselves, that is, how we "feel" about our incessantly undulating, swinging and serving, and ambulating body. Our proprioceptors inform us and our motility gives us a sense of where we are in space, if our feet are in contact with turf, bare ground, vinyl tile, thick carpeting, or a mud puddle, where our arms are, how our shoulders are positioned, the rigidity or lack thereof of the torso, whether our stomachs are full or empty, whether we have an itchy spot on the upper left side of our back, whether we are approaching defecation time, and so on. This sense, unlike the concrete world of touch, cannot be more than vague: it is far from accurate. As a result, we customarily take on an exaggerated sense of our body and of our self, due to our inflated egos and all. However, that is another story.[1]

For now, suffice it to say that to the query "How are you?," unlike Kafka's hapless anti-hero, we can usually respond quite well with a "Fine," "Miserable," "Uh-huh," or perhaps merely a grunt. Nobody expects us to go into detail regarding what our proprioceptors tell us about the state of our lungs, heart, nasal mucosa, blood pressure, and so on. This expected answer is of the most vague of vagues if we consider raw language use. In terms of sign 322, in our response there is strictly speaking no genuine syntax or meaning, no argument, just a couple of syllables that, if taken out of context, are of hardly any consequence. Yet the response is quite sufficient, given the context of its utterance. And context is of utmost importance here. It carries a replete bag of implicit meanings along with it, perhaps something like: "Ah, yes, here we are again; our daily encounter, this casual renewal of our friendship over the past decade; I've come to know you well over the past couple of decades, and you me; you're O.K. with me and me with you; well, I enjoyed seeing you once again, take care." All this is quite vague, of course, a matter of signs 322 to 111, signs of de-engenderment, signs with implications of something that would require many screens full of e-mail to describe and many more to explain and interpret. But all that explicitness—that is, signs 331, 332, and 333— is not really necessary at the moment of our contact during a busy day at the office or wherever. What is important is the contact (Jakobson's "phatic" communication), a little vague proprioception, and a minimum of language. It all happens within the stream of semiosis, that ongoing, ever transient flow of happenings in which nothing is permanent and everything is in flux. This is what Oliver Sacks's "languageless" patients knew so well, often considerably better than we do.

Which brings us back to the self, and identity. It is the self that allows for proprioception; in fact, it is the self that propriocepts, the self that is neither exclusively mind nor body but bodymind. There simply cannot be any distinction here. The overriding question that emerges, then, is: "Is the self permanent or transient?" If it is permanent, then it must stand as a breed apart from the flow, but I have in so many words discounted this idea in all the above pages. If it is transient, then it is inside the flow; in this event, it stands nary a chance of enjoying an objective, detached view from "outside." Consensus has it that from the Peircean view the self is radically transient—another convergence of Peirce and Oriental thought (Fisch 1986, Colapietro 1990). This transience has, in Western societies, taken the self to a point from which there is virtually no return, in the eyes of Baudrillard and a host of observers.

How so?

II. RADICAL MISCONCEPTIONS:
OR, HOW BAD IS IT, REALLY?

Allow me to attempt a response to the question thus. In spite of my disclaimer at the outset of the previous section, the fact remains that communication, in the West, has evolved from oral to chirographic to typographic to electronic. During this process, the system of exchange has moved from barter to money whose value is approximately equivalent to the face value of the metal coined to paper currency enjoying representation in bullion to currency without one-to-one representation in bullion elsewhere to bank notes, and, finally, to a rectangular piece of plastic with a name and a number that allows its carrier to come into possession of x commodities with the stipulation that they be paid for in y increments. In each case there has been successive abstraction. In each case the individual has him/herself suffered successive loss of self: the ego diminishes, the self tends to fuse into the massive rush of signs within which it finds itself, and the body tends to vanish, becoming of lesser and lesser importance. The cybernetic world consisting of video, internet, images on TV and the movies and in magazine and newspaper and billboard ads that are engulfing our more familiar world, is like Borges's planet Tlön in the process of overtaking the earth in his short story, "Tlön, Uqbar, Orbis Tertius" (1962). Customary boundaries between biological and inorganic, life and death, self and other, what is mine and what belongs to the globalized economy, what is body and what is not, all are becoming fuzzy and fused. Artificial body images have begun displacing the felt body, and proprioception, motility, soma, and kinesthetics are losing ground in the process.

Cybernetic technology obsessed with the bits and nothing but the bits threatens to engulf the self and body in a tide of flashing two-dimensional images. What was once taken to be inalienable bastions of self and body rights become threatened by multilayered images of rootless, free-wheeling, artificial, and sham instantiations of rapid-fire action and reaction in the face of whatever happens to pop up. This is life as a vast video-game, life within a virtual world, life without a body and rushing along within the cascade of artificial images that come and go in staccato fits and jerks whose rhythm, if genuine living rhythm there indeed be, is measurable in bits of information rather than the syncopated beat of life and of full-blown semiosis.[2] Confusion within this apparently incomprehensible milieu becomes clarity when surveillance breaks it down and quantifies it into Boolean binary values. Consequently, life begins to come under the control of the new mechanism exercising an abstract form of power that was unimaginable according to the dictates of classical science and its accompaniment, the lumbering totalitarian state. Fragmentation becomes the norm, with the perverse image of the body and desire deconcretized and converted into an abstract mechanism for sadistic-masochistic violence the likes of which lie beyond the wildest dreams even of a Marquis de Sade. The value of flesh-and-blood human beings sinks to the same level as that of commodities. All is a matter of signs rushing about to be ephemerally taken and consumed and then tossed—for recycling into more signs, one hopes—which is tantamount to a devaluation of the individual. This is a far cry from Lucien Goldmann's (1975) loss of the individual in corporate capitalism, or the loss of the self in the nouveau roman art and architecture during the 1940s, 1950s, and 1960s (Sypher 1962), or in the antipsychiatry of R. D. Laing (1965, 1969, 1971), David Cooper (1967) and Thomas Szasz (1988). The new upswing of homeless bodies gnawing out a rodent existence on the city streets and in the gutters make way for computer stores and video rentals and banks and fast-food franchises and shopping malls, and for new offices where through the internet money is pushed around so that the rich can get richer. Yes, this grave new world of the cyborg.

The old social body is taken over by a hybrid form of multiplicities, a pluralism of discourses, an identityless cyborg, an automaton form threatening to become like the "replicants" of the cult film *Blade Runner*. From linearity there is multiperspectivism, and certainty loses ground to uncertainty, God to a random gush of signs, truth to a mindless taking of whatever happens to be at hand, human interrelations to a rush of disengaged signs virtually devoid of all relations, reality to sham simulacra, imagination to the same old things over and over again, feeling to a zombified and impersonal consumptions of signs, the will to a manipulation of signs by just more signs, the body to artificial video images, and the self to a strange nihilistic-solipsistic sort of nonself. At least this seems to be the message given us from various and sundry angles. And it is quite in line with the quite natural outgrowth of that mechanical paradigm founded in the times of Galileo, Bacon, Newton, Hobbes, Descartes.

However, perhaps the outlook is not as dire as it might seem to some of our current prophets of the apocalypse. In light of the previous chapter, perhaps a distinction should be established between (1) the idea of information and control as a direct result of technology and as the exclusive product of that very technology, and (2) the idea that the evils of control were already there as a product of the machine age and the classical world-image, evils that were exacerbated and brought to a shrill pitch by the facilities offered it with the technologization of culture. According to (2), the technological cyberscape is conceived as an extension of the machine age; according to (1) it is considered to be a newcomer on the scene and to have brought new methods and resources to bear on and to rejuvenate a tired and burned-out culture. View (1) includes the Jürgens Habermas (1983) thesis regarding contemporary times as an opportunity to dream of those venerated goals of the Enlightenment, yet without the expectation ever of reaching that goal. View (2) consists of a spectrum: one end has those who often present an antipathetic, apocalyptic view of postmodernism-post-modernity; at the other end, a sympathetic view of our contemporary milieu is either celebrated (Hassan 1987, Jencks 1977, Lyotard 1984) or patronized (Huyssen 1984, Jameson 1992). Regarding (2), Donna Haraway (1989) quite optimistically goes a step further, suggesting the image of the cyborg as a hybrid body capable of integrating, from the margins, the free flow of multiple narratives and discourses, institutionalized and idiosyncratic values, and transcultural, syncretic private and public practices, thus harnessing forces and tendencies in new ways and creating novel responses to novel problems within novel contexts. Over the long haul, everybody should be able to cope in one form or another with whatever unexpected contrivances, collusions, corroborations and collaborations, and even catastrophes that might arise.

And yet, . . . and yet, by and large this trend continues to place unwarranted priority on the image, the visual, the icon: ocularcentrism! What is usually taken for granted is that there is above and beyond everything else perception, that is, signs viewed, seen, gazed upon: the omniscient icon (eyecon), the icon-eye of the eidos, that which sees and that which is seen, the icon-eyed in the eidetic tradition. To repeat myself—I'm afraid it is really necessary in order that my message be foregrounded to the utmost—primacy in the West has been obsessively placed on sight. The long tradition from Aristotle in *Metaphysics* (1966) to Hans Jonas's *The Phenomenon of Life* (1966), among a host of works, has assumed without further ado that sight is the most noble of the sensory channels. The trouble with sight, however, is that it must always be focused on something. As observed above, it must be directed, it cannot turn corners, like sound and smells and touch. For that reason vision tends to be more of a tunnel nature than the other senses. This, plus its overwhelming binary, digital character with which it is endowed thanks to the Grand Age of the Machine, renders it the favored candidate for reception of doctrinaire, dogmatic philosophies, attitudes, and everyday behavior. Moreover, with respect to the modes of sensation, seeing is most clearly of something "out there," hence its likeliness as the grounding for the Cartesian mind-body split, for objectivism, for optimism that the world is "out there" and ripe for the plucking by the most logically and rationally prepared mind. Sight is in this sense by its very nature a distancing, judgmental act.

The primacy of sight appears to correspond with remarkable fidelity, and quite conveniently, to typographs, linear writing, phonocentric displays of words. This is even more the case of our recent electronic culture that has heightened and extended our senses, that has culminated in the promotion of a new form of orality with greater prospect for verbal communication (Ong 1982). However, Donald Lowe (1982:8–9) writes that with the extension of signs in the electronic age the image has become more "realistic"; that is, at least it is taken for real. Actually, Lowe maintains, perception involves: (l) the perceiver, (2) the act of perceiving, and (3) the content—idea, thought, concept—of the perceived. This notion of perception, if and only if we exercise the proper mind-shift, can come to cohere with the above formulation regarding dancer-dance-dancing. The dancer is the dance and the dance the dancer, and the two are engaged in the flowing process of dancing. The presence of the absent creator of the dance as well as the present director of the performance are themselves signs interrelated and interacting with and codependent upon the dancer-dance-dancing signs. The same can be said of the spectators as well. All is semiosis, signs, ongoing fluxes and flows, process.

Now, if we widen the parameters of our sensing the entire process to the nth power, it can include the very act of feeling, sensing, perceiving, and conceiving, which involves: (4) the media, (5) the variegated modes of feeling, sensing, and perceiving (smelling, tasting, touching, etc.), and (6) the presuppositions and prejudices involved in all these activities. This second triad of images, interrelations, and thinking, which complements that triad outlined in the previous paragraph, is also of the nature of the range of possibilities (Firstness), the engagement of a minuscule portion of those possibilities (Secondness), and the mediative interaction of these portions as signs and their respective others in terms of ongoing, continuous process (Thirdness). The medium dances the sensations, the recipients of the sensations are the dancers that dance the dance, and they are in turn danced by the dance; all is in a process of dancing, dancing, dancing. . . .

In this sense if we bring (1) to (6) together in an interrelated package, they relate to Firstness, Secondness, and Thirdness. In Peirce's conception, the perceiver—the semiotic agent—is him/herself a sign among signs. Like the dancer, he/she interrelates, interacts, and collaborates with his/her signs, and they reciprocally do the same with him/her. During this process, he/she is immanently within some semiotic media or other, as are the signs with which he/she is involved. There is simply no all-or-nothing separability between semiotic agent and signs and media and messages.

Allow me to cite a media illustration. José Martín-Barbero, author of the seminal *Communication, Culture and Hegemony* (1993), wrote a letter to his colleague Armand Mattelart describing his experience while with a group of students viewing a popular movie in a neighborhood theater in Colombia. He expressed his disturbance, his "epistemological shudder," when the students realized that what they took to be trite, humdrum action on the screen actually moved the audience to tears:

> After twenty minutes of viewing, we had begun to feel such great boredom—the film was so elementary and stereotypical—that we began to laugh loudly. The people around us (the theater was full, mostly with men; this film was breaking records in Colombia and that is why we were there) became angry, shouted insults at us and wanted to force us to leave. For the rest of the projection, I watched these men, moved to tears, as they "lived" the drama with remarkable pleasure . . . and when leaving I asked myself: "What does the film I saw have to do with the film they saw?" because what brought me such boredom induced such pleasure in them. What had they seen in it that I had not? And of what use was my "ideological reading," even if I manage to translate it into their words, since that reading will always be of the film I saw, not the one they saw? . . . I wrote a hundred pages that I dare not publish, in which I do nothing more, in the end, than ask and re-ask in every form a question . . . : Why do popular classes "invest desire and extract pleasure" from a culture that denies them as a subject? . . . And today this question leads me to conclude that it is an inescapable necessity to interpret mass culture from a different standpoint that allows one to formulate another question: What, in mass culture, responds not to the logic of capital but to other logics? (in Mattelart and Mattelart 1992:92)

Mattelart and Mattelart write that such observations as that of Martín-Barbero have led to a reevaluation of the studies of the past thirty years that focus on the tastes and habits of so-called mass culture from the angle of "ideological injunction." New questions must be asked regarding the nature of the media, the messages sent and the manner in which they are received, the daily practices of the receivers and their roles in processing the product, and the way the institutions package signs for public consumption from the perspective of certain givens and the way the public takes these signs.

As I see it from my own neo-Peircean perspective—which, I would hope, is not irremediably presupposition-laden—in the Martín-Barbero episode the medium and the mode in terms of the signs of Secondness presented to the audience were basically the same both in the cases of the "mass audience" and the presumed "neutral observers." In contrast, the presuppositions—product of Peircean "habits" of feeling, thought, and

action—diverged widely. Which is to say that the two groups of per-
ceivers, as themselves so many signs among signs, were well-nigh incommensurable with one another, hence their acts of perception were distinct,
as were their signs' contents, that is, the processed messages given through
and by the medium.[3] The "mass audience" to which the above film was
intended formed a community at the level of feeling—pleasures, pains,
joys, sorrows, desires, fears. As a consequence, they processed their sensations and perceived the signs around them as a rather coherent community, and the content of their signs, their interpretants, their meanings as
a process of mediation regarding the community's feelings and acts of perception was to a large extent shared by the entire community. In this regard, semiotic agents and their signs became fused into one; there was no
longer any appreciable distinction between them. The entire community
was involved as if it were one complex sign, the complex of signs was involved as if all the signs made up a whole. Ordinary borders became fuzzy.

Martín-Barbero and his investigators, of course, formed their own community, a community of observers led by a set of internalized "ideological
injunctions." They read their signs insofar as they were filtered through the
lens of their intellectually constructed presuppositions and prejudices, and
they processed their signs accordingly. Their community, in other words,
was as such more basically at the level of Thirdness—thought, cognition,
intellect, control—than at the level of Firstness—feelings, gut responses—
hence their perception and their acts of perception differed radically from
those of the "mass community" surrounding them. They filtered the film
and they filtered the community watching the film into one semiotic receptacle, and they processed their signs according to their preconceived
views in terms both of the signs and the community. The investigators'
logic was that paper logic of Secondness and Thirdness and of generality
of which I have written above: it was relatively more binary in orientation
and divorced from Firstness in its implementation, and, I must reiterate,
it was destined to remain incomplete as a set of signs depicting what there
was "out there." The community that made up part of the semiotic objects
observed by the investigators, in contrast, saw the film, while giving the
other community composed of the presumptuous investigators hardly any
mind. In fact, it was not a matter of mind at all but of bodymind—while
the investigators thought they were doing exclusively "mind work." The
"mass audience" followed entrenched, embedded, automatized habits of
thought and of action, to be sure. But their response to their signs was
guided by another "logic" entirely, as Martín-Barbero himself acknowledges. Their's was a logic of vagueness, of the bodymind, which was more

in tune with Firstness than was the classical logic of the investigators—in addition to its capacity of this logic of vagueness to hold contradictions and inconsistencies within its embrace.

Now I must confess that I have no idea what film the people in the theater were watching. Insofar as I know Latin American audiences, it could have had a rural peasant or an urban slum setting, it could have been a comedy or a high drama film, or it could have revolved around a power struggle between upper-class clans of the "Dallas" or "Dynasty" sort. In whichever case, the film could well have been so far removed from the daily lives of the audience that there were no rational and consistent lines of correspondence between the two. Yet the audience was quite clearly moved by it. The logic of vagueness, at the level of feeling and Firstness, is of the "reason of the heart" and knows relatively little of the "reasoning of the mind" presumably within the domains of Secondness and Thirdness.[4]

However, not even the most rational, objective, and scientific acts of perception and sign contents are ever entirely divorced from Firstness. Take Norwood Hanson's (1958) account of the Ptolemaic and Copernican scientists seeing the sun one bright morning. Hanson asks the question: Do they see the same sun? "Of course they do," the hopeful realist would like to respond. "The sun is the sun in terms of its brute physical existence, as hard-core Secondness. Hence basically the same set of photons strike both scientists' retinas." But that is not what Hanson has in mind. What he asks is: Do they see the same "sun"?—in which case "sun" is the semiotic object, not the real physical thing. After much deliberation, Hanson concludes that they see virtually the same sun but do not see the same "sun." They see the same physical object, but for one scientist what is seen is a mobile body while what the other scientist sees is a static body. So the two "suns" the pair of scientists see are not really the same "sun," for, given the nature of the semiotic object, its meaning is always subject to alteration. One "sun" has one meaning and the other "sun" another meaning, and there always exists the possibility of many other "suns" popping up further to confuse the issue regarding which "sun" is the "true sun."[5] I have synthesized Hanson's argument drastically, and I hope without doing it injustice. The upshot is that not even the most cold and impersonal and dispassionate scientist is entirely divorced from the feeling of Firstness, which is precisely where his/her most deeply embedded presuppositions and prejudices lie. He/she desired, wished, hoped, expected to feel, sense, perceive, and to be able to cognize, intellectualize, and articulate "sun" in a particular and quite impressive way, and, sure enough, we would expect he/she would have been capable of doing so. He/she would have been so capable because his/her knowledge had become entrenched, part of his/her tacit knowing, implicitly knowing how to process his/her signs and explicitly know and be able to say that they are signs of such-and-such characteristics.

In other words, his/her knowing would consist of a form of personal knowledge (Polanyi 1958). He/she would belong to a community of like-minded and therefore "right-minded" knowers; he/she would, in terms of his/her acts of perception and practices, move within a paradigm (Kuhn 1970), which would allow for much security and much certainty, though it would tend to enshroud any and all alternative forms of knowing in a fog of learned ignorance.

III. A BRIEF OVERVIEW

Of course, I am alluding to the new turn in philosophy of science and aspects of popular culture that generally go by the name of "postmodernism." Postmodernism, or the same contemporary milieu by any other name, is with us whether we like it or not.

The postmodern scene, as summarily discussed in the previous chapter, is multiply ambivalent, giving rise to a plethora of interpretations. Some observers from the academic heights rejoice in its consumerism, others condemn it from some apparently neutral zone; some celebrate its obsession with pluralism, others decry its directionlessness; some laud the subservient "guerrilla tactics" it spawns, others reduce it to a game of hegemonic powermongers and the powerless disenfranchised masses; some revel in its inconsistencies, others remain nostalgic for the golden age of stability and certainty; some take it as a break from modernism-modernity, others argue that it is nothing more than an extension of bygone modes; some see novelty in it, others see it as old hat with a few frivolous frills; some look for depth, for others it is simply surface glitter and glitz. And the debate goes on. The term "postmodern" is an umbrella covering a bewildering disarray of cultural artifacts and manifestations, political, social and economic practices, and theoretical postures presuming the capacity to articulate the whole mess. In short, the debate gives expression to the last gasp of a tired century.

From the real estate aggressively appropriated by the voracious and occasionally imperialistic evangelists of so-called cultural studies, it might appear that postmodernism must be taken for granted (for example, Denzin 1991, Grossberg 1992). The assumption has it that we are in the postmodern age, and that's that. Hardly any questioning, specific details, substantive and systematic analyses, or comparisons or contrasts are necessary, we are told in so many—too many!—ways. We should go with the flow, observe what we can, render a personal narration of it, and enjoy it to the best of our ability. Those propagators of cultural studies who make a stab at defining the term more often than not list a few arbitrary characteristics classifying our contemporary milieu as "postmodern," usually along with a few binary oppositions that are thrown into the bin for good measure with the label "modern," and they assume their task has been brought to its conclusion, as if the academic air were thus purified and now we could enjoy some clear sailing into the open horizon. Those are usually the observers that overdefine "postmodernism" as virtually everything that has happened since World War II. Those who underdefine the term tell us that virtually everything during that period is the most reasonable extension of "modernism." At any rate, so much for "postmodernism." It is actually not to be placed in the spotlight here, though it merits a passing look.

Regarding cultural studies, per se, the focus for many scholars has rested on so-called popular cultures.[6] Traditionally it has been "high brow" art and culture and "low brow" art and culture, and solely the former was considered worthy of the academician's sacred time. The Frankfurt School, inaugurated in the 1930s and consisting of Theodore W. Adorno, Walter Benjamin, Max Horkeimer, and others takes this view with its analysis of music, radio soap operas, magazines, and other items of mass culture (Jay 1973). This was a beginning. One of the chief problems with the Frankfurt School is that it established and maintained a distinction between the "high brow" that is the "real" culture, and that other culture that can hardly be dignified by the name "culture." This view is often—though not always, and here Walter Benjamin is one of the most salient exceptions—elitist, erecting binary oppositions between "genuine culture" and the concept of "mass culture" as if mass culture were a monolithic dissolution of many practices into one, as if it had become a faceless, characterless, homogeneous, and quite bland expression of common folk incapable of comprehending the subtleties of "genuine art." Raymond Williams, and the Birmingham school led by Stuart Hall and others and building on the theory of Antonio Gramsci, are responsible for revealing this unfortunate cut between "genuine culture" and the babble and innocent images and sounds of the ignorant.[7] The idea now has it that the powers that be exercise hegemony over the general populace engaged in their own cultural expression. It is the responsibility of the learned academicians to set things straight. They are endowed with the charge of highlighting social production and reproduction, of outlining the means and methods by which cultural forms and expressions are a slave to hegemonic powers. At the same time, the academicians can serve the subordinate class, gender, and ethnic make-up of society by giving them a means to bring out their own expression of opposition to, contempt for, and rebellion against those at the peak of the hierarchical structure. British cultural studies has been innovative, then, chiefly insofar as it foregrounded the importance of media culture in our contemporary milieu and how it reveals the processes of domination and resistance within societies.

While battles over hegemony within the domains of academia itself have raged regarding cultural studies, the question of terminology has often emerged. The labels "mass culture" and "popular culture" carry an overload of presupposition-laden baggage with them that renders them too biased for my blood. They still tend to be elitist, heavy with binary oppositions and antagonisms, and hierarchical. I prefer Douglas Kellner's concept of "media culture." This term

> has the advantage of signifying both the nature and form of the artifacts of the culture industries (i.e., culture) and their mode of production and distribution (i.e., media technologies and industries). It avoids ideological terms like "mass culture" and "popular culture" and calls attention to the circuit of production, distribution, and reception through which media culture is produced, distributed, and consumed. The term breaks down artificial barriers between the fields of cultural, media, and communication studies and calls attention to the interconnection of culture and communication media in the constitution of media culture, thus breaking down reified distinctions between "culture" and "communication" (Kellner 1995:34–35)

The dichotomy customarily established by "mass culture" or "popular culture" and the "dominant culture" is problematic, and it should give way to a view that there is and there will always be some filling in of the middle between the two poles of the dichotomy.

IV. AND A DIFFERENT THRUST

However, a problem persists in some circles. The assumption often has it that there is a "dominant culture" and a "subservient" or "popular culture," and that the former exercises "hegemony" over the latter.[8] This assumption is flawed in ways that are becoming increasingly evident, especially in light of Michel de Certeau's (1984) contention that the would-be dominant group of capitalist societies are perpetually subjected to contestations and negotiations by the guileful ruses, subversive trickery, and "guerrilla tactics" of the so-called subaltern groups.

The dominant classes are powerful, but they are also laden with bureaucratic baggage; they are overweight and sluggish. In contrast, the underprivileged are lean and mean, nimble and flexible, creative and mobile. The powerful construct the fortresses of capitalistic might: shopping malls, schools, parks, recreation areas. The weak make their own space in and leave their mark on these memorials to the virtues of capitalism: graffiti; shoplifted goods; and defacing of shrubs, signs, windows, and painted surfaces. This requires amazing acts of improvisation. There are numerous ways of altering standard procedures and methods that

> characterise the subtle, and stubborn resistance activity of groups which, since they lack their own space, have to get along in a network of already established forces and representations. People have to make do with what they have. In these combatants' stratagems, there is a certain art in placing one's blows, a pleasure in getting around the rules of a constraining space. . . . Even in the field of manipulation and enjoyment. (de Certeau 1984:18)

Shoplift an item worth ten dollars and buy a package of gum and you've doubly manifested your contempt—often in large part implicit—for those that wield the power. Plagiarize for your term paper and get an A, and you're rewarded for your craft. Cheat during the final exam and two weeks later you can still receive a diploma for your efforts. Take a couple of tools from the auto repair shop where you work, and soon you'll have a well-equipped workshop in your garage. You may never belong to the power elite, but you'll give them enough pricks in their buttocks when their back is turned to help make life miserable for them. You are not a producer of cultural artifacts, nor are you a full-blown consumer. You are somewhere in between. That is precisely the art. The dominant culture must have everything given either in blacks or whites. But you, you are superior to such binary imperatives. In a rather tacit sense you know everything is neither the one thing nor the other, or it is both the one thing and the other, take your pick. That is to say, you neither exclusively buy nor do you exclusively not buy when you shoplift and purchase some gum. You engage in another activity entirely. You do buy, after a fashion; you don't buy everything you take, but you buy a portion of it, however small. And you do not *not* buy, for much or most of what you take remains unpurchased.

From another, complementary, perspective, you both buy and you do not buy. Put the two activities together and we have the sphere of Firstness and that of Thirdness, to complement that of Secondness of the dominant culture's either/or imperatives.

According to standard logic, there are simply the powerful and the weak, those in control and those who have no say, the dominant and the subaltern. It is an either/or proposition. According to "guerrilla logic," in contrast, it is possible to don a different mask for each occasion. One can be all things to all those who are in control. One is a sort of Forrest Gump, Woody Allen's Zelig, de Andrade's Macunaíma, and Robert Musil's "man without qualities"—even Oliver Sacks's patient suffering from Tourette syndrome—wrapped into one. One can be intermittently both one thing and the other, buying a little and stealing a little, showing civic responsibility by throwing trash in the proper receptacle and later that night strewing the contents of that same receptacle along the sidewalk, catering to the boss in the morning and stealing from the company in the afternoon. Concomitantly, one is, like a picaresque anti-hero, neither the one thing nor the other on a permanent basis, for there is always the possibility of engaging in some act that falls neither within the *neither* nor the *nor:* it is something else entirely, emerging from within the interstices. So between the *either* and the *or* one always seems capable of finding something to fill in a portion of the excluded-middle, thus bringing it into the equation.

All this is to say that the ordinary concept of "popular culture" is that of a teeming cauldron of aesthetically senseless, intellectually trivial, morally bankrupt, and virtually chaotic activity. But this is an impoverished notion. "Popular culture" in this manner presents itself not as a monolithic mass of faceless dough but as a radically heterogeneous, ongoing flux of humanity and cultural artifacts. This renders it thoroughly contradictory, and it is always in transition, with no readily apparent purpose or direction. "Guerrilla culture" is anything but simplistic or reducible to any set of descriptive features. It is in a manner of speaking identityless; it lacks identifying features; it eludes every effort conceptually to pin it down. Yet there is identity; it is like the Peircean self, forever transient. It is, in a word, process. It defies all labels and all definitions. Once it has been labeled, it contradicts that very label; once it has been defined in terms of what it is in contrast to what it is not, it has already altered itself to the extent that it is neither the *is* nor the *is not* but now something else.

In this sense Kellner's "media culture" as an alternative to "mass culture" and "popular culture" to a great extent avoids the "high-low" elitism from "above," and it expands on the idea that the "culture of the people" is strictly from "below." I would agree with Kellner that the ordinarily pre-supposed dichotomy between "culture" and "communication" is arbitrary and incapable of accounting for what I have tentatively called "guerrilla logic" within "guerrilla culture." Kellner's alternative helps do away with high/low and popular/elite categories and sees all "forms of media culture and communication as worthy of scrutiny and criticism" (Kellner 1995:35). Yet I would disagree with him regarding his emphasis on the "culture industry" and on "production, distribution, and consumption." He rightly points out that culture is both the mediator and is mediated by multiple channels of communication, and at the same time communica-tion is the mediator and is mediated by culture. Culture and communica-tion are more multiply and rhizomically interrelated and interdependent than Kellner reveals. Thus what he calls "media culture" is not merely a creation of production and distribution on the part of industry and con-sumption on the part of the public. Culture was always there, and it con-sists of signs—which include both the media and the messages. Without already existing cultural processes the culture industry would not be what it is, and without the culture industry the existing culture would have taken on many of the industry's myriad masks. Neither the industry nor its target can stand alone; take away one and the other falls in a heap.

As was mentioned above, today's milieu is that of what Mark Poster calls "modes of information" rather than "modes of production and con-sumption." But this doesn't quite do the trick either, I would submit. Today's "postmodern scene," by whatever name, is yet something else. That is, any name for it is by its very nature false to itself. Granted, Kell-ner (1995:26–28) acknowledges the "theoretical multiplicity," "contextual pragmatism," and "transdisciplinarity" of media culture. Yet the problem is that, in the long run, Kellner and virtually all scholars speeding in cir-cles in hot pursuit of first prize in the cultural studies Grand Prix are guilty of the sin of linguicentrism. Their media appear to be largely made up of sight and sound, primarily insofar as language is concerned. I would sug-gest that any reliable form of media culture studies must demand a radical look at multiple sensory modes, especially kinesthetics, from the semiotic perspective.

V. WHERE TO, THEN?

Well, then, in this regard, what have we? Take a look at figure 23. The first observation to be made is that we must keep in mind that the zones are ac-tually cloudy, with no precise lines of demarcation between one sign and

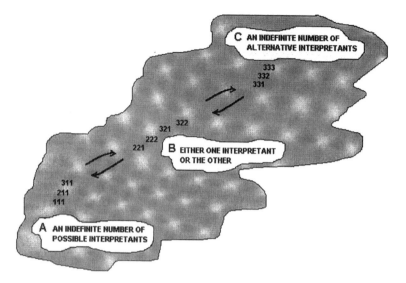

Figure 23

another, between one category and another, or between one class of inter-pretants (alternately taken as interpretations of conglomerate signs) and another. This condition is necessary, given the fluctuating, constantly en-gendering, de-engendering, and re-engendering nature of semiosis and subsequently of Peirce's sign decalogue as outlined in the first chapters of this inquiry.

A, of figure 23, is what I have dubbed the sphere of chiefly iconicity. Here, we have the senses at their most fundamental: smells, tastes, kines-thetics, and such. This is where the body does what it knows how to do and what it does best. Here, we find the basics of music and of dance, where there are continuous wholes, with hardly any relationship of the parts—as in a roundabout way we also saw in our observations of ciga-rette, perfume, and deodorant ads in chapter 7. Here is where "tacit knowing" is at its most proficient, whether level-headed or muddle-headed. This is, we would expect, where Oliver Sacks's aphasiacs under-stood Reagan's nonverbal messages without being clear on the digital message. Here is where Tourette syndrome finds its most customary semi-otic expression. Here is where touch is at its most sensitive, as are all those signs without the possibility of their enjoying accompanying linguistic signs but are still able to compensate for this apparent loss with the aid of other senses. Here is, finally, where we might hope to find Baudrillard's simulacra.

In the middle portion of figure 23 we encounter chiefly indexical signs, usually found in the form of linear strings of digitally engendered semiotic entities. Here, there is no awareness of the totality of things, there is very little generality. In its extreme form, it is much like the case of the "Funes syndrome" suffered by Oliver Sacks's disembodied person, the aphasiac with no body image to speak of; the disembodied person experiences linear streams of sensations, with either total memory or hardly any memory at all. There is a linear array of parts, without necessary awareness of their past, of their history. At C of figure 23 we find chiefly symbolic signs, signs of generality, signs of underdetermination, signs making up corporate bodies of semiosis whose interpretations are destined in this world of finite and fallible semiotic agents to remain incomplete. These signs are the counterpart of the chiefly iconic signs of the lower left-hand portion of the figure that cannot hope but to remain vague, radically overdetermined, and, when taking the whole of their possible manifestations into account, schizophrenically inconsistent. Thus, as we shall note in more detail below, we have in figure 23 the abrogation of the principle of noncontradiction—at A—and of the excluded-middle principle—at C—while within a subdomain of the figure—at B—classical logic can still manage to exercise its hegemonic reign.

Toward the lower level of the chiefly iconic signs we have the complement of the upper level of that same class of signs. Here, we have he/she who sees all but possesses little to no consciousness of the parts. This sphere of semiosis can be available to those who are fundamentally without language, like the so-called idiot savants who see the whole but can't relate the parts—i.e., Sacks's autistic twins. So there is gravitation toward utter vagueness at the bottom and toward the ultimate of generality at the top, consciousness of virtually nothing at the bottom and consciousness of many things, and in the most ideal of worlds, consciousness of virtually everything, at the top. Between the two extremes, we have the sphere of parts and nothing but the parts—of Boolean classes, of classical logic, of clapped-out binary thinking (chiefly Peircean Secondness). Abduction below and Deduction above, with Induction sandwiched in between; aesthetics and ethics held together by a most often loosely practiced form of inferential thinking; acceptance of contradiction below and awareness of limitations and incompleteness above, with wild-eyed and wide-eyed dreams of reason and totalization in the middle. Figure 23 apparently, and to the chagrin of the most stalwart of analytical minds, holds the virtues and the vices, and the euphoria of success and the despondency of failure, in one fluid embrace. Nevertheless, it should, I would hope, give us a feel for the semiosic process.

Of course, things are never as simple as we would like. For an illustration of how complex the issue actually is when including our notions of nothingness and emptiness into the equation, take a look at figure 24. Along the hair-line at Y dividing A from -A (Not-A), we have A-ness thanks to the presence of Not-A-ness, and we have Not-A-ness as a consequence of its complementary, A-ness. In other words, in a manner of speaking, the hair-line consists of A-ness (since it is not Not-A-ness) plus Not-A-ness (since it is not A-ness). When these values are combined they become tantamount to A-Not-A-lessness (A-lessness coupled with Not-A-lessness). This, in view of the discussion of Table 1 and the "cut" or "mark" in chapter 1, makes way for the initiation of asymmetry, irreversibility, and transitivity, and, ultimately, of temporality. When relating figure 24 to the middle portion of figure 23, somewhere there exists the becoming of awareness that something is neither black nor white, neither A nor Not-A, but most likely, according to the prevailing conditions, something else. In other words, the hair-line is not A but A-less, and not Not-A but Not-A-less. It is neither the one thing nor the other, yet, like emptiness (pure emptiness) or nothingness (the noticed absence

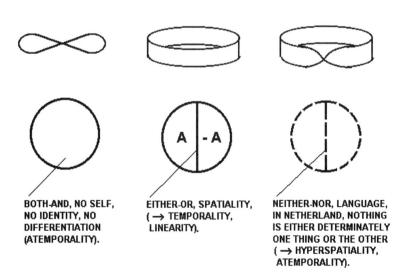

BOTH-AND, NO SELF,
NO IDENTITY, NO
DIFFERENTIATION
(ATEMPORALITY).

EITHER-OR, SPATIALITY,
(→ TEMPORALITY,
LINEARITY).

NEITHER-NOR, LANGUAGE,
IN NETHERLAND, NOTHING
IS EITHER DETERMINATELY
ONE THING OR THE OTHER
(→ HYPERSPATIALITY,
ATEMPORALITY).

Figure 24

of "something") it contains, within itself, the possible manifestation as either A or Not-A, or of both A and Not-A; yet it is, in and of itself, neither A nor Not-A. And the principle of noncontradiction and that of the excluded-middle have hardly any alternative but to begin their dance of death.

Within this massive sphere, where the answer to a problem can be "Yes but no," "No but yes," "Yes and no," or "Neither yes nor no," and "None of the above" and "All of the above," we are within the domain, quite appropriately speaking, and in light of chapters 1 through 3, of "hyperspace." As a consequence, at Z of figure 24, the circle (or sphere) and hair-line should actually consist of broken lines to illustrate the intractable vagueness of any and all boundaries. For, ultimately—that is, at the infinite horizon—Z doubles back on itself to become X; that is to say, it all collapses to the equivalent of a line, infinite in extension, with no "warp" or "twist" in space to mar the continuum. In fact, that is what Z has the potential to become, at the end of the asymptotic approximation in the best of all ideal worlds: continuous, tantamount to X.

But in our "real semiotic world" of semiotically limited souls, we can't have everything. In fact, we can't even have a single sign without another sign, without all signs. In a manner of speaking, it might seem to be like that old song of the happy, innocent, and carefree times: "Love and marriage / You can't have one without the other." Well, not quite; in fact, not by a long shot. Granted, it might appear that at X you can have both one sign and the other sign and at Z you can have neither the one sign nor the other but something else altogether. However, in either case, one sign is nothing without the coexistence, the codependence—whether possible or actualized—of another sign, and the emergence of one is accompanied by that of the other, or if it does not emerge, it is nonetheless there, aiding and abetting or conspiring and contriving against the other. For everything is codependent while in the process of self-organization. So it is true, we can either have the one sign without another one or we can't, or we can have both the one sign and the other one—at Z and X. It is also true that none of the above really applies at all from yet a broader feel for the whole of semiosis, when there is subsumption of a greater part of the whole within one's sensing and feeling—this occurring at the lower level of figure 23, of course.

That is to say, we must resign ourselves to our living within Y, the brute physical world and all our various semiotic worlds engendered from it, but a certain feel must also persist in regard to X. To a certain extent we can articulate that feel coupled with the existence in the physical world of raw Secondness within Z. However, no matter how far in the direction of Thirdness we wish to go or that we can actually proceed, our task of reaching the end of the nonlinear endpoint is always incomplete. But, fortunately for us, the world continues to turn, and, fortunately, life continues to go on and we continue to make do with what we have. So we dwell partly within Y, which is dependent upon X, and to an extent we think and talk within Z—which is as dependent upon X and Y as X is upon Y—though there is no way we can with absolute certainty know what we are thinking and talking about. And, in a figurative sort of way, it's all in figure 24.

"But," my skeptic asks, "how, precisely? You really must explain yourself better." That, of course, is difficult; in fact, it is well-nigh impossible. I should at least give it try, however. In the first place, at Y, "within" the hair-line so to speak, we have not merely a line but the implication of what holds promise as the possibility for rhizomicity. Take, for example, that quite unique but now well-worn Nike slogan, "Just do it." Just do what? What is meant by *it*?—reminiscences of the "Coke is it" ad. Ultimately, I would suggest that *it* can be none other than the line, mere nothingness or emptiness. *It* is what, where, when, and who everyone wants to do and be. There-then, we have no individuality, no self, no time in the strict sense of the word. There is only possibility, pure possibility. The possibility for realizing hopes and desires, dreams and fantasies. Yet there is nothing, emptiness. Between one extreme and the other, what one is and what one is not, there is just that, *it*. Yes, "Just do it," and you can do it, if you just hop, skip, and do slam-dunking jumps along the yellow brick road in a pair of Nikes. In fact, you can leap 25 feet high and dunk a basketball in a ridiculously heightened rim. You can be all you can and want to be and don't really have to work to get it, or at least that often seems to be the implication.

"But what, really, are the implications of the hair-line other than fuzzy images and inordinately vague allusions?" Well, take our Grueworlder-Realworlder thought experiment from chapter 3. X of figure 24 can contain both "Grue" and "Green" as a set of possibilities (recall the terms from chapter 2). Y can be either the one or the other but not both at the same time, with no absolute certainty that in a given world we will necessarily have the one or the other—we are speaking of the "new riddle of induction," after all. "But how, actually, do we get to Z? To the Thirdness of signification? To mediation? To synthesis?" Once again, in a sort of metaphorical sense through the hair-line, I would suggest. There, we have "Grue-Greenlessness," that is, either "Grueness" or "Greenness," and at the same time, from another perspective, we have both "Grueness" and "Greenness." But, of course, that is not all there is. From the above formulations, it can be said that we have neither "Grueness" nor "Greenness," but something else. Now, this requires a mind-shift, to be sure, as per chapter 3, from sign 331 through 311 to 111 and beyond, then through the ranks in the inverse order to 331. This is like seeing the Necker cube as now pointing upward, now downward, and back again. It is Escher's ambiguous prints as now one thing, now the other. It is Wittgenstein's drawing now as a duck, now as a rabbit. It is, as well, Ehrenzweig's dedifferentiated of the differentiated and then a redifferentiated of the dedifferentiated, all by a synthetic scanning operation, with mergence of the one thing into the other: they become as one, they are both one with the world and at the same time each is within its particular made world. Thus, by a de-engendering reversal of sign engenderment in rapid succession, by a reversal of that engenderment that ordinarily occurs over much time and much practice within a given community, a sign is seen for what it is: the Grueworlder sees the way she sees because she somehow undergoes a perceptual and conceptual switch, while we do not. Then, re-engenderment can transpire, with the semiosic processual development of a slightly to radically new perception and conception.

This entire process is pictured in the topological forms coinciding with the circle-spheres in X, Y, and Z. X is a line of an infinity of points; it is smooth, with no spatial distortions to indicate anything other than the possibility of linear one-dimensionality. Y is two-dimensional, a band sporting clearly delineated "inside" and "outside" qualities: there is either the one or the other, with no other possibility in between. Z, in terms of its Möbius strip qualities, mars the continuum of X and the crisp digitality of Y with fuzzy ambiguities. Here emerges—that is, possibly emerges—awareness that the world, consisting of myriad many possible worlds, is not limited to mere "Grueness" and/or "Greenness," but also awareness that many worlds can be held up as forthright candidates offering the good life for all, along with those other less desirable worlds that are even more numerous.

Now take the two halves of the split circle in the middle of figure 24—the cosmic egg—and collapse them into one, while spreading the hair-line fracture to a smear and including all possible signs of chiefly indexicality within the two adjacent and mirror-image spaces, as in figure 23. We are now in the void: there is no self, no other, no distinctions or divisions. If there is sound, it is no more than, say, a sustained high C note with no variation, no differentiation, and with no past (memory) containing anything other than the same note. If there is sight, it is no more than, say, a sensation of "blue," with no variation and no past. If there is smell, it is no more than the prolonged aroma of, say, Chanel 5. And so on. Spatiality, differentiation between the self and the other and between one thing and the other begins with the introduction of Secondness. Now there is distinguishable spatiality, something separated from something else. Asymmetry is ushered in, there is linear directionality, irreversibility, and hence temporality. The hoary universe of binaries—their compelling attraction, their power, their rendering everything that is complex so apparently simple—make their grand entry. Since there is time, there is a past, history, memory. There are reminders of something other than high C, other than mere blueness, other than Chanel 5, and so on. The world begins to become kaleidoscopic. At the smeared dividing line, we have language, that netherland where a sign is neither what the thing is nor what it is not, but something else, where the self is neither itself nor its other but a mere inference, where what was perceived to be high C a moment ago may now be seen as a mistake, for it is now perceived to be C-sharp. Here, between what is taken for one thing and not the other, at a future moment might be taken for something else entirely. That is, the excluded-middle of the either-or becomes a vast field of possibilities, one of which might stand a chance of popping up at the next moment.

For example, at X of figure 24, the pop star Madonna is nobody; that is, she is indistinguishable from anybody or anything else, she has not (yet) become a differentiated sign-event of something or other for somebody in some respect or capacity. At Y she is now somebody: she is Madonna. Ah, now we know, that infamous icon. But this icon is not an icon for us until there is some element of indexicality. Madonna must be distinguished and indicated as something or somebody apart from everything else in her surroundings. She has been so distinguished and indicated and is now there for our approval or disapproval, for our gaze or our disinterest, or whatever. Yes, definitely Madonna. Or at least Madonna as she is right here and now. That is to say, she is no fixed essence in the venerable Western-Platonic tradition; she is not herself what she is, was, and will be. She is timebound, a set of irreversible, asymmetrical space-time events, happenings, flashes in the cosmic pan. In the next moment Madonna might well be somebody else, say, brunette instead of blond, passive instead of aggressive, a virgin saint instead of a material girl, braless instead of sporting conical breasts, or perhaps something else altogether different. As no more than a strung-out series of sign-events, whatever self might characterize Madonna is perpetually transient, there is no permanence about her. Perhaps she could even be Evita Perón. But then we would make a hasty retreat. No. Madonna is no Evita, and she never will be—to say nothing of Frida Kahlo who she purportedly wishes to play in a future movie. But that's another story.[9]

The same goes for all of us, for all living organisms, for the entire universe. At Z of figure 24 we have that intoxicating, that enticing capacity of language to attach labels to ephemeral sign-events in such a way that they appear in some respect or other fixed for all time. But they do not. That is why Madonna-blond and Madonna-not-blond can be-become Madonna-brunette, or Madonna with green hair or Madonna with an afro or a shaved head or a wig. With each change a new symbol, and with each new symbol, the temptation to pin Madonna down. But, of course, she is elusive. She writhes and wiggles and frees herself from our mental grasp to do her own thing. She becomes yet something other, something we didn't expect, something surprising, as she perpetually strives to reinvent herself so as to keep the public guessing and the millions of bucks coming in. And for some, life takes on a bit more interest as a consequence.

Now, if I might test your patience even further, consider figure 25. It has to do with time, we might call it cyclical time and linear, irreversible time. Anthropologist Edmund Leach (1961) suggests that outside chronometric or clock time, which exercises its undeniable hegemony over us inhabitants of modern and postmodern societies, the basic human sense of time comes in two forms: (1) repetition of certain natural phenomena, and (2) irreversibility of life processes. Our modern and postmodern mind-set favors the second form, but in a rigid mechanical rather than organic sense: time as a cussed succession of one damn thing after another. Religions, in contrast, both ancient and modern and even postmodern, vary widely in their account of time, but in general there is an attempt, largely outside Christianity, to flatten the upward-bound succession of events to a series of cycles. One of the most common devices is to assert that birth and death are two sides of the same coin (Eliade 1965). Birth follows death just as death follows birth. This form of religious time is a "timeless time," so to speak. Leach concludes that time in traditional cultures is not experienced as a linear succession of events at all, but "as something discontinuous, a repetition of reversals, a sequence of oscillations between polar opposites: night and day, winter and summer, drought and flood, age and youth, life and death. In such a scheme the past has no 'depth' to it, all past is equally past; it is simply the opposite of now" (Leach 1961:126).

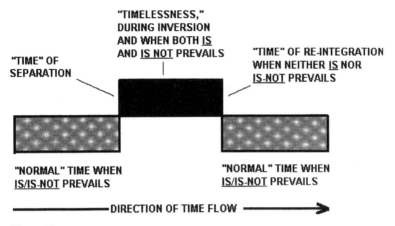

Figure 25

In other words, this time is somewhat comparable to J. M. E. McTaggart's (1927) B-series time (recall the allusion to McTaggart in chapter 10). There is only a before and an after, with no knife-edge now in a linear race from past to future. The before is one discontinuous increment or cycle and the after is another one; there is no fundamental irreversible movement; in fact, it can be said that there is really no movement at all outside the oscillations. Time in this conception is no more than a set of oscillations, zig-zags up and down or right and left. In order for such oscillations to exist in the first place there must be something and its other, what it is not. There also must be something else, something that is capable of bringing about the reversibility, the inversion of one thing into its opposite in order that the oscillation can begin anew. This something else is comparable to the complementary principle that limits the *this* to its being *this* for *now*—which is now a *then*—and nothing but *this,* and when it passes into the *that* it no longer exists, it is the before after which the *that* forced its way onto the scene as *this.* In addition to the before and after of the B-series there is something else that brings about the oscillation. This something else, then, is the complementary principle according to which the before contains the seeds of the after and that after the seeds of another before. In other words, the Yin has a smudge of Yang and the Yang has a smudge of the Yin, and the Yin/Yang diagram keeps them in eternal agonistics. It is the principle, the scheme, the diagram that symbolically brings about the movement. Like the myths of early cultures, what we have here is a story of the beginning of temporal process, of the beginning of beginning itself.[10]

Leach goes on, observing that since this oscillation view of time is discontinuous and reversible, there are sequential markings, which have their manifestation in rituals and myths whose vestiges are found in our modern-day societies. In the Leach-inspired figure 25, we have "normal" or humdrum "secular" time and its inversion, "sacred" time, with discontinuous breaks that bring about the transition from one to the other. In traditional cultures, during a separation rite the subject is transferred from the profane world to the sacred "timeless" realm. While in that "timeless" state, everything that would ordinarily exist in the profane world is mirror-imaged, a carnivalesque inversion. Chaos prevails, as all the norms of profane life fall by the wayside and virtually anything and everything goes. After the proper initiation into the other world, another rite of re-integration brings the subject back to his/her "normal" existence in profane time, a rite that in its own turn must be an inversion of the separation rite. Leach suggests that in our modern-day societies vestiges of separation rites are found in formal occasions such as weddings, coronations, and graduation ceremonies, when dress, etiquette, and customary rules are rigorously and ostentatiously obeyed. Post-separation carnivalesque atmospheres encourage role reversal: paupers dress and act like aristocrats, men like women, adults like children and vice versa, and orgy becomes the normless norm. Masquerades are of the nature of re-integration, wherein the subject dons a mask concealing his/her real social self and at the propitious moment removes it to become a full-fledged member of ordinary customs and modes of conduct once again.

The figure 25 scheme gives us another view of the "guerrilla" warrior using his/her "guerrilla tactics" by means of "guerrilla logic." "Normal" existence within the "cultural logic of late capitalism" entails rampant consumption of signs-commodities-simulacra within a hyped, sham hyperreality—to use the standard jargon. The guerrilla puts on airs of playing the game, bowing to the proper rules and strategies. This is no more than an act, however, for below the mask of conformity is the face of the guerrilla carnivalizing, parodying, satirizing, and ridiculing the hollow simulacra parading around as if they were genuine articles. In the process the actor subverts, ransacks, vandalizes, debases the system, in the process manifesting his/her contempt for the standard conventions and regulations. The malls, parks, schools, streets, and other public places are the arenas of guerrilla carnivalization. Then, later, outside the mall and in the parking lot, "normal" living within "normal" time begins to re-assert its "hegemony," though it is never entirely dominant, given the guerrillas' indomitable countenance. The guerrilla is a force to be reckoned with but cannot be reckoned with by logical means, for he/she is not what he/she appears to be. Yet he/she is and is not precisely what he/she is; and at the same time he/she is neither the one thing nor the other but at any moment can become something else. Without such subversions society would be considerably more dull than droll, more tedious than enticing.

However, I have a bone to pick with Leach. Things are actually not so cut and dried as they might appear. The problem is that the scheme is indelibly binary: time/timelessness, sacred/secular, linear/nonlinear, and so on. In order to flow with the general tenor of this inquiry, it must be properly "triadized." Instead of the fiesta or carnival as a time when society escapes from its secular existence and finds refuge in the sacred realm, I would, following Argentine anthropologist Néstor García Canclini (1993), propose that it is a moment when society "goes into its deepest self, that part that normally escapes it, in order to understand and restore itself." The distance between regular humdrum existence and fiesta life lies in the former's incapacity to reveal the deeper meaning of things.[11] The excesses, waste, and copiousness of fiesta time can be looked upon as compensation for the absence of all this during everyday existence, in the first place, and in the second place, it is a sudden outburst or hidden realization of desires ordinarily repressed or outlawed. Fiesta is not simply nothing more than an escape from rules and regulations and taboos and mores in search of a space without restrictions, however. Quite the contrary, it is a time when one can exercise certain power over forces that ordinarily lie beyond one's control, when alternative social practices are explored and often practiced. The fiesta

> prolongs daily existence to such an extent that its development reproduces society's contradictions. It cannot become a place for subversion or egalitarian free expression, or if it does it is with reluctance, because it is not just a movement of collective unification; it duplicates social and economic differences. . . . [Thus] the *fiesta* reasserts social differences and offers another opportunity of internal and external exploitation of the village. (García Canclini 1993:32)

The fiesta does not bring about a "leveling effect." It is not a means by which those who have the pecuniary means are burdened with the responsibility of financing the fiesta for the benefit of the less fortunate. Actually, those who are more economically endowed enjoy the means for good modernist, capitalist entrepreneurship and can profit quite handily from the venture.

Brazilian anthropologist Roberto DaMatta (1991:213–17), while by and large sticking to Leach's three categories with their attendant binaries, alludes to them nonetheless as a "triangle of dramas" and argues that the categories make up a continuum rather than discontinuous sets. This is closer to the mark. I would go so far as to take a giant step further, positing that, in light of figures 18 and 20, a genuine triad of relations more adequately exemplifies the flow of ordinarily life and fiesta or carnival time and the interplay between them. That is to say, the semiotic object of everyday life becomes during fiesta time a sign, a representamen, giving rise to a radically distinct, and even an inverted, semiotic object, and an interpretant that would hardly be expected to surge forth during the give-and-take of everyday affairs arises. But this hardly gives the picture of a fiesta or carnival, of course. It is a minuscule microcosm of the rampant outpouring of signs constantly bordering on chaos, but with some vague and tenuous sort of order always maintaining tender priorities. Signs are always on the go, nothing is ever at a standstill; everything is always already something other than what it was-is; things are both what they are and something other than what they are, they are neither what they are nor something other than what they are, but something else. In short, semiosis, the semiosis of fiesta or carnival time, is a matter of flow, of converging, diverging, involuted, convoluted, nonlinear whirls, vortices and spirals in incessant process.[12]

VI. TRANSGRESSIONS

Mikhail Bakhtin's (1968, 1981) theory of the carnival also pays heed to the distinction between the life imposed by the hegemonic controlling body that represses the pleasures of the subordinate or subaltern groups. But, in light of the preceding section, the flow, the interrelated, interacting, codependence of ordinary existence and carnival is a triadic process.

In Rabelais's world, during carnival time the established order is subverted, and laughter, gaiety, mockery, parody, satire, excesses, what would ordinarily be considered bad taste, and violation of sexual taboos emerges and pervades. It becomes a question of constant struggle between two languages: the presumably "high," validated language of formal learning, enshrined social, political, and religious respectability on the one hand; and on the other, the "low," vulgar, obscene, subversive vernacular of the common folk. Carnival time is when this struggle surfaces and bears witness to the guerrilla rites, rights, and might of the people.[13] Another unrepressed world and another liberated life reveal themselves, and the established order is temporarily suspended. Carnival is exaggerated sport, games, play, language, when rules fall and spontaneous strategies and free-for-all tactics temporarily replace them. It has been suggested that white-knuckle rides at amusement parks are the epitome of the carnivalesque in the sense that they invert the extracarnivalistic relationship of the body to machine-induced artificial stimulation (Bennett 1983). The same has been said of video games, which require intense concentration and release through the body, all by means of simulacra rather than the "real" (Fiske 1989b). In this manner, the body's "momentary release from its social definition and control, and from the tyranny of the subject who normally inhabits it, is a moment of carnivalesque freedom" (Fiske 1989a:83). The phenomenon so described appears closely aligned with Roland Barthes's (1973) wrestling as a spectacle and his general notion of *jouissance*—spontaneous carnivalesque pleasure—in contrast to *plaisir* (1975), which is relatively controlled, measured, and socially prescribed.

From another vantage point, and focusing specifically on figure 25 once again, separation is seen in the TV series "Star Trek" in its various reincarnations, as well as other comparable series. It is also present in programs such as "Cops" and "Rescue 911," in which everything is so "irreal" that it is "real." Or perhaps we might say, it is more "real" than the real, because it is "eerily" and "irreally real," for it is what happens, yet it happens as it happens because cameras are focused on what happens and not because in retrospect and with plenty of editing it becomes something other than what happened. In other words, it is both "real" and "irreal," from one perspective, and neither "real" nor "irreal," from another perspective. There need be no suspension either of belief or of disbelief, for what there is is "real," for sure, because it is what happens-happened. At the same time it is sham; since it is "real" but at the same time "irreal," it is an artificial depiction of what would under the circumstances be the most reasonable and logical world imaginable.

There is, for sure, carnival with respect to Leach's formulation in TV wrestling, in which the action is grossly exaggerated. Moreover, carnival can be found in situation comedies that are so ridiculous as to be laughable not because they are funny but, rather, because they are exceedingly stupid. It can also be found in "The X-Files" and such productions, in which the events are so outlandish that they are simply consumed without any credibility, yet with a sort of suspension of disbelief such that they are simply received and consumed as if they were as "real" as could be. "The

X-Files" phenomenon escalated during the 1996/97 television season with the introduction of two dramas, "Profiler" and "Millenium," that were the sort of wholesome entertainment that would send Pat Buchanan into a frenzy. Fantasmagoric scenes, eerie music, camera lenta and chiaroscuro effects, quotes from Nostradamus and verses from the Apocalypse all frustrated any lingering desires for a happy ending. From another view, that of certain sitcoms, we have a complementary effect. "Rosanne," "Coach," "The Nanny," "Home Improvement," and such, and, even more so, "The Simpsons" and "Beavis and Butthead," are so preposterously "irreal" that they manage to strike a responsive chord tuned to the ridiculous facets of the real. As simply "irreal," the lines and actions are so silly as to provoke little laughter, but when placed in the context of the real, they are laughable insofar as they relate to the sorts of events we quite often take seriously, however bizarre, silly, and foolish they may be. Here, I suppose, we may have something in the order of referenceless signs, the "floating signifiers" of which Baudrillard writes, at their level-headed best.

Leach's re-integration is evidenced in the likes of "Hill Street Blues," "NYPD Blue," "Law and Order," "Murder One," "ER," "Chicago Hope," and to a greater degree, certain soaps, in which things are taken quite seriously, and they appear to be on the level, but everybody knows they are not really "real," for there are obvious giveaways once in a while. In other words, suspension of disbelief is temporarily unsuspended such that the signs are taken as if they were "irreal," but they could easily be "real" in an "irreal" sort of way. These types of programs bring us back into the "real" world, the fake world, the world that is really a fake, the fake that is really "real." This world is like that of the ad: "You're living in real time—Seiko time," and "Miller Genuine Draft—As real as it gets." Ah, yes. Seiko time and Miller draft are "real"; they are commodities that occupy space, fill up space, and are genuine and "real." Yet we all know they are "irreal," don't we? They are "irreal," because the context within which the two ads are placed is too "real" to be "real"; that is, the ads are "irreal," but at the same time they are the kind of "real" we would like them to be, so they are "irreally real." We damn-well know they are "irreal." Or at least we know we should know they are, yet chances are we would rather continue in our ignorant bliss, taking them provisionally as "real," giving in to our penchant for suspending disbelief. That possibility, at least, is apparently what motivates Seiko and Miller.[14]

This move puts us even more dangerously close to Baudrillard's simulacra, unrepresentation and unserialization of pseudo-real commodities that have been transformed into a deluge of signs among signs and nothing more: "floating, referenceless signifiers." These are, of course, Baudrillard's third order simulacra. But they are third order simulacra of the most extreme sort; they are carnivalesque inversions gone wild, pure fantasy, the "hyperreal." For example, the NYPD Blue sort of program consists of first order simulacra of representation; "Star Trek" and other serials are the separation rite; and programs of pure fantasy are simulacra of the third order. In between, as simulacra of the second order, we have at one end, "The Simpsons" and "Beavis and Butthead," the "irreal real" caricaturized such that it is literally more "real" than we might like to take our suspension of disbelief, and at the other end, the likes of "Walker, Texas Ranger" and "Dr. Quinn, Medicine Woman," with their amusing "reality" pretentions that might succeed in unsuspending our propensity to suspend disbelief, and they are taken for just what they are, "irreal." A chief difference between this characterization of TV programs and Baudrillard is that there is no historical progression. For Baudrillard, the three orders came chronologically. In contrast, in terms of today's TV, we can take them forward or backward, however we like, because Baudrillard is looking back to the future— back toward the "end of the world," as he writes in the title of one of his books. TV programs, on the other hand, know of no time.

Granted, Baudrillard's first level simulacra (representation, in the area of symbolicity), second level simulacra (serialization, of indexicality), and third level simulacra (signifiers only, hyperreality, mere iconicity) actually interrelate quite closely to the three different manifestations of signhood. What we seem to have here is genuine semiosis, first de-engenderment, and second de-engenderment. In a nutshell, these three processes consist of (1) symbols in the full-blown sense, subject to the conscious and conscientious interpretation of their makers and takers, (2) symbols made and taken either as if they were indices or as symbols the interpretation of which has become habitualized, entrenched, virtually automatized, and (3) symbols made and taken either as if they were icons or as symbols in a tacit, noncognitive fashion, and with a certain loss of awareness that they are being so taken. With progressive de-engenderment, signs tend to drop out of consciousness; they become relatively mindlessly processed. However, the process is not one-way only. Signs mindlessly made and taken can re-emerge into the light of awareness at a moment's notice, thus becoming genuine symbols. The problem with Baudrillard is that he flattens all signs and their meanings in contemporary cultures to third-level simulacra, comparable to signs of second de-engenderment. In regard to Baudrillardian simulacra, there is surface and little to no depth; time has been "spatialized"—Jameson also stands out in this regard—and we are met with a barrage of superposed images from many different eras of the past and many different geographical locations both in the past and in the present. Meaning is collapsed to a point such that there is no difference that makes a meaningful difference; signs are no more than so many signifiers relating to other signifiers, simulacra are lost in a buzz of other simulacra. There is no need to give up the ship regarding meaning, however, unless meaning is conceived in terms of those obstinate guests of the classical paradigm who are still hanging around in spite of the fact that the party exhausted itself long ago: cause and effect sequences, linearity, Boolean binarism. The trouble is that Baudrillard is definitely a Boolean binarist, an admirer of the cybernetic digital machine within the ghost of a deceased worldview, with its attendant linear thinking in the order of pushes and pulls of signs—in the guise of simulacra—that are now standing in proxy for the billiard ball items of the Cartesian-Newtonian corpuscular-kinetic model of the universe and mechanical thinking.

I would argue that signs apparently squashed to a two-dimensional plane are not simply meaningless, gutless signifiers, but the surface of rhizomicity. Semiosis in the Peircean sense composes an intricate rush of interrelated, interdependently emerging and submerging signs the meaning of each of which is dependent upon the whole concoction. There is no "Here one sign, there another sign," or "Now this sign, now that sign," or "Here the sign there the object and further on the meaning." Or even "Here the cause, there the effect," as per Marxist and classical interpretations of postmodernism, especially in the order of Fredric Jameson (1984) and his postmodern turn as the "cultural logic of late capitalism," with nary a hint as to what he means by "cultural logic." No, classical thought is simply inadequate to the task. Time and space are wedded together and the consummation of their marriage has no conceivable beginning or ending, nor is it possible to know where it is taking place, for it is taking place everywhere and nowhere, and at this time and at every time. The so-called flattening of meaning marks the demise of a tired worldview and an emergence into the light of day of unlimited possibilities for signs, semiotic objects, and interpretants—all of them signs in their own right—to combine and interact in new ways and by nonlinear, non-Boolean, contradictorily complementary means. Spacetime—recall the above on Wheeler—is the stage upon which the interplay unfolds itself. The drama is comparable to Chantal Mouffe's (1988) "subject" at some spacetime juncture within a "radically democratic" society who intersects and interacts and communes with a multiplicity of other "subjects" in their own spacetime juncture.

This drama highlights the incessantly altering and being altered, emerging and submerging, coming and going of the many faceted hybrid, rhizomic character of present cultures (García Canclini 1995). It falls somewhat in line with Donna Haraway's (1989) "cyborg" metaphor of a new social body capable of going with the flows of the universe of signs and capable of bringing about the emergence of signs hitherto marginalized or suppressed. It is commensurate with Deleuze and Guattari's (1987) hero, the schizophrenic, nomadic mind that knows no boundaries and gives no respect, who wanders in and out of discourses at will and who can survive whatever context the world has in store. All this is wrapped into one massive flow of signs, I would submit. (However, I am by no means presuming to offer a catch-all view of everyone everywhere and anytime, but, rather, I believe a thoroughgoing concept of semiosis falls in line with much of the current narrative of the most daring sort, and I would like to articulate this insofar as I am capable.)

Richard Nixon often cited that all too familiar adage, "When the going gets tough, the tough get going." We have occasionally heard a variation on that melody in recent years with respect to consumer hype: "When the going gets tough, the tough go shopping." But this variation is a much more general issue, which involves Deleuze and Guattari's favorite character, and goes something like this: "When the going gets uncertain along nonlinear pathways, he/she who is capable of becoming a genuine guerrilla warrior gets schizoid." This move facilitates a dispersion and diaspora of desires and subjectivities, deliriously giving him/herself up to the disintegration of the worn-out subject of modernity. This, then, is a more genuine image of signs squashed to two-dimensionality while at the same time allowing for a virtual infinity of interrelations along noncausal, nonlinear paths. If flattening there be, it is the result of de-engendered signs, signs made and taken as if they were signs of lesser complexity, signs that under certain conditions might be made and taken in the order of Baudrillard's zombified masses mindlessly traveling along their one-dimensional, tunnel-focused, digitalized road of lifelessness. They are not irretrievably controlled, however. For their signs, rather than merely hollow signifiers, are signs of de-engenderment, most of which can be re-engendered at the proper spacetime juncture to open out and into an infinity of possible alternative roads.

Let me, then, turn to this issue by way of discussion of postmodernism's kitsch, but from a very special point of view.

13

A SEMIOTICS FOR
EVERYDAY LIFE

I. WHEN THINGS ARE AS
THEY APPEAR, OR ARE THEY?

To recap, space, things in space, and isotropic time and their specification in terms of cause and effect, linearity, and the reversibility of their actions and reactions all collapse with irreversible time, with nonlinearity. If we place space in the classical sense of the term within the framework of chiefly indexical signs (221, 222, 321, 322), and signs of subjective and anisotropic temporality and mediation within the framework of chiefly symbolic signs (331, 332, 333), there still remains a vacuum to be filled: signs of chiefly iconicity (111, 211, 311).

If considered merely as signs of simulation—which they are, no doubt—nonetheless, they are not signs of the Baudrillardian sort of simulacra about which some observers of postmodernism wax ebullient. They are, more properly put, signs of "em-bodiment," of "in-corpora-tion," of "in-carnation." They include corporeal semiosis of quality before quantity, feeling before form, intuition before reason. But, just as for Peirce abduction is an absolutely necessary precursor to the formation of hypotheses (by deduction) and their being put to the test (by induction), so also are signs of corporeality, of iconicity, necessary forerunners to in-dices and symbols. Iconicity (or simulation, if you wish) is the being of the becoming, and in the same process the becoming of the being, of semiosis, which includes indexicality and symbolicity in addition to iconicity. In this manner, just as space and time and indexicality and sym-bolicity and Secondness and Thirdness are all collapsed into one, so also simulation (iconicity, Firstness) merges with and loses itself within them. At the same time it exercises its influence on the nature of semiosis: the symbolic and the indexical become imaginary, become the oneness of iconicity, become bodymind and mindworld.

Thus mind and body, and mind and world "out there," free themselves of that abstract line of demarcation that in the Western mind has separated them for generation after generation. To re-evoke concepts used in passing above and developed elsewhere in Merrell (1991, 1995a, 1996, 1997a), classical obsession with indexicality (extension, reference, primary qualities) and symbolicity (description and explanation, and a mathematization of the universe) has been mired in underdetermination, generality of the most abstract order, and the rage for consistency of knowledge. Now, thanks to, among a host of others, Heisenberg in physics and Gödel in metamathematics, underdetermination, generality, and consistency have given way to their complements. These complements consist of the Firstness of things: overdetermination (a virtual infinity of irreversible, nonlinear, radically nonbinary paths are available at each and every juncture), vagueness (new meanings and interpretations are always possible), and inconsistency (contradictory and incompatible meanings and interpretations can learn to live together, and quite comfortably at that, in peaceful coexistence).

With the inclusion of Firstness, iconicity, simulacra, and corporeality as integral actors on the stage of semiosis, the conglomeration of any and all hybrid sorts of signs becomes possible, no matter how apparently incompatible and how bizarre they may be. There exists the possibility that any and all signs may take on virtually the same value, hence they may be ultimately in some form or fashion interchangeable. In other words, given multiple times and places, no sign is necessarily superior or inferior to any other sign. All signs are thrown into the same democratic mess—i.e., the so-called depthlessness of which the revelers from within their joyous free play of postmodern signifiers blissfully write. This, then, introduces us to the idea of kitsch and other comparable postmodern phenomena, whether we like it or not.

Celeste Olalquiaga, in *Megalopolis: Contemporary Cultural Sensibilities* (1992), reveals—albeit unfortunately from a Saussurean-Baudrillardian semiological framework—the features of kitsch that, I would suggest, fit more nicely within the Peircean semiotic view. Olalquiaga recalls her walks along Fourteenth Street in New York City, which previously sported the appearance of hyperreal kitsch iconography. The street exploded into

> a frontierlike bazaar, a frantic place of trade and exchange, a truly inner-city
> port where among cascades of plastic flowers, pelicans made with shells,

rubber shoes, Rita Hayworth towels, two-dollar digital watches, and pink electric guitars with miniature microphones, an array of shrine furnishings is offered. Velvet hangings picturing the Last Supper are flanked on one side by bucolic landscapes where young couples kiss as the sun fizzles away in the ocean and on the other by 1987's "retro" idol, Elvis Presley, while the Virgin Mary's golden aura is framed by the sexy legs of a pin-up, and the Sacred Heart of Jesus desperately competes in glitter with barrages of brightly colored glass-bead curtains. (Olalquiaga 1992:36–37).

Later, Catholic iconography was brought to the United States from Puerto Rico, the Dominican Republic, Mexico, Cuba, and Central America. Eventually, sacred images profaned the erstwhile profane images, or perhaps it is the converse, profane images profaned the sacred images, in a delightfully delirious mix: punk crucifix earrings; rosaries that glowed in the dark; Jesus sweatshirts; the Pope, Christ, and the Virgin on clocks and pins, snowstorm globes, and lampshades; and such. Sensibilities (i.e., feelings, visceral attractions, sentimental leanings, all of the sphere of Firstness, the imaginary, overdetermination, vagueness, inconsistency) became syncretically fused and de-fused and fused once again in new and infinitely diverse ways. These were vicarious sensibilities that followed inclinations toward images that were not real yet they were taken in as if they were real. In fact, to repeat the now tired phrase, they were more "real" than the real, for they exuded an attraction and provoked a feeling the likes of which the real was incapable (a variation on the "guerrilla" theme).

Kitsch, of course, is ordinarily considered that which is of "bad taste." It is aesthetic values gone rotten, once noble metaphors now abused, potentially effective parody exaggerated to the extreme, a deluge of artificial and recycled images. Kitsch is the yield of the rootless, happy-go-lucky bricoleur: signs are taken at random and thrown together in a quasi-chaotic mix, with little regard for original sources and the signs' previous values. It is melodrama at its tacky best, replete with hilarious, disrespectful, and at times contemptful and even rebellious superpositions. Olalquiaga points out, and rightly so I believe, that Christianity, and perhaps especially Catholicism, has always left itself open to kitschification. The imagery is a visual sort of *glossolalia* that embodies otherwise intangible qualities. Mystical fervor is translated into eyes turned toward the heavens, gaping mouths, and levitation. Goodness always feeds on the image of white sheep; virginity is surrounded by auras, clouds, and smiling cherubim; passion is a bleeding heart. In contrast, evil is a matter of goulish faces and snakes, horns, and flames. In kitsch, "this dramatic quality is intensified by an overtly sentimental, melodramatic tone and by primary colors and bright glossy surfaces" (Olalquiaga 1992:41).

I will deviate somewhat from the letter of Olalquiaga's three degrees of kitsch (corresponding quite closely to Baudrillard's three orders of simulation), while, I hope, maintaining the spirit of her exposition. My motives are not necessarily subversive. Rather, I wish to illustrate how kitsch, according to Olalquiaga's rendition of it, is actually more conducive to the Peircean mold of sign de-engenderment than Baudrillardian binarily focused simulation. Olalquiaga's "first-degree" kitsch keeps "representation," which is "based on an indexical referent." The difference between the "real" and her conception of "representation" is quite straightforward: the "real" is the real and kitsch is a mere substitute that has no reality of its own; it has iconic, but no intrinsic indexical, that is referential, value. But this iconic value regarding religious imagery is certainly valid and valuable for the user. In fact the relationship between sign and perceiver is an intimate one of ritual or quasi-ritual value. As art, on the other hand, first-degree kitsch is definitely on the "low" side, since, if considered art at all, it is usually of the popular or folk variety and hardly worthy of taking its place among genuine art forms.

In terms of Peirce's decalogue of signs, and his conception of iconicity, I would place first-degree kitsch in the category of hypoiconic metaphors. A metaphor in its most proteanly iconic form is actually a Peircean "hypoicon" (*hypo* = beneath, not yet a full-blown icon). That is to say, as a hypoicon, a verbal metaphor is still in the iconic state. It is at most sign 311. It has not been given a linguistic label, which would place it in the bag with signs 331, then if given a definition, with signs 332, and if embedded in an argument or text, with signs 333. But that's another story. For the moment we should stick to sign 311, the hypoiconic and nonlinguistic stage of metaphoricity. A metaphor as hypoicon can be a sign in the process of engenderment, in which case it has high hopes of slithering its way up the semiosic stream to span signs of more complex sorts. It can also be a sign of de-engenderment, from a text to a sentence to a solitary word and then on down to the iconic stage—i.e., the universe as a "machine" metaphor, which became firmly entrenched in Western discourse. Thus in terms of Olalquiaga's first-degree kitsch iconography, a particular saint's moment of epiphany and the verses surrounding it in Catholic texts is presented as a vulgar piece of art depicting the saint with eyes toward heaven and mouth in awe. From the symbolism of religious doctrine to indexical relations, compulsions, and evocations, at this stage we have an icon that is hardly more than a visual metaphor for the original sign. The shells of the onion in figure 4 have been peeled away to leave no more than a pale memory of what it once was.

First-degree kitsch maintains in the good tradition of signs 311 the relation between sign or representamen and the semiotically real object. In other words, the metaphorical relation is in play; there is interaction between the sign and that to which it relates, where the difference between the sign and its object is maintained. Olalquiaga writes that in first order kitsch the semiotic object is of no intrinsic value in and of itself; it is sold only for its iconic (hypoiconic, metaphorical) value. In the case of the Christ clocks, when checking the raw physical item for the time of day, Christ as an icon becomes a mere backdrop, and when gazing upon the countenance of Christ as a religious figure, the clock as icon falls into the background. There is no "representation" in the Fregean or logical sense. Rather, there is no more than relations, or better, interactions. The term interaction is relevant in this context. In fact, philosopher Max Black (1962) uses it as his chosen concept of the metaphor while rejecting the traditional comparison view (I. A. Richards, et al.) and the substitution view (Roman Jakobson, et al.) as inadequate. The utterance "Those homeless rats of the urban complexes . . ." brings together into interaction, within a specific linguistic and semiotic world context, humans and rats, impoverished people and scavenging rodents, in such a way that the ordinary meanings of both terms change. During this process, all the words of the discourse within which they are found suffer minor to major alterations, as do the physical objects, both human and living and inorganic, on the city streets. Black's theory of metaphoricity placed within the sense of semiosis developed here breeds signs in an incessant effervescent dance that allows no words or any other signs a moment's rest—which in this respect actually departs radically from Black's original formulation.

Olalquiaga also writes that while her first-degree kitsch maintains a distinction between reality and representation—or in other words, between the real and the semiotically real—second-degree kitsch collapses this distinction: there is only representation and no other referent to be had. First-degree kitsch familiarized the unspeakable by rendering a saint a sort of caricature but at the same giving him a countenance the populace could at least get a feel for and identify with. Second-degree kitsch defamiliarizes its object of representation, for it sneaks out of the scene altogether, leaving only representation. Now, rather than tackiness and vulgarity for the purpose of representing something—a purpose that is not entirely devoid of a certain charm—tackiness and vulgarity are presented simply and self-reflexivity for the sake of tackiness and vulgarity, nothing more, nothing less. I would suspect that, in spite of her folksy and provocative exposition, Olalquiaga goes a little too far here. It is not so much that there is no reference except representation looking at itself, but rather, there never was any legitimate representation in the first place, nor was there any reference in the classical sense. Representation, reference, correspondence, and comparable labels, all belong to a mind-set of foregone days—though still tossed around by too many poststructuralists and cultural critics. What there is, as I have argued in greater detail (Merrell 1997a), is, more appropriately put, relations, interrelations, and interrelatedness. The representamen relates to, it does not refer to, its object, for that object can in a future moment also become a representamen in its own right, and then it will relate to another object; and both representamen and object will relate to, or better, their interpretant will relate to and mediate between them. In this manner, if we could just discard the pig-headed idea that there is a sign here and a thing there and a meaning either embodied in the sign or in the thing or in the head or somewhere else, then we might come to an awareness of the radical wholeness of the sign and of the codependent interrelatedness of all signs.

I would submit that Olalquiaga's second-level kitsch is a further de-engenderment of the Peircean sign. As de-engenderment of an iconic sign after it has already been de-engendered from a symbolic sign, we have second-level kitsch or a de-engendered iconic sign, which is best illustrated by the hypoiconic diagram (sign 211). This is a sign of the Secondness of the hypoicon to complement its Thirdness in the hypoiconic metaphor. Olalquiaga (1992:46) calls second-degree kitsch "a fad, something fun to play with," such that what matters is only "iconicity itself; the 'fad's' worth is measured by its icon's traits—the formal, technical aspects like narrative, color, and texture." Kitsch now consists of poststructuralism's favorite conceits, that of floating images, simulacra, signifiers devoid of any mooring in the real world. As a matter of fact, as "floating signs, they can adhere to any object and convey onto it their full value, 'kitschifying' it" (Olalquiaga 1992:46). In contrast, the hypoiconic diagram bears a definite relation to the real, however schematic and abstract that relation may be. What might give it the appearance of a "floating sign" is the vagueness of this relation; it is, perhaps better said, relativity more than concrete relation, form rather than content. It is, nonetheless, relation. It is a relation of a sign and that which it is an icon of, a relation of Secondness without the mediating effect of Thirdness.

Meanwhile, back in Max Black's theory of metaphoricity, what we have in second-degree kitsch and in first-degree de-engenderment—from a relatively genuine, although nonlinguistic, metaphorical sign to a de-engendered sign—is tantamount to the Jakobsonian substitution theory of metaphor. One thing for another thing, one sign for another sign: what we have is a sign and one of its others that can in its own turn become a sign with its own other—i.e., Jakobson's (1960) paradigmatic interjection along the syntagmatic chain. Two-way relations are highlighted and triadic relations wane. Olalquiaga's example of plastic bottles in the shape of the Virgin Mary filled with holy water and sold in the marketplace are a propos in this regard. Bottles ordinarily provide a mere practical function. The image, the bottle, is colorless, and the material of which it is composed is merely functional. The sacred icon is no more than an abstraction in relation to its conventional manifestation. When the receptacle takes on this abstract form and is filled with religious meaning, it becomes charged with indexicality-diagrammaticity. In Black's critique of the substitution model he points out that a new word is put in an old flask, like "orange" as a color from "orange" as a fruit, or "lion" as Richard from "lion" as a brave animal. In like fashion, to replace "homeless people" with "rats" is to say something about homeless people, it seems. But what? "Rats" are still virtually the same rats, and homeless people remain basically unaffected. The semiotic object becomes a sign, and that's that. Nothing substantially changed, hardly anything gained. The signs are just taken for what they were, without suffering appreciable alteration. In this relatively unthinking way of making and taking signs, as Olalquiaga puts it, the products can be more effectively mass marketed. Thus the signs of second-order kitsch can be recycled to become even further commodified, now consumed much in the order of Baudrillardian simulacra—alas, I must concede at least that much to him—given the market interchangeability of all such signs designed specifically for immediate consumption.

Olalquiaga tells us that with signs of third-order kitsch, commodification is raised to a screaming pitch. These signs take on either new or foreign sets of meanings, in the process becoming hybridized, syncretized, a blending of the various facets of United States' culture and Latin American cultures. Altars to the Virgin might be presented in quite ordinary fashion except that instead of the Virgin's face one might find that of Frida Kahlo or Mexican movie star Dolores del Río, or perhaps in the case of an artwork even the artist's grandmother, aunt, or sister. Or perhaps the Virgin and saints and Christ may be more overdramatized even than in Medieval and Baroque times, thus parodying and caricaturizing them. Or traditional Catholic figures and images may be vulgarized in gaudy colors, phosphorescent paint, and glitter dust. In such cases, high culture, popular culture, and even the immediate family are integrated with sacred images, all in, logically speaking, contradictory and irrational fashion. Conventional iconicity is invested with foreign images and their attendant meanings (Kahlo's face instead of the Virgin's) at the most anarchic level of similarity. Indeed, as Nelson Goodman (1972) forcibly argues, similarities can be found anywhere anytime; it's simply a matter of sensing and letting the mind take its course—abduction at its loosest. This is a play chiefly of images (hypoicons of Firstness, signs 111), which finally opens the door to hyperreality. Such acts of third-order kitsch or profanization create new values, revealing that the old patriarchical hierarchization of society is no longer valid.

Black's critique of the comparison view of metaphoricity is well taken in the sense that it is virtually an "anything goes" enterprise. This doesn't necessarily tell us much. These are signs of de-engenderment (iconization) to the extent that virtually anything can be taken for anything else. Which can be the virtue and the vice of hypoiconic images. Vice, for if taken for something else unthinkingly and unknowingly, they are mere simulacra in the Baudrillard vein sopped up by somnambulistic, clapped-out brains hardly capable of thinking and sensing otherwise. And virtue, in the event that the semiotic agent is aware of her making and taking her signs. It is the difference between homeless people taken for "rats" and nothing but "rats" and their being construed as "rat-like, unfortunately, because of the prevalent conditions of society that allow for such marginalization, but with proper measures taken, perhaps . . ." It is the difference between gut reaction without giving it a moment's thought, on the one hand, and, on the other, thoughtful contemplation of the semiosic array of signs that have presented themselves.

Olalquiaga quite rightly claims Baudrillard ascribes a nostalgic function to such radical alterations of religious simulacra, though he assigns the desecraters of these images little to no semiotic power—Olalquiaga calls it "discursive power." Unlike both Olalquiaga and Baudrillard, however, I prefer a more nonlinguicentric posture. Actually, upon appropriating icons from radically distinct frames of reference for kitsch purposes, they can be recycled such that new meanings may be forthcoming. In other words, the signs (hypoicons) are taken from a conception of comparison to substitution to interaction, and they are de-engendered to bring about increased awareness of semiosis from within a larger scope. There is no implosion or loss of meaning in the Baudrillard sense, but the possibility—the potentially infinite possibility, since we are within the sphere of Firstness—of an expansion of meaning through recycled icons along multiply nonlinear lines.

This entails an act of subversion, a cannibalization of images, "guerrilla warfare" in the sense of de Certeau (1984), especially as outlined by García Canclini (1993, 1995). It is the way of subalterns to get back at those who wield overpowering hegemonic influence. It entails, as Olalquiaga puts it:

> the collapse of the hierarchical distinction between the avant-garde and kitsch—and, by extension, between high and popular art—a collapsing of what modernity considered a polar opposition. According to this view, sustained principally by Clement Greenberg, the avant-garde revolution transferred the value of art from its sacred function (providing access to religious transcendence) to its innovative capabilities (leading to a newly discovered future via experimentation and disruption). Since kitsch is based on imitation and copy, countering novelty with fakeness and artificiality, it was consequently understood as the opposite of the avant-garde and considered reactionary and unartistic. (Olalquiaga 1992:50)

The upshot is that:

> Religious imagery in third-degree kitsch surpasses the distance implied in second-degree kitsch. Instead of consuming arbitrarily, it constitutes a new sensibility whose main characteristic is the displacement of exchange by use. The consumption of images has been qualitatively altered: images are not chosen at random; they must convey a particular feeling, they must simulate emotion. Third-degree kitsch is the result of that search. Whether its potential destabilization will have a concrete social result before it is annihilated by a systematic assimilation that hurries to institutionalize it—making it into second-degree kitsch, for example—is debatable. Still, it is not a question of this assimilation seeping down into the depths of culture and carrying out some radical change there. After all, American culture is basically one of images, so that changes effected at the level of imagery cannot be underestimated. Since commodification is one of the main modes of integration in the United States, it can certainly be used as a vehicle of symbolic intervention. (Olalquiaga 1992:54)

Yes, religious imagery of third-degree kitsch "surpasses the distance," because it is so close to the visceral, to feeling, sentiment, quality (signs 111). Hence, there is constitution of a "new sensibility" (via signs 211 and 311), for the consumption of signs "has been qualitatively altered." The images, of course, must convey a "particular feeling," and for this reason I would prefer to replace "symbolic intervention" with "semiosic intervention," in keeping with my somewhat self-indulgent presumption of a radically non-linguicentric posture.

In this vein, and for the fun of it, let's place the present variation on the Olalquiaga theme within the sphere of Peirce's signs as presented in the first two chapters. I have suggested that metaphors involve chiefly the Thirdness, diagrams the Secondness, and images the Firstness of hypoiconicity. Within the sphere of Thirdness, any and all signs of generality that might be engendered by a finite semiotic agent or community of semiotic agents are destined to remain incomplete. Metaphors are signs that require that the images (of Firstness), and their relation (of Secondness) to other images, and ultimately to the words (of Thirdness) in question, be taken in terms of their ordinarily literal, conventional sense, in order that their figurative meaning may emerge so they can function as metaphors. Yet, since this generality is always and invariably incomplete generality, the metaphors must remain open into the indefinite future—even though they have become "dead metaphors," there is the possibility of their revival and alteration. Hypoiconic images as images of the possibility of Firstness before there has been any actuality (of Secondness) and mediation or interpretation (of Thirdness), can present themselves as a superposition of images of different to radically inconsistent sorts. Such combinations, ordinarily maintained in separation at all cost since they are hierarchized binaries with one end of the pole prioritized, can nevertheless exist as strange but quite compatible bedfellows within the sphere of Firstness in the subsphere of the imaginary, of hypoicons as images. In this sense, the images remain exceedingly vague, of the vagueness of which I wrote in the first two chapters of this inquiry.

"And vague signs?" Well, what can one say, given their indelible element of unsayability due to their very vagueness? They are just vague, and as such can hardly be more than felt, according to the sensitivities of the semiotic agents that happen to be at hand. We are now undoubtedly close to the bottom line of semiosis, or at least we have bottomed out to the extent of our finite capacities—unless we wish to garner pretensions of mysticism, or of having been chosen to speak with God or the angels. Within this sphere of existence, we and our signs enjoy a virtual infinity of possibilities (that is, possibilities if we are finite; were we to enjoy infinitude, those possibilities would be necessities, since everything would be there all at once in the eternal now). That is to say that we are not condemned to that somnambulistic existence of Baudrillard's helpless and hapless robotic souls. There always exists the possibility, however remote, of our raising ourselves by our own bootstraps, our signs included, into the light of a new dawn—well, at least it will be new for us. So it is that semiosis is an open field inviting an open game. Whatever closures there may be, outside biological constraints are for the most part of our own making.

In sum, signs may suffer de-engenderment from 333 toward those more basic signs. When they reach 311, they are closing in on hypertrophied body-signs while mind-signs are atrophied—though there is always at least a modicum of mind-signs in the deepest of body-signs, just as there is always a degree of embodiment in the most hyperintellectual mind-signs. From this more fundamental sphere of semiosis there can be further de-engenderment toward hypoiconicity: metaphors, diagrams, images. Each of the subspheres of hypoiconicity in collaboration with the other subspheres gives flavor to the otherwise bland meat-and-potatoes diet of further engendered icons and indices of Firstness and Secondness, which can then be digested with gusto within the sphere of mediating signs of symbolicity, of Thirdness. Each sign, without all other signs in the semiosic process, will surely suffer a quick death; and the composite of all signs, if suffering the loss of only one sign, no matter how insignificant it may be, nonetheless suffers a significant loss of some sort or other.

II. WHEN THINGS ARE DEFINITELY
NOT AS THEY APPEAR: CULTURAL CLASH

Let us take the case of a particular human response to the other of another culture as illustrated by the Spanish conquest and colonization of the Americas.[1]

As far as Hernán Cortés was concerned, the religion, beliefs, rites, and in general the customs of the Aztecs were no less than abominable, practices of barbarians, evidence of the anti-Christ. It is significant that in his letters he tells of human sacrifices while referring to the Aztec temples as "mosques," thus suggesting that the wars against the Amerindians were in essence an extension of the "Reconquest of Spain" against the Moors who invaded in the year 711, a "Reconquest" that finally culminated in the expulsion of the "infidels" in 1492, the very year Columbus disembarked in the Americas.[2] Christianity, in this and a host of comparable manifestations of the Spanish mind, presents itself as the ideological legitimation of the conquest that can justifiably impose itself on the indigenous cultures and religions. In large part, the march of feudal Europe toward capitalism realized its motivating force in the conquest and colonization of the Americas. The pillage of Aztec and Inca treasures, and, later, exploitation of gold and silver deposits in Mexico, Peru and Bolivia; the dramatic rise in production of sugar cane and other products of the soil; the increasingly lucrative slave trade; all these activities filled the coffers of the emerging capitalist nations, England, France, Italy, and Holland, more than they did those of Spain, which remained for the most part mired in the relatively immobile hierarchy of feudalism. According to one of the admittedly more negative reports, 18,000 tons of silver and 200 tons of gold were transported from America to Spain between 1521 and 1600. During the same period, it has been estimated that the indigenous population diminished by 90 percent in Mexico and 95 percent in Peru (Beaud 1981:19, see also Gibson 1966). This dramatic reduction of raw labor stimulated an equally dramatic increase in the importation of slaves from Africa. As an accompaniment to this destruction of lives, there was a concerted effort on the part of the colonizers to prevent the practice of indigenous religious customs. Nevertheless, as the Amerindians were converted to Catholicism, whether of their own accord or by force, they in turn converted the Catholic saints and Mary into pre-hispanic deities and virgin-mothers.

Putting this in the manner of "subversive acts" as presented in the first three chapters and later in terms of "guerrilla acts," according to the conquerors, the idea of culture and religion was a matter of two incommensurable (differentiated) systems, one right and the other wrong, one destined to become the norm, the other destined to vanish. It was basically an either-or situation. Catholicism was right, so it would persevere; the pre-Hispanic religious practices were heretical, hence they should go the way of all other manifestations of ungodliness. From the indigenous (undifferentiated) point of view, in contrast, transculturation became the rule: both the one set of practices and the practices of the other were in effect, since according to their mind-set old practices were never shed while at the same time new practices were either given a show of their being willfully embraced or they were the product of imposition by skillful tactics or ruthless force. Yet, from a complementary (dedifferentiated) perspective, what eventually came about was something entirely new, emerging from within what would otherwise have been regarded as the excluded middle. This novel practice would be best termed neither the practice of hegemonic forces nor the practice of the other, but something else, something different, something unexpected.

Yet, as far as the Spanish Crown was concerned, it was business as usual and full speed ahead. The religion of the conqueror operated on the basis of the theological, cultural, ethical and moral inferiority of the indigenous peoples and of the necessity of fulfilling God's will by evangelizing them and bringing them into the Catholic fold, rendering them vassals of the King, molding them into upright subjects either by loving inculcation or as a byproduct of ofttimes sadistic castigation. Indeed, José de Acosta wrote in *De procuranda indorum salute* (1954:392) that there are three classes of "barbarous nations": Oriental cultures (India, China, Japan), urban American cultures (Aztec, Maya, Inca), and those nomadic "savages, hardly different from animals," that roam the American continent. The heated polemic between Bartolomé de las Casas, defender of the Amerindians, and Ginés de Sepúlveda, imbued with Aristotelian thought and arguing that "inferior" peoples are "inferior" because that is their lot in life, brought some carefully hidden Spanish presuppositions and prejudices out in the open (Zea 1987).

Bartolomé de las Casas, a precursor of modernity, proposed emancipation for all human beings: nobody is either superior or inferior to anybody else, but thinking (and circumstances) can quite often serve to make it so. In other words, it is not a matter of Spanish ways being right and indigenous ways being wrong, so the former must rub out the latter, but, rather, both stand on equal ground at the outset, and now it is the charge of the Spaniards to show by their noble deeds and kind words that their ways are worthy of emulation (las Casas 1942:19; see also Hanke 1949, 1959; Zavala 1964). It might be said that las Casas won the debate. But, of course, nobody really wins in such encounters; each side tries to verbally beat the other into submission, then when all involved parties are exhausted, a decision is made, a few new laws are enacted, and by and large it's back to many of the old abuses as usual. To make a long story short, there were noble champions of the masses and there were exploiters, systematic persecutors, and ruthless inquisitors for three centuries. That has been quite well documented (in general, Burkholder and Johnson 1994, Gibson 1966). So much for the travails of human history in the Americas.

The important point to be made regarding the present inquiry involves the religious response on the part of the so-called subaltern peoples (Amerindians and African Americans) to the Spanish hegemony. By and large the response depended on the human interrelations established shortly after the conquest. Chilean sociologist Christian Parker divides the various responses into four general categories: (1) an attitude of rebellion accompanied by an attempt to revindicate ancient deities, (2) a submissive attitude, leading to an embrace of Christianity, (3) active resistance to the colonial order, often culminating in messianic movements, and (4) partial submission, involving an outward show of accepting the Christian religion but with a syncretic perseverance of ancestral beliefs and clandestine practices (Parker

1993:26–38). However, things are not as clear-cut as they might appear or as we would perhaps like. Category (1) has the forces of colonization saying "A," but the subalterns saying "Not-A." While the overpowering force of the colonizer evokes an outrage of negation on the part of the colonized, the latter are soon pounded into a state of resignation and compelled to adopt their victor's ways, overtly saying "A," but perhaps covertly returning to their previous ways—category (4).[3] According to (2), the submissive semiotic agent says "Not-A," and then by force of attraction she may be drawn toward "A"—for if not, after the decimation of her culture she would remain in a sort of limbo, without identity or direction. Such was often the case of the so-called religious conquest (Ricard 1966) by example and humility rather than by the sword, epitomized in the utopian ideals of Bartolomé de las Casas and especially Vasco de Quiroga and his work with the Tarascan Amerindians of Mexico (Zavala 1965). Quite often, to the chagrin of the Spanish clergy, (4) eventually came to predominate (Wolf 1959).

Category (3) entails saying "Neither A nor Not-A," and fanaticism often takes over in an attempt to fill the vacuum that inevitably remains. Fanaticism is fanaticism, however, and it usually solves few problems in the long run other than in the minds of a handful of opportunistic leaders. This response does, however, bring about a necessary subversion of the excluded middle of classical principles. It thus introduces an element of underdeterminism: to the same conditions there can be many possible alternatives, with none of them necessarily enjoying priority over any of the others, given the prevailing conditions. This range of possible alternatives, any one of a number of which stands an outside chance of emerging at hardly a moment's notice, gives rise to ever-increasing generality in regard to the range of any given response. That is, the task of determining the range of general applicability of a particular response is left to the pragmatic capacity of the subject of the response to negotiate a modus vivendi regarding the circumstances within which she is caught—her imagining how to cope with whatever circumstances that might make their appearance and her conceiving of new strategies geared toward the success of such coping (recall the brief words on Peirce's "pragmatic maxim"). Category (3) came into its own as the colonial period slowly made its way through history. The paradigm case is found in the rebellion of Túpac Amaru II of Peru during the final years of the eighteenth century. The rebellion arose in reaction to generation after generation of abuses. However, rather than an exclusive return to pre-Hispanic modes and models, there was a proclamation of and a continued adherence to Christianity (Mires 1988:15–58).[4]

Syncretism, operating chiefly within (4), is what gives life to the other three classes of responses. Containing, within itself, both one possible response and another, . . . and possibly another, . . . and yet another, it can get along quite comfortably with the inclusion of inconsistent alternatives to the same prevailing conditions. The paradigm case in this regard is that of the Virgin of Guadalupe of Mexico. Shortly after the conquest of the Aztecs, the Catholic Virgin mysteriously appeared to a humble Amerindian peasant, Juan Diego, at Tepeyac, ancient sanctuary dedicated to Tonantzin, Amerindian goddess of fertility. The profound significance of what later became known as the guadalupana myth consists of the combination of the Virgin Mary, Mother of God, and Tonantzin, Earth Mother who was given the charge of comforting the Amerindians during the traumatic experiences suffered at the hands of the conquerors. A shrine dedicated to the Virgin of Guadalupe was constructed at the very site of the ancient sanctuary of Tonantzin, bringing together the two traditions into a syncretic whole and giving sustenance to the mestizo or hybrid ethnic make-up of what was to become today's Mexican culture and society (Lafaye 1976).

Response (4), then, is radically overdetermined; at least two and usually many alternatives, some of them mutually exclusive, are brought together in what evolves into a peaceful to not-too-peaceful coexistence. Thus the atemporal sphere of (4), bringing together both one response and another, and another, and another, . . . complements (3), which allows for neither one of a pair of mutually exclusive answers to a particular contextualized problem situation nor the other; but, over time, there may be a nod to either one of them or to both of them. Putting the whole package together, from the sphere of overdetermination the entire gamut of (1)–(4) is taken in one massive gulp, timelessly, so everything and anything enjoys a possibility of arising. From the other side of the mirror and from within the sphere of underdetermination conceived in the most radical sense, none of the above can go, that is, neither (1)–(4) taken as individual possibilities nor all of them taken together is viable. Putting it all together, taking either (1) or (2) or (3) or (4), or all of them, or none of them, there can hardly be more than emptiness, sheer emptiness. And we are back to that again.

In short, we have a general, noncognitive, nonscientific, apparently "irrational" and "illogical" (at least according to Western reason and classical logic) set of responses within the pragmatics of human conduct. Inferential processes are there, for sure, but they are tacit inferences rather than consciously devised strategies for coping. Thought is there as well, but it is "thought" at the gut, and almost instinctive, level, at the level of "deep culture"; chiefly symbolic signs (331, 332, 333) are there, but so also are those signs and the others to which they interrelate (221, 222, 321, 322), in addition to signs that appeal most to the inner self, the self and its inner other (111, 211, 311). Since the baser signs play a prominent role in the pragmatic give-and-take of categories (1)–(4) above, an overriding element of unsayability pervades amongst symbolic signs, just as in the case of signs of extralinguistic nature emerging through smells, tastes, touches, sounds, and sights. This is, essentially, nonlinguicentricity at its level-headed best.

"What about simulacra?" our hopeful disciple of postmodernism chimes in. Well, yes. But if simulacra are taken merely as "A," there is always already the possibility of the emergence of complementary signs: "Not-A," "Both A and Not-A," and "Neither A nor Not-A." "Is there no cognitive, rational, logical, and conscious and intentional employment of the 'pragmatic maxim' or some facsimile thereof?" Yes again. But the same process is always already flowing at tacit levels as well. "And what about language as the index of what is a distinctively human semiotics? Does it not push its way into the scene?" Most likely. But obsessive stress on language eventually evokes the hollow question, "Is that all there is?" which in turn provokes a solid: "No! There is everything that *is not* what there *is*." And other than that? "Emptiness, cussed emptiness." But, . . . no, that's not right, for without emptiness there would be nothing (no-thing) at all.

It may be said in this regard, then, that the media is in the message and the message is in the media. At the same time, the message is in the making and taking of signs, signs of whatever category, whether linguistic or not. And the meaning of the signs is in their making and taking and interpreting, that making and taking and interpreting having emerged as no more and no less than so many more signs, whose making and taking and interpreting consists of yet more signs, and so on, without conceivable end. Signs make themselves less vague in collaboration with their makers; they make themselves signs of more general application in terms of their entering into greater interrelations with other signs in collaboration with their takers.[5]

This is the case whether we are speaking of the colonized subaltern's response to the colonizer, or the other way 'round. A linguistic message, a command, is in the air—assuming there is now a common language between colonizer and colonized. The addressee can comply, simply rebel, actively resist after an outward show of compliance, or covertly and clandestinely resist in the form of a syncretic fusion of what the addresser demanded and expected and what the addressee needed and desired. Or the addressee may hold all the options open as a set of possibilities for any and all future acts. Or (s)he may embrace none of the above, which would be possible in death, coma or catatonia, or the most pure form of passive resistance. But such passive resistance could not actually be called resistance, for from within the sphere of such resistance, there would be nothing against which that resistance could resist; it would be simply resistance without relation of similarity to anything (Firstness), relation to something as other (Secondness), or mediation of what simply is and its other that gives rise to something else (Thirdness). All this is, most properly speaking, appropriate for the flux and flow of semiosis. It knows no suffocating predominance of linguicentrism or ocularcentrism or bifurcation into dichotomies. It asserts them and simultaneously denies them, it includes them and simultaneously excludes them. Semiosis: possibly both any sign and all signs and yet neither exclusively any particular sign nor any other sign, both sign and nonsign and yet neither sign nor nonsign. To say what something is is to say what it is not; to say what it is not is to say what it is. Yes, I know, it's perplexing. But, I would suggest, that is the way of semiosis, whether we like it or not.

With this in mind, a turn to a certain aspect of our present-day condition of hoopla, hype, and hypersemiotics is a must.

14

INTO THE POSTMODERN
MAELSTROM OF SEMIOSIS

I. MEDIA AND MESSAGE ARE
IN THE SIGN, THEY *ARE* SIGNS

I trust it is time for an assessment. We have, in light of the last section of chapter 13, signs of assertion, "A"; signs of denial, which point toward or imply some other, "Not-A"; signs of inclusion, often culminating in contradiction, "Both A and Not-A"; and signs of inclusion denied, often yielding contradictory complementarity, "Neither A nor Not-A, but something other." Of course all this is in language, in spite of my penchant against linguicentric practices. For the purpose of convenience and in an attempt to find at least a modicum of sayability, let us, nonetheless, stick to language for the time being.

"A" in its baldest manifestation is no more and no less than what it is, without relation to any other. It is simply assertion, without there existing any form or fashion of what the assertion is an assertion of, without memory of past assertions of comparable or contrasting ilk, without hope or expectations regarding the reason for and purpose of such assertion, and without that assertion being mediated by other signs of assertion or of any other sort. In other words, a bald and unrelated "A" is no more than the Firstness of signs of assertion. This would appear simple enough. That which "A" implies or to which it implicitly relates, "Not-A," cannot emerge into the light of day in simultaneity with "A," but only a split moment after there has been the emergence of "A." After there is "A," then the possibility exists that there will have been during a successive moment the emergence of "Not-A." What "A" asserts is something other than "A," purely and simply, and that something other is the Secondness in its basest form of its respective sign of assertion, or it is a flat denial of "A," possibly giving rise to an alternative assertion that "A" *is not*. This still appears clear enough: first there is "A," what *is*, then there is what "A" *is not*, which is that to which "A" relates. Our smug knowing has been ephemeral, however. "A *and* Not-A" unites sign and *other*, whether they are compatible or not and whether they like it or not.

Consider, for example, "Earth" as a raw assertion. That, we have already noted, tells us very little. Earth what? When? Where? In what capacity? With respect to some other celestial body or considered as a relatively autonomous entity? In keeping with the spirit of Peirce, what we have in "Earth" is merely a word, or in technical terms a *rheme*, which, if separated from any and all forms of embedment in any form of statement and from any and all contexts of human interaction, depends upon its engenderer for further determination. There is at this stage little to no Secondness, and even less Thirdness. It is merely a sign of 331. But what is this solitary sign anyway? It could be "Earth," "is the center of the universe about which the sun revolves," or "revolves about the sun, which is the center of the universe." Or perhaps something entirely different. We could have "Neither of the two statements is correct," which is quite in line with contemporary scientific theory. In fact, we could potentially have an infinity of different alterations to and aberrations of the sentence in question. But for the sake of simplicity and our own sanity, let us stick with the first two sentences. What we have here is two assertions that have much bearing on the history of scientific thought. The two sentences are not ordered in the mathematical sense. The integers consist of a linearly ordered series, from 1 to infinity. If we know the order, we know the basics of the series. Someone says, "5!" Well, 5 what? "Just 5," we are told in response. Furthermore, we are told that we don't really need any more information than that in order to derive meaning from the number. We should know that its immediate predecessor is "4" and that its immediate successor is "6," and that if we subtract "2" from "5" we have the immediate predecessor of the immediate predecessor of "5," and that if we add "2" to "5" we have the immediate successor of the immediate successor of "5," and so on. Simple enough. Any elementary school graduate is able to tell us so much.

What about the order of "The sun revolves about the Earth" and "The Earth revolves about the sun"? There is none, that is, not necessarily. Or, better said, the two sentences are contextually relative to one another: if the Earth is at a standstill, the sun moves; if the sun is at a standstill, the Earth moves (recall the above words on "sun" via Norwood Hanson). This is like saying of John and Jim locked in a chess match: if John wins, Jim loses; if Jim wins, John loses. In fact, according to contemporary relativity theory, we could say that neither does the sun go around the Earth nor vice versa, for their motion is relative. Or we could say that both the sun goes around the Earth and vice versa, for their motion is relative. We could even say none of the above, for the earth is actually on an elephant's back, and the elephant is standing on a giant tortoise. To take the next monolithic and apparently crazy step further, we could finally claim that all the above are true. Is this overdetermination gone mad? Not really. For signs, to be signs, must be actualized for us in some respect or capacity. They begin this trek toward actualization within the sphere of just-a-mite-beyond-pre-Firstness, at least, and according to whichever of the possible injunctions with respect to "Earth" is taken to be either true or false at a particular spacetime juncture, depending upon the prevalent conditions and the reigning conventions with a particular community of semiotic agents. However, there appears to be no sense of order of the sort with which we have become quite comfortable in numbers. No necessary order, that is. If order there be, it exists within a particular set of cultural conventions, not across cultures. What consists of the facts and nothing but the facts de-pends upon conventions, and what determines the conventions depends upon whatever facts there were upon which to build conventions. With this apparent chicken-and-egg dilemma, we are getting ourselves in deep waters. So let's just leave things at that, since our central concerns should be with signs of Firstness and their self-engenderment into other signs.[1]

At this most primitive level of the Firstness of "Earth," there can be no more than one sign. That is why it is hardly more than pure Firstness: the sign is all there is; there has not (yet) been any form or fashion of relation to any other. It is a matter of "A and Not-A" and nothing else. Well, actu-ally, if Not-A includes everything in the universe that is not A, then there is nothing other with which to establish a relation anyway. On the other hand, if "A and Not-A" is a sphere within the sphere of the universe, then there is possibly something other, but it is not available, at least not yet. Yes. "A and Not-A." Something and its possible other, its opposite, both of which are not (yet) anything at all, that is, anything at all as a sign re-lated to something else for someone in some respect or capacity. Just "A and Not-A." Yet, if we want to be able to say anything at all about this con-coction that supposedly makes up a unary unrelated sign, we must talk about its parts. But actually there are no parts, for the existence of two parts implies something and something other, which cannot be the case if the sign is just that, a sign, and a not-yet-actualized sign at that. Nonethe-less, that is all we can come up with at the bottom line of Firstness. But that simply won't do; it is not enough to satisfy our compulsive need to cognize everything. We really must take matters into our own hands and somehow get a handle on this problem.

II. EVERYDAY LIFE AGAIN?

Well, then, consider Murphy Brown. I am of course referring to the character in that popular television sitcom. On May 19, 1992, shortly after the Los Angeles riots, with many parts of the world in turmoil, children starving in Africa, and the Federal deficit ballooning, Dan Quayle argued in a speech at San Francisco that Murphy Brown's decision to become a single mother had aided and abetted the disintegration of traditional American family values (for a detailed account, see Fiske 1994).

The press throughout the country immediately waxed as euphoric as it did hyperbolic. This was precisely what it needed after the uprising in Southern California to keep its listeners, readers, and views on the edge of their seats. In fact, the episode became an issue in the presidential campaign and a focal point around which debates on "family values" gyrated. Four months later, Murphy Brown gave a reply to Dan Quayle on her show. As a TV journalist herself for a current affairs show called "FYI," she presented a rebuttal to the then vice president. But at a particular moment in her reply, there was a switch. Murphy Brown looked straight at her audience, the viewers of "Murphy Brown." All signs did an about-face, Murphy Brown suddenly became Candice Bergen the actress, and the audience became not a fictitious audience but the "real" addressees of a "real" message about a "real" vice president. Following her address, the addresser left her set and entered the floor of the "real" studio, then this "real" Candice Bergen who had recently posed as Murphy Brown and entered the "FYI" studio addressed herself to some "real" single parents and their children in order that they substantiate the actions of the fictitious "actress," Murphy Brown, while in the presence of the "real" actress, Candice Bergen, who was now making explicit and implicit reference to a vice president who had now become somewhat more cardboard than "real." A couple of months later George Bush lost the election to Bill Clinton, perhaps with at least an iota of help from Murphy Brown. Or should I say Candice Bergen? Or was it really Murphy Brown?[2] So much for the anecdotal, and back to the central issue at hand.

During the Brown-Quayle confrontation, one icon-image, the "fictitious" Murphy Brown, at a quite opportune moment submerged into the soup of semiosis, and another icon-image, the "real" Candice Bergen, became "fictitious" and at the same time bigger than the "real," more "real" than the "real," for she was daring to do what no "real" person would ordinarily attempt: virtually taking on the White House itself. Candice Bergen, now more "real" than the "real" in Baudrillard's own terms, addressed herself to an audience the majority of which it is probably safe to say was somewhat more than amused, perhaps in some cases even spellbound, for that audience in a certain sense also become more "real" than the "real." Murphy Brown and the "FYI" set and what would ordinarily be her fictitious audience became one with Dan Quayle, who, as Murphy Brown's antagonist, was thrown into the "fictitious" sphere as well. Meanwhile, back on the set-having-become more "real" than the "real," Candice Bergen responded to the vice president, while addressing herself to a now transformed public. We have, then, Bergen ("A") and Quayle ("Not-A") as opposites, and the addressees who could interpret the signs in proper binary fashion, if they so desired. But wait. What about the other signs? Swirling around in the semiosic stream we also have the composite of Brown and Quayle and addressees now as a set of possibilia, as an alternative virtual "reality," where "A" and "Not-A" and any other sign that might wish to enter the game exist in a lovely embrace without any distinctions or dichotomies having (yet) been enacted. So within the sphere of actuality (Secondness) there is "Either A or Not-A," and in the sphere of possibility (Firstness, vagueness, inconsistency, overdetermination) there is "Both A and Not-A."

That is to say, a sign of Secondness cannot logically and rationally take on the guise of both one thing and the other thing. However, there is no preventing it over time from being first one thing and then another thing (i.e., first my car was shiny and smooth, now it is rusty and perforated). In this sense, and regarding above sections, Firstness is at the outset of the order of an image, then it can become the Secondness of Firstness or a diagram, with that to which the diagram relates remaining as a possibility. Then the rudimentary makings of a metaphor, the Thirdness of Firstness, enters the scene, which brings two or more otherwise incompatible elements together to highlight their commonalities over their differences. And, of course, speaking about all this puts us within the sphere of symbols, of full-blown Thirdness. If we reverse the direction, the sign can become de-engendered to a sign of Secondness and then of Firstness (or "kitschness," if that be the case) at any of the three subspheres (hypoicons: images, diagrams, metaphors). It is from within these baser spheres of Firstness, I would submit, that syncretism emerges, and cultural hybridism is initiated. In other words, there is movement from signs 333 to 111, and back again. The signs are in part or as a whole presented in inverse fashion with respect to their interpretants—i.e., tantamount to the reversal of the Grueworlder's "grue" emeralds from our "green" to our "blue." The Thirdness of the interpretant of one sign (333) de-engenders to the Firstness of representamen, semiotic object, and interpretant (111), where the sign can become other than what it was, even the inverse of its former self. Then the representamen, semiotic object, and interpretant can begin the slithering road toward engenderment into their Thirdness once again, thus taking on the appearance of a new sign. In this sense, the image of Candice Bergen as Murphy Brown talking from within a fake, fictional, or metaphorical world was re-engendered to emerge as Candice Bergen talking "real" talk. Then, things became normal, with the "real" person, now having become more "real" than the "real," taking her dutiful place in the intricate gush of semiosis.

Another incident in Los Angeles, the beating of Rodney G. King by white LAPD officers, gives us additional insight into the semiosic slush of things. On March 3, 1991, King was brutally assaulted. George Holliday, a nearby resident, videotaped the incident, which was during the following months replayed time and time again throughout the TV media, clips of which were seen repeatedly in newspapers and magazines. John Fiske (1994) presents the convincing case that there was not merely one video but two, and arguably four. There was the low-tech video shot by George Holliday (videolow), and there was the technologized (videohigh) version of it used in the trials and on the media. The videohigh version was doctored by computers, slowed and reversed, frozen at individual frames, and inscribed with arrows and circles. What the public saw, of course, was the version of the beating made accessible by high tech society, that very society that was inaccessible to the Rodney Kings of Los Angeles and the majority of the United States citizens. The videolow version was of poor and unsteady focus, unplanned position and angles, and, of course, it was unedited. It all remained vague and indeterminate. Yet of the two versions it remained "closer to the action"; it was the version of the people, whether African Americans or blue-collar workers like George Holliday. The videohigh version, in contrast, produced clarity and definition. Distinctions became evident because they were made evident by careful editing; the tape had been properly de-differentiated and re-differentiated to fit the biases and presuppositions of the hegemonic powers that were. In other words, the visual signs were returned, de-engendered, to their semiosic soup (322 → 321 → 311 → 211 → 111) and then re-engendered as reprocessed signs. Subsequently, during the courtroom procedures and throughout the media, every move was put into words and re-categorized (111 → . . . →

331 → 332 → 333) with the utmost of precision and control (i.e., like "grue" signs doing a somersault from "green" to "blue").

During a key moment of the action, encircled by police officers after having suffered the agony of hundreds of volts from the Taser gun, and from batons and boots, King rose up and moved forward either in an attempt physically to confront one of the officers or to escape—Rush Limbaugh in graphic language claimed he "lunged" at the cop. This scene was described in terms of a "bear" of a man 250 pounds and 6'3" tall threatening the officers, who were then supposedly forced to do what they did in the face of a threat. The doctored videotape and its discursive window-dressing was in Fiske's terms logorational, and it presented an appeal on the part of the cops to all "decent" citizens out there (that is, the white Anglo-American public). What those without access to the doctoring and those who sympathized with the victim (the African American public and certain other groups and individuals) saw was something else, a man victimized. This was what Fiske dubbed the hypervisual interpretation (chiefly 111–322). The logorational approach (chiefly 331–333) could not possibly cope with King's refusal to submit to such overwhelming odds as anything other than a "man-animal" crazed out of his mind with drugs and alcohol who was threatening all that was well and good about American society. The hypervisual approach, in contrast, was witness to inspiring heroism, an individual who simply refused to cave in—as King himself remarked: "I was trying to stay alive sir" (in Fiske 1994:135).

What we have here, it would appear, is videolow as Firstness (i.e., "grue" as "green"), which remains vague and overdetermined and plagued with inconsistencies and ambiguities. Consequently it presents a plethora of possibilities for interpretation. The forces that be, primarily the defense for the white police officers, pulled some of those interpretations into Secondness by constructing a set of distinctions and categories in them. In so doing they symbolized them, rhetorically dressed them in language, discursivized them, thus introducing them to the well-prepared and carefully tilled grounds of Thirdness. And videohigh (i.e., "grue" as "blue") gave birth to an argument that at least temporarily got Sergeant Stacey C. Koon and officers Laurence M. Powell, Theodore J. Briseno, and Timothy E. Wind off the hook. Then those other "threatening" forces of "disorder," those African American citizens who had seen nothing but the hypervisual, videohigh manifestations of the tapes, rebelled.

Where, actually, did the "truth" lie? Within the sphere of the two different tapes and the two different interpretations of the carefully prepared tapes, it might be said that the "truth" is either the one ("grue" as "green") or the other ("grue" as "blue"), depending upon the eye and mind and heart and guts of the beholder. At a "deeper" sphere, all interpretations are interlaced in a congenial relationship as a massive set of possibilities, with none of them (yet) enjoying any priority over any other one.

III. WHAT HAPPENS SEMIOSICALLY?

But matters quickly become murky. We must at some turn in the road take on the idea of "Neither A nor Not-A," which places us in the sphere of generality, underdetermination, incompleteness, the indeterminate, indecisive, and undecidable. Regarding the sphere of vagueness, with all its attendant defining terms and their properties, we saw, in view of Peirce's concept of the sign, that it is up to the addresser to endow his/her signs with enough specification to render them intelligible and relatively unambiguous. Within the sphere of generality it is the addressee's responsibility to further determine the sign.

Now, subversion on the part of the addressee is brought into the picture. This subversion is of that variety put forth by de Certeau's "guerrilla warfare" and our "guerrilla logic" into which the marginalized, the subservient, the dispossessed, the exploited, in short the subaltern, enters. It entails use and abuse of established values, norms, and conventional practices, in which case there may or may not be any awareness of the fact that the act is a subversive act by subaltern groups and individuals in order to bring about the emergence of signs specifying the nature of the implicit dominance/subservience interrelations in question (i.e., teen-agers in the video arcade, at a rock concert, shoplifting, spewing graffiti in public places). Yet the signs are there. Graffiti bears witness to the fact that something is awry in the system, that the sets of eithers and ors that according to the established equations should function like a well-oiled machine are moving off in tangential directions and threatening to spin out of control.

Awareness of the act as an act of subversion and rebellion that reveals the signs for what they are is awareness that the eithers and the ors are not all there is to the machine. For the machine is not a nuts-and-bolts machine at all, nor is it even a software machine, which, in collaboration with a hardware machine, possesses the capacity to generate an infinity of fractal displays. No. It is a "soft machine," a vacillating, indecisive, uncertain, pliable, slithering, sliding, flowing "organism-machine" much of the Deleuze-Guattari (1987) variety. It is more than mere mind or mere body. It is bodymind. The bodymind's awareness of the futility of the eithers and the ors to bring about the emergence of a solution to the problems at hand entails some sort of awareness of the neithers and the nors. It entails an act of dedifferentiation such that the eithers and the ors are scanned within the same perceptual grasp to reveal that there is something else, many other things. The classical excluded-middle principle falls out of the picture, and between any two signs and their interpretants there exists at least one other sign and its respective interpretant.

Thus it is that the notion of either "grue" emeralds or "green" emeralds simply does not fly: emeralds can also go by the labels "gro" or "gree" or "gue" or "goo" or whatever other variety we might have at hand. There are unlimited possibilities. A "gro" emerald might be "green" up to time t_0, then it is "turquoise"; a "gree" emerald might be "turquoise" up to time t_0, then it is "chartreuse," and so on. It all depends on what color terms a particular community of semiotic agents happens to have projected onto-into emeralds such that they became part of that community's entrenched practices. For the Copernican the Earth must be either the center of the universe or it must revolve about the sun; it revolves about the sun, therefore it cannot be the center of the universe. During a later stage in the history of the Western community neither the one sign nor the other is the case, but something else, . . . and then there will be something else, . . . and then something else, with no conceivable end in sight. Here also, at the level of the neithers and the nors, we have the resistance level of the colonized as described in the previous chapter coupled with category (4), which implies a denial of "A," of "Not-A," and of "Either A or Not-A," and an affirmation of "Neither A nor Not-A," with the potential emergence of something else.

From this broader vantage, then, Rodney King was neither a victim nor a hero, but something else, part of which came out in the subsequent trial in which the previously acquitted white police officers were found guilty of certain charges. Yet, that "something else" was never really resolved to the satisfaction of all interested parties. Nor can it be entirely resolved, for, commensurate with the sphere of the neithers and the nors, any and all signs must remain to a degree open and incomplete, for as signs of generality they are inexorably indeterminate, undecidable. (The O. J. Simpson trial, by the way, unlike the original Rodney King trial, had the presumed subaltern as a rich celebrity icon with the best lawyers available and a jury dominated by African Americans and other minorities and women. The outcome should have been no surprise to anyone, yet there was to a large extent either jubilance or outrage. Actually, from the neither-nor perspective, according to the evidence as presented to the public, Simpson was neither entirely guilty nor entirely innocent, but somewhere in between, which the subsequent litigations might reveal—though such revelation will remain partly indeterminate, undecidable, incomplete.)[3]

IV. SO FAR FROM THE HEGEMONIC BODY OF LINGUICENTRIC DISCOURSE

Yes, the haves and the have-nots, those who are on the top of the world and the subaltern peoples, the dominant and the subservient, the superordinate and the subordinate. "But," my skeptic protests, "are you not merely erecting twin columns of binaries? Where is legitimate triadicity? Why are you traveling along what appears to be a self-defeating path?" Hm. I see, and I really must take the next step.

This next step entails consideration of the subversive act on the part of the marginalized—the body in Western discourse, and, in light of previous chapters, those other senses, smell, taste, touch, and nonlinguistic sound and sight. What is conceived to be the central core of the power structure operates on the basis and is governed by rules of practice, and the attendant activity is chiefly objective. It follows carefully designed, institutionalized, and implemented strategies. Take commodity consumption, for instance. The market economy is quantitative and calculable. It is objectively and rationally determined by abstract theory—"game theory" must be counted amongst the worst offenders—mathematical formulas, statistics, computer simulations, and hard-nosed empirical analyses. Consumption of marketed goods is calculated to operate in terms of the public's desires—programmed by market propaganda—more than biological demands or psychological needs. Houses, cars, furniture, clothing, food, all is presented as a means toward status, comfort, recreation, entertainment, leisure, the good life. At least that, is the dream.

Everyday life proves to be another matter, de Certeau argues, which is in virtually all cases far removed from the dream. Many of the marginalized groups within contemporary societies can enjoy little of the hotly pursued "good life" outside the most essential furniture, a beat-up car, TV, a few CDs, fast-food restaurants, a movie once in a while, small-change video games, and a few pieces of clothing—and the vast majority of the world's populace cannot even afford these barest of "essentials."[4] Their consumption of what little they can afford is often converted into subversive acts. They engage in a carnival of "guerrilla tactics," following their whims, vague wishes, desires, intuitions, inclinations, and feelings (i.e., Firstness, body, and the "irrational" in contrast to Thirdness, mind, and the "rational" of the power elite). For those in power, following the entrenched strategies, "time is money" and must be used judiciously, for both time and money are instruments of control. Those of the subaltern, the other, buy what they can, but they do not merely consume what they buy and then leave things as they were. The marketplace is there for their pleasure, for their leisure (wasting time is no problem), for their rebellion. As a prime example, the video palaces in the malls are precisely the spot where the marginalized (youth, most of them of minority groups in the cities) can exercise their own degree of power and control. There, the video player can become the Emperor of the Emporium. He is in charge of that alternate world in front of him, which, with practice, he can manipulate at will.

It is in such everyday life of postmodern Western societies that the contradictions inherent in the capitalist system allow for incessant negotiation and contestation. It might appear at the outset that the power elite has all the cards stacked in its favor. If one takes Baudrillard at face value, the elite has the soporific masses, the silent majority, blindly and tunnel-mindedly buying and consuming signs as simulacra that make the rich richer and the poor poorer and the middle class what it has always been, that tired bourgeoisie under the illusion that it is buying into at least a small part of the life of the beautiful and the famous people. For de Certeau, in contrast, Baudrillard is under the illusion that the weak are powerless, whereas they actually exercise their own form of control by quite devious means. De Certeau writes that the powerful and their institutions are lumbering giants dragging cumbersome baggage along with them; they are conservative, slow to learn new ways, and tend more often than not to resist all forms of change. They construct shopping malls, schools, churches, factories, offices, and places of leisure in order to set their power in concrete and keep the common folk under their surveillance. Their control comes in the form of rules and regulations—the law—exercised in terms of set-in-stone strategies designed to control by instilling desires, drives, and compulsion for commodities of consumption. To make matters worse, they constantly carry out objective studies in order to discover better means for manipulating the public.

The presumably weak other, the subaltern, however, have their own ways that do not conform to the motives, means, and methods of the strong. They travel light; they are mobile, wily, full of tricks, flexible, nimble, and creative. They carve out bits and pieces of territory within the malls, schools, and other public places designed by the powerful to control them, and, engaging in hit-and-run "guerrilla tactics," they find ever-newer ways to subvert the rules and regulations placed before them. They must "make do with what they have," much in the fashion of *bricoleurs*. They do not simply and passively consume the signs around them, they put them to use for their own purposes, and they abuse them whenever they can do so and thereby manifest their contempt, whether explicitly or implicitly, of the system. De Certeau observes that this practice has been around for quite a while. He evokes as a paradigm case that of the Amerindians shortly after the conquest and colonization by the Spaniards—recall the last chapter. The victory of the colonizers over the colonized

> was diverted from its intended aims by the use made of it: even when [the Amerindians] were subjected, indeed even when they accepted their subjection, the Indians often used the laws, practices, and representations that were imposed on them by force or by fascination to ends other than those of their conquerors; they made something else of them; they subverted them from within—not by rejecting them, or by transforming them (though that occurred as well), but by many different ways of using them in the service of rules, customs or convictions foreign to the colonization which they could not escape. They metaphorized the dominant order: they made it function in another register. They remained other within the system which they assimilated and which assimilated them externally. They diverted it without leaving it. Procedures of consumption maintained their difference in the very space that the occupier was organizing. (de Certeau 1984:31–32)

The strategies of the conqueror were by design—one need only take a look at the original symmetry of a Spanish colonial plaza—and ideally carried out by the rigid protocol of the colonial guidelines set down by the Spanish crown. The Amerindians' tactics, in contrast, were amorphous, a matter of incessantly altering, alternating, and self-organizing semiosis. The example of the Amerindians, de Certeau assures us, is by no means extreme. To a degree the same processes can be found in the everyday life of our contemporary milieu, "in the use made in 'popular' milieus of the cultures diffused by the 'elites' that produce language" (de Certeau 1984:32; see also Eco 1986). We find the paradigm case of this amorphous semiosic process in the Virgin of Guadalupe of Mexico, as described at the end of the previous chapter.

Now, in the manner of Peirce's semiotic decalogue, to subvert a sign is to translate it into another sign. In order for this to occur, a sign, let's say a symbol, must travel the path of de-engenderment to the barest of iconicity (111), the field of possibility, where it can discard its worn luggage and grab a new satchel of meaning. It is back to Firstness, to imagery and the imaginary, tacit signs, signs of sense and feeling and quality, signs of the body more than the mind, signs of desire more than convention, intuition more than logic and reason. In fact, there must be a plunge into the abyss in which everything is possible before anything novel can stand a chance of emerging—once again as John Cage put it, between one and another word there is a vacuum, a moment of silence; the same can be said of any and all boundaries (recall also the words by Wheeler in chapter 3). Once the field of possibilities has been reached and sign translation is in progress, the sign, if it is to attain the status of symbol once again, must make its way along the stream and catch up with its former self in order that the translation may become manifest.

"Guerrilla warfare": signs incessantly becoming other signs. Signs turning around and showing another face on their backside. The "guerrillero" is a warrior in the morning and in the afternoon he/she takes on the role of an innocent peasant. The graffitist in the local high school receives his/her diploma with a knot of emotion in his/her throat. The drug dealer is an amiable employee at the corner drugstore. The shoplifter becomes a neutral bystander when confusion erupts. The Pueblo Native American of New Mexico enters into the community corn dance during the week, and Monday morning he dons a suit and tie and is off to Sandia Base where he is employed as an engineer. The North African living in Paris creates a little Africa in the low-class neighborhood that is imposed on him due to his race and his background. The Mexican slum dweller buys a "hot cake" on the street and rolls it up and eats it like a taco. College students inject oranges with hypodermic needles filled with vodka and sneak them into the football stadium where alcohol is prohibited. The blue-collar worker leaves the factory with his lunchbox full of nuts and bolts and wire and tools. The white-collar employee takes a handful of diskettes in his attaché case. From minuscule to sweeping, the examples are inexhaustible. All "guerrillas" are engaged in playing both sides of the court at once. First they are honest Johns and Janes, then they are pilferers and poachers, and then back to their previous roles. For the boss they are either one thing or the other: honest until they get caught and contemptible when their two-faced practice is revealed.

De Certeau's example of *la perruque* (the wig), is apropos in this regard:

La Perruque is the worker's own work disguised as work for his employer. It differs from pilfering in that nothing of material value is stolen. It differs from absenteeism in that the worker is officially on the job. *La Perruque* may be as simple a matter as a secretary's writing a love letter on "company time" or as complex as a cabinetmaker's "borrowing" a lathe to make a piece of furniture for his living room. . . . With complicity of other workers . . . he succeeds in "putting one over" on the established order on its home ground. For from being a regression toward a mode of production organized around artisans or individuals, *la perruque* re-introduces "popular" techniques of other times and other places into the industrial space (that is, into the present order). (de Certeau 1984:25)

Thus, the very success of the commodity-consumerist oriented commercial system, and the making and selling and using of the objects of production, has created the means of, and even invited its own, subversion. From the view of the established order, guerrilleros are laudable laborers until their practices become known, then they are canned. It is an either-or logical and rational affair. From the field of Firstness, the guerrilleros are both honest and crooks, and whichever side of them that happens to surface depends on the context and the situation. From the guerrilleros' own point of view, they are neither entirely honest nor are they entirely crooks; they are simply and without regrets doing what they can or what they want to a system that in their opinion has done them no favors. They do not necessarily have any truck against their boss, the struggling owner of a franchise at the mall they frequent, the good-natured underpaid and overworked teacher at their high school, the local cop who sometimes prefers to look the other way. They are guerrilleros, subverting the system as a whole in their own small way.

Indeed, de Certeau addresses himself to an "alternate logic." The problem is that it is linguicentric through and through; in fact, it is hyperlinguistic. This characteristic, endemic in French thought, does not, nevertheless, reduce the importance of de Certeau's argument; that is, if we include all signs up to 331. If so much is taken for granted, de Certeau's "alternate logic" is context-dependent rather than context-free in the order of classical logic and Chomskyan natural language. We read that a "rich elucidation" of this logic is found in Sun Tzu's *Art of War* (1963) and in the *Book of Tricks* (Khawam 1976) of the Arabic tradition. But, de Certeau continues, we need not look that far abroad, for all societies contain, within themselves, the seeds of this "subversive logic," which emerges itself somewhere from the formal rules of daily practices. However, there is a problem:

[W]here should we look for [these practices] in the West, since our scientific method, by substituting its "own" places for the complex geography of

social ruses and its "artificial" languages for ordinary language, has allowed
and even required reason to adopt a logic of mastery and transparency? Like
Poe's "purloined letter," the inscriptions of these various logics are written
in places so obvious that one does not see them. (de Certeau 1984:22)

I find de Certeau's line of thought compelling, in spite of its obsessive
focus on language and virtually language alone, especially in his reference
to the "purloined letter" as a counterpart to the "tacit dimension" to which
I have alluded in this inquiry. Expanding the field of de Certeau's account
to include the whole of Peirce's semiotic decalogue, I would suggest that
what we have is the four-fold set of possibilities for a "logic," which at one
and the same time overthrows classical logic and contains classical logic:
"A," "Not-A," "Either A or Not-A," "Both A and Not-A," and "Neither A
nor Not-A."

"My God! Back to that. This is all becoming tedious." But this time the
move is from within a larger, all-embracing, all-encompassing sphere,
which is: "All of the above" (in other words, "Both this, and . . . and . . ."
and "Either this, or . . . or . . ." (in the sense of Deleuze and Guattari
1983). But then, as also suggested above, we are forced to make the next
move, which is, in addition to "Neither this, nor . . . nor . . ." (Deleuze
and Guattari 1983), "None of the above." One injunction is all-inclusive,
the other all-exclusive. Both, ultimately, are the same: everything thrown
together in one massive mix becomes in essence nothing at all, everybody
becomes nobody, the infinitely large is virtually tantamount to the infinitely small (this we so emphatically learn from Buddhist thought).

"Why do you insist on getting us into these tangles?" In response, I can
do no more than say: Because if we think about the issues long enough and
hard enough we will arrive at the conclusion that we have nowhere else to
go. We can go only so far, then we smash our nose into the periphery of
the circle and cannot smell, taste, touch, hear, or see any further. Perhaps
another example may help at least to illustrate my message.

V. WHEN WHAT IS, IS NOT WHAT IT IS

I allude once again to the strange but nonetheless unsurprising case of
Madonna. To put it in the most brief, on the surface Madonna lends herself beautifully to a play of dichotomies of the structuralist and even the
poststructuralist and postmodern sort.

Depending on the eye of the beholder, Madonna is a tart and a slut, a
desecrater of sacred images, egomaniacal and excessively aggressive, and

weighed down with too much jewelry—she once garnered second place in a "Turkey of the Year" contest. That is the negative side. On the positive side, most often from the minds and mouths of teen-age young women who closely identify with her seditious attitude, she is liberating, a woman who knows what she wants and gets it, sexy in all the right ways, exuding a funkiness that is appealing. Madonna in "Material Girl" is taken in by commodity culture, yet she is nonmaterialistic within other contexts. In "Like a Virgin" she is a saint and a sinner. She alternates between the white dress of Madonna the bride and the black, provocative cut of Madonna the singer. There is the saintly name, and the ever-wiggling navel; there is a crucifix on a fleshy bosom; there is the woman to be worshipped by men—the Marianist cult—and the woman giving lustful men what they really want. And there is the actress who claimed only she could understand the passion and pain of Evita.

Madonna mimics and mocks. She knows the image she portrays is artificial, and she knows her audience knows it is, so she makes the very best of it. It is not a matter of her being either "A" or "Not-A," although she is most often categorized in that fashion. In fact, in parodying the societal contradictions of our times, she is actually "Both A and Not-A." Oh, . . . no, that's not exactly right either. She cannot be both at the same time from two contradictory perspectives. So she must be "Neither A nor Not-A." In which case interpretation of the Madonna sign remains unresolved, indeterminate, undecidable, and hence incomplete. But, of course, in good keeping with all that has been said and done in this inquiry, we must declare: "All of the above." And in virtually the same moment, we must admit, with some misgivings: "None of the above."

Madonna is not linked to her audience like Candice Bergen-Murphy Brown. Bergen and Brown each retained her own persona within distinct semiotic spheres, while Madonna, well, she's just Madonna: How could she be anything other than what she is? Neither is her image comparable to that of Rodney King. As a sign he was thoroughly doctored, and he was not simply there to be interpreted by his audience. He had hardly any say about how he, as a sign appearing to the public, would be reconstructed. Madonna, on the other hand, was/is author of her own self-image as sign. And now, she is apparently in control, though her audience is free to do with her self-sign as they may. In other words, Madonna as a vague sign is presented to the public in a manner that tends to evoke either one response or the other, or another, or . . . , depending upon the perspective. Rodney King as sign was already interpreted as a general sign that left considerably less to the interpretive imagination and freedom of the public. Madonna grabs her viewers at a relatively primitive level of semiosis; Rodney King is served up on a platter in such a way that the consumers tend simply either to take it or leave it. Madonna, her very becoming as sign, embodies what she is; Rodney King as sign had already been injected with a strong dose of language and all its inherent dichotomizing force. The Madonna phenomenon can be seen in a host of other signs: in Michael Jackson; in Madonna's presumably former bed partner, that hyperbolic cross-dresser Dennis Rodman; in performances by Ronald Reagan or Bill Clinton or Newt Gingrich when at their best, and in other celebrities who play two or more games virtually at once.

What, in the final analysis, do we have? Madonna, Rodney King, subaltern guerrilla warriors, the Amerindians and African Americans of Latin America during the Conquest and Colonial Period and thereafter, kitsch in New York, simulacra and their makers and takers—signs all, signs that include and corroborate and collaborate with their respective semiotic agents, and those semiotic agents do the same with them. What are signs that they may allow us the presumption that we know them, and what are we, signs ourselves, that we may somehow know the signs in our vicinity as if we were somehow set apart from them, though actually we are not and can never be so detached? Or, in the most general way of putting it: What are signs that they may come to know themselves? Peirce's sign decalogue is at once much more marvelously simple and more marvelously complex than that which initially meets the nose, the tongue, the hand, the ears, and, finally, the eye.

NOTES

CHAPTER 1

1. I should mention at the outset that there have been various and sundry outlines of Peirce's sign typology, from Sebeok's (1994) expansion of the basic triad of icons, indices, and symbols into six signs, Peirce's own set of ten signs (Merrell 1995a, 1995b, 1996), and an expansion of those into twenty-seven or 33 signs (Marty 1982), and into sixty-six signs (Weiss and Burks 1945). By virtue of their *ars combinatoria*—each of Peirce's ten signs possessing, as it were, its own triads—Peirce's signs are capable, Peirce himself tells us, of engendering 310, or 59,049 signs (*CP*:8.343–47). For quite obvious reasons, I would suspect, I limit myself in this disquisition to the ten basic signs.

2. In brief, Firstness is monadic: it stands alone, without relation to any other sign or thing. Secondness is dyadic, enjoying relation to some other. Thirdness is triadic, providing mediation between Firstness and Secondness in order to bring them into relation with one another and at the same time with Thirdness itself. A more detailed discussion of Peirce's categories will appear in chapter 5, after the terrain has been properly tilled.

3. See Abbott (1952), Dunne (1927), Gardner (1964), Henderson (1983), Hinton (1987, 1988), Kaku (1994), Merrell (1991b), Rucker (1977, 1983, 1984).

4. In this vein, see Dirac (1963) on the physicists'—or at least one physicist's—conception of the importance of mathematical "beauty" in physical theories, and Wigner (1969) on the "unreasonable effectiveness of mathematics in the natural sciences."

5. Riemann uses pairs of numbers while I, following Peirce, use triplets. By taking Riemann "metric tensors" as an elaborate metaphor, a conceit, if you will, I have brought about the figure 1 mapping.

6. In this regard, see Hartshorne (1970) and Merrell (1991a) on the initiation of asymmetrization by way of Secondness or indexicality in the semiosic process.

7. Elsewhere (Merrell 1996) I have attempted to demonstrate that sign 311 is of central importance since it is the first sign to bring about the realization of Thirdness—that is, of the representamen. By the same token, 331

is the first sign to introduce the Thirdness of the semiotic object, such that language in the genuine sense, consisting of symbols related to their semiotic objects not by iconicity or indexicality but by social convention, becomes possible.

8. Another possible source of Peirce's ten sign types from three sets of three signs may be found in the ancient *tetraktys*. The Pythagoreans saw a "holy fourfoldedness" in the tetraktys that supposedly corresponded to the four elements: fire, water, air and earth. The holy ten derives from the first four numbers by a union of 1, 2, 3, and 4 dots in rows and columns to give 1, 4, 9, and 16 dots respectively, and the union of 1, 3, 6, and 10 dots in triangles. Thus they had the combination of square numbers and triangular numbers. The square number of any rank, say 16 (the fourth generation of squares), is equal to the triangular number of the same rank, or 10 (the fourth generation of triangles) increased by its predecessor (that is, 6, hence 10 + 6 = 16, equal to the fourth generation of squares). In this manner, and turning the equation around, from rectangular fours (four rows and four columns of dots = 16 dots) minus triangular threes (a base of three dots and an apex of one dot = 6 dots) we have triangular fours (a base of four dots and an apex of one dot = 10 dots). While this generation of ten from threes is in tune with ancient number worship that enjoys vestiges in modern day astrology and certain other practices, all of which gives much food for thought, I would like to believe that Peirce's ten signs come to us from a more appropriately modern Riemann geometry. (I might add that an informal method for the generation of Peirce ten sign types from his three sets of three signs is offered in Merrell 1991a.)

9. See especially Butler (1994), Henderson (1983), Kern (1983), Shlain (1994), Szamosi (1986), Waddington (1970), and, as related to semiotics, Merrell (1995b).

10. For the moment it must be said that sign de-engenderment actually goes by the name of "de-generacy" in Peirce's semiotics. Peirce uses "de-generacy" in the strict mathematical sense, and it has nothing to do with the negative connotations of the term in ordinary spoken English. In fact, Peirce pointed out that de-generate signs of the indexical and iconic sort are no less important than symbols, for if it were not for these de-generate signs, symbols could not have existed in the first place. In the present inquiry I have substituted "de-engenderment" for "de-generacy" and "engenderment" for "generacy" in order to avoid mechanistic or quasi-mechanistic implications and to highlight the organicity of Peirce's semiotics. See Gorlée (1990), Buczynska-Garewicz (1979), and Merrell (1995a) for a more detailed discussion of de-generate signs, and Tursman (1987), who discusses de-generacy within a mathematical context.

11. Out of Peirce's idea of the "cut," and insofar as he developed his "logic of relatives," he anticipated what was later called the "stroke function," put

forth by Henry Sheffer (1913), which is fundamental to modern logic and modern variations of Boolean algebra. Interestingly enough, Whitehead and Russell (1910:xvi) demonstrated that the logical connectives can be defined by the "stroke," and subsequently it is possible to "construct new propositions indefinitely." Moreover, since the "stroke" implies incompatibility or inconsistency in the most fundamental sense, Whitehead (1938:52) writes that it provides for "the whole movement of logic." And Hutten (1962:178) remarks that: "It is the very essense of rationality to abolish contradictions; but logic—being the most rational thing in the world—is generated by contradiction."

12. See Merrell (1997a, 1998), Lee (1986), Thompson (1986).

13. In Peirce's terms, "[a]n *Index* or *Seme* is a Representamen whose Representative character consists in its being an individual second. If the Secondness is an existential relation, the Index is *genuine*. If the Secondness is a reference, the Index is *degenerate*. A genuine Index and its Object must be existent individuals (whether things or facts), and its immediate Interpretant must be of the same character" (*CP*:2.283; italics in original). For a comparison of the three types of signs with regard to genuine signs, see *CP*:2.309–10, 4.448.

14. I would ask that you be tolerant of Peirce's occasional submission to the temptation of "ocularcentrism." After all, he, like you and me and everyone else, was to an extent a child of his times.

15. Peirce writes that genuine signs involve purpose, as in A gives B to C with some intention in mind, which entails Thirdness (*CP*:1.366–67). First-degree de-engenderment—such as billiard ball 2 hitting 3 and 3 hitting 4 or a brain-numbed drunk bumping into a woman as he leaves a bar—involves Secondness, mere action and reaction without conscious intention. An example of second-degree de-engenderment is the sensation of an orange spot without there (yet) existing any explicit acknowledgment of the color's relation to red on the one side of the spectrum and yellow on the other (*CP*:1.473). Nevertheless, Peirce asserts, even the most de-engendered forms of Thirdness still have some aspect of mind (*CP*:8.331).

16. Sebeok (1976:24) defines a symptom (index) as "*a compulsive, automatic, nonarbitrary sign, such that the signifier is coupled with the signified in the manner of a natural link*. (A syndrome is a rule-governed configuration of symptoms with a stable designatum) (italics in original)." A symptom as compulsive, obsessive behavior is comparable to Milic Capek's (1961) "Newtonian unconscious": the after-effects of an index-icalization and iconization of the "Universe ª Machine" metaphor-model of the universe that reigned supreme during the classical period. In this regard, a symptom is to be taken as any other mental disorder, whose history must be traced in order to discover the events that played a part in its development. The mental patient suffers from the "figments" of his

own imagination, which he takes to be real; the "Universe ª Machine" equation was, in the beginning, the figment of Descartes's imagination, and over time, became literally construed in Western culture as the way things are, clearly and distinctly.

CHAPTER 2

1. I take my cue here from Nelson Goodman's (1979) notorious "thought-experiment," his "new riddle of induction," designed to make a shambles of induction as it had generally been conceived in Western thought.

2. Geometrically this orthogonal switch is illustrated by what is called an "Argand plane." I have addressed myself to the implications of the Argand plane for semiotics elsewhere (Merrell 1995a, 1997a, 1998) and will briefly return to it in Section IV of this chapter.

3. At your leisure you might compare this formulation to an illustration of sign engenderment in Merrell (1995a, 1995b), from 111 to 333, where I put forth a detailed outline of the semiotic-pragmatic case of Shakespeare's Macbeth confronting the dagger that suddenly appears before him.

4. Interestingly enough, in this regard, composer John Cage once remarked that one must go back to zero ("nothingness" or "emptiness") in the interim between saying one word and another word, or between playing one musical note and another one.

5. Polanyi will be given further discussion at various junctures below. For more detail, see Merrell (1991a, 1995a, 1995b, 1996).

6. I say "pure possibility," since no sign is considered actualized. A conception of actualized signs, which calls for consideration of an entirely different spacetime system, will be briefly discussed in Section V.

7. Recall, in this light, our discussion of the "Grue-Green" phenomenon with respect to figure 8.

8. See Dilworth (1969), for a comparison of and contrast between James and Nishida.

9. See Merrell (1991a, 1995a, 1995b, 1996, 1997a).

10. We must not forget that Peirce also had a hand in this turmoil, this doubt and self-questioning, given his radical anti-Cartesianism (*CP*:5.213–310).

CHAPTER 3

1. In regard to this query on the generality of Peirce's sign decalogue and of his theory of semiotics, see Colapietro (1991) and Fisch (1986).

2. See, for a general introduction and survey, Huntington (1989), Kalupahana (1986), Moore (1960), and Nishitani (1982, 1990).

3. I should point out that elsewhere (Merrell 1995a) I have made a distinction between the "empty set" of set theory, conceived as a "noticed ab-

sence," and, in contrast to "noticed absence," "emptiness," as "that" which "is" prior to there having been anything at all: there is simply "emptiness," no more, no less.

4. "Diddley," you will most likely have noticed, is the consequence of an ambiguity: it is the blues artist's surname, and it is also from the colloquial expression, "You don't know diddley shit."

5. If you may be so inclined, at your leisure please relate this notion to the concepts of sign engenderment and de-engenderment as discussed above.

6. For a standard, yet excellent, "linguicentric" interpretation of the maxim, see Nesher (1983, 1990), and a critique of the "linguicentric view" in Merrell (1997a).

7. Consequently, if we wished to be so perverse, we might observe that the maxim could thus be subject to the same rigorous inquiry that Nagarjuna, in the above example, subjected ordinary logical procedures.

8. What we can do, in view of the above remark on Gödel, is assume our knowledge of whatever and in whatever guise is incomplete, and if it proudly takes on a countenance of apparent completeness—i.e., it is capable of accounting for all signs within certain specified parameters—then it must be inconsistent.

9. Among a scattering of other scholars, most notably George Lakoff (1987) and Mark Johnson (1987) have begun such a defense of the importance of the body in the sign (also Lakoff and Johnson 1980).

CHAPTER 4

1. Figure 15 should be taken as a dynamic illustration, a relatively simple icon, so to speak—though it is kinesthetic in addition to its visuality—by means of which the semiosic process in the best of semiotic worlds of Firstness can be sensed, felt, intuited. Hence I would not go so far as to label it an icon as a model or even a metaphor, for, I would suggest, it is not to be cognized or intellectualized, much less rationalized in the most respectable sense of Thirdness.

2. See my discussion of Spencer-Brown in Merrell (1995a).

3. It might appear that this "somewhere else" with each return of a cycle contradicts Wheeler's self-reflecting "nothingness" of the "boundary of the boundary" that takes things back to where they began. However, here I am including time in its barest form, as the initiation of irreversibility as a product of the "asymmetrization" of the semiosic process (see note 6 of chapter 1).

4. If the oscillations were considered in terms of three dimensions, thus describing an indeterminate number of spheres rather than circles, they would describe a hypersphere of the sort of which the four-dimensional space-time continuum consists.

5. It bears mentioning at this juncture that the relationship between quantum theory and Oriental thought has been notoriously put forth by, among others, Capra (1975), Talbot (1980), and Zukav (1979), and Oriental thought and quantum theory have been brought into the view of process philosophy by Bohm (1980) and Griffin (1988).
6. The problem, as is now notorious, is that the valued binaries tend to be hierarchized, with one pole of the opposition prioritized over the other.
7. Merrell (1996, 1997a), Varela (1984), Maturana and Varela (1980, 1987).
8. Merrell (1996, 1997a), Putnam (1981, 1983).
9. I might add that in Wittgenstein's "language games" (1953) the rules are often up for grabs to a much greater extent than in conventional games because for the most part they are not clearly specified.
10. Elsewhere (Merrell 1995a, 1996, 1997a) I have expounded from various angles on a most general form of nonstandard "semiosic logic." Here, as I have intimated, I am in the process of offering a non-Boolean, nonlinear, ortho-complementary "cultural logic" in an attempt to clarify, insofar as my limited faculties will allow, what is meant by the various allusions to some ill-defined "logic" of culture.

CHAPTER 5

1. I wish to acknowledge my debt to John Post and his "paradox of the possible liar" (1987) for the basis of this section. This "possible liar paradox" should be taken as an extension of the case of little Johnny's fib in chapter 4.
2. See Fiske (1989a, 1989b, 1994), Kellner (1995).
3. See Merrell (1991a, 1995a, 1995b, 1996, 1997a).
4. Please relate, if you will, this Borromean knot aspect of figure 18, as well as the other figures later to appear in this chapter, to the discussion regarding figures 5, 6, and 7 from chapter 1, for, I would suggest, the arguments, as well as the figures, are tightly interwoven.
5. One would do well also to relate figure 20 to the words in chapter 1 with respect to figures 6 and 7.

CHAPTER 6

1. It bears mentioning that physicist Erwin Schrödinger in 1945 suggested that at its most fundamental life consisted of "aperiodic crystals," a prediction that in an uncanny way proved to be quite the case with the discovery of DNA (Schrödinger 1967).

CHAPTER 7

1. I begin with the sense of smell, unlike Aristotle, who placed taste and touch, which require bodily contact, at one end of the spectrum, and sight

and sound at the other end, with smell equidistant between the two extremes. Consequently, I locate smell at the most basic level of semiosis, for it is more corporeal, intimate, it requires no contact, like taste and touch; it does not penetrate, like sight; and, as we shall observe, it is the most direct of the senses.

2. See also in this regard Brill (1932) and Classen et al. (1994:1).

3. For an excellent study of the senses and their interaction in the literature of the Western tradition, see Vinge (1975).

4. The Aztecs called it *xocoatl* (Spanish, *chocolate*).

5. According to more recent studies the high is equivalent to a very mild ingestion of marihuana fumes.

6. For a more detailed study of taste, see Brillat-Savarin (1949).

7. For an excellent series of studies, see Teevan and Birney (1961).

8. Interestingly enough, here one might speculate that the color wheel, in order to be sensed as an optical harmony, must include another "dimension" capable of fusing the various color categories of the wheel, in much the manner in which, as we noted in chapters 1 and 2, Peirce's decalogue of signs is graphically presented as a two-dimensional spread curved in three-dimensional space, with our making and taking of signs in our three-dimensional existence implying yet another dimension for such sign processing.

9. The obsession with sight, contrary to many recent observations, is not unique the Western thought. Other cultures, namely, the Desana people of the Colombian Amazon region, believe the cosmos functions on the basis of color. All people receive an equal concentration of color energies at birth, and at death they return to the Sun, the repository and source of all energy and all color. It seems that this culture is as visually oriented, albeit in a much different way, as the West (Classen 1993:131–37).

10. In this regard, see E. T Hall's *The Hidden Dimension* (1969), a study of variations in the perception and conception of space in different cultures.

CHAPTER 8

1. Recall note 10 chapter 4, in which I make mention of a complementary or semiotic logic I attempt to develop for Peirce's decalogue of signs.

2. Haptic space, I should also point out, though it goes virtually without saying, plays a central role in all sorts of creativity in the arts (see Ehrenzweig 1967, Heelan 1983, Löwenfeld 1939).

3. However, for a critique of Piaget with respect to his concept of the younger child as a non-Euclidean "savage" and the older, "enlightened" child as having been taught the proper principles of Euclidean geometry, see Wilden (1980).

4. However, I would take issue with the notion of the "immediately and directly *experienced*," for there is no immediacy, no direct experience in the here, now, no presence.
5. For further, see also Laban (1948, 1960, 1984).
6. In this respect, see also the discussion of studies by William S. Condon on synchrony, resonance, and rhythm in face-to-face human communication, in Hall (1973).

CHAPTER 9

1. One problem with a serious study of scents is the low status to which they have been relegated—which for obvious reasons makes them so susceptible to taboos. Classen, Howes, and Synnott (1994:5) write in this regard that "Academic studies of smell have tended to suffer from the same cultural disadvantages as smell itself. While the high status of sight in the West makes it possible for studies of vision and visuality, even when they are critical, to be taken seriously, any attempt to examine smell runs the risk of being brushed off as frivolous and irrelevant" (on the senses in general, see also Howes 1991; Stoller 1989; Synnott 1993; for earlier work, Straus 1963).
2. For a study of the senses, that includes smells and tastes to complement Gardner, see Synnott (1993).
3. Recently, women critics, philosophers, and theorists such as Luce Irigaray (1985) write that women are more in tune with touch than with sight, the Foucauldian "gaze." This helps reveal the mind-as-mirror-of-nature metaphor, that "picture that held us captive" as the later Wittgenstein put it, for the sham it is (Rorty 1979).
4. For example, Rajchman and West (1984), Bernstein (1983), Dasenbrock (1993), Davidson (1984), Goodman (1978), Hacking (1983), Putnam (1981, 1988), Roth (1987)—and within a semiotic context perhaps also even Merrell (1996), if I may be so presumptuous.
5. Actually, I have said nothing from within a semiotic context about McLuhan's linear, pseudo-evolutionary chain of media history, but there is no time for that story here.

CHAPTER 10

1. Sacks (1987, 1990, 1995); see also Susan Schaller's fascinating *A Man Without Words* (1991).
2. As a visual counterpart to Christina, Sacks (1995:3–41) describes the dilemma of a painter, Mr. I, who after a concussion discovers he is color-blind and must compensate by artificially fabricating colors in his paintings.

3. As is notorious, the word "camel" does not appear in the *Koran,* though we must suppose that the de-engendered, tacit, implicit sign is in the minds of all members of the Islamic community.

CHAPTER 11

1. In this sense it might be surmised that the sole remaining superpower, the United States, is now in search of a respectable replacement for its erstwhile antagonist.
2. This, then, is the general thrust of my study of signs and life processes in Merrell 1996.

CHAPTER 12

1. The story, I should at least mention, thought there is neither time nor space to delve into the issue here, bears on the relations between semiosis as Peirce on the whole perceived and conceived it and much Oriental thought. This topic has captivated me of recent, and if the cards that are dealt me are of the nature that they might permit it, in the future I would cherish the opportunity to continue this line of research. For the moment, however, allow me to recommend in particular the work by Jacobson (1983, 1988) and Unno (1989).
2. The notion of "genuine semiosis," I should be quick to add, does not exclude the Boolean world, which is primarily of Secondness, pure nominalism, so to speak, or at least as purely nominalistic as we can get (Bolter 1984), and is therefore included as a part of the entire semiosic process. Consequently, on one hand, without the Boolean world semiosis could not be "genuine." On the other hand, the Boolean world without the rest of the semiosic process cannot but remain severely handicapped.
3. Recall the distinction between the "Grueworlders" and us "Realworlders" in the Nelson Goodman inspired thought experiment from chapter 2.
4. For another, entirely distinct, case study, see Douglas Kellner's (1995:62–75) analysis of the public's view of Rambo films and the Ronald Reagan rhetoric during the early 1980s, in which the analyst analyses what the general media audience sees with one set of presuppositions, while the audience sees what it sees with its own set of presuppositions. We would assume that the analyst is at least somewhat aware of his presuppositions, while the audience behaves as it behaves in blissful ignorance. However, that is not necessarily the case, for the audience, in its own way, might be able to articulate its feelings and fears and desires and motives quite effectively. (I do not single Kellner out for any perverse reason; comparable examples of presupposition-laden views are numerous, and I obviously in the past and most

certainly at present have committed the same academic sin of presuming "Immaculate Perception.")

5. The problem of one referent (the physical sun in this case) coupled with ambiguous sense (Copernican "sun" and Ptolemaic "sun") is in modern times due primarily to the work of Gottlob Frege. Since Frege's time, however, most philosophers, linguists and semioticians make little to no distinction between the physically real *an sich* and what is considered from a particular vantage point to be the merely semiotically real. The difference is important, since in the Peircean sense the semiotically real may approximate, but never exactly reduplicate, unmediated reality as it is. In making this distinction, consequently, I prefer to use "relate to" rather than "refer to," since the latter brings rhetorically loaded baggage evoking the image of the physically real *an sich* (see Merrell 1998).

6. To cite a scattering of notable examples, Fiske (1989a, 1989b); Grossberg (1988, 1992); Grossberg, Nelson, and Treichler (1992).

7. See Gramsci (1992), Bocock (1986), Hall (1980), Williams (1961, 1977).

8. For the notion of the dominant culture's control over the subservient culture, see Said (1993); for a critique of this view, see Bhabha (1994).

9. Admittedly, Madonna and Evita share an impressive resume: ambitious, physically attractive, and charismatic blondes, eye-popping performance artists, legendary icons having arisen from tragedy and poverty to become revered and ridiculed and loved and despised by millions. Some Argentines welcomed Madonna-as-Evita, while many others were livid that the pop-tart who desecrates Catholic images was to portray their martyred mother figure. Nevertheless, it was hoped that the movie would haul in millions, which is what the industry is all about.

10. Leach doesn't actually use this argument, but, rather, he bases it on Greek myths and modern psychoanalytic theory—i.e., semen as the third property between male and female that brings about a "little death" of both and gives rise to new life—though his explanation is not incompatible with the one presented here.

11. García Canclini uses the term "fiesta" rather than "carnival." I will use them somewhat interchangeably, especially in light of the following section on Bakhtin.

12. I by no means wish to imply that there is some set of universal constants delineating rituals, ceremonies, fiestas, and carnivals, both modern and traditional (see García Canclini [1993] and DaMatta [1991] for important distinctions). What I have suggested is that the processual, ever openended semiosic flow of the universe finds its expression in the phenomena herein foregrounded, as it does in all other phenomena.

13. Of course, de Certeau's guerrilla has no need of any special carnival time to engage in what he/she does best. As for as he/she is concerned, it is al-

ways "carnival time"; there's no better time than each and every present to invent new ways to subvert the system.

14. I would invite your contemplating, at your convenience, the interrelations between "real" and "irreal" and suspension and unsuspension of belief and disbelief in regard to the "pragmatic possible liar paradox" as presented in chapter 5, which would, of course, be another tale of binaries subverted.

CHAPTER 13

1. I would also recommend Todorov's *The Conquest of America* (1984), one of the first studies to focus from at least a semiological, if not a semiotic, view on this topic (for a critical post-Todorov view, see Jara and Spadaccini [1992]).

2. And thus the "invention of America" began, to evoke Mexican historian Edmund O'Gorman's (1958)seminal and creative approach to the beginnings of cultural hybridism in the Americas—however, I might add that rather than O'Gorman's Heideggerian interpretation, I prefer a "constructivist-conventionalist" approach as outlined in Merrell (1997a).

3. A good case in point regarding this phenomenon in the present century is found in the religious syncretism found in Amerindian communities in Mexico after the Revolution of 1910–17 as described by Brenner (1929).

4. Three noteworthy alternatives are found among Peruvian thinkers in the present century. José Carlos Mariátegui offers a variation of the Marxist solution for the Latin American continent, Victor Raúl Haya de la Torre proposes a rather vague socialist-communal alternative based on a mix of Western and ancient Amerindian models, and José María Arguedas places greater emphasis on Amerindian cultures as viable local responses to global Western trends (for specific treatises, see Arguedas [1975], Haya de la Torre [1973], Mariátegui [1971]; for an overview, see Stabb [1967], Pike [1992]).

5. This distinctively Peircean idea that it is up to the sign's maker to render a vague sign more specific for the benefit of the addressee, and that it is the responsibility of the addressee to further generalize a sign of generality handed to her by the addresser, is a quite complex issue to which I turn attention in Merrell 1997a.

CHAPTER 14

1. It bears mentioning before we leave this topic, however, that Henri Poincaré (1952), for instance, offers arguments to the effect that such a hardrock science as geometry is conventional, and there are some, most notably Wittgenstein (1956), who teach that even our number system is a matter

of convention, but of course, that, I'm afraid I must say, is yet another story.

2. Actually, at the time of Murphy Brown's rebuttal the Republican campaign was in trouble, yet the general "family values" issue had backfired and might have contributed to the fact that Bush was at the time trailing Clinton by ten points in the polls.

3. And then, the civil trial began, with a self-repeating plethora of questions: "How many times did he hit Nicole?" ("Never," was O. J.'s response.), "How many times did he slap her?" ("Never."), "How many times did he kick and beat her?" ("Never."). Charismatic denials. And many questions remained. Was the infamous glove real or not? Did O. J. actually own a pair of those exotic Bruno Magli shoes? When, actually, did he cut his hand and how? What was really behind the *camera lenta* Bronco chase along the freeway? And why was he carrying a fake goatee and a passport and several thousand dollars in cash? Had the breakup with his girlfriend, Paula Barbieri, been acknowledged or not? And so on. And so on. When one concluded that the public had finally wearied of O. J., some new enticing piece of news would pop into the headlines and into the CNN drone of voices. Books on the comedy kept climbing best-seller lists, and the celebrity's friends were still giving prime-time interviews. And now, it's all over. And it's by no means over. TV coverage of the "hot news" has never been the same. Since the O. J. Simpson debacle, television has been starving to find another story to galvanize the public. So the vultures as of this writing have converged on Washington. And why not? The "news" is chiefly driven by market-place economics. With dozens of channels competing for shrinking ratings, the stakes are high. It's eat or be eaten. The "news" gives the people what they want. Or is it more a matter of the "news" creating in the people a desire for the spectacular? The interpretations go both ways. Wherever the truth may lie, the O. J. Simpson case was indeed a turning point in TV coverage.

4. Indeed, at the Habitat 2 Conference at Turkey during the summer of 1996 it was pointed out that 500,000 of the world's inhabitants are homeless and 2 billion have no electricity. Fidel Castro observed in his wildly applauded speech at the Conference that the very idea of the so-called consumer culture of our times is hypocritical, for it excludes roughly 4/5 of the world's population, and that this hypocrisy is given testimony by the fact that not a single representative from the seven richest countries of the world was present.

REFERENCES

Abbott, Edwin A. (1952). *Flatland.* New York: Dover.

Ackerman, Diane (1990). *A Natural History of the Senses.* New York: Random House.

Acosta, José de (1954). *Obras del Padre José de Acosta.* Madrid: BAE.

Adorno, Theodore W. (1973). *Philosophy of Modern Music.* New York: Seabury.

Amoore, John (1971). *Olfaction.* New York: Springer-Verlag.

Arguedas, José María (1975). *Formación de una cultura indoamericana.* México: Siglo XXI.

Aristotle (1966). *Metaphysics,* trans. H. G. Apostle. Bloomington: Indiana University Press.

Arnheim, Rudolf (1969). *Visual Thinking.* Berkeley: University of California Press.

Baer, Eugen (1988). *Medical Semiotics.* Lanham: University of America Press.

Bakhtin, Mikhail (1968). *Rabelais and His World.* Cambridge: MIT.

—— (1981). *The Dialogic Imagination.* Austin: University of Texas Press.

Barthes, Roland (1972). *Mythologies,* trans. A. Lavers. New York: Hill and Wang.

—— (1975). *The Pleasure of the Text.* New York: Hill and Wang.

Bartley, William Warren III (1962). *The Retreat to Commitment.* New York: Alfred A. Knopf.

Bateson, Gregory (1972). *Steps to an Ecology of Mind.* New York: Chandler.

Baudrillard, Jean (1975). *The Mirror of Production,* trans. M. Poster. St. Louis: Telos.

—— (1981). *For a Critique of the Political Economy of the Sign,* trans. C. Levin. St. Louis: Telos.

—— (1983a). *Simulations.* New York: Semiotext(e).

—— (1983b). *In the Shadow of the Silent Majorities,* trans. P. Foss, J. Johnston, and P. Patton. New York: Semiotext(e).

—— (1988a). *The Ecstasy of Communication,* trans. B. Schutze and C. Schutze. New York: Semiotext(e).

—— (1988b). *America.* London: Verso.

Beaud, Michel (1981). *Histoire du capitalisme de 1500 á nos jours.* Paris: Seuil.

Beckett, Samuel (1955). *Molloy, Malone Dies, The Unnamable.* New York: Grove.

Benedict, Ruth (1946). *The Chrysanthemum and the Sword.* New York: Meridian.

Bennett, Tony (1983). "A Thousand and One Pleasures: Blackpool Pleasure Beach." In *Formations of Pleasure,* 138–45. London: Routledge and Kegan Paul.

Bergson, Henri (1911). *Creative Evolution,* trans. A. Mitchell. New York: Henry Holt.

Berman, Morris (1981). *The Reenchantment of the World.* Ithaca: Cornell University Press.

Bernstein, Richard (1983). *Beyond Objectivity and Relativism: Science, Hermeneutics, and Praxis.* Philadelphia: University of Pennsylvania Press.

Bhabha, Homi (1994). *The Location of Culture.* New York: Routledge.

Bianconi, Lorenzo (1982). *Music in the Seventeenth Century,* trans. D. Bryant. Cambridge: Cambridge University Press.

Birdwhistell, Ray L. (1970). *Kinesics and Context.* New York: Random House.

Black, Max (1962). *Models and Metaphors.* Ithaca: Cornell University Press.

Bocock, Robert (1986). *Hegemony.* London: Tavistock.

Bohm, David (1980). *Wholeness and the Implicate Order.* London: Routledge and Kegan Paul.

Bolter, J. David (1984). *Turing's Man: Western Culture in the Computer Age.* Chapel Hill: University of North Carolina Press.

Borges, Jorge Luis (1962). *Labyrinths, Selected Stories and Other Writings,* D. A. Yates and J. E. Irby (eds.). New York: New Directions.

———— (1964). *Other Inquisitions,* trans. M. L. Simms. Austin: University of Texas Press.

Bourdieu, Pierre (1990). *The Logic of Practice,* trans. R. Nice. Stanford: Stanford University Press.

Brenner, Anita (1929). *Idols Behind Altars.* New York: Harcourt, Brace.

Brill, A. A. (1932). "The Sense of Smell in Neuroses and Psychoses." *Psychoanalytical Quarterly* 1, 7–42.

Brillat-Savarin, Jean Anthelme (1949). *The Physiology of Taste,* trans. M. F. K. Fisher. San Francisco: Northern Point Press.

Bruner, Jerome (1956). *A Study of Thinking.* New York: Wiley.

———— (1986). *Actual Minds, Possible Worlds.* Cambridge: Harvard University Press.

———— (1987). *Making Sense: The Child's Construction of the World.* London: Methuen.

Buczynska-Garewicz, Hanna (1979). "The Degenerate Sign." *Semiotics Unfolding* (Proceedings of the Second Congress of the International Association for Semiotic Studies), T. Borbé (ed.), vol. 1, 43–50. Berlin: Mouton de Gruyter.

Bunn, James (1981). *The Dimensionality of Signs, Tools, and Models.* Bloomington: Indiana University Press.

Burkholder, Mark A. and Lyman J. Johnson (1994). *Colonial Latin America.* New York: Oxford University Press.

Butler, Christopher (1994). *Early Modernism: Literature, Music and Painting in Europe 1900–1916.* Oxford: Clarendon.

Cabrera Infante, Guillermo (1970). *Three Trapped Tigers,* trans. D. Gardner and S. J. Levine. New York: Harper and Row.

Cain, W. S. (1981). "Educating Your Nose." *Psychology Today* 15 (7), 48–56.

Calvino, Italo (1969). *T Zero*. New York: Harcourt Brace Jovanovich.

———— (1981). *If on a Winter's Night a Traveler*. New York: Harcourt Brace Jovanovich.

Capek, Milic (1961). *The Philosophical Impact of Contemporary Physics*. New York: American Book.

Capra, Fritjof (1975). *The Tao of Physics*. Berkeley: Shambhala.

Carpenter, Edmund and Marshall McLuhan (eds.) (1960). *Explorations in Communication*. Boston: Beacon.

Carter, Robert E. (1989). *The Nothingness Beyond God: An Introduction to the Philosophy of Nishida Kitaro*. New York: Paragon House.

Cataldi, Sue L. (1993). *Emotion, Depth, and Flesh: A Study of Sensitive Space*. Albany: SUNY Press.

Certeau, Michel de (1984). *The Practice of Everyday Life*, trans. S. Rendall. Berkeley: University of California Press.

Chow, Rey (1993). *Writing Diaspora: Tactics of Intervention in Contemporary Cultural Studies*. Bloomington: Indiana University Press.

Classen, Constance (1991). "The Sensory Orders of 'Wild Children'." In *The Varieties of Sensory Experience: A Sourcebook in the Anthropology of the Senses*, D. Howes (ed.), 47–60. Toronto: University of Toronto Press.

———— (1993). *Worlds of Sense: Exploring the Senses in History and Across Cultures*. New York: Routledge.

————, David Howes, and Anthony Synnott (1994). *Aroma: The Cultural History of Smell*. New York: Routledge.

Clifford, James (1986). "Introduction: Partial Truths." In *Writing Culture: The Poetics and Politics of Ethnography*, J. Clifford and G. E. Marcus (eds.), 1–26. Berkeley: University of California Press.

Clynes, M. (1978). *Sentics: The Touch of Emotions*. New York: Doubleday.

Cohen, Richard A. (1984). "Merleau-Ponty. The Flesh and Foucault." *Philosophy Today* 28, 329–38.

Colapietro, Vincent (1990). *Peirce's Approach to the Self*. Albany: SUNY Press.

Cole, K. C. (1984). *Sympathetic Vibrations: Reflections on Physics as a Way of Life*. New York: Bantam.

Comfort, Alex (1984). *Reality and Empathy: Physics, Mind, and Science in the 21st Century*. Albany: SUNY Press.

Conze, Edward (1962). *Buddhist Thought in India*. Ann Arbor: University of Michigan Press.

Cooke, Deryck (1987). *The Language of Music*. London: Oxford University Press.

Cooper, David (1967). *Psychiatry and Anti-Psychiatry*. London: Tavistock.

Cytowic, R. E. and F. B. Wood (1982). "Synesthesia II: Psychophysical Relations in the Synesthesia of Geometrically Shaped Taste and Colored Hearing." *Brain and Cognition* 1 (1), 23–35.

Cytowic, Richard E. (1989). *Synesthesia: A Union of the Senses*. New York: Springer-Verlag.

DaMatta, Roberto (1991). *Carnivals, Rogues, and Heroes: An Interpretation of the Brazilian Dilemma.* Notre Dame: University of Notre Dame Press.

Dantzig, (1930). *Number: The Language of Science,* 4th ed. New York: Free Press.

Dasenbrock, Reed Way (ed.) (1993). *Literary Theory After Davidson.* Pennsylvania: The Pennsylvania State University Press.

Davidson, Donald (1984). *Inquiries into Truth and Interpretation.* Oxford: Clarendon.

DeBellis, Mark (1995). *Music and Conceptualization.* Cambridge: Cambridge University Press.

Deleuze, Gilles (1990). *The Logic of Sense.* New York: Columbia University Press.

───── (1993). *The Fold: Leibniz and the Baroque,* trans. T. Conley. Minneapolis: Minnesota University Press.

─────and Félix Guattari (1983). *Anti-Oedipus: Capitalism and Schizophrenia I,* Minneapolis: University of Minnesota Press.

─────and Félix Guattari (1987). *A Thousand Plateaus: Capitalism and Schizophrenia II,* trans. B. Massumi. Minneapolis: University of Minnesota Press.

Denzin, Norman (1991). *Images of Postmodern Society.* London: Sage.

Derrida, Jacques (1974). *Glas.* Paris: Galilée.

Dilworth, David A. (1969). "The Initial Formations of 'Pure Experience' in Nishida Kitaro and William James." *Monumenta Nipponica,* 24 (1/2), 93–111.

Dirac, Paul A. C. (1963). "The Physicists's Picture of Nature." *Scientific American* 208 (5), 45–53.

Dobbs, H. A. C. (1972). "The Dimensions of the Sensible Present." In *The Study of Time,* J. T. Fraser, F. C. Huber, and G. H. Miller (eds.), 274–92. New York: Springer-Verlag.

Douglas, Mary (1966). *Purity and Danger: An Analysis of Concepts of Pollution and Taboo.* London: Routledge and Kegan Paul.

───── (1975). *Implicit Meanings.* London: Routledge and Kegan Paul.

Downey, J. E. (1912). "Seeing Sounds and Hearing Colors." *Independent* 78, 315–18.

Duhem, Pierre (1954). *The Aims and Structure of Physical Theory,* trans. P. P. Wiener. Princeton: Princeton University Press.

Dunne, J. W. (1927). *An Experiment with Time.* London: Faber and Faber.

Eco, Umberto (1968). *Apocalípticos e integrados ante la cultura de masas,* trans. A. Boglar. Barcelona: Lumen.

───── (1976). *A Theory of Semiotics.* Bloomington: Indiana University Press.

───── (1984). *Semiotics and the Philosophy of Language.* Bloomington: Indiana University Press.

───── (1986). *Travels in Hyperreality.* San Diego: Harcourt Brace Jovanovich.

─────and Thomas A. Sebeok (eds.) (1983). *The Sign of Three: Dupin, Holmes, Peirce.* Bloomington: Indiana University Press.

Eddington, Arthur S. (1958). *The Philosophy of Physical Science.* Ann Arbor: University of Michigan Press.

Ehrenzweig, Anton (1967). *The Hidden Order of Art: A Study in the Psychology of Artistic Imagination.* Berkeley: University of California Press.

—— (1975). *The Psychoanalysis of Artistic Vision and Hearing: An Introduction to a Theory of Unconscious Perception.* London: Sheldon.

Eliade, Mircea (1965). *The Myth of the Eternal Return: Or, Cosmos and History.* Princeton: Princeton University Press.

Escher, Maurits C. (1971). "Approaches to Infinity." In *The World of M. C. Escher,* 15–16. New York: Abrams.

Evarts, Edward V. (1973). "Brain Mechanisms in Movement." *Scientific American* 229, 96–103.

Feher, Ferenc and Agnes Heller (1983). "Class, Democracy, and Modernity." *Theory and Society* 12 (2), 211–44.

Finnegan, Ruth (1988). *Literacy and Orality: Studies in the Technology of Communication.* Oxford: Basil Blackwell.

Fisch, Max (1986). *Peirce, Semeiotic, and Pragmatism.* Bloomington: Indiana University Press.

Fiske, John (1989a). *Understanding Popular Culture.* London: Routledge.

—— (1989b). *Reading the Popular.* London: Routledge.

—— (1994). *Media Matters: Everyday Culture and Political Change.* Minneapolis: University of Minnesota Press.

Flay, Joseph C. (1985). "Experience, Nature, and Place." *The Monist,* 68 (4), 467–80.

Foster, Susan Leigh (1986). *Reading Dancing: Bodies and Subjects in Contemporary American Dance.* Berkeley: University of California Press.

Franz, Marie Louise von (1974). *Number and Time,* trans. A Dykes. Evanston, IL: Northwestern University Press.

Fraser, J. T. (1979). *Time as Conflict: A Scientific and Humanistic Study.* Basel, Germany: Birkhäuser.

—— (1982). *The Genesis and Evolution of Time: A Critique of Interpretation in Physics.* Amherst: University of Massachusetts Press.

Gadamer, Hans-Georg (1975). *Truth and Method.* New York: Crossroads.

García Canclini, Néstor (1993). *Transforming Modernity: Popular Culture in Mexico,* trans. L. Lozano. Austin: University of Texas Press.

—— (1995). *Hybrid Cultures.* Minneapolis: University of Minnesota Press.

Gardner, Howard (1983). *Frames of Mind: The Theory of Multiple Intelligences.* New York: HarperCollins.

—— (1987). *The Mind's New Science: A History of the Cognitive Revolution,* 2nd ed. New York: Basic Books.

Gardner, Martin (1964). *The Ambidextrous Universe.* New York: Basic Book.

Geertz, Clifford (1975). *The Interpretation of Culture.* New York: Basic Books.

Gibson, Charles (1966). *Spain in America.* New York: Harper and Row.

Goldmann, Lucien (1975). *Towards a Sociology of the Novel,* trans. A. Sheridan. London: Tavistock.

Gombrich, Ernst H. (1979). *The Sense of Order: A Study in the Psychology of Decorative Art*. Ithaca, NY: Cornell University Press.

Goodman, Nelson (1972). "Seven Strictures on Similarity." In *Problems and Projects*, 437–47. Indianapolis: Bobbs-Merrill.

———— (1978). *Ways of Worldmaking*. Indianapolis: Hackett.

———— (1979). "The New Riddle of Induction." In *Fact, Fiction, and Forecast*, 4th ed., 59–83. Cambridge: Harvard University Press.

Goody, Jack (1977). *The Domestication of the Savage Mind*. Cambridge: Cambridge University Press.

Gorlée Dinda (1990). "Degeneracy: A Reading of Peirce's Writing." *Semiotica* 81 (1/2), 71–92.

Gramsci, Antonio (1992). *Prison Notebooks*. New York: Columbia University Press.

Granet, Marcel (1968). *La Pensée chinoise*. Paris: Albin Hichel.

Gregory, Richard L. (1966). *Eye and Brain: The Psychology of Seeing*. London: Weidenfeld and Nicolson.

———— (1970). *The Intelligent Eye*. New York: McGraw-Hill.

———— (1981). *Mind in Science: A History of Explanations in Psychology and Physics*. Cambridge: Cambridge University Press.

Griffin, David Ray (1988). *The Reenchantment of Science: Postmodern Proposals*. Albany: SUNY Press.

Grossberg, Lawrence (1988). *Marxism and the Interpretation of Culture*. Urbana: University of Illinois Press.

———— (1992). *We Gotta Get Out of This Place: Popular Conservatism and Postmodern Culture*. New York: Routledge.

————, Cary Nelson, and Paula Treichler (eds.) (1992). *Cultural Studies*. New York: Routledge.

Habermas, Jürgen (1983). "Modernity—An Incomplete Project," trans. S. Ben-Habib, 3–15. In *The Anti-Aesthetic: Essays on Postmodern Culture*. Port Townsend, WA: Bay Press.

Hacking, Ian (1983). *Representing and Intervening: Introductory Topics in the Philosophy of Natural Science*. Cambridge: Cambridge University Press.

———— (1985) "Styles of Scientific Reasoning." In *Post-Analytic Philosophy*, J. Rajchman and C. West (eds.), 145–65. New York: Columbia University Press.

Hadamard, Jacques (1945). *An Essay on the Psychology of Invention in the Mathematical Field*. Princeton: Princeton University Press.

Hall, Edward T. (1969). *The Hidden Dimension*. New York: Doubleday.

———— (1973). *The Dance of Life*. New York: Doubleday.

Hall, Stuart (1980). *Culture, Media, Language: Working Papers in Cultural Studies, 1972–79*. London: Hutchinson.

Hanke, Lewis (1949). *The Spanish Struggle for Justice in the Conquest of America*. Philadelphia: University of Pennsylvania Press.

———— (1959). *Aristotle and the American Indians*. Chicago: University of Chicago Press.

Hanson, Norwood R. (1958). *Patterns of Discovery.* Cambridge: Cambridge University Press.

Haraway, Donna (1989a). *Primate Visions: Gender, Race, and Nature in the World of Modern Science.* New York: Routledge.

—— (1989b). "A Manifesto for Cyborgs: Science, Technology, and Socialist Feminism in the 1980s." In her *Primate Visions: Gender, Race, and Nature in the World of Modern Science.* New York: Routledge.

Harris, Lauren J. (1978). "Sex Differences in Spatial Ability." In *Asymmetrical Functions of the Brain,* M. Kinsbourne (ed.), 405–522. Cambridge: Cambridge University Press.

Hartshorne, Charles (1970). *Creative Synthesis and Philosophic Method.* LaSalle, IL: Open Court.

Hassan, Ihab (1980). *The Right Promethean Fire. Imagination, Science, and Cultural Change.* Urbana: University of Illinois Press.

—— (1987). *The Postmodern Turn: Essays in Postmodern Theory and Culture.* Columbus: Ohio State University Press.

Haya de la Torre, Víctor Raúl (1973). *Aprismo: The Ideas and Doctrines of Víctor Raúl Haya de la Torre.* Kent: Kent State University Press.

Heelan, Patrick (1983). *Space-Perception and the Philosophy of Science.* Berkeley: University of California Press.

Henderson, Linda Dalrymple (1983). *The Fourth Dimension and Non-Euclidean Geometry in Modern Art.* Princeton: Princeton University Press.

Hiley, David R., James F. Bohman, and Richard Shusterman (eds.) (1991). *The Interpretive Turn: Philosophy, Science, Culture.* Ithaca, NY: Cornell University Press.

Hinton, C. Howard (1987). *What is the Fourth Dimension?* London: Sonnenschein.

—— (1988). *The New Era of Thought.* London: Sonnenschein.

Hofstadter, Douglas R. (1979). *Gödel, Escher, Bach: An Eternal Golden Braid.* New York: Basic Books.

Howes, David (1989). "Scent and Sensibility." *Culture, Medicine and Psychiatry* 13, 121–19.

—— (1990). "Controlling Textuality: A Call for a Return to the Senses." *Anthropologica* 32 (1), 55–73.

—— (1991). "Introduction: 'To Summon all the Senses'." In *The Varieties of Sensory Experience: A Sourcebook in the Anthropology of the Senses,* D. Howes (ed.), 3–21. Toronto: University of Toronto Press.

Huntington, Jr., C. W. (1989). *The Emptiness of Emptiness.* Honolulu: University of Hawai'i Press.

Hutten, Ernest H. (1962). *The Origins of Science: An Inquiry into the Foundations of Western Thought.* London: George Allen and Unwin.

Huyssen, Andreas (1984). "Mapping the Postmodern." *New German Critique* 33, 5–52.

Irigaray, Luce (1985). *This Sex Which Is Not One.* Ithaca: Cornell University Press.

Jackson, Michael (1989). *Paths Toward a Clearing: Radical Empiricism and Ethnographic Inquiry.* Bloomington: Indiana University Press.

Jacobson, Nolan Pliny (1983). *Buddhism and the Contemporary World: Change and Self-Correction.* Carbondale: Southern Illinois University Press.

────── (1988). *The Heard of Buddhist Philosophy.* Carbondale: Southern Illinois University Press.

Jakobson, Roman (1960). "Linguistics and Poetics." In *Style and Language,* T. Sebeok (ed.), 350–77. Cambridge: MIT.

James, William (1948). *Some Problems of Philosophy.* London: Longmans, Green and Co.

────── (1950). *The Principles of Psychology,* 2 vols. New York: Dover, 1950 (first published 1890).

────── (1955). *Pragmatism, and Four Essays from The Meaning of Truth,* ed. R. B. Perry. New York: New American Library (first published 1890).

────── (1967). *Essays in Radical Empiricism and a Pluralistic Universe.* Gloucester, MA: P. Smith.

────── (1976). *Essays in Radical Empiricism.* Cambridge: Harvard University Press.

Jameson, Fredric (1979). "Reification and Utopia in Mass Culture." *Social Text* 1, 130–48.

────── (1983). "Postmodernism and Consumerist Society." In *The Anti-Aesthetic: Essays on Postmodern Culture,* H. Foster (ed.), 111–25. Port Townsend, WA: Bay Press.

────── (1984). "Postmodernism: Or, the Cultural Logic of Late Capitalism." *New Left Review* 146, 53–92.

────── (1992). *Postmodernism, Or, The Cultural Logic of Late Capitalism.* Durham: Duke University Press.

Jara, René and Nicholas Spadaccini (ed.) (1992). *Amerindian Images and the Legacy of Columbus.* Minneapolis: University of Minnesota Press.

Jellinek, J. S. (1975). *The Use of Fragrance in Consumer Products.* New York: John Wiley and Sons.

Jencks, Charles (1977). *The Language of Postmodern Architecture.* New York: Rizzoli.

Johnson, Mark (1987). *The Body in the Mind: The Bodily Basis of Meaning, Imagination, and Reason.* Chicago: University of Chicago Press.

Jonas, Hans (1966). *The Phenomenon of Life: Toward a Philosophical Biology.* New York: Dell.

Jung, Carl G. (1958). *Psychology and Religion.* In *Collected Works,* vol. 11. Princeton: Princeton University Press.

Kaku, Michio (1994). *Hyperspace.* New York: Doubleday.

Kalupahana, David J. (1986). *Nagarjuna: The Philosophy of the Middle Way.* Albany: SUNY Press.

Kauffman, Louis H. and Francisco J. Varela (1980). "Form Dynamics." *Journal of Social Biological Structure* 3, 171–216.

Kearney, Richard (1988). *The Wake of Imagination.* Minneapolis: University of Minnesota Press.

Keller, Helen (1909). *The World I Live In.* New York: Century.

Kellner, Douglas (1995). *Media Culture: Cultural Studies, Identity and Politics Between the Modern and the Postmodern.* New York: Routledge.

Kern, Stephen (1983). *The Culture of Time and Space, 1880–1918.* Cambridge: Harvard University Press.

Khawam, R. K. (ed.). (1976). *Le Livre des ruses. La Stratégie politique des Arabes.* Paris: Phébus.

Klee, Paul (1959). *The Inward Vision: Watercolors, Drawings and Writings by Paul Klee,* trans. and ed. N. Gutterman. New York: Abrams.

Klein, A. B. (1926). *Color Music: The Art of Light.* London: Crosby, Lockwood and sons.

Kline, Morris (1980). *Mathematics: The Loss of Certainty.* Oxford: Oxford University Press.

Kuhn, Thomas S. (1970). *The Structure of Scientific Revolutions.* Chicago: University of Chicago Press.

Laban, Rudolf von (1948). *Modern Educational Dance.* London: Macdonald and Evans.

———— (1960). *The Mastery of Movement.* London: Macdonald and Evans.

———— (1975). *Laban's Principles of Dance and Movement.* London: Macdonald and Evan.

———— (1984). *A Vision of Dynamic Space,* comp. L. Ullmann. London: Falmer.

Lacan, Jacques (1977). *The Four Fundamental Concepts of Psycho-Analysis,* trans. A. Sheridan. New York: W. W. Norton.

Lafaye, Jacques (1976). *Quetzalcóatl and Guadalupe: The Formation of Mexican National Consciousness, 1531–1813,* trans. B. Keen. Chicago: Chicago University Press.

Laing, Ronald D. (1965). *The Divided Self.* Middlesex: Penguin.

———— (1969). *The Politics of the Family.* New York: Random House.

———— (1971). *Self and Others.* Middlesex: Penguin.

Lakoff, George (1987). *Women, Fire, and Dangerous Things: What Categories Reveal About the Mind.* Chicago: University of Chicago Press.

————and Mark Johnson (1980). *Metaphors We Live By.* Chicago: University of Chicago Press.

Lao Tzu (1963). *Tao Te Ching,* trans. D. C. Lau. Middlesex: Penguin.

Las Casas, Bartolomé de (1942). *Del único modo de atraer a todos los pueblos a la verdadera religión.* México: Fondo de Cultura Económica.

Leach, Edmund R. (1961). *Rethinking Anthropology.* London: Athlone.

———— (1972). "Anthropological Aspects of Language: Animal Categories and Verbal Abuse." In *Reader in Comparative Religion: An Anthropological Approach,* W. Lessa and E. Z. Vogt (eds.), 206–19. New York: Harper and Row.

Lee, Harold N. (1986). "Discourse and Event: The Logician and Reality." In *The Philosophy of W. V. Quine*, L. E. Hahn and P. A. Schilpp (eds.), 295–314. LaSalle: Open Court.

Levin, David Michael (1985). *The Body's Recollection of Being: Phenomenological Psychology and the Deconstruction of Nihilism*. London: Routledge and Kegan Paul.

Lévi-Strauss, Claude (1966). *The Savage Mind*. Chicago: University of Chicago Press.

——— (1976). *Tristes Tropiques*. Harmondsworth: Penguin.

Lowe, Benjamin (1977). *The Beauty of Sport: A Cross-Disciplinary Inquiry*. Englewood Cliffs, NJ: Prentice-Hall.

Lowe, Donald M. (1982). *History of Bourgeois Perception*. Chicago: University of Chicago Press.

Löwenfeld, Victor (1939). *The Nature of Creative Activity*. New York: Harcourt and Brace.

Luria, A. R. (1968). *The Mind of a Mnemonist*. New York: Basic Books.

Lyotard, Jean-François (1984). *The Postmodern Condition: A Report on Knowledge*, trans. G. Bennington and B. Massumi. Minneapolis: University of Minnesota Press.

Macrae, Janet (1988). *Therapeutic Touch: A Practical Guide*. New York: Alfred A. Knopf.

Mariátegui, José Carlos (1971). *Seven Interpretive Essays on Peruvial Reality*. Austin: University of Texas Press.

Marks, L. E. (1974). "On Association of Light and Sound: The Mediation of Brightness, Pitch and Loudness." *American Journal of Psychology* 87, 173–88.

Martin, Jay (1973). *The Dialogical Imagination: A History of the Frankfurt School and the Institute of Social Research, 1923–1950*. Boston: Little, Brown.

Martín-Barbero, José (1993). *Communication, Culture and Hegemony: From the Media to Mediations*, trans. E. Fox and R. A. White. London: Sage.

Martland, Thomas R. (1963). *The Metaphysics of William James and John Dewey: Process and Structure in Philosophy and Religion*. New York: Greenwood.

Marty, Robert (1982). "C. S. Peirce's Phaneroscopy and Semiotics." *Semiotica* 41 (1/4), 169–81.

Marvin, Carolyn (1988). *When Old Technologies Were New: Thinking About Electric Communication in the Late Nineteenth Century*. New York: Oxford University Press.

Mattelart, Armand and Michèle Mattelart (1992). *Rethinking Media Theory*, trans. J. A. Cohen and M. Urquidi. Minneapolis: University of Minnesota Press.

Maturana, Humberto and Francisco Varela (1980). *Autopoiesis and Cognition: The Realization of the Living*. Dordrecht, Holland: D. Reidel.

——— (1987). *The Tree of Knowledge: the Biological Roots of Human Understanding*. Boston: Shambhala.

McClary, Susan (1995). "Music, the Pythagoreans, and the Body." In *Choreographing History*, S. L. Foster (ed.), 82–104. Bloomington: Indiana University Press.

McLuhan, Marshall (1962). *The Gutenberg Galaxy*. Toronto: University of Toronto Press.

───── (1964). *Understanding Media*. New York: New American Library.

McTaggart, J. M. E. (1927). *The Nature of Existence*, vol. 2. Cambridge: Cambridge University Press.

Merleau-Ponty, Maurice (1962). *Phenomenology of Perception*, trans. C. Smith. London: Routledge and Kegan Paul.

───── (1964). *L'Oeil et l'esprit*. Paris: Gallimard.

───── (1968). *The Visible and the Invisible*, ed. C. Lefort, trans. A. Lingus. Evanston, IL: Northwestern University Press.

Merrell, Floyd (1983). *Pararealities: The Nature of Our Fictions and How We Know Them*. Amsterdam: Johns Benjamins.

───── (1991a). *Signs Becoming Signs: Our Perfusive, Pervasive Universe*. Bloomington: Indiana University Press.

───── (1991b). *Unthinking Thinking: Jorge Luis Borges, Mathematics, and the "New Physics."* West Lafayette, IN: Purdue University Press.

───── (1991c). "Thought-Signs, Sign-Events." *Semiotica* 87 (1/2), 1–58.

───── (1995a). *Semiosis in the Postmodern Age*. West Lafayette, IN: Purdue University Press.

───── (1995b). *Peirce's Semiotics Now: A Primer*. Toronto: Canadian Scholars' Press.

───── (1996). *Signs Grow: Semiosis and Life Processes*. Toronto: University of Toronto Press.

───── (1997a). *Peirce, Signs, and Meaning*. Toronto: University of Toronto Press.

───── (1998). *Simplicity and Complexity: Some Questions from Literature, Science, and Mathematics*. Ann Arbor: Michigan University Press.

Mires, Fernando (1988). *La rebelión permanente*. México: Siglo XXI.

Montagu, Ashley (1971). *Touching: The Human Significance of the Skin*. New York: Columbia University Press.

Moore, Charles A. (ed.) (1960). *The Japanese Mind: Essentials of Japanese Philosophy and Culture*. Honolulu: The University Press of Hawaii.

Morris, Edwin T. (1986). *Fragrance*. New York: Scribner's Sons.

Mouffe, Chantal (1988). "Radical Democracy: Modern or Postmodern?" In *Universal Abandon? The Politics of Postmodernism*, A. Ross (ed.), 31–45. Minneapolis: University of Minnesota Press.

Murphey, Murray (1961). *The Development of Peirce's Philosophy*. Cambridge: Harvard University Press.

Nabokov, Vladimir (1949). "Portrait of my Mother." *New Yorker* April 9, 33–37.

Nagel, Ernest and James A. Newman (1958). *Gödel's Proof*. New York: Columbia University Press.

Neisser, Ulric (1967). *Cognitive Psychology.* Englewood Cliffs, NJ: Prentice-Hall.

Nesher, Dan (1983). "A Pragmatic Theory of Meaning: A Note on Peirce's 'Last' Formulation of the Pragmatic Maxim and its Interpretation." *Semiotica* 44 (3/4), 203–57.

———— (1990). "Understanding Sign Semiosis as Cognition and as Self-Conscious Process: A Reconstruction of Some Basic Concepts of Peirce's Semiotics." *Semiotica* 79 (1/2), 1–49.

Nishida, Kitaro (1960). *A Study of Good,* tr. V. H. Viglielmo. Tokyo: Japanese Government Printing Bureau.

Nishitani, Keiji (1982). *Religion and Nothingness,* trans. J. van Bragt. Berkeley: University of California Press.

———— (1990). *The Self-Overcoming of Nihilism,* trans. G. Parkes. Albany: SUNY Press.

Ogden, C. K. and I. A. Richards (1923). *The Meaning of Meaning.* New York: Harcourt, Brace, and World.

O'Gorman, Edmundo (1958). *La invención de América.* México: Fondo de Cultura Económica.

Olalquiaga, Celeste (1992). *Megalopolis: Contemporary Cultural Sensibilities.* Minneapolis: University of Minnesota Press.

Ong, Walter (1967). *The Presence of the Word: Some Prolegomena for Cultural and Religious History.* New Haven, CT: Yale University Press.

———— (1971). *Rhetoric, Romance, and Technology: Studies in the Interaction and Expression of Culture.* Ithaca, NY: Cornell University Press.

———— (1977). *Interfaces of the Word.* Ithaca, NY: Cornell University Press.

———— (1982). *Orality and Literacy.* New York: Methuen.

———— (1991). "The Shifting Sensorium." In *The Varieties of Sensory Experience: A Sourcebook in the Anthropology of the Senses,* D. Howes (ed.), 25–30. Toronto: University of Toronto Press.

Parker, Christián (1993). *Otra lógica en América Latina: Religión popular y modernización capitalista.* México: Fondo de Cultura Económica.

Peirce, Charles Sanders (1931–35). *Collected Papers of Charles Sanders Peirce,* C. Hartshorne and P. Weiss (eds.), vols. 1–6. Cambridge: Harvard University Press (reference to Peirce's papers in the text will be designated *CP*).

———— (1958). *Collected Papers of Charles Sanders Peirce,* A. W. Burks (ed.), vol. 8. Cambridge: Harvard University Press (reference to Peirce's papers in the text will be designated *CP*).

———— (1976). *The New Elements of Mathematics by Charles S. Peirce,* 4. vols, C. Eisele (ed.). The Hague: Mouton (reference to the *New Elements* in the text will be designated *NE*).

Piaget, Jean (1973). *The Child and Reality.* New York: Grossman.

Pike, Fredrick B. (1992). *The United States and Latin America: Myths and Stereotypes of Civilization and Nature.* Austin: University of Texas Press.

Plotnitsky, Arkady (1994). *Complementarity: Anti-Epistemology After Bohr and Derrida.* Durham, NC: Duke University Press.

Poincaré, Henri (1952). *Science and Hypotheses,* trans. F. Maitland. New York: Dover.

Polanyi, Michael (1958). *Personal Knowledge.* Chicago: University of Chicago Press.

Popper, Karl R. (1962). *The Open Society and Its Enemies,* 4th ed., vol. II. New York: Harper and Row).

—— (1972). *Objective Knowledge.* London: Clarendon.

Post, John F. (1987). "The Possible Liar." In *Evolutionary Epistemology, Theory of Rationality, and the Sociology of Knowledge,* G. Radnitzsky and W. W. Bartley, III (eds.), 217–20. LaSalle, IL: Open Court.

Poster, Mark (1990). *The Mode of Information: Poststructuralism and Social Context.* Chicago: University of Chicago Press.

—— (ed.) (1988). *Jean Baudrillard, Selected Writings.* Stanford, CA: Stanford University Press.

—— (ed.) (1989). *Critical Theory and Poststructuralism: In Search of a Context.* Ithaca, NY: Cornell University Press.

Putnam, Hilary (1981). *Reason, Truth and History.* Cambridge: Cambridge University Press.

—— (1983). "Vagueness and Alternative Logic." *Erkenntnis* 19, 297–314.

—— (1988). *Representation and Reality.* Cambridge, MA: MIT.

Rajchman, John and Cornel West (eds.) (1985). *Post-Analytic Philosophy.* New York: Columbia University Press.

Révész, Geza (1957). "Optik und Haptik." *Studium Generale* 6, 374–79.

Ricard, Robert (1966). *The Spiritual Conquest of Mexico,* trans. L. B. Simpson. Berkeley: University of California Press.

Riemann, Bernhard (1854). "On the Hypotheses that Lie at the Basis of Geometry," trans. W. K. Clifford. *Nature* 8, 14–17.

Rivlin, R. and K. Gravelle (1984). *Deciphering the Senses: The Expanding World of Human Perception.* New York: Simon and Schuster.

Roberts, Don (1973). *The Existential Graphs of Charles S. Peirce.* The Hague: Mouton.

Rochberg, George (1971). "The Avant-Garde and the Aesthetics of Survival." *New Literary History* 3 (1), 71–92.

Romanyshyn, Robert (1989). *Technology as Symptom and Dream.* London: Routledge.

Rorty, Richard (1979). *Philosophy and the Mirror of Nature.* Princeton, NJ: Princeton University Press.

Roth, Paul A. (1987). *Meaning and Method in the Social Sciences: A Case for Methodological Pluralism.* Ithaca, NY: Cornell University Press.

Rotman, Brian (1987). *Signifying Nothing: The Semiotics of Zero.* New York: St. Martin's.

Rucker, Rudolf v. B. (1977). *Geometry, Relativity and the Fourth Dimension.* New York: Dover.

Rucker, Rudy (1983). *Infinity and the Mind: the Science and Philosophy of the Infinite.* New York: Bantam Books.

——— (1984). *The Fourth Dimension: Toward a Geometry of Higher Reality.* Boston: Houghton Mifflin.

Russell, Bertrand (1910). "The Theory of Logical Types." In *Principia Mathematica,* by Alfred North Whitehead and Bertrand Russell, 37–65. Cambridge: Cambridge University Press.

Sacks, Oliver (1984). *A Leg to Stand On.* New York: HarperCollins.

——— (1985). *Migraine,* revised and expanded ed. Berkeley: University of California Press.

——— (1987). *The Man Who Mistook His Wife for a Hat, and Other Clinical Tales.* New York: HarperCollins.

——— (1989). *Seeing Voices: A Journey into the World of the Deaf.* New York: HarperCollins.

——— (1995). *An Anthropologist on Mars.* New York: Vintage.

Said, Edward W. (1993). *Culture and Imperialism.* New York: Knopf.

Sartre, Jean Paul (1989). *No Exit, and Three Other Plays.* New York: Vintage.

Savan, David (1987–88). *An Introduction to C. S. Peirce's Full System of Semeiotic* (Monograph Series of the Toronto Semiotic Circle 1). Toronto: Victoria College.

Schafer, R. Murray (1977). *The Tuning of the World.* New York: Knopf.

Schaffer, Peter (1981). *Amadeus: A Drama.* New York: S. French.

Schaller, Susan (1991). *A Man Without Words.* Berkeley: University of California Press.

Schechner, Richard (1982). *The End of Humanism: Writings on Performance.* New York: Performing Arts Journal Publications.

Schonberger, Martin (1979). *The I Ching and the Genetic Code,* trans. D. Q. Stephenson. New York: ASI Publishers.

Schrödinger, Erwin (1967). *What is Life?* and *Mind and Matter.* Cambridge: Cambridge University Press.

Sebeok, Thomas A. (1976). *Contributions to the Doctrine of Signs.* Bloomington: Indiana University Press.

——— (1994). *An Introduction to Semiotics.* Toronto: University of Toronto Press.

Seigfried, Charlene H. (1978). *Chaos and Context: A Study in William James.* Athens: Ohio University Press.

Seneca (1962). *Epistulae Morales,* trans. R. M. Grummere. Cambridge: Harvard University Press (written A.D. 63–65).

Sheffer, Henry M. (1913). "A Set of Five Independent Postulates of Boolean Algebra." *Transactions of the American Mathematical Society* 14, 481–88.

Sherrington, Charles S. (1940). *Man on His Nature.* Cambridge: Cambridge University Press.

Shlain, Leonard (1991). *Art and Physics: Parallel Visions in Space, Time, and Light.* New York: William Morrow.

Singh, J. A. L. and R. M. Zingg (1966). *Wolf-Children and Feral Man.* Hamden, CT: Archon Books.

Smart, Barry (1992). *Postmodernism.* New York: Routledge.

Spencer-Brown, G. (1979). *Laws of Form.* New York: E. P. Dutton.

Sperber, Dan (1975). *Rethinking Symbolism,* trans. A. L. Morton. Cambridge: Cambridge University Press.

Sperry, Roger W. (1969). "A Modified Concept of Consciousness." *Psychological Review* 76, 532–36.

——— (1970). "An Objective Approach to Subjective Experience: Further Explanation of a Hypothesis." *Psychological Review* 77, 585–90.

Spivak, Gayatri Chakravorty (1988). "Can the Subaltern Speak?" In *Marxism and the Interpretation of Culture,* C. Nelson and L. Grossberg (eds.), 271–313. Urbana: University of Illinois Press.

——— (1990). *The Post-Colonial Critic: Interviews, Strategies, Dialogues,* S. Harasym (ed.). New York: Routledge.

Stabb, Martin (1967). *In Quest of Identity: Patterns in the Spanish American Essay of Ideas, 1890–1960.* Chapel Hill: University of North Carolina Press.

Stoller, Paul (1989). *The Taste of Ethnographic Things: The Senses in Anthropology.* Philadelphia: University of Pennsylvania Press.

Straus, Erwin (1963). *The Primary World of Senses: A Vindication of Sensory Experience,* trans. J. Needleman. London: The Free Press.

Stravinsky, Igor (1956). *The Poetics of Music in the Form of Six Lessons.* New York: Vintage.

——— (1971). *Conversations with Robert Craft.* London: Pelican.

Synnott, Anthony (1993). *The Body Social: Symbolism, Self and Society.* London: Routledge.

Sypher, Wylie (1962). *Loss of the Self in Modern Literature and Art.* New York: Random House.

Szamosi, Géza (1986). *The Twin Dimensions: Inventing Time and Space.* New York: McGraw-Hill.

Szasz, Thomas Stephen (1988). *Schizophrenia: The Sacred Symbol of Psychiatry.* Syracuse, NY: Syracuse University Press.

Talbot, Michael (1980). *Mysticism and the New Physics.* New York: Bantam Books.

Teevan, Richard C. and Robert C. Barney (eds.). *Color Vision.* New York: Van Nostrand.

Thomas, Lewis (1980). *Late Night Thoughts on Listening to Mahler's Ninth Symphony.* New York: Viking.

Thompson, Manley (1986). "Quine's Theory of Knowledge." In *The Philosophy of W. V. Quine,* L. E. Hahn and P. A. Schilpp (eds.), 537–68. LaSalle, IL: Open Court.

Todorov, Tzvetan (1984). *The Conquest of America.* New York: Harper and Row.

Turner, Victor W. (1967). *The Forest of Symbols: Aspects of Ndembu Ritual.* Ithaca, NY: Cornell University Press.

Tursman, Richard (1987). *Peirce's Theory of Scientific Discovery: A System of Logic Conceived as Semiotic.* Bloomington: Indiana University Press.

Tyler, Stephen (1987). *The Unspeakable: Discourse, Dialogue, and Rhetoric in the Postmodern World.* Madison: University of Wisconsin Press.

Tzu, Sun (1963). *The Art of War,* trans. S. B. Griffith. Oxford: Clarendon.

Unno, Taitetsu (ed.) (1989). *The Religious Philosophy of Nishitani Keiji.* Berkeley: Asian Humanities Press.

Vaihinger, Hans (1935). *The Philosophy of "As If"; A System of the Theoretical, Practical and Religious Fictions of Mankind,* trans. C. K. Ogden, 2nd ed. London: Kegan Paul, Trench, Truber and Co.

Varela, Francisco J. (1984). "The Creative Circle: Sketches on the Natural History of Circularity." In *The Invented Reality,* P. Watzlawick (ed.), 309–23. New York: W. W. Norton.

Verrill, A. H. (1940). *Perfumes and Spices.* Boston: L. C. Page.

Vinge, L. (1975). *The Five Senses: Studies in the Literary Tradition.* Lund, Sweden: Publications of the Royal Society of Letters.

Waddington, Conrad H. (1970). *Behind Appearances: A Study of the Relations Between Painting and the Natural Sciences in this Century.* Cambridge: MIT.

Weiss, Paul and A. W. Burks (1945). "Peirce's Sixty-six Signs." *The Journal of Philosophy* 42, 383–88.

Weyl, Hermann (1952). *Symmetry.* Princeton, NJ: Princeton University Press.

Wheeler, John Archibald (1980). "Beyond the Black Hole." In *Some Strangeness in the Proportion: A Centennial Symposium to Celebrate the Achievement of Albert Einstein,* H. Woolf (ed.), 341–75. Reading, MA: Addison-Wesley.

——— (1990). *A Journey into Gravity and Spacetime.* New York: Scientific American Library.

Whitehead, Alfred North (1929). *Process and Reality.* New York: Macmillan.

——— (1938). *Modes of Thought.* New York: Macmillan.

——— (1948). *Science and the Modern World.* New York: New American Library.

———and Bertrand Russell (1910). *Principia Mathematica.* Cambridge: Cambridge University Press.

Whitrow, G. J. (1961). *The Natural Philosophy of Time.* Oxford: Clarendon.

Wiener, Norbert (1956). *The Human Use of Human Beings.* Cambridge: MIT.

Wigner, Eugene P. (1969). "The Unreasonable Effectiveness of Mathematics in the Natural Sciences." In *The Spirit and the Uses of the Mathematical Sciences,* T. L. Saaty and F. J. Weyl (eds.), 123–40. New York: McGraw-Hill.

Wild, John (1969). *The Radical Empiricism of William James.* Garden City, NJ: Doubleday.

Wilden, Anthony (1980). *System and Structure,* 2nd ed. London: Tavistock.

Wilhelm, Richard (1960). *I Ching or Book of Changes,* trans. C. F. Baynes (London: Routledge and Kegan Paul).

Williams, Raymond (1961). *The Long Revolution.* London: Cox and Wyman.

———— (1976). *Keywords: A Vocabulary of Culture and Society.* Oxford: Oxford University Press.

———— (1977). *Marxism and Literature.* Oxford: Oxford University Press.

Wittgenstein, Ludwig (1953). *Philosophical Investigations,* trans. G. E. M. Anscombe. New York: Macmillan.

———— (1956). *Remarks on the Foundations of Mathematics,* trans. G. E. M. Anscombe. New York: Macmillan.

———— (1961). *Tractatus Logico-Philosophicus,* trans. D. F. Pears and B. F. McGuinness. London: Routledge and Kegan Paul.

Wolf, Eric (1959). *Sons of the Shaking Earth.* Chicago: University of Chicago Press.

Wood, Thomas (1936). *True Thomas.* London: Cape.

Yourgrau, Wolfgang (1966). "Language, Spatial Concepts and Physics." In *Mind, Matter, and Method,* P. K. Feyerabend and G. Maxwell (eds.), 496–99. Minneapolis: University of Minnesota Press.

Zavala, Silvio Arturo (1964). *The Defense of Human Rights in Latin America, Sixteenth to Eighteenth Centuries.* Paris: UNESCO.

———— (1965). *Recuerdos de Vasco de Quiroga.* México: Porrúa.

Zea, Leopoldo (1987). *Filosofía de la historia americana.* México: Fondo de Cultura Económica.

Zuckerkandl, Victor (1956). *Sound and Symbol: Music and the External World,* trans. W. Trask. Princeton, NJ: Princeton University Press.

———— (1959). *The Sense of Music.* Princeton, NJ: Princeton University Press.

Zukav, Gary (1979). *The Dancing Wu Li Masters: An Overview of the New Physics.* New York: William Morrow.

INDEX